CHINA

ITS HISTORY AND CULTURE

Bactrian horse. Tang dynasty, eighth century.

This superb horse of dignity and power represents an import to China from Ferghana in Central Asia, quite distinct from the Mongolian pony. Even the sculptors of the Parthenon frieze did not exceed the skill of the Tang artist who made this figure, an unusually large one over 26 inches tall, covered in the typical three colors of glaze: cream, chestnut brown, and green. The imperial stables and pastures numbered their steeds in hundreds of thousands about this time, and poets and artists celebrated them with names such as Flying Dragons and Horses of Heaven. Some were trained to give exhibitions of dancing at the palace.

CHINA

ITS HISTORY AND CULTURE

THIRD EDITION

W. SCOTT MORTON

McGraw-Hill, Inc.

New York   St. Louis   San Francisco   Auckland   Bogotá   Caracas
Lisbon   London   Madrid   Mexico City   Milan   Montreal
New Delhi   San Juan   Singapore   Sydney
Tokyo   Toronto

First hardcover edition by Lippincott & Crowell Publishers

Second McGraw-Hill paperback edition, 1995

9 10 FGR/FGR 0 5 4 3

Grateful acknowledgment is made for permission to reprint:

Excerpts from *The Analects of Confucius,* translated by Arthur Waley. Copyright 1938 by
George Allen & Unwin Ltd. Reprinted by permission of George Allen & Unwin (Publishers) Ltd. and the Macmillan Publishing Co., Inc.

Excerpts from *Book of Songs* (Shih Ching), translated by Arthur Waley, 1960. Reprinted by
permission of George Allen & Unwin (Publishers) Ltd. and Grove Press, Inc.

Excerpts from *Life and Times of Po Chu-i* by Arthur Waley. Reprinted by permission of
George Allen & Unwin (Publishers) Ltd.

Excerpts from *The Way and Its Power* by Lao-tzu, translated by Arthur Waley, 1958.
Reprinted by permission of George Allen & Unwin (Publishers) Ltd. and Grove Press, Inc.

Maps by Paul J. Pugliese

ISBN: 0-07-043424-7

Sponsoring Editor: Jeanne Flagg
Production Supervisor: Leroy Young
Editing Supervisor: Patty Andrews

This book is printed on acid-free paper.

Library of Congress Cataloging-in-Publication Data

Morton, W. Scott (William Scott)
   China: its history and culture / W. Scott Morton.—3rd ed., 2nd
McGraw-Hill pbk. ed.
      p.   cm.
   Includes bibliographical references and index.
   ISBN 0-07-043424-7
   1. China—History. 2. China—Civilization.   I. Title.
DS735.M64 1995   94-37610
951—dc20   CIP

Hunc libellum
Phyllidi carissimae
dono dedit scriptor

CONTENTS

ILLUSTRATIONS

MAPS

FOREWORD

Understanding of China has advanced tremendously since the Second World War. Many more courses on China have been offered in American schools and colleges. Many more Americans have lived in or visited China. And more students have studied the Chinese language. As a result, they can learn about China from direct sources and can view China from within. American views of China have become more objective and more balanced. Gone are the old clichés that the Chinese have no respect for life and know of no dignity of the individual, that China has always been backward in science, that the Chinese language has no grammar or has no word for this or that, that the Chinese family is always harmonious, that the word of a Chinese is always as good as gold, and so on.

But true understanding of China requires more than doing away with old clichés and having a more objective and balanced viewpoint. It requires some basic knowledge of Chinese history and culture, for China is essentially a country of history and culture. China is not really a very old country, but it does have a long and fully recorded history to which the Chinese have always looked back. Few aspects of China can be detached from this history. Ideologically China turned a complete somersault in 1949, and yet the political structure of provinces and counties is 2,000 years old. When a Chinese talks about friendship, for example, he will quote Confucius, from the sixth century B.C. The Chinese have always looked back to history, not because they are backward looking or are simply conservative; they do so for concrete evidence and past experience, not much different from the American legal system, which insists on precedents to show why a certain decision has been made. It is not an exaggeration to say that the Chinese are among the most historically minded people to be found anywhere. Details of life in the second millennium

B.C., conversations of the sixth century B.C., and letters of the first century A.D. and the like have been preserved, and thousands and thousands of local gazetteers about local conditions have been published by prefectures and counties for centuries. The average Chinese family has a recorded genealogy going back at least 800 years, in addition to traditional records of perhaps a thousand years more. Therefore, no aspect of China can be genuinely appreciated out of context of its long history. Perhaps it is an oversimplification to say that Chinese history can only be studied vertically, just as Western history can only be studied horizontally. Nevertheless it is true that the historical perspective is necessary in any study of China.

Equally indispensable is the study of Chinese culture. Because China printed books several hundred years before the Gutenberg Bible, because Chinese landscape painting emerged as an independent art form several hundred years ahead of that in Europe, many Westerners have the idea that Chinese culture is very old and superior to most others; and many Chinese are quick to accept the honor. But China is weak in a number of cultural components, such as harmony in music, and Chinese culture is actually not very old. The bronze age came comparatively late, for instance. What can be said is that Chinese culture matured rapidly, for its political institutions and concepts, social organization, and religious attitudes and practices reached great heights 2,000 years ago. There is ample justification for the Chinese to call their country "a country of cultural matters." Just as one needs to know Chinese history in order to know China, so does one need to know its culture.

To help the Westerner know China, many excellent books on Chinese history and culture have been written, particularly in recent years. However, there is a dire need for a simple, concise, factual, and yet comprehensive, penetrating, and readable account for the great and rapidly increasing number of nonspecialist but sophisticated readers. Dr. W. Scott Morton's book meets this need.

Unlike books on Chinese history which deal chiefly with political and economic changes, or books on Chinese cultural history which proceed from one dynasty to another, thus breaking one particular cultural development into different periods, or books on Chinese culture which treat Chinese culture topically, Professor Morton's work combines history and culture as a continuous and well-integrated phenomenon. Along with a historical account in chronological order, he has woven Chinese culture into the different dynasties, often concentrating on one or more cultural areas. Poetry, for example, is singled out for discussion in the Tang period, Buddhism in the Six Dynasties, technology in the Song, the novel in the Qing, and so forth. In this way the reader receives a simple but clear and deep impression. As an illustration, take landscape painting. It is difficult to find in only a few pages as penetrating an interpretation of the spirit of Chinese landscape painting as in this book.

It is hoped that with rapidly widening contact between China and the United States, the American public will not limit their reading to travelers' accounts, however informative they may be. One needs to know China's history and culture to appreciate fully and intelligently what one sees and hears. This is also true for the interested student. Dr. Morton's book will contribute to this appreciation.

Wing-tsit Chan

Professor of Chinese Philosophy and Culture Emeritus, Dartmouth College; Gillespie Professor of Philosophy, Chatham College; Adjunct Professor of Chinese Thought, Columbia University

ACKNOWLEDGMENTS

The sources of this book lie far back in my life and thinking. I am more grateful than I can say to family, friends, and teachers during happy days in Peking and Manchuria, and to colleagues and students more recently in Seton Hall University in the departments of History and Asian Studies.

Among those who have given me invaluable aid in the writing of the book itself I am particularly grateful for the generosity and support of Professor Wing-tsit Chan, who not only wrote the Foreword, and suggested improvements, but also gave me encouragement in my early years in the United States. Annette Juliano enlarged and refined my thoughts on Chinese art and introduced me to art collectors and museums, as well as providing me with photographs of her own. Mr. and Mrs. Ezekiel Schloss kindly opened to me their invaluable collection of Chinese ceramic figures and allowed me to reproduce illustrations scarcely obtainable elsewhere in such richness. John M. Crawford, Jr., was most generous in welcoming me to view his outstanding collection of Chinese paintings and calligraphy and gave me, in some pleasant and memorable conversations, ideas as to which examples might best suit an introductory history of Chinese culture. Takanaru Mitsui of Tokyo graciously allowed me to reproduce a picture from his private collection. Professor Paul Tsai of Seton Hall University also provided me with illustrations. Marge Lin kindly inscribed the Chinese characters used in the text.

Michael Loewe of the Department of Oriental Studies in Cambridge University was of the greatest assistance in the early planning of the book.

No one could have been pleasanter to work with than Hugh Rawson, now twice my editor. My thanks are due to all; responsibility for the opinions expressed is my own. Finally, I am most grateful to my son, Keith Scott Morton, whose professional skill produced the jacket illustration and many of the other pictures.

W. SCOTT MORTON

Bloomfield College
New Jersey
January 1980

For some emendations and improvements in the present paperback edition I am much indebted to the prompt and unstinting help of L. Carrington Goodrich, professor emeritus, Columbia University.

W.S.M.

New York
Fall, 1981

For this second paperback edition of the book I have made a number of changes in the existing text, rewritten chapter 15 and added three new chapters, 16, 17, and 18, to bring the text up to the beginning of 1994. So much has altered in China since the events covered in the previous edition (up to Fall 1981), including the economic reforms, the democracy movement of Tiananmen Square, and the new opening of China to the West, that a considerable amount of material had to be added.

In this regard I am immensely indebted to Professor Charlton M. Lewis of Brooklyn College, City University of New York, who kindly read both the former text and the new material, and made many invaluable suggestions for correcting, clarifying and better integrating the subject matter. I am responsible for the final form of the book. Friends in the Columbia University Faculty Seminars on Traditional and Modern China have been a continual stimulus. John Carleo, John Aliano, Jeanne Flagg, and Patty Andrews at McGraw-Hill have again given me steady support. Finally my wife and fellow-historian, Phyllis Stock-Morton, has been a loving, understanding and discriminating critic.

W.S.M.

New York
Spring, 1994

A NOTE ON
SPELLING AND PRONUNCIATION

In this book the new form of romanization in use in the People's Republic of China and introduced by *The New York Times* on March 1, 1979, has been adopted. It is known as *pinyin* as opposed to the Wade-Giles romanization, which has been the usual form of the spelling of Chinese words and names in English since the nineteenth century.

In the following table the pinyin form is given first, the Wade-Giles second, and an approximate English equivalent third. It should be noted that in books in French, German, and other languages the spelling of Chinese words has followed the form which, in the pronunciation of the country concerned, would yield the best approximation to the Chinese sounds. Now most countries are adopting the pinyin form as standard (for example, Gernet, *Le Monde Chinois*). Unless one already knows spoken Chinese, it is impossible to reproduce the exact pronunciation, including the tones, by the use of the Western alphabet in any form.

Two consonants in pinyin at first cause difficulty, *q* for *ch'* and *x* for *hs*, a thin *sh*. One must realize that these consonants are used purely as arbitrary symbols. The pinyin system is on the whole clearer than the Wade-Giles, but even in the pinyin system, vowels remain confusing: *a* (pinyin) often corresponds to *e* (Wade-Giles) and *o* (pinyin) to *u* (Wade-Giles), as in German *jung*. Also, in pinyin two quite different sounds for *u* are not distinguished, *u* as in *too* and the thin *ü* as in *München* or the French *tu*. The distinction is not important in place names, since *ü* does not occur often, but in personal names and in the language generally the sound *ü* is quite common. Compare *yü*, "fish," and *yung*, "use."

For the benefit of those accustomed to the Wade-Giles, Chinese words in the list of place names accompanying the map are given first in pinyin and then the Wade-Giles form.

A Note on Spelling and Pronunciation

Table of Pronunciation

PINYIN	WADE-GILES	ENGLISH EQUIVALENT
a	a	vowel as in *far*
b	p	consonant as in *be*
c	ts'	consonant as in *its*
ch	ch'	consonant as in *church,* strongly aspirated
d	t	consonant as in *do*
e	e	vowel as in *her*
f	f	consonant as in *foot*
g	k	consonant as in *go*
h	h	consonant as in *her,* strongly aspirated
i	i	vowel as in *eat,* or as in *sir* (in syllables beginning with *c, ch, r, s, sh, z,* and *zh*)
j	ch	consonant as in *jeep*
k	k'	consonant as in *kind,* strongly aspirated
l	l	consonant as in *land*
m	m	consonant as in *me*
n	n	consonant as in *no*
o	o	vowel as in *law*
p	p'	consonant as in *par,* strongly aspirated
q	ch'	consonant as in *cheek,* used preceding the letter *i* and sometimes the letter *u;* otherwise *ch* is used
r	j	consonant, a soft *r,* halfway between the *r* in *right* (not rolled) and the *z* in *azure,* or the *j* in French *je*
s	s, ss, sz	consonant as in *sister*
sh	sh	consonant, a full *sh,* as in *shore*
t	t'	consonant as in *top,* strongly aspirated
u	u, ü	vowel as in *too,* also as in French *tu* or German *München*
v	—	consonant used only to produce foreign words, national minority words, and local dialects
w	w	semi-vowel in syllables beginning with a *u* sound when not preceded by consonants, as in *want*
x	hs	consonant as in *she,* a thin *sh,* with tongue far forward, just above front teeth
y	y	semi-vowel in syllables beginning with *i* or *u* when not preceded by consonants, as in *yet*
z	ts, tz	consonant as in *zero*
zh	ch	consonant as in *jump*

To aid the reader I have occasionally given the old Wade-Giles form in parentheses after personal names such as Jiang Jieshi (Chiang Kai-shek), where the divergence is considerable and due to differences in dialect as well as method of spelling. Quotations from published books and journals, of course, follow the spelling used in the work being quoted. In the later chapters, post–1949, Beijing has been substituted for Peking. In each case the Chinese characters are the same.

CHINA

ITS HISTORY AND CULTURE

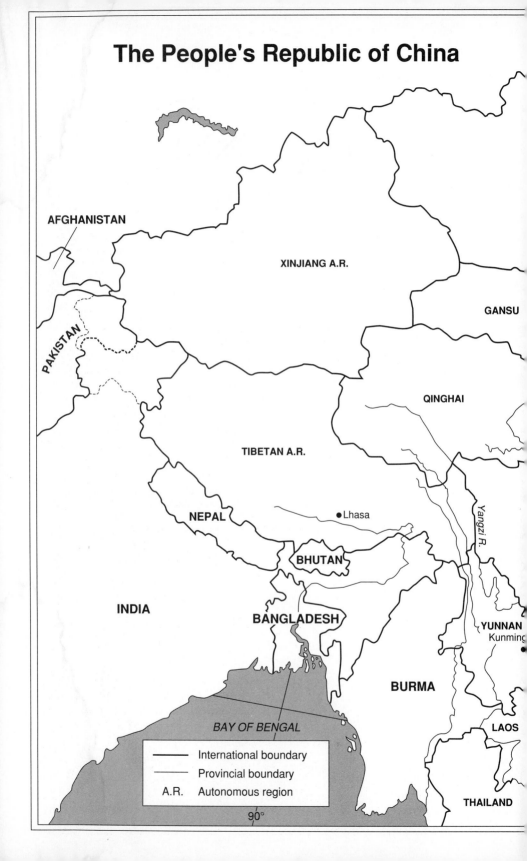

The People's Republic of China

AFGHANISTAN

XINJIANG A.R.

GANSU

PAKISTAN

QINGHAI

TIBETAN A.R.

NEPAL

●Lhasa

BHUTAN

INDIA

BANGLADESH

YUNNAN
Kunming

BURMA

BAY OF BENGAL

LAOS

Yangzi R.

	International boundary
	Provincial boundary
A.R.	Autonomous region

THAILAND

90°

The People's Republic of China

PROVINCES (approximately N. to S.)		CITIES (approximately N. to S.)	
pinyin	*Wade-Giles*	*pinyin*	*Wade-Giles*
Heilongjiang	Heilungchiang	Harbin	Harbin
Jilin	Kirin	Jilin	Kirin
Liaoning	Liaoning	Changchun	Ch'angch'un
Hebei	Hopei or Hopeh	Shenyang	Shenyang, Fengt'ien,
Shandong	Shantung		or Mukden
Shanxi	Shansi	Anshan	Anshan
Shaanxi	Shensi	Tangshan	T'angshan
Gansu	Kansu	Lüda	Dalien, Talien,
Qinghai	Ch'inghai		or Dairen
Henan	Honan	Beijing	Peking
Anhui	Anhui	Tianjin	Tientsin
Jiangsu	Kiangsu	Taiyuan	T'aiyuan
Sichuan	Szech'uan or	Jinan	Tsinan
	Szechwan	Qingdao	Ch'ingtao or
Hubei	Hupei or Hupeh		Tsingtao
Zhejiang	Chekiang	Lanzhou	Lanchou
Guizhou	Kueichou or	Kaifeng	K'aifeng
	Kweichow	Xian	Sian (Hsi-an)
Hunan	Hunan		ancient Ch'angan
Jiangxi	Chianghsi or	Luoyang	Loyang
	Kiangsi	Nanjing	Nanking
Fujian	Fukien	Shanghai	Shanghai
Yunnan	Yünnan	Hangzhou	Hangchow
Guangxi, now		Wuhan	Wuhan, including
Guangxi			Hankou (Hankow)
Zhuang		Chengdu	Ch'engtu
A.R.	Kwangsi	Chongqing	Chungking
Guangdong	Kwangtung	Changsha	Ch'angsha
		Nanchang	Nanch'ang
		Fuzhou	Foochow
		Kunming	K'unming
		Xiamen	Hsiamen or Amoy
		Guangzhou	Canton
		Xianggang	Hongkong
		Aumen	Macao

INTRODUCTION

To the average Westerner, China has always been, ever since Marco Polo, a mysterious and fascinating country. The cloud of mystery which began to be dispelled after the forcible opening of China in the nineteenth century descended once again with the emergence of the Communist regime. Now the cloud is thinning once more, and there is a surge of interest in China to be felt not only in Europe and America but in almost every country in the world.

The new China has been deeply affected by Western modes, culture, and technology for three main reasons. First, the changes in China are part of a worldwide process going on everywhere for, to a greater or lesser degree, all countries are adopting the Western bag of tools and the ideas which go with them. Second, the People's Republic of China (PRC) is the present culmination of a political and social revolution which has been developing in that country for over eighty years, since 1911, a revolution provoked even earlier by the impact of Western trade and technical advances operating from the middle of the nineteenth century onward. Third, China today is affected in a special way by the West because its Communist ideology is rooted in the French Revolution, in the labors of Karl Marx writing in the British Museum in London, and in the blood of the Russian Revolution. Communism is, to begin with, a Western product.

Would it not be sufficient, then, for a student of modern China to start with Mao Zedong or with Sun Yat-sen, or at the earliest with the Opium War of 1839? It does not take much reflection to conclude that this rhetorical question must receive a negative answer. Although the West has influenced modern China, that nation cannot be understood without reference to all the major phases of its long past. We are here dealing with the evolution of a proud and largely self-sufficient civilization. The attitudes of Chinese alive today are, to an unusual degree, rooted in a history consciously present to their minds.

Chinese history is not the oldest in the world. We have records of developed civilizations in the valleys of the Nile, the Euphrates-Tigris, and even the Indus which are older than that of the Yellow River. But peoples and languages have changed out of all recognition in those other centers of early civilization. Chinese civilization, by contrast, has remained recognizably the same in essentials and is thus the oldest continuous, homogeneous, major culture in the world today.

This fact often leads to the assumption that Chinese history is static, that the passivity, even stagnation, visible in the Chinese scene at the end of the Qing (or Manzhou/Manchu) dynasty in the nineteenth century is true of all Chinese history. This is far from being the case. Numerous changes, some of them violent, many of them innovative and creative, took place in the course of the centuries. Yet through all these changes, including the recent ones set off by Western contacts, the Chinese people, their language, and the indefinable essence of their culture have maintained certain constant characteristics.

How are these constants and these changes to be captured in the compass of a small book? It is obviously necessary first to provide the outlines of a political framework and then to weave into this framework some account of the main cultural and social trends in Chinese history.

The political framework is conventionally divided by dynasties. Traditionally, Chinese historians have viewed their history from the angle of Confucian moralism. It is family history, determined by family succession in dynasties, and it is personal history, determined by the character of the ruler and his officials at the apex of the vast autocratic government pyramid. Thus the first ruler of a dynasty is seen as good, the dynasty rises and ultimately declines through moral weakness, and the last ruler is seen as evil. A new line of dynastic rulers appears, often as the result of popular demand, sometimes as the result of foreign conquest (which itself may be perceived as the result of moral failure in the rulers of China).

Much of Chinese history does divide actually and naturally into dynastic periods. But modern historians see other factors operating: social and economic changes and external threats, beginning part way through a dynasty, contributing to its downfall, and shaping the political forms of the succeeding dynasty. They would therefore mark the divisions of history at the points where the new factors begin to affect the course of events and where they cease to count. Neither of these points may happen to coincide with the beginning or end of a dynasty. For example, some historians see a change so important as to deserve being labeled the transition from medievalism to modern times occurring not between the Tang and Song dynasties but at the time of the rebellion of An Lushan in A.D. 755, some 150 years before the close of Tang. Nevertheless it is necessary to become thoroughly acquainted with the names and dates of the dynasties, since these are used as reference points in all Chinese history, cultural as well as political.

Since there is such a wealth of material in China's cultural history, it is not possible here to explore with any amplitude the origins and rise of each form of art, literature, or cultural expression, but only to introduce a brief consideration of each form at the approximate point in the chronology when it is at its height. The mention of poetry during the Tang dynasty and of landscape painting during Song does not imply that great painters and poets did not exist at other periods in Chinese history, any more than consideration of the romantic novels of Walter Scott and Victor Hugo would be taken to indicate that novel writing began and ended with these two authors.

Scientific history must perforce specialize. General history should aim to present the story of a people's development as far as possible as a unity and not consent to split history into discrete components such as constitutional, military, economic, social, and art history. The extent to which our understanding of history has become compartmentalized is scarcely appreciated until we turn to the history of Asia, and of China in particular. The Chinese scholar thought of himself* not as a specialist ("the gentleman is not a tool"—Confucius), but as an all-around person. He expected to acquire some proficiency not only in the art of government, which as a member of the bureaucracy he had to attend to as his main job, but also in such polite accomplishments as calligraphy and painting. He could give a good account of himself as a musician, as a poet, and as a writer of essays or belles lettres. His training included field sports such as archery, and he was expected to know something of military tactics, since his duties as a magistrate included both civil and military responsibilities. In presenting a history of China it is therefore necessary to attempt, however inadequately, to include at least some mention of all the significant elements in Chinese life and culture.

The task of compressing such a variety of material into a short account which is to any degree readable presents problems. Some short histories of China stress the modern period and give only a sketchy treatment of the past. Others deal more thoroughly with the imperial period and do less than justice to the Chinese Revolution in its Nationalist and Communist phases. The present work attempts to give approximately equal treatment to all periods, believing that each has its importance in the evolving story of the Chinese experience. The 1980s and early 1990s have perforce been accorded fuller attention.

Events in any country can be recorded, and trends in any society examined, in words which are intelligible to all. But the interpretation of the Chinese experience in terms which make sense, which clear up deep-lying confusions and leave a clear impression on Western minds, is a formidable challenge. It is hard for Westerners to understand the Chinese, their motives and their modus operandi, just as it must be hard for Chinese to understand us and our unconscious assumptions. The best road to understanding is to live in the other society for a long period of time, but this is only possible for a few.

*Over most of Chinese history, the word *scholar* refers to men. There are notable exceptions, such as the woman historian Ban Zhao, but they are few. Confucianism dictated confinement of women to the home.

I have tried to write this book for the average educated Western reader, using terms, parallels, and illustrations from the West which may illuminate the Chinese scene, proceeding from the known and the common to the unknown and the distinctive. I have also tried to let the Chinese speak for themselves, to illustrate their own history through their anecdotes and ways of thought. I am conscious of many gaps and inadequacies in my account. I have one positive factor to cite: I came to the task slowly. I lived in China for some years, with the people on the land, in Peking and in the small towns, speaking nothing but Chinese for weeks at a time; then, captivated by China, I began to study Chinese thought, art, and history; and lastly I spent a good many years teaching these subjects to Western students who had no background whatsoever in Chinese studies. At length I have tried to put the results together, in the hope that the book may serve as an introduction to one of the great civilizations of the world, and to a people of great vitality, charm, and wisdom with whom we now, in the present political circumstances, have a better chance to become truly acquainted.

Those who wish to pursue the study of China will find books in English and other European languages available for both generalists and specialists, covering different aspects and periods of Chinese history and civilization, a number of which are listed in the bibliography. University and community classes in the subject are being more widely offered, but it is also possible to obtain considerable knowledge and much enjoyment by becoming self-taught. For instance, reading a book such as George Rowley, *Principles of Chinese Painting,* will not make one an art expert, but it will open up the subject. Then one can begin a lifelong process of "soaking," immersing oneself in the contemplation of Chinese pictures, which is in itself infinitely rewarding. Similarly, Chinese verse is now accessible in good English and other translations. A thorough study of the Chinese language, written and spoken, is necessary for those who will become scholars, able in turn to train the diplomats, businessmen, and students whom we shall require in large numbers for our future intercourse with China. But for every single scholar, we shall need a hundred amateurs of the subject of Chinese studies, in the best and most literal sense of the term *amateur.* This book is for them.

1
THE LAND AND
THE PEOPLE OF CHINA

China, 3,600,000 square miles in extent, is about the same size as the United States and second only to Soviet Russia in area. It extends some 2,300 miles from north to south. Canton is within the tropical belt, while northern Manchuria has temperatures of 40 degrees below zero Fahrenheit in winter and lies only 13 degrees from the Arctic Circle. The country is so large and regional differences are so great that it might easily in the course of its history have broken up permanently into separate nations, as Europe did after the decline of the Roman empire. What seems to have prevented this breakup in China was a relatively stable and very powerful bureaucracy, which was the guardian of a common script and a common, highly prized culture.

China has frontiers which touch all the main countries of Asia except those of West Asia (the Middle East and the Near East). Yet in spite of this fact, China throughout its history has been comparatively isolated owing to geographical barriers. The vast Pacific Ocean on the east, the impassable gorges of the Burma border and the inhospitable plateau of Tibet to the south and west, and the arid and sparsely populated lands of Central Asia and Mongolia to the northwest and north have caused China to have less than average contact with other major civilizations and to develop its own way of life in relative isolation. Contacts with other lands undoubtedly took place: with India through the northwest corridor, as in the coming of Buddhism along trade routes; with the Arab world by sea to Canton; with Southeast Asia by constant seaborne trade; and with the West in a small trickle overland through Central Asia and, much later, in a flood by world sea routes. The tendency of recent scholarship has been to emphasize certain foreign contacts, particularly in the prehistoric and early historical periods, but the predominant facts, long recognized and still true, are that China developed her own culture from the beginning in her own way, with few decisive influences from abroad, and that this was due in the main to factors of geography.

THE LAND

The land of China slopes down from west to east, from the mountains of Tibet, some four miles high, to the shores of the Pacific. Much of the country is mountainous or hilly, and the true plains are found mainly in Manchuria, in a large area of north China, in the Yangzi river system, and in the Sichuan basin. All rivers flow into the Pacific Ocean, except the Huai River in the north China plain, which empties into inland lakes with no outlet.

The principal rivers are but five in number: the Sungari in north Manchuria, only navigable for six months of the year; the Liao in south Manchuria; the Yellow River in north China; the Yangzi in central China; and the West River, flowing out at Canton. The Yellow River (Huang-he) is 2,700 miles long, rising in the Tibetan plateau, flowing east through gorges, turning north, then south, to make a great loop around the Ordos desert, and swinging sharply east again. After this point it has changed course several times in its lower reaches to the north and the south of the Shandong peninsula, and with disastrous effects. It flows at present north of the Shandong mountains into the great gulf known as the Bo Hai. The Yellow River has been called "China's Sorrow" because it is liable to extensive flooding. The fine soil of north China, known as loess, is carried in suspension in the river and deposited to such an extent that the level of the riverbed has been elevated above the surrounding land. When the banks or dikes give way, the floodwaters spread devastation far and wide. The Yellow River is not navigable for most of its length save by small native boats. The Yangzi, on the other hand, China's greatest river, 3,200 miles long and sixth in length in the world, is navigable for a thousand miles, up to Hankou, by large steamships all year round. Oceangoing vessels of as much as 10,000 tons can reach Hankou in the summer season of high water. Junks, launches, and smaller vessels can proceed upstream for another 600 miles, although the fourteen-knot current in the gorges above Yichang makes navigation difficult and dangerous. The Gezhou Dam, completed in 1981, now lies athwart the river above Yichang. Another, greater dam is planned within the gorges.

The mountain ranges and clusters are somewhat indeterminate in shape and direction, but the most important is the Qinling range, extending out east from the great Kun Lun system of north Tibet. The Qinling range divides north from south China, and the numerous differences thus produced between the northern and southern halves of the country form the most distinctive social and political features of China's history. The north has dry, cold, desert winds in winter; the south has the moist climate of the southeastern summer monsoon. The farmers of the northern

The Yangzi (Yangtze) River Gorges. Photographed by B. W. Kilburn about 1900.

Where the vast river emerges from the mountains onto the flatland there are currents in the narrow gorges against which for centuries men have painfully hauled junks upstream by ropes on a rocky towpath.

Library of Congress

plains produce millet, *gao liang* ("tall grain," a form of millet), and wheat; those in the southern hills and valleys grow rice, tea, mulberry trees for silkworm feed, and bamboos. The growing season in the north is from four to six months and one crop, in some places two, can be produced; in the south the season may last from nine months to a year and two or even three crops are possible. The northern farmers tend to stay at home; many men of the south are fishermen and traders and have ventured overseas in considerable numbers. When one meets a Chinese in New York, London, Brussels, or Kuala Lumpur, the chances are that his or her family originated in south China.

THE PEOPLE

Chinese society has always been predominantly rural rather than urban, and perhaps 80 percent of the population still lives in the countryside, in villages and small towns, rather than in large cities. The present government of the People's Republic of China (hereafter PRC) takes account of this fact and has decentralized industry and attempted to interfuse it with the rural communes. A large afforestation program has of recent years been undertaken to attempt to check the serious problem of soil erosion. The problem has existed for centuries, especially in the north, where timber has been used for building, cooking, and heating without adequate replacement of trees. Even in south China, where vegetation is more abundant, many slopes have been eroded because the very roots of crops have been dug out for use as fuel. The peculiar loess soil of the northern plains, though very fertile when properly watered, has the characteristic of vertical cleavage, so that deep gullies are formed during floods and the light grains of soil are washed away by water and even carried by the wind in thick storms of dust. So great is the tendency to vertical cleavage that cart tracks are quickly worn down to the point where cart, horse, and all disappear in sunken roadways below the level of the surrounding fields. (Environmental problems of drought, flooding, and pollution are mentioned again in Chapter 18.)

The population of China is not easy to calculate, in spite of the existence of a sophisticated bureaucracy from early times. Since population figures formed the basis for taxation, there was a temptation to alter the figures. At times, boys under one year and girls under five were not included. Major discrepancies occur when remote areas such as Tibet and Outer Mongolia are included in one count and omitted in another. Nevertheless the census for China taken over the centuries is probably more accurate than for most countries. The figures in the following table, derived from G. B. Cressey, *China's Geographic Foundations* (1932), and certain modern estimates, are probably as reliable as any others obtainable.

The figures for population density (also from Cressey, *China's Geographic Foundations*) show an enormous range, reflecting the widely varying nature of the terrain in its suitability for agriculture.

The population has been traditionally reckoned as consisting of five groups: Han, Chinese; Man, Manchus; Meng, Mongolians; Hui, Muslims; and Zang, Tibetans. The Han, or pure Chinese, constitute probably 94 percent of the total. The government of the PRC has instituted a program of birth control by encouraging late marriages (age twenty-five for women and twenty-eight for men being considered optimum) and by the provision of

Population of China

YEAR	POPULATION IN MILLIONS
A.D.　　1	57
1712	120
1900	440
1926	485
1953	583 (PRC census)
1975	close to 800 (estimate)
mid-1979	almost 960 (PRC census)
1988	1.07 billion

Population Density of China

AREA	DENSITY PER SQUARE MILE
China overall, including Tibet and Mongolia	120 persons
China excluding Farther Tibet and Outer Mongolia	156 (comparable to Scotland or Ohio)
China, eastern half	326 (comparable to Germany)
North China plain	647
China, total of actual cultivated land	1,479 (0.43 acre per person)

contraceptive devices and medication. The practical aim ended up as one child per family in the cities, two in the countryside. On the other hand, increase of fertility among the minority ethnic groups is said to be favored by the government.

The Chinese belong to the racial type known as Mongolian, a group which also includes the Koreans, Japanese, Mongolians, Eskimos, and American Indians. The type is marked by slightly yellow skin pigmentation, relatively flat faces, high cheekbones, almond-shaped dark eyes, and black hair. Within this type there are considerable variations between the northern and southern Chinese. Those in the north are taller by an average of two inches, have a ruddier and less yellow complexion, a less-evident almond shape to the eye, and a slightly larger head in proportion to the body than those in the south.

The culinary art has been highly valued in China from ancient times, and here also regional differences are evident. A Chinese proverbial saying points to a sweet taste in the south, a preference for salt in the north, a sour or vinegar taste in the east, and a hot, pungent taste in the west. The west China taste for hot foods has spread to New York and other cities, where menus appear in Sichuan restaurants with the names of the very hot dishes printed in red and the remainder in black, a salutary warning to the unwary foreign guest.

However, the principal regional differences are marked by wide variations in dialect. The written language is held in common and can be read by all scholars, but dialect pronunciation is so different as to make the spoken language mutually unintelligible to natives of, say, Canton and Peking. Geography has played a large part in the emergence of the dialects. The former official and court language spoken in Peking—in the past called "mandarin" and now "the national language"—was used all over the great north China plain, where intercommunication was relatively easy. It was also spoken in the southwest. But the broken nature of the mountainous terrain of south China favored the rise of different dialects. Communication downriver to the sea was much easier than it was over the steep mountains to strange villages in the next valley only a few miles away. Language thus developed in different linguistic directions and at varying rates in small isolated communities. There are said to be 108 dialects in the province of Fujian alone. One may compare the differences of speech in America between the inhabitants of the remote Kentucky hills and those in the rest of the country, and the retention in these faraway valleys of words and idioms from Elizabethan and Jacobean England.

The spread of modern popular education in both the PRC and Taiwan has led to an almost universal use of the national spoken language among a large majority of the population of both sections of China. This fortunately makes secure a common heritage for all Chinese in the future.

2
ORIGINS AND EARLY HISTORY

The human or near-human species has lived in China for a very long time. In 1923 there were discovered in a limestone cave near Peking remains of a creature, *Sinanthropus pekinensis,* or Peking man, who certainly walked upright, who used fire, and who had a brain capacity about two thirds that of modern man. Whether any physical features of Peking man were transmitted to the modern Mongoloid populations of the area remains doubtful. At the same level were found primitive stone tools and the remains of animals, including those of buffalo, deer, sheep, wild pig, and rhinoceros. Indications are that these finds date from a warm, dry, interglacial period of the Middle Pleistocene Age, some 500,000 years ago. In 1963 a further discovery was made at Lantian near Xian in Shaanxi province of another hominid perhaps 100,000 years older than Peking man, whose brain was somewhat smaller but still considerably larger than that of the most advanced anthropoid ape. He has been named *Sinanthropus lantianensis.*

EARLY CULTURES

The date of Peking man corresponds approximately to the Acheulean culture and is assigned to Lower Paleolithic. An immense interval of time passes, and then human remains or traces of human occupation in Guangdong in south China, in Hubei in central China, and in the Ordos region in the north are tentatively assigned to Middle Paleolithic, from 200,000 to 100,000 B.C. The appearance of Late Paleolithic man, by now *Homo sapiens* without question, occurs in the upper cave at Zhoukoudian, above the site of Peking man, around 35,000 B.C., at a point which would correspond to Cro-Magnon man. There are a number of other sites containing tools and human bones of the Old Stone Age in China, extending in space from Manchuria to south China and running in time down to c. 10,000 B.C. Similar tools have been found north of Lake Baikal in Siberia, indicating a single Sino-Siberian Late Paleolithic culture. Some sites contain microlithic tools formed of small flints made to be set in rows in wood or bone. This type of tool is found all over Europe and Asia and usually appears just before the onset of the great revolution betokened by the Neolithic period of polished stone tools, the practice of farming, and the making of pottery.

The social scene changed vastly in Neolithic times. Neolithic man lived a comparatively settled life in villages, such as that discovered at Banpo in Shaanxi, which measures 200 by 100 meters and is surrounded by a deep ditch that served for both defense and irrigation. Houses were semisubterranean, round or rectangular, with central pillars supporting a roof of clay and thatch. The walls were of pounded earth, and inside were ovens, cupboards, and benches, all formed of clay, while in some cases the floor was finished in white clay. The population engaged in agriculture, hunting, and fishing. Stone tools and weapons, including axes, chisels, and adzes, were of both chipped and polished varieties. There were arrowheads, harpoons, and needles of bone. Millet, the chief grain, was stored in pear-shaped ground pits. Protein diet must have been varied, for bones of pigs, dogs, sheep, goats, and deer have been found. Near Banpo are 250 tombs in which adults are buried in individual rectangular graves, while children are interred in jars beside the houses.

Types of pottery form convenient distinguishing marks of early cultures, in China as elsewhere. Following upon early simple pots with cord markings impressed upon them, the Yangshao Neolithic culture shows reddish pottery with black designs of considerable sophistication—some geometric, some natural. Some vessels have free-flowing curved designs executed with skill upon a surface itself curved. One bowl from Banpo has a fish of a highly satisfying semiabstract design in opposing triangles and subtle curves of red and black, with prominent snout and eyes and open mouth. It is highly stylized, yet it exhibits the vitality and rhythm which is to characterize all Chinese art.

The Yangshao culture is to be found in sites, usually near the fertile soil of rivers, along the middle course of the Yellow River, on the west-central plain, and up into the northwest of China and the tributary valleys of the Yellow River. The Longshan culture, which overlaps and seems to succeed it, is centered farther to the east, in northeast China, the Shandong coastal region, and part of the central plain. In some places, particularly in Henan, Longshan pottery remains are found above Yangshao items on the same site, but the exact chronological sequence of the two cultures as a whole is still not clear. Longshan ware is thin, hard, black, and burnished. It was formed on a potter's wheel, which is not the case with Yangshao ware, and the profiles are more angular than those of Yangshao.

It has not been possible so far to assign dates with any certainty to these Neolithic cultures of north China, but a rough approximation can be reached with the aid of a Japanese parallel. The earliest pottery in Japan has been dated

Neolithic pottery jar. Yangshao stage, after 5000 B.C.

This vessel, 17 inches in diameter, was found at Ban Shan in Gansu, in the far northwest. The geometric design, far from primitive, shows the successful treatment of a large curved surface and is much more effective because the lower portion is left plain.

Buffalo Museum of Science

by the carbon-14 method to the eighth millennium B.C. It is thought highly unlikely that the first pottery on the continent would be any later in date. If that is so, then the developed cultures of Yangshao and Longshan probably arose after the year 5,000 B.C., by which time the megalithic cultures were flourishing in Europe.

Chinese scholars of a later date, always inveterate annalists and recorders, assigned the beginnings of their history to the year 2852 B.C. and said that China was first ruled by the Three Sovereigns, who were followed by the Five Rulers. To these mythical kings are attributed such beneficent inventions as the gift of fire, the building of houses, the invention of farming, and, by the Yellow Emperor's wife, the invention of silk culture. From the kings also came the discovery of medicine and the inventions of the calendar and the Chinese script. The last of the Five Rulers were the model emperors Yao and Shun. Then another great benefactor, Yu the Great, is said to have founded the first dynasty, the Xia dynasty.

THE XIA DYNASTY

Among these culture heroes admired by the Chinese, Yu is particularly interesting, for his contribution was flood control and irrigation. He is said to have been so devoted to his work that when he came to his own district after an absence of nine years, he saw his home near the river but walked past and would not take time to go in. These myths, which cannot be fitted into any time framework established by archaeology, show that, although China has fought many cruel wars, the ideal has always been that of peaceful cultural achievement rather than feats of battle. The legend of Yu demonstrates that the needed culture hero is one who can organize men and make them combine to combat the natural disaster of a flood on a vast scale. Chinese society recognizes the survival value of working together for community ends, whereas the individualist credo dictated by the circumstances of the American frontier believes in the lone pioneer who, with family help, can carve out a piece of the wilderness to enjoy in freedom. A few individuals are of no use in the north China plains; there it takes tens of thousands, each carrying a spade and a sandbag, to tame the raging of China's Sorrow, the Yellow River.

The Xia dynasty (attributed dates 2205–1766 B.C.) cannot be linked with any known archaeological evidence. There was a tendency for the later annalist officials to push back as far as possible into the past the appearance of the Chinese state as a centralized, bureaucratic, and dynastic system. The historicity of Xia is thus in doubt, but scholars are becoming more cautious. It was thought at one time that the Shang dynasty, also known as the Yin dynasty (traditionally 1766–1122 B.C., more correctly 1523–1027 B.C.) was also to be considered as legendary. Yet the list of kings of this dynasty recovered from inscriptions of known Shang date was found to agree almost exactly with the traditional list as given by the great historian of the second century B.C., Sima Qian (Ssu-Ma Ch'ien), thus entirely vindicating in this case the literary sources. Judgment on the Xia must therefore be reserved until further evidence is in.

THE SHANG DYNASTY

The story of the oracle bones of Shang is one of the most exciting in the annals of archaeology, in view of the flood of light it has shed upon the early history of China. It is a story comparable in its wider aspects to that of the decipherment of Linear B writing in Minoan Crete, where the dates of the originals happen almost to correspond. (This is also the period of the pharaoh Tutankhamun.) Just before the end of the nineteenth century, Chinese scholars became aware that so-called "dragon bones" were turning up in apothecaries' shops and being used in the preparation of traditional Chinese medicines. The bones were valued as magic because they had symbols inscribed upon them. Serious work on the bones began in 1903, but fuller results were only to come after extensive excavations from 1928 to 1937 at Anyang, near the great bend in the Yellow River, the area known as the cradle of Chinese civilization. Altogether 100,000 of these bones—shoulder blades of deer and oxen and the carapaces of tortoises—have been unearthed and the results of research upon 15,000 of them published. The characters inscribed upon them, dating from about 1300 B.C., and some of the signs found on Yangshao pottery represent the earliest known form of the Chinese language. Some 5,000 characters have been distinguished and 1,500 of these deciphered. A major reform of Chinese writing in the second century B.C. is the reason why the meanings of many of the older characters have been lost.

Royal priests used the oracle bone writing in their divination methods to get in touch with the spirit world. These practices underlie the more sophisticated ones used later in the Yi Jing, *Book of Changes,* or *Book of Divination* (see p. 33). All are based on the belief in an intimate correlation between the natural and human worlds found throughout Chinese history.

The oracle bones, the superb bronze vessels, and the tombs of Shang reveal a civilization of splendor and of violence. Their kings were buried in coffins in immense pits with two or four sloping access ramps. A dog was sacrificed and placed immediately under each coffin, and numerous treasures (5,801 articles in one particular tomb) were buried along with the monarch. Among the most valuable of these objects, and ranking as status symbols, were cult vessels of bronze and war chariots, with horses and charioteers previously killed and buried along with them. The chariots are similar to those described by Homer in the *Iliad* as existing in 1200 B.C. and were constructed with a high degree of skill in carpentry. The two wooden wheels are slender and have sixteen or more spokes. The box body, supported on axle and shaft running forward between the two or four horses, was small and light but of sufficient size to carry a charioteer and spearman as well as the king or noble owner. The hubs had to be long in order to distribute the heat generated by the friction of wood on wood, although pitch or animal fat was employed to lubricate them. Fine bronze fittings for chariot and harness have been preserved in the tombs.

A grim feature of Shang burials was the sacrifice of large numbers of human victims in groups of ten. They were ceremonially beheaded with large axes, also found in the tombs. These were prisoners taken in war or captured from nomad shepherd tribes on the western borders of Shang. This slaughter and the fact that the victims were sometimes chained has caused Chinese Marxist historians to attach the name "The Slave Society" to this period. William Watson notes a resemblance between Shang and the states of ancient Mesopotamia in the institutions of kingship and priesthood, sacrifice and oracle-taking, the use of the bow and the chariot, and "hypertrophy of the funeral rite accompanied by human sacrifice. Beneath was a vast peasantry hardly advanced beyond their old neolithic economy."*

---

*William Watson, *Cultural Frontiers in Ancient East Asia* (Edinburgh: Edinburgh University Press, 1972), p. 38.

Shang seems to have been organized as a form of city-state under a monarchy which in the beginning was strong. There were satellite villages not far away from the central capital, and the state had a measure of control over communities at a greater distance. More than fifty sites of Shang finds, nine of them principal ones, have been identified, centered on the Yellow River and the north China plain. The location of the walled capital shifted, and two of the most noteworthy sites were Zheng Zhou (probably the ancient Ao), a capital founded under the tenth king and occupied from c. 1500 to 1300 B.C., and Anyang, also known as Great Shang, which dates from the time of the nineteenth king in 1300 B.C. until the fall of the dynasty in 1027 B.C.

The wealth and the command of skilled labor displayed in the tombs, comparatively great for this early stage in Chinese history, indicates that the Shang kings and nobles held positions of considerable power and prestige in society. The kings were able to put into the field armies of from 3,000 to 5,000 strong. It is clear from the oracle bone inscriptions that hunting was a major preoccupation of the leaders, and, as in the Mongol dynasty, hunting with organized drives for game was used as a means of training bodies of soldiers. Indeed, hunting, fishing, and food gathering remained an important part of the economy for the whole population, even although agriculture was long established as the mainstay.

The Shang tombs also give us a good idea of the weapons in use at this period, which was the beginning of China's Bronze Age. The chariots already mentioned were apparently used mainly to transport warriors to the battle site, where they dismounted to fight, again as in Homeric warfare. Among the weapons were spears with bronze blades and the great axes used also for ceremonial decapitation of victims. Bows of wood and horn are perishable and no examples have been found, but characters on bronze vessels hint that Shang bows were of the reflex or compound type, which deliver great power for a shorter bow length than the simple longbow. The compound bow with its double curve is thus valuable in the cramped quarters of a war chariot and was used with great effect at a later date by both nomads and Chinese on horseback. Swords were not in use in the Shang age. They occur first during the Zhou dynasty in the sixth century B.C.

A peculiarly Chinese weapon found in large numbers from the Shang period is the *ge,* or halberd. This pole weapon has a blade mounted at right angles to the shaft, with a tang at the rear passing through the shaft. Later a guard extended down the shaft to give rigidity to the blade fitting, and a spear point continuing in the line of the shaft was added. Ceremonial examples of the *ge* are numerous, some with blades of jade and with decoration on the tang, guard, and ferrule at the bottom of the shaft.

The chief glories of Shang art and craftsmanship are the magnificent vessels of bronze. These vessels, in a number of carefully prescribed shapes, were designed primarily for use in sacrifice to ancestors and gods, but they were also used to mark occasions of royal favor, such as the granting of a fief or an honor to a noble. Possession of bronze vessels was a conspicuous sign of wealth and a means of preserving it in the family.

The forms of the bronzes, in many cases derived from earlier pottery shapes, are solid, dignified, and satisfying. The ornament is highly elaborated and beautifully adapted to the shape of the vessel. A main motive is that of the *taotie* monster mask, a stylized, symmetrical form of animal face viewed from the front. Minor decoration in the form of fretted or geometrical designs fills in the spaces of the main pattern. The vessels were cast in pottery molds. A higher than usual proportion of lead was added to the copper-and-tin mix in order to produce a free flow of the molten metal into the fine portions of the design and to prevent the formation of gas bubbles. The workmanship of these bronze pieces is so fine that the grooves can be seen under a lens to be not V-shaped but showing a full, open, square section with perpendicular sides, thus: ⊔ .

Shang <u>bronze-working</u> attained an extremely high standard, scarcely excelled anywhere else at any date. The rise of Shang bronze techniques appeared until recently to have been very rapid, and this led to speculation that knowledge of bronze casting might have been introduced from West Asia, then applied and developed in China. But discoveries in the 1970s have revealed examples of earlier, thinner, and much more primitive bronzes, which point to a long development within China itself. It now seems likely that the Chinese invented the casting of bronze independently.

Bronze wine vessel *(cun, ts'un)*, inlaid with black lacquer. Shang dynasty, 1523–1027 B.C.

Note the satisfying shape and the extremely fine lines of decoration, which are cast, not incised. Shang bronze craftsmanship, although so early, has never been surpassed.

The Metropolitan Museum of Art, Rogers Fund, 1943

THE CHINESE LANGUAGE

It is certain that the Chinese form of writing is an entirely distinct and native product. Chinese script first appears about 1300 B.C., as has been mentioned, on the oracle bones discovered chiefly at Anyang, the later Shang capital. These bones were found in large numbers and therefore form a significant sample for the study of the evolving Chinese language. The oracular procedure was as follows: On one side of a shoulderblade bone or piece of tortoise shell a slight oval hollow was cut, and heat was applied with a bronze point at the side of this hollow. The bone on the other side cracked, usually in a long line with a shorter spur going off at an angle. This is clearly indicated by the Chinese character ⼘ "to divine," "foretell." It is not known exactly what angles or positions of crack determined the answer of the oracle as being yes or no, favorable or unfavorable, to the question put. This method of divination was also practiced, as has been said, in pre-Shang Neolithic times, but the bones from this early period bear no writing. In the Shang period many of the bones have inscribed upon them with a sharp point characters which give in laconic form the question or subject reference of the oracle, occasionally the answer as interpreted by the soothsayer, and very occasionally the actual outcome of the event in question. The questions cover a variety of topics, including acceptable sacrifices, propitious days, weather, crops, and journeys, and success in war or the hunt.

The important points for the historian in all this are, first, that the script on the bones is clearly the ancestor of modern Chinese and essentially the same in character structure, and, second, that the written language, when it

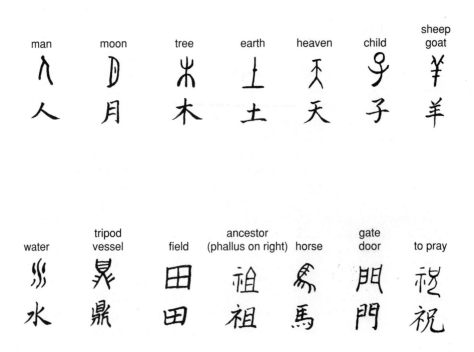

first appears in Shang times, is already developed and no longer primitive. As may be seen from the accompanying figure (based on William Watson, *Early Chinese Civilization*), the basic idea is the representation of objects by pictures, pictograms. Other peoples, such as those of ancient Egypt and the North American Indian tribes, also used this method. But before the Anyang period of Shang the Chinese had taken the decisive step forward of combining pictures to represent abstract ideas, as in the character "to pray" at the right of the illustration, a man kneeling before a divine symbol. Here a pictogram becomes an ideogram, and the Chinese language is launched upon a developing course of infinite variety and richness. Proceeding for a moment beyond the oracle bones, other examples of such combinations are 明 日 "sun" and 月 "moon" together meaning "bright" or "brilliant," the quality shared by the heavenly bodies; or 東 the sun coming up behind a tree 木 (third from left in illustration), meaning "the east"; or 安 an^1, a woman under a roof, meaning "peace."

The next step is the sorting out and arrangement of characters by category. Water words, such as "sea," "river," and "lake," all have the signific or radical 水 "water" contracted to 氵 written alongside another character. This second character is the phonetic which gives a clue to the sound of the word; thus 河 he^2, "river" (phonetic 可 ke^3). Because pronunciation has altered greatly over the centuries, and for other reasons, the phonetics unfortunately do not always live up to their name. Trees and wood words have the radical 木 "tree" alongside, and so on. The 214 radicals are used in a Chinese dictionary to group the characters. The number of strokes in the remaining part of the character determines its place in the group. So in order to read Chinese and be able to find a word in a dictionary, it is necessary to be able to write it and thus know the exact number of strokes required.

This is obviously a cumbrous method, and written Chinese is a difficult language, not only for foreigners but for the Chinese themselves. But the system does secure precision in meaning. How necessary this is may be seen by turning for a moment to the spoken language. In spoken Chinese, monosyllables, each signified by a written character, are used as building blocks for polysyllabic words, phrases, and sentences. The spoken language also employs tones. The "national language" or standard dialect of Peking has four tones, Cantonese as many as nine in all and six in common use, designated by a number above the last letter of a word. The tones are obtained by employing rising or falling pitch on a syllable. The employment of tones increases the range of possible voice sounds, but even so the human mouth can only form a certain number of single syllable sounds, and thus the range of possible meanings is limited. Spoken Chinese overcomes this difficulty in part by the context supplying the meaning, and in part by the use of two words in combination. Thus the sound an^1 (first tone) can mean "peace," but it can also mean other things, as, for example, "a saddle." However, when $ping^2$, "level," "tranquil," is combined with an^1 in the phrase *ping an,* the meaning is clearly defined by the two referents. It is somewhat like pinpointing a position by x and y coordinates on a graph.

In written Chinese there is no doubt as to the meaning of 安 *an*[1], "peace," or 鞍 *an*[1], "saddle." In the second character the radical on the left-hand side, *ge*[2], means "hide," "leather," giving the category, and the phonetic *an*[1] on the right-hand side gives the pronunciation. Thus Chinese is one of the few languages in the world where the common man is more prolix, because he has to employ circumlocution, and the scholar's expression is more terse and economical. By assigning one distinct written character to each meaning or monosyllabic word, Chinese in its literary form avoids ambiguity, and over the centuries the language has become one of great terseness, vitality, and flexibility, as well as artistic charm. (The characters themselves are precise in the sense described, but the meaning of a sentence may not be as exact and unambiguous as in an inflected language such as Greek.)

Written Chinese, moreover, acts as a cultural bond between those in different regions of the country who have come in the course of time to speak mutually incomprehensible dialects. It is also a unifying factor for all of East Asia, between China and the peripheral areas which have borrowed its culture: Korea, Japan, Vietnam, Tibet, and Mongolia. Throughout all the changes which the language has undergone, rich overtones of an aesthetic and spiritual nature still dwell in written Chinese and add immeasurably to its artistic and literary appeal. "Leisure," for instance, is represented by moonlight through the opening of a door, and "good" by the picture of a woman and a child. This is humanism at its best, woven from the beginning into the very stuff of thought and expression.

The foregoing discussion should make clear why Chinese cannot easily be alphabetized in Western form, since chaos in communication would result from too many words which are similar in sound. However, something has been done to simplify the writing of Chinese characters by the use of contractions to eliminate a number of strokes, and by encouraging the use of selected basic characters. In spite of what has been said above, the PRC authorities are introducing alphabetized Chinese for everyday use. Literacy levels have been significantly raised in the population, first under the Republic and then under the Communist government.

Word order is most important in Chinese, since the language is uninflected. There is no difference made in a word for number or gender, and verb tenses are indicated by auxiliaries comparable to the English "will" and "did." Word order in fact determines grammar and syntax. A character may function as a noun, verb, or other part of speech depending upon its place in the sentence. Horace or Virgil may displace and rearrange words in a sentence to secure dramatic poetic contrasts, in the knowledge that case, number, and tense are securely indicated by inflection and thus the meaning is preserved. This is not possible in Chinese. Effects are obtained in poetry and prose by the shape and associations of the characters, by their spoken sound in verse, by striking parallelisms, and perhaps above all by echoes and literary allusions. Chinese civilization depends upon writing and calligraphy; there are great authors and books, but no tradition of great orators and speeches.

As an appendix to this short discussion of the Chinese language, it may be well to clear up some practical points for those unfamiliar with Chinese names. Modern Chinese use a system called *pinyin* for the transliteration of Chinese terms into Western alphabets. But historical works in English have generally employed an older form, the Wade-Giles romanization. Pinyin was adopted officially by *The New York Times* on March 1, 1979, and is used here (see A Note on Spelling and Pronunciation at the front of the book). This is all less confusing in fact than it sounds. Care in acquiring correct pronunciation pays dividends in communication and memorization later.

Chinese throughout history have placed the surname first, followed by the given name, and that practice is used here. Many Chinese are adopting the Western form, now almost universal in Japan, of placing the surname last. Chinese emperors are usually distinguished by the name of their dynasty when first mentioned, followed by their reign name, which was actually given posthumously but is customarily used to refer to them when alive.

3

THE FORMATIVE PERIOD

Zhou Dynasty: 1027–221 B.C.

Where the Yellow River ends its southern flow and takes a sudden bend north of east, it is joined by an important tributary, the Wei River, flowing in from the west. Out of the Wei valley in 1027 B.C. came a vigorous and warlike people known as the Zhou to conquer the Shang and take over their territory. The Zhou were not "barbarians" but Chinese, although their western origin had brought them into contact with the nomads of the steppes and given them training in the warfare of movement. They had already had contact with the Shang and their culture and, in fact, probably supplied the Shang with horses from their upland pastures.

WESTERN ZHOU PERIOD

King Wen of Zhou prepared the attack, and King Wu successfully completed it by a victory at Mu. The Duke of Zhou, brother of Wu, had to return soon after to suppress a revolt by some of the defeated Shang, supported by other disaffected persons, but thereafter the Zhou were in full control. So great was the vigor of the Zhou attack that before long they had penetrated to the eastern seaboard of north China. In order to control this extensive territory, the Zhou kings assigned various cities and regions to their relatives to rule. For this reason the period has sometimes been called the "feudal age," but the term in its developed meaning is scarcely applicable, for there is no evidence of feudal contracts at this time, in the sense of grants of defined amounts of land in return for levies of so many fighting men.

The Shang, though reduced to a very minor position after their revolt, were allowed by the Zhou to retain a small amount of land, in order that their ancestral sacrifices might be continued. The importance of landholding in

China from the beginning may be seen here. It was considered necessary for a noble house to be based upon some territory of its own in order to perform the religious rites of ancestor worship on which its welfare depended. While this provision of land by the Zhou to their defeated enemies may be deemed chivalrous, it was also a sensible precaution, since neglected ghosts of former powerful personages could cause considerable harm to the living.

The importance of the change from Shang to Zhou rule consists not only in the event itself but also in the interpretation put upon it by the Zhou. Their chief deity was Tian, or Heaven, and the new ruling family maintained that their authority was acquired through the Mandate of Heaven. (From this time on in Chinese history each new dynasty claimed legitimacy by possession of this Mandate of Heaven.) Much, therefore, is made of the wickedness of the last Shang ruler, Zhou Xin (the name is confusing, but he is, of course, not of the new Zhou line), and the goodness, unselfishness, and restraint of Kings Wen and Wu and the Duke of Zhou. Confucius himself is known to have shared this feeling, for he said, "How utterly things have gone to the bad with me! It is long now indeed since I dreamed that I saw the Duke of Zhou."* Zhou Xin in the traditional accounts appears as a monster of evil and sunk in debauchery, for he entertained his court around a lake of wine by forcing naked youths and maidens to chase one another amid a forest of trees hung with portions of meat. Modern anthropologists with a different eye see this as a spring fertility festival, designed by sympathetic magic to promote fruitfulness in the earth (groves of trees are associated with fertility), success in the hunt, and the growth of the tribe.

For the first three centuries of Zhou rule, society and culture continued along the lines established by the Shang. Houses were built in much the same form, although roof tiles of earthenware were being used. Magnificent bronze vessels were still cast, but toward the end of the period accuracy of workmanship declined slightly and inspiration in design began to flag. The inscriptions on bronzes became longer and more detailed. Some vessels were made in sets, as, for instance, three discovered recently: a square bronze vessel for wine, another for water, and a vessel with a lid in the form of a grotesque animal, all bearing identical inscriptions in eighteen characters: "Precious ritual vase dedicated to Zhe Qi. May his sons and grandsons for 10,000 years make eternal and precious use of it." Jars of protoporcelain have been found, made of the same clay as the later renowned porcelain of the imperial factories at Jingdezhen in Jiangxi province. One of the oldest carillons of nine bronze bells, the carillon of the Marquis of Cai, dates from this period. Bells formed an important part of Zhou ritual music, as did also musical stones which sounded when struck.

The use of ink and the writing brush were known in Shang, and the existence of bamboo books consisting of slats bound by a cord is deduced from the Shang character ▦. But in Zhou, writing was more prevalent and

---

Analects, VII, 5, Waley's translation.

Bronze Grain vessel. Late Zhou
(Chou) Dynasty, about 770–
256 B.C.

The cover with intertwined dragon
ornamentation forms a cup.
*The Metropolitan Museum of Art,
Rogers Fund, 1925*

records were kept in much greater quantity. There are known to have been
Zhou lists of valuable objects, account books, written instructions to subordi-
nates, and royal edicts issued in formal language by trained scribes. By the end
of the Zhou period there were works on history, music, ritual, archery, and
other topics, as well as collections of poetry (see chapter 4). Most of these
records were kept on bamboo or wood, the most popular materials for writing
before the invention of paper in the second century A.D.

As a part of the Confucian idealization of the early Zhou dynasty, the
degree of central control exercised by the kings has been exaggerated. But
even the limited amount of control actually put into effect declined by the
ninth century. A popular revolt drove out the king in 841 B.C., and the subsequent setting up of the Gong He regency gives us the first completely firm
date in Chinese history. From this point on the dates are considered reliable.

EASTERN ZHOU PERIOD

Soon thereafter, in 771 B.C., the Zhou king suffered a severe defeat by a
nomad tribe, the Chuan ("Dog") Rong. It is said that the monarch had previously had the alarm beacons lit for raising the levy of troops simply in order to
see his favorite concubine laugh, for she was a petulant lady. When the real
attack came, the soldiers disregarded the beacon fires and refused to muster.
After this disaster the Zhou kings were forced to transfer their seat out of the

Wei River valley to a new capital farther east near Luoyang. The Western Zhou subperiod was over and the Eastern Zhou had begun.

From this point on, the allegiance of the various states and cities to the Zhou became merely nominal. The Zhou court alone had the right and duty to perform the sacrifices to Heaven and was still in theory the fount of all honors, but the kings were figureheads and virtually powerless. In the traditional view this represents a sad decline from the earlier legitimate and glorious rule of the Zhou. In actuality the ensuing period up to the official end of the dynasty in 221 B.C., although full of violence and intrigue, was a time of fresh creativity and inventiveness in the realms of thought, technology, and social change. This was the great formative period in Chinese philosophy, when, as we shall see in the next chapter, a number of schools covering a wide spectrum of thought were contending for the minds of men in the areas both of theory and of practical politics. Accompanying the revolution of thought were sweeping changes in society and greatly improved techniques in agriculture and the economy.

The Zhou dynasty is by far the longest in Chinese history, and the conditions of life and the state of society at the beginning and end of it are vastly different. The only bond is the existence of the Zhou house, which starts as conqueror and ends a long 800 years later as a neglected family of priest-kings with scarcely the vestiges of power. The second half, or Eastern Zhou period, is in turn usually subdivided into two sections, which cover most but not all of the years involved. The first is the Chunqiu, or Spring and Autumn period, 722–481 B.C., so called from the title of a work, the earliest chronicle in Chinese history, which records the annals of the state of Lu between these dates. The second is the period of the Warring States from 403 to 221 B.C., when the Qin dynasty began, the Zhou line having already been deposed some years earlier.

The situation during Eastern Zhou was one in which ten to a dozen major states, later reduced to seven, were contending for territory and leadership in a changing series of alliances, intrigues, and open wars. In addition there were countless smaller states, some consisting only of a walled town and a few square miles of territory, which were gradually swallowed up by larger ones. The states turned from being principalities under the Zhou to becoming independent kingdoms. Their chiefs, who had been divided into five grades of nobility, equivalent to duke, marquis, count, viscount, and baron, had all by the middle of the Warring States period taken the title of *wang,* king, formerly reserved for the Zhou sovereigns alone. None of the contending kings, however, arrogated to himself the title "Son of Heaven" or claimed the right to offer the sacrifices to Heaven. Some of the signs of power and status which tended to raise the ruling family of a state, large or small, above its rivals were military strength, measured in numbers of chariots; prestige, seen in connections with the Zhou house, long ancestry, and acknowledged religious privileges; and wealth, exhibited in treasures and symbols of rank, such as bronze vessels, bells, jade, and other precious objects.

The nature of warfare underwent change during the long period of the Zhou dynasty. At the end of the seventh century the earlier idea of war as a gentleman's activity to be pursued with some moderation and respect for Heaven's decrees still prevailed. The Duke of Song allowed his enemy Zhu to cross a river and draw up his forces in battle array before launching his attack. He was soundly defeated. When taken to task by his advisers for what seemed to them an excess of chivalry, the duke replied, "The sage does not crush the feeble, nor give the order for attack until the enemy have formed their ranks." But attitudes began to change, and as rites, ceremonies, and hierarchy of rank were less respected, the niceties of combat were neglected. Men fought less for honor and more for territory and gain. War *à outrance* became commoner. By the time the Qin conquered the whole of China, war was ruthless not only in practice but also in Qin theory.

Tactics and weapons also changed. The first innovation was the sword, known in the West much earlier. Probably adopted from the nomads of the steppes, it was not in use in China in bronze form until the sixth century B.C. and in iron when the Qin used it with effect in their conquests at the end of the third century B.C. In the fifth century the crossbow was introduced. This weapon, which could be stretched for cocking and loading by the foot, was more powerful and more accurate than the compound bow. The trigger-release mechanism was gradually improved until at a later period it attained a high degree of efficiency. With levers arranged in three moving parts, it could hold a heavy-tension load yet be easily and smoothly released. The removal of two pins dismantled the mechanism in case of capture by the enemy, and it could not be easily reassembled by anyone unfamiliar with its operation. Then in 307 B.C. the King of Zhao took a lesson from his nomad neighbors in the north and replaced war chariots with cavalry, which was both faster and more mobile. This in turn involved a change in dress, and the wearing of trousers and tunic in China dates from this time.

But the greatest change in warfare was the new importance given to the use of infantry. In mountainous terrain or among the lakes and marshes of the Yangzi valley, chariots were of little use. Cavalry alone was insufficient and was also unable to operate in certain types of country. More reliance had to be placed on large bodies of infantry, either supporting chariots and cavalry or by themselves. This carried wider social consequences, as it did also in the West at the end of the Middle Ages.

*L'état centralisé est contemporain d'une promotion de la paysannerie au rang de cultivateurs indépendants et à celui de combattants. Le droit à la terre et le droit aux honneurs acquis sur le champ de bataille vont de pair.** [The centralized state is contemporary with the promotion of the peasantry to the rank of inde-

---

*J. Gernet, *Le Monde Chinois*, p. 65. Translation by present author.

pendent farmers and to that of combatants. The right to the soil and the right to honors acquired on the field of battle go together.]

The work of the peasant in peace was encouraged as well as his place in war, for this Warring States period of unrest deplored by later Chinese scholars as the breakup of the old order was also the period of encouragement of the clearing of new land, of the use of fertilizer, of the study of types of soil and the best dates for sowing, and of the increased employment of drainage.

Better farming led to population growth. A census in A.D. 2 showed a population of 57,671,400, slightly more than the numbers in the whole Roman empire at Augustus's census a few years later.

Again, technical invention was of aid in agriculture as it was in war. A chest harness for horses, which increased efficiency, was invented at this time, and this was followed sometime after the fifth century A.D. by the rigid harness collar. These two devices enabled a single horse to do what two or even four had done before, when the neck harness had tended to strangle the animals if they put too much weight on the pull. The greatest technical advance of all was the introduction of the smelting and casting of iron, first mentioned 513 B.C. and found in dated objects from 400 B.C., by which time iron was in fairly general use. An early use of iron in China was for the cutting edge of wooden spades and for other agricultural implements such as hoes, knives, and sickles. But hoes made of stone were still in use in Han times and even later, since iron was costly. Profiting by their bronze-casting experience, the Chinese made rapid advances in iron production, including reproduction of several examples at one time from one compound mold. In Rehol province in the far north, the site of a foundry has been uncovered, showing 87 molds for iron spades, chisels, and chariot parts, dating from the fourth century B.C.

Iron was forged in Europe long before it was cast, but in China the two treatments seem to have arisen at about the same time. It is possible that improved harness and the casting of iron, known in Europe only centuries later at the end of the medieval period, were in fact both brought originally from China through intermediate stages.

An important adjunct to metallurgy, improved bellows, was introduced in the Warring States period, and by the Han dynasty these had developed into bellows with a double piston and valves, which would deliver a continuous forced draft and enable higher furnace temperatures to be reached. This made possible the production of steel, which was practiced in China as early as the second century B.C.

Not only industry but also trade was on the increase in the Warring States period, and it proved to be another agent of social change. In earlier periods trade had been for the most part confined to luxury goods such as silk, pearls, and jade. Now enterprising merchants began to deal on a large scale in general bulk commodities such as grains, salt, metals, furs, and leather. They operated boats on the rivers and carts on land in convoys of some size. Their activities were furthered by the new availability of coinage, albeit often not in very convenient forms. There were four main types of currency used in different parts of the country: miniature spades of iron; knives; cowrie-shaped pieces, which were used as charms and ornaments as well as coins; and, lastly, circular copper pieces with a central hole for stringing them together. These last, the copper "cash," were the only type to survive and continued in use until the nineteenth century.

Returning in conclusion to the political situation at the end of the Zhou dynasty, we may note that the central states, such as Zhou, Song, Lu, and Jin (after 403 B.C. Jin split into three: Han, Wei and Zhao), affected to despise the peripheral states, such as Qi in the east, Chu in the south, and Qin in the west, as being semibarbarous. But it was in these freer, larger, less tradition-bound states that many of the above-mentioned innovations first occurred, particularly in the military sphere.

The state of Qi in the seventh century, by improving its administration and incorporating new territory, became powerful. The Duke of Qi was appointed in 651 B.C. as *ba,* or hegemon, to defend a loose confederacy of the central states against the rising power of Chu. Wu, on the lower reaches of the Yangzi River, became a major force in 482, only to be defeated a few years later by Yue, farther south in modern Zhejiang province. Chu prevailed over Yue in the next century, in 334, and some of the smaller states were absorbed by their more powerful neighbors. The result of these kaleidoscopic changes, spread over several centuries, was to leave the way clearer for the rapid rise of Qin, which ended the long series of wars and fastened a single central rule upon all the divided Chinese states. Qin, reinforced by the addition of two territories in distant Sichuan province and organized for total war, wiped out the sacred Zhou in 256 B.C. and in swift moves from 230 to 221 B.C. conquered all the other states and emerged as undisputed master of China.

4

RELIGION AND PHILOSOPHY

We have looked briefly at how the Chinese lived in the early days; we must now try to see how they thought. When the lineaments of Chinese prehistory, of the first historic dynasty, the Shang, and of the second, the Zhou, are combined, the main pattern of Chinese life has already emerged. Interaction with the nomads of the north and west, it is true, keeps providing new impetus. Important accretions are still to come from outside: Buddhism from India, technology and new ideas from the West. There will be many internal changes and alterations of balance in Chinese society. But by the end of Zhou in the third century B.C. the basic pattern is set.

RELIGION

The religion of China has usually been described as beginning in ancestor worship, but this is only partially true. Ancestor worship was present from the earliest time of which there is any record, but only as one element in Chinese religion. The other element is the worship of the spirits of Nature.

The Chinese approached the riddle of human life by supposing that a person has two souls, the *po,* animal soul or life soul, and the *hun,* spiritual soul or personality soul. Both souls become separated from the body at death, and both can be kept alive by sacrifices upon which they feed. The life soul, however, gradually decays with the body, while the personality soul survives as long as it is remembered and receives due sacrifices from the living. It can become a deity of power and influence, can respond in divination to the questions and requests of its descendants, and can even postpone their deaths. If the *po* is neglected, it may become a *gui, demon,* and haunt the living, while the neglected *hun* in like case will become a pitiable ghost but also capable of working harm. Hence the paramount importance of having male descendants to perform the family ancestral sacrifices. The downfall of a kingdom or a dynasty is described in Chinese histories in the phrase, "The sacrifices were interrupted."

The Supreme Being was possibly conceived of as the Supreme Ancestor, for the human and spirit worlds were closely connected. Under the Shang the Supreme Being was known as Shang Di, the Lord on High, but under the Zhou the term used was Tian, Heaven. In course of time Tian came to be thought of as the guardian of the moral order of the universe.

In addition to the ancestors, certain spirits of Nature also received honor in ancient China. There is mention during Shang of the Eastern Mother, the Western Mother, the Ruler of the Four Quarters, the Dragon Woman, the Snake Spirit, and the Wind as deities who were reverenced. Mere mention of these names is enough to indicate that we are here dealing with nature spirits and deities of fertility. The loess soil of North China is very fertile, but only when it receives sufficient rainfall. On the other hand, we have seen that the Yellow River flowing through loess country has by silt deposits built up its bed above the surrounding land in such a way that, when floods do occur, the damage is enormous and widespread. Thus the balance of Nature, between too little rain and too much, was clearly seen to be a delicate one, and it was the duty of the Son of Heaven to preserve it by due sacrifices, not only to Heaven but to the gods of the earth.

The cruder and more primitive forms of worship of the life force proved something of an embarrassment to the puritan Confucian scholars of a later day, who were eager to minimize them or explain them away. But the presence of this element of nature worship with an emphasis on fertility is clearly attested in China, as elsewhere in the world. The characters for *zu*, ancestor, and *she*, god of the soil, both contain a phallic symbol. Both forms of worship enjoyed equal honor, with shrines placed east and west of the entry to the palace, as if designed to ensure good crops of sons to the ancestors and of grain in the fields.

The Book of Songs, which reflects society before the days of Confucius, contains many songs of courtship which point to a much freer and more natural relationship between the sexes than that obtaining at a later date. For example (Waley's translation):

> Out in the bushlands a creeper grows,
> The falling dew lies thick upon it.
> There was a man so lovely,
> Clear brow well rounded.
> By chance I came across him,
> And he let me have my will.
> Out in the bushlands a creeper grows,
> The falling dew lies heavy on it.

There was a man so lovely,
Well rounded his clear brow.
By chance I came upon him:
"Oh, Sir, to be with you is good."*

In another poem from this book a woman says:

By the chestnut trees at the Eastern Gate
Where there is a row of houses.
It is not that I do not love you,
But that you are slow to court me.†

Later scholars viewed the *Book of Songs* as they did the primitive cults, trying to purge what they conceived to be its grosser elements. They endeavored to give the songs of courtship and marriage an allegorical meaning to inculcate such virtues as loyalty to the prince, in much the same way as allegorical significance was attributed to the biblical love song, the Song of Solomon, in the West.

As Chinese religious practice developed, the absence of a priestly class, enjoying a position of power in the society, is notable. There were advisers in matters of ritual and etiquette, but the sacrifices and cult services themselves were performed by state officials or the heads of families, as the case might be. Animals sacrificed included cattle, sheep, pigs, and dogs, usually in small numbers (under ten at one time). A "great sacrifice" to three former kings was recorded, in which three hundred cattle were offered. The character for *li*, ritual, courtesy, indicates that flower offerings were also made. Wine when offered was poured on the ground as a libation. Sacrifices were most commonly burned but were also buried or thrown into water. Rich persons when crossing a certain river used to throw a jade ring into the stream as an offering to the river spirit. The poor joined together to celebrate the river festival, in which a beautiful girl was chosen and sent off to float away in a boat and ultimately drowned as the "bride of the river." Human sacrifice as a general rule, however, was abolished by the end of the Zhou period.

It should be emphasized that the common people had no part in the ceremonies of ancestor worship, which were reserved for the families of the gentry, corresponding as a class to the *gentes* of ancient Rome. The common folk in China did not even have surnames, much less recorded ancestors. Their religious customs, including that of marriage, were completely different from those of the upper class. They did not celebrate individual marriage rites but took part in a common spring festival. If a girl was pregnant by autumn, she and her man would settle down to married life in an arrangement acknowl-

---

* *The Book of Songs,* tr. Waley, A. *Chinese Poems.* p. 17.
† Ibid.

edged by both families and the community. The religion of the peasant farmer was marked by worship of the local deities of the soil, and of fertility, and by shamanistic cults involving spirit mediums, exorcists or sorcerers called *wu*, who danced in frenzy.

This shaman element, found all over northeast Asia, including Japan, was early eliminated from the religious practice of the upper class, and their objects of worship became basically Heaven (this cult confined to the sovereign), Earth, the gods of the soil and the crops, and the spirits of rivers and mountains, in addition to their respective ancestors. It was to a man of the gentry group, united by religious practice and social attitudes, and not to the Chinese people as a whole nor to aliens, that Confucius referred when he said, "All within the four seas are his brothers."* The phrase is universalistic in its reference up to a point, but not to the extent often assumed by modern idealists. Confucius was also representing the group of "gentlemen" and their disassociation from popular shamanism and superstitious forms of religion when it was said that he "never talked of prodigies, feats of strength, disorders or spirits [*shen*, gods]"†. This phrase has also been misunderstood, in the sense that it is taken for granted that Confucius was opposed to religion as a whole, which is far from being the case. As one example to the contrary, he seems to regard morality as having some kind of religious sanction when he remarks, "He who offends against Heaven has none to whom he can pray.‡

PHILOSOPHY

Cosmology, an account of the universe and how it came to be, lies at the base of philosophy in many cultures. Chinese thought about origins is different from the creator religions of the West. In China there was no creation myth, no source of divine law outside nature. Nature thus partook of the divine, and moral law was securely fixed in human authority, as represented by the sage kings, the Zhou founders, and Confucius.

Religion for the Chinese has a practical rather than a highly mystical concern; likewise, Chinese philosophy has to do primarily with ethics and conduct in actual life, and not to any great degree with abstract questions such as are dealt with in Western metaphysics. There are notable exceptions: Buddhism, coming from India, is both mystical and intellectually complex, while Daoism does deal with Being and Nonbeing. But the practical, this-worldly tendency is inherent in Chinese religion and philosophy and finds its fullest expression in the dominant school of Confucius.

---

*Analects, XII, 5, Waley's translation.
†Analects, VII, 20, Waley's translation.
‡Analects, III, 13, Legge's translation.

Confucianism

Confucius more than any other single man formed the thought of China and was responsible through his followers for the main outlines of both its ethics and its political theory. His authority was enormous and his appeal extraordinary. Yet he was rather a prosaic person. His philosophy was far from exciting. How did this man, surely the least romantic among the world's great leaders, exert such a deep and long-continued influence? Perhaps it was because he understood his countrymen and mirrored for them the best in their own civilization. He believed in and practiced the highest standards of morality, yet did it all in the spirit of moderation and harmony so admired by the Chinese. As Arthur Waley says, "He contrived to endow compromise with emotional glamour."

Before considering the Confucian and three other representative philosophical schools in somewhat more detail, it is necessary to mention the early sources upon which subsequent Chinese thought depended. The best known of these are always referred to as the Five Classics *(Wu Jing)* and the Four Books *(Si Shu)*.

The Five Classics comprise:

The *Book of Changes (Yi Jing)*, a book used for divination built on the oracle bones tradition, which combines, in one interrelated whole, all of human life and fate and the physical elements of the world in symbolic form, represented by the *ba gua* diagram of whole and broken lines. The contents of the Book of Changes include ancient cosmological beliefs of the Chinese antedating the separate philosophical schools. Appendices giving amplifications and interpretations were added by early Han times.

The *Book of History or Documents (Shu Jing)*, short sections of material of varying date and authenticity ascribed to early sovereigns and officials.

The *Book of Odes or Songs (Shi Jing)*, a collection of ceremonial and folk verse, probably of early Zhou date (already referred to, see p. 30).

The *Book of Ritual*, a compilation usually dated from middle Zhou down to the first part of the Han dynasty. The best-known section is the *Li Ji* (Book of Rites).

The *Spring and Autumn Annals (Chunqiu)*, chronicles of Confucius's state of Lu covering the years 722 to 481 B.C., with appended commentaries.

The Four Books are all post-Confucian. They are: two important sections of the Book of Rites, the *Great Learning (Da Xue)*, on self-cultivation as the key to the good society, and the *Mean (Jung Yung)*, on moderation in man's conduct which enables him to live in harmony with the universe; the *Analects (Lun Yu)*, a collection of sayings of Confucius and incidents from his life, compiled by students of his disciples; and the *Mencius*, the sayings of Confucius's great successor (who was born about 100 years after Confucius's death and who lived from 372 to ?289 B.C.), probably written by Mencius's disciples. These Four Books were singled out, grouped together, and published in A.D. 1190 by Zhu Xi, the Neo-Confucian philosopher, as especially important and became the basis of study for all civil service examinations from about 1300 to 1900, thus exerting enormous influence upon Chinese thought and life.

Kung Fu Zi (Master Kung) (551–479 B.C.), or Confucius, in the latinized form of his name used by the Jesuits in the seventeenth century, was born and raised in the state of Lu in Shandong province in northeast China. The materials on his life are meager, after a due purge of all the laudatory and imaginary accretions of his later admiring biographers. His ancestors may have been of the aristocracy, but Confucius himself was born to a family of comparatively humble status, his father possibly a minor official in the state of Lu.

There is a tradition that Confucius before long became an orphan, and in fact no early work mentions his father or mother. As a boy and a young man he probably received the elements of education as an apprentice official engaged in clerical work. Mencius, his later disciple, wrote, "Confucius was once keeper of stores, and he said, 'It is only necessary that my accounts be correct.' He was once in charge of pastures, and said, 'It is my duty only to see that the oxen and sheep are well-grown and strong'" (V,2,v,4). He also practiced archery and music, two of the polite accomplishments of the gentleman class. His passion for knowledge and aptitude for study made him in the end one of the most accomplished scholars of his day. He had a son, who died while Confucius was still living, and a daughter. No mention whatever is made of his wife.

Confucius has been credited with a number of literary works, but there is no hard evidence that he wrote anything at all. (The same holds true for Gautama Buddha, Socrates, and Jesus.) It is possible that Confucius did some editing of the *Spring and Autumn Annals* and the *Book of Songs*. His abiding influence was attained not through books but through his effect upon the men who gathered around him in an informal way, reminiscent of the friends surrounding Socrates, although in Confucius's case some students paid fees for their instruction.

Confucius would doubtless have liked to exert a direct influence upon affairs through holding office under the state. The *Analects,* an early collection of his *obiter dicta* and anecdotes of his life, hints that he was disappointed at being passed over in the official appointments. He may have held a post in his own state for a period at some time between 502 and 492 B.C., when he was already fifty years of age. It is possible that this is a different and later post than those mentioned by Mencius. But lack of recognition did not affect the steadiness of his own inner development.

The Master said, At fifteen I set my heart upon learning. At thirty, I had planted my feet firm upon the ground. At forty, I no longer suffered from perplexities. At fifty, I knew what were the biddings of Heaven. At sixty, I heard them with docile ear. At seventy, I could follow the dictates of my own heart; for what I desired no longer overstepped the boundaries of right.*

---

*Analects, II, 4, Waley's translation.

Even making allowances for the favorite Chinese literary device of schematic progressions of this type, one receives the impression of a man of conviction and independence of mind.

Confucius, however, according to Mencius, felt he was "not used" in Lu and left home to seek a prince who would be more prepared to adopt his principles. This period of travel began not earlier than 498 B.C. and not later than 493 B.C., and the states of Wei, Song, Chen, and Cai are cited among those visited by Confucius and his students. Twenty-two names of these students, probably an inner group, are mentioned in the *Analects,* but the number must have varied considerably as some came and others left. Although Confucius on these journeys was not appointed to office, perhaps because the princes may have felt his moral challenge was inconveniently high, we know that several of his students did receive official posts. They were in some demand, not only because of their general education but also because they had received training in the forms of state ritual so important in the establishment of claims to leadership on the part of princes in the Spring and Autumn period (722–481 B.C., the years covered by the *Spring and Autumn Annals*).

As pioneers in higher education, Confucius and his school may be compared to the sophists in Greece. Elementary education was, of course, already in existence in some form in both societies; for where there is a written language, both it and the use of numbers must be passed on to each new generation. But the organized pursuit of higher knowledge—knowledge as power, knowledge as virtuosity and special skills, and knowledge for its own sake—this is a much later and distinct development in civilization. The first clear traces of it seem to emerge in China with Confucius and in Greece with the sophists.

Since this is such a crucial comparison, it may be worth while to pause and consider it briefly in rather more detail. The sophists were professional educators and what we should call "consultants" in fifth-century Greece. They traveled from city-state to city-state instructing classes of young men who were prepared to invest the money for fees in order to get on in political life. Since the popular assemblies were becoming more powerful, and since there were no professional barristers or attorneys in the law courts, it paid an ambitious young man to be able to speak effectively in public for himself and his policies, to defend himself when attacked, and to down an opponent. Thus the instruction of the sophists centered on the arts of persuasion, oratory, and the marshaling of arguments. This led to the discussion of logic and the use and implications of language, topics of concern in China also at about the same time. It also led to argument for practice, to putting up a thesis to be defended and attacked, such as the idea that killing your father was justifiable because it happened in Nature. Does not the young bull in time drive out the old bull from headship of the herd of cattle?

Many of the more reputable sophists performed a valuable service in higher education and contributed to the study of logic and linguistics. Yet it is scarcely surprising that the sophists as a class received a bad press, for the average Greek farmer or sailor was conservative and suspicious of specious argument, of "making the worse appear the better reason." Much of our information about the sophists comes from Plato, who, in defense of his master, Socrates, pointed out that Socrates differed at two crucial points from the sophists; first, he did not pursue his philosophical inquiries and his informal instruction of youth for money; and, second, he engaged in demolishing false and vaguely held opinions on ethical matters only in order to reach solid ground for the establishment of true justice and goodness. In spite of the skepticism of the age, Socrates was convinced that the sophists' subjective relativism in morals was pernicious and that a true grasp of morality could be attained by inquiry, for "the unexamined life is not worth living for a man."

Confucius (551–479 B.C.), living about a century earlier than Socrates (470–399 B.C.) and in somewhat parallel circumstances, was also deeply concerned about morality. The rival "consultants" with whom he had to contend were the new class of advisers to the hereditary aristocrats who were heads of the various states in the loose Zhou confederacy. Some of these advisers traveled from court to court, as Confucius did. Their counsels to the princes tended to be of a Machiavellian character, aimed at the securing of *li*, profit, direct and immediate advantage to the prince and his state without regard to any consideration of accepted moral standards. They were doubtless able to cite a number of currently plausible arguments for such policies, since the Spring and Autumn period was a time of intellectual ferment and widespread questioning of traditional standards, which was also the case in fifth-century Athens. (There was less stress in China on verbal and more on written disputation, since Chinese civilization has always depended to a high degree on the written word.) Because the later ascendancy of Confucianism as a state orthodoxy became so complete, one is apt to forget that at this time of the "hundred schools contending," Confucius could claim no special place or privilege for his views on morals. It was perhaps for this reason that he emphasized so strongly his dependence on the past and the example of the sage-kings. "A transmitter and not an originator, believing in and loving the ancients, I venture to compare myself with our old Peng'* (Peng is a wise old man, the Chinese Nestor). The morality which Confucius believed had created the golden age in early Zhou and preserved society thereafter was the answer, he contended, to the moral relativism, internecine rivalries, and chaos of the period in which he lived.

Confucius's methods were different from those of Socrates, but his aim was the same, the definition of morals with a view to their application to life in the state. And both men owe their enormous subsequent influence on the societies of East and West in part to the fact that they lived out in their own experience the morality they so consistently advocated. Among the methods employed by Confucius was the outlining of an ideal character whom he called the *junzi*, the "gentleman" or "noble man." The Chinese ideograms originally signified "son of a prince or nobleman," and Confucius himself was responsi-

---

*Analects, VII, 1, adapted from Legge's translation.

ble for the deliberate transfer of the phrase from an aristocratic social meaning to an ethical one, a transfer which can be perfectly represented in English as the change from "nobleman" to "noble man."

The character of the gentleman is subtle and beautifully balanced, but it is basically simple. He is what we would call a well-integrated personality. Here is a man both resolute and gentle, conscious of his place in a society where all men are interconnected, a man who counts deeds of more import than words, and with whom form and order are so inbred as to have become instinctive. He is trustworthy and shows moderation in all things. He is saved from being a prig because he is conscious of his own faults and aware of the need for self-discipline. He follows the Way, a pattern of behavior the sages saw as naturally right, and this is his deliverance. Ultimately responsible to Heaven, he is independent, unafraid, ready for whatever may come.

The Confucian gentleman places more emphasis on propriety than even the most meticulous Westerner.

> When Master Tsêng was ill, Mêng Ching Tzu came to see him. Master Tsêng spoke to him saying, When a bird is about to die, its song touches the heart. When a man is about to die, his words are of note. There are three things that a gentleman, in following the Way, places above all the rest: from every attitude, every gesture that he employs he must remove all trace of violence or arrogance; every look that he composes in his face must betoken good faith; from every word that he utters, from every intonation, he must remove all traces of coarseness or impropriety. As to the ordering of ritual vessels and the like, there are those whose business it is to attend to such matters.*

This is to say that in personal bearing no detail is unimportant. Attitudes, gestures, looks, words, intonation—all these are a clue to the man within. In contrast to the spirit of Confucius's age and to the behavior of those addicted to the pursuit of selfish whims, the gentleman must banish from his conduct and even from his manner or expression anything savoring of violence, arrogance, or impropriety. It is not a question only of open indecency or tyrannically overbearing acts toward others. It is a question rather of "avoiding all appearance of evil"† and, in the expressive popular phrase which reflects the Chinese as well as the English mentality, "not throwing your weight around."

Among the virtues which Confucius singled out for particular attention were *ren,* "humanity," and *li,* "courtesy," the latter being the kernel of the passage just quoted. These are entirely Chinese in conception and not easy to translate. The ideogram for *ren* consists of "man" and "two," or the way two men ideally should behave toward one another in mutuality and human-heartedness. (The Latin word *humanitas* gives the exact sense.) Confucius accords

---

Analects, VIII, 4, Waley's translation.
†I Thessalonians 5:22. Compare the Chinese proverb, "Do not tie your shoe in a melon-patch nor adjust your hat under a plum-tree" (*Mathews Dictionary,* no. 3504). Someone will be looking and will misinterpret your innocent conduct as stealing.

such a high place to this attitude that some have seen in his use of the word an almost mystical sense of Goodness, with a capital G. The left half of the second ideogram, *li*, places the word in the category "spirit," while the right half represents two kinds of sacrificial vessel. The concept thus begins as ritual toward the gods or spirits but goes on to mean ritual or correct conduct toward men. Etiquette, "doing the proper thing," carries little weight as a virtue in the West; indeed, as "conventional conduct" it may even seem opposed to true morality. But in China the overtones are different and much more impressive. To behave with "courtesy," in a spirit of live and let live, may be crucial to the harmony of society; and the Chinese, in a tightly packed society, value harmony above all else. Lin Yu-tang has called *li* the virtue which erects a dam against social chaos and the law of the jungle.

Three more virtues have their importance in the earliest Confucian teaching and were combined with the first two to make up five, a favorite number in Chinese schemata. They are *yi*, "uprightness" or "honesty," *zhi*, "knowledge" in the sense of moral wisdom, and *xin*, "faithfulness," "integrity." The ideogram for *yi* contains the elements "I" or "my" (bottom half) and "sheep" (top half), a relic of early nomadic, pastoral days when wealth was reckoned on the hoof and the honest man claimed only the animals which were his own. *Zhi,* knowledge, is not abstract learning but knowledge for the sake of goodness, the study of the past in order to form character by means of moral example and warning. The last ideogram, *xin*, represents a man standing by his word or, as in the Book of Psalms, "he who sweareth to his own hurt and changeth not." A virtue often stressed by Confucianists, namely *xiao,* or filial piety, does not occupy a prominent place in the earliest tradition of the *Analects,* becoming important only in the Han dynasty.

The group virtue of steadfastness or loyalty, *zhong,* was not only stressed by Confucius but clearly exemplified in his life of moral courage and devotion to principle. Physical courage in battle, the soldier's virtue, on the other hand, receives little mention, although it is a basic virtue in the whole Western tradition, from Homer and the Greeks through the Romans and Germanic tribes to the medieval knight.

Daoism

Unlike Confucianism, with its stress on human relations, Daoism is preoccupied with man's place in the natural world. In this form of Nature mysticism, the secret for man is simply to abandon self-effort and ease himself into the rhythm of the universe, the cycle of the seasons, and the inevitable progression of day and night, life and death. Although the term *dao*, "way" and also "word," can be used of the beliefs of any philosopher—and Confucius used it of the "way" as he saw it–in Daoism it is used in a semimystical sense as "the Way of the Universe."

The origins of this philosophy are attributed to one Laozi (Lao Tzu), who is reputed to have lived about the time of Confucius. (The name means "Old

Master.") Little is known about his life. He is said to have left China for the fabled land of the west, riding on a purple buffalo. Before he passed through the gate at the frontier, the guard is said to have asked him to leave a short account of his philosophy, and Laozi obliged with the work known as the _Dao De Jing (Tao Te Ching)_, "The Classic of the Way and Its Power."

Fantastic as the legend sounds, there may have been an individual Laozi who lived probably in the sixth century B.C., but possibly in the third, and was the author of the _Dao De Jing_. Whatever its origins, this is one of the most remarkable of the Chinese classics and the one, incidentally, most frequently translated into European languages. It is a prose poem full of brief aphorisms and comparisons highly stimulating to the imagination. The work begins by saying that the Dao is ineffable but then suggests some similes which hint at its nature. The Way is humble like water which flows downward and seeks the lowest place. "The highest good is like water. Water benefits all things generously and is without strife. It dwells in the lowly places that men disdain. Thus it comes near to the Tao."* The Way is like empty space, but emptiness has been undervalued, since the hollow in the center of a bowl, the space in a wheel between rim and hub, or the empty space of a window or door in a room are the very things which give these objects their point and their usefulness. Thus Nonbeing as well as Being has a positive value. The mutuality of this pair of opposites in the universe, matter and space, being and nonbeing, must be recognized. The Way also may be likened to the _yin_ component in the ancient _yin-yang_ dualism, which is the paired harmony of female and male, dark and light, low and high. Both members of the duality are needed, but _yang_ has been overemphasized and _yin_ must be restored to its rightful place. The Way is like the _yin_ or female because it is passive, yielding, receptive, not active and dominating.

---

*_Dao De Jing_, chapter 8, Y. P. Mei's translation.

Yin-yang circle.

The ancient symbol for the complementary forces of _yin_ and _yang_. (See above.)

> The Valley Spirit never dies.
> It is named the Mysterious Female.
> And the Doorway of the Mysterious Female
> Is the base from which Heaven and Earth sprang.
> It is there within us all the while;
> Draw upon it as you will, it never runs dry.*

Consideration of the female leads on to that of the infant. Man must return to the state of the child, which is pure potential and thus nearest to the Way. The inanimate image corresponding to the child is that of the uncarved block, the primal unity not yet formed or differentiated or "improved" in any way.

> He who knows the masculine but keeps to the feminine,
>   Becomes the ravine of the world.
> Being the ravine of the world,
>   He dwells in constant virtue,
>   He returns to the state of the babe.
> . . . .
> He who knows glory but keeps to disgrace,
>   Becomes the valley of the world.
> Being the valley of the world,
>   He finds contentment in constant virtue,
>   He returns to the uncarved block.†

The Dao thus has the capacity of resolving all relative differences and contradictions, and this capacity gives rise to a mystical admiration of the Dao amounting almost to worship, although there is no suggestion whatever that a personal deity is involved.

> The Way is like an empty vessel
> That yet may be drawn from
> Without ever needing to be filled.
> It is bottomless; the very progenitor of all things in the world.
> In it all sharpness is blunted,
> All tangles untied,
> All glare tempered,
> All dust‡ smoothed.
> It is like a deep pool that never dries.
> Was it too the child of something else? We cannot tell.
> But as a substanceless image it existed before the Ancestor.‡

Dao De Jing, chapter 6, Waley's translation.
†*Dao De Jing,* chapter 28, Mei's translation.
‡Dust, Waley notes, is the Daoist symbol for the noise and fuss of everyday life.
‡*Dao De Jing,* chapter 4, Waley's translation.

The most famous successor to Laozi was Zhuangzi (Chuang Tzu), who lived and wrote in the fourth century B.C. He went even further than his predecessor in stressing the relativity of the attributes of all things. The wren and the cicada mock at the claims of a fabulous bird to be able to fly hundreds of miles at a stretch; which of them is right is a relative matter and depends entirely on the definition of what is long and what is short.

In view of all this, Zhuangzi seems to say, efforts to regulate life and improve the world are not only useless and absurd but positively harmful. The Confucian attempts to organize society by rules and precepts are self-defeating, for men want to do evil chiefly when they are forbidden to do so, and they are only conscious of the need to be good when evil is already rampant.

> It was when the Great Way declined
> That human kindness and morality arose . . .
> It was when the six near ones[close relatives] were no longer at peace
> That there was talk of "dutiful sons."*

The sage in charge of government should therefore aim to keep the people in a state of nature, where they are content. He should "fill their bellies and empty their minds." He should "govern the country as you would cook a small fish"—interfere with either and it will fall apart. This is the famous Daoist prescription of *wu wei, nonaction.*

By nonaction Zhuangzi apparently did not mean total inaction, laziness, or defeatism. Rather he is describing the approach to government adopted by an ideal sage who is fully alert, aware of the processes of nature and the needs of men, prepared to keep the life force in himself and others going, but wary of interfering in any way with what is "natural." The sage is marked not by resignation but by an "ecstatic acceptance" (Waley) of the Way of the Universe as the guideline for his own life and that of society. This eager awareness and acceptance of natural laws is well exemplified in a famous anecdote concerning Zhuangzi in mourning:

> When Chuang Tzu's wife died, the logician Hui Tzu came to the house to join in the rites of mourning. To his astonishment he found Chuang Tzu sitting with an inverted bowl on his knees, drumming upon it and singing a song. "After all," said Hui Tzu, "she lived with you, brought up your children, grew old along with you. That you should not mourn for her is bad enough; but to let your friends find you drumming and singing—that is really going too far!" "You misjudge me," said Chuang Tzu. "When she died, I was in despair, as any man well might be. But soon, pondering on what had happened, I told myself that in death no strange new fate befalls us. In the beginning we lack not life only, but form. Not form only, but spirit. We are blent in the one great featureless, indistinguishable mass. Then a time came when the mass evolved spirit, spirit evolved form, form evolved life. And now life in its

*Dao De Jing, chapter 18.

turn has evolved death. For not nature only but man's being has its seasons, its sequence of spring and autumn, summer and winter. If someone is tired and has gone to lie down, we do not pursue him with shouting and bawling. She whom I have lost has lain down to sleep for a while in the Great Inner Room. To break in upon her rest with the noise of lamentation would but show that I knew nothing of Nature's Sovereign Law."*

Mozi

He would say to himself, "I have heard that to be a superior man one should take care of his friend as he does of himself, and take care of his friend's parents as he does of his own." Therefore when he finds his friend hungry he would feed him, and when he finds him cold he would clothe him. In his sickness he would minister to him, and when he is dead he would bury him. Such is the word and such is the deed of the advocate of universality.[†]

It is surprising to many to discover such a close parallel to the New Testament ethic some 400 years earlier in the works of a Chinese philosopher. Mozi (Mo Tzu, 470–?391 B.C.), moreover, founded his advocacy of universal love as the way for men on the fact that "Heaven loves the people dearly, Heaven loves the people inclusively."

The doctrine of Mozi (or Mo Di) gained considerable influence in his own time and for almost two centuries thereafter, but it was subsequently eclipsed by the triumph of orthodox Confucianism. His idea of universal love was strenuously opposed by the Confucianists for a curious reason, as subversive of the natural order of things, which to a Confucian meant love for parents, affection for friends, loyalty to the state, and so on in a sensible, graded progression of attachments.

Although Mozi was an idealist, he was also a pragmatist in a very down-to-earth manner. He was opposed to waste and extravagance in all its forms and hence disapproved of ceremonial, feasting, music, and especially the wastefulness of aggressive war, which he characterized as a form of brigandage. The disturbed conditions of the Warring States period favored the rise of military experts, sometimes called knights-errant, from among the minor nobility or gentleman class (shi), who hired out their services to ambitious princes. Mozi seems to have been such an expert, but his objective was totally different from that of the rest of his class. He gathered a body of like-minded disciplined men who went to danger points in the wars between the states and tried to effect reconciliation. Where this proved impossible, they frequently took the side of the weaker party and gave their expert help in siege warfare to withstand the attacks of a more powerful enemy.

*Zhuangzi, XVIII, 2, Waley's translation, in his *The Way and Its Power.*
[†]Mozi, chapter 16, translated by De Bary et al. in *Sources of Chinese Tradition*, Vol. I p. 41.

Legalism

The school of Legalism, on the other hand, came out strongly in favor of war as a legitimate means of strengthening the power of the state and imparting discipline to the people. Its proponents maintained that the notion that men are by nature good is purely visionary, and that the only way to establish a stable and peaceful kingdom is by means of rewards and punishments.

> Within the frontiers of a state there are no more than ten people who will do good of themselves; nevertheless if one brings it about that the people can do no wrong, the entire state can be kept peaceful. He who rules a country makes use of the majority and neglects the few, and so does not concern himself with virtue but with law.*

Shang Yang, also known as Lord Shang (d. 338 B.C.), was the first known exponent of this school of thought, and he laid the foundations of the Qin state, which ultimately came to power over a century later by the conquest of all its rivals.

The theory of Legalism, one of the most thoroughgoing statements of totalitarianism in world history, was worked out by Han Fei Zi (d. 233 B.C.). He advocated laying down a complete code of laws, which were to be crystal clear in their delineation of rewards and punishments and which must then be applied impartially to rich and poor alike. To try by methods of persuasion to "win the hearts of the people," as the Confucianists did, is a vain endeavor. Drastic methods alone will work and, in the end, will prove to everyone's advantage. Just as a baby, kicking and screaming, has to be held firmly to have a boil lanced, the body politic may have to undergo a small pain to reap a great benefit. Rewards and punishments are thus "the two handles of the ruler, due to the fact that it is the nature of man to seek profit and avoid harm."

The Legalists disagreed with the Confucian school not only in their view of human nature and in their method of ruling society but also in their reading of history. They refused to interpret history as being a constant degeneration from a hypothetical Golden Age in the past. They drew this consequence from their realistic view of the life of men.

> The sage does not seek to follow the ways of the ancients . . . he examines the circumstances of his own time. . . . Indeed ancients and moderns have different customs; the present and the past follow different courses of action. To attempt to apply a lenient and benevolent government to the people of a desperate age is about the same as trying to drive wild horses without reins or whips. This is the affliction of ignorance.†

Han Fei Zi, chapter 50, see Fung Yu-lan ed. Bodde, D. *A Short History of Chinese Philosophy,* p. 160.
†*Han Fei Zi,* translated by De Bary et al. in *Sources of Chinese Tradition,* Vol. I, pp. 130 and 131–132.

So to rule the people of today by the methods of the early kings is like the farmer of Song (proverbially a backward state of simple rustics) who once, while ploughing, saw a hare killed by running against the stump of a tree. He thereupon left off ploughing and waited for another hare to do the same, only to become the laughingstock of his neighbors. This developmental insight of the Legalists—namely, that new days require new methods—marked a radical departure from past thinking, but it was not destined to survive. Their immediate practical success in the military sphere was, however, spectacular, and this we shall examine in the next chapter.

Chinese philosophy includes a number of other schools, such as the School of Names, which contributed to the development of semantics and logic. However, the four schools mentioned previously were in the long run the most significant, while varying in their destiny. Confucianism became dominant. Daoism made a strong if less direct contribution through the arts of poetry and painting and through its effect on the Buddhist school of Chan (Zen). The school of Mozi did not last as a separate movement. Legalism is being reassessed and is now seen to have had a considerable effect on Confucians and their state policies at various periods of history.

5

UNIFICATION AND EXPANSION

Qin Dynasty: 221–206 B.C.
Han Dynasty: 206 B.C.–A.D. 221

The dramatic conquest of the ancient China of separate kingdoms was carried through by the state of Qin with despatch and completed by 221 B.C. Qin (pronounced "chin," which gave us the present name "China") had a double advantage, in theory—the pragmatic and ruthless philosophy of Legalism— and in practice—an efficient military machine under strong leaders, possessing cavalry and superior iron weapons, both comparatively new developments at the time. Although the final stages of mastery were rapid, the preparation had been going on for a long time.

THE QIN DYNASTY

The foundation of Qin strength had been laid by Lord Shang between the year 361 B.C. and his death in 338 B.C. At the upper level of society, his reforms had aimed at establishing a new aristocracy of men rewarded for prowess in war, in place of the old hereditary leading families; at the lower level, a system of rewards and severe punishments, the formation of groups mutually responsible for one another, and the strict reporting of misdemeanors to the authorities had tightened state control over the whole population. A century later, when the future emperor of all China, Qin Shi Huang Di, came to the local throne of Qin in 246 B.C., he was ably served by an ex-merchant, Lu Buwei, as chief administrator, and he in turn was succeeded by the prominent Legalist Li Si, who applied the Qin pattern of control to the whole of China. The methods of reorganization and of the fastening of central authority over the independent kingdoms had thus been worked out and applied in a limited sphere by a few forceful personalities prior to the Qin military conquest.

When the victory was complete in 221 B.C., all weapons of those not in the Qin army were confiscated and the metal melted down. It was sufficient in quantity to make twelve gigantic statues at the new capital, Xianyang. To indicate his intention of making an entirely new beginning, the ruler adopted the ambitious title of Shi Huang Di, "The First Emperor." The country was divided into thirty-six, later forty-eight, commanderies, or military districts, each with three officials who acted as checks upon one another: a civil governor, a military governor, and a direct representative of the central government. All officials were methodically divided into eighteen orders of rank. Uniform laws and taxation were put into operation throughout China, regardless of former boundaries.

The vital difference in the organizing of the general population under Qin was that the people were detached from their former allegiance to individual landowning lords and brought under the direct control of the new centralized government. This gave the government access to a manpower potential hitherto unknown, both in the army and in a conscript labor force. With this abundance of workers, a network of roads radiating from the capital was constructed. As in the Roman empire these roads, built primarily for strategic purposes, also served the ends of trade. Canals were built for irrigation and transport, and emphasis placed on increasing agricultural production. To meet the

The Great Wall.

China's most famous feature, with its solid construction, towers, and crenellated ramparts, the Great Wall marches over the mountains for over 1,400 miles. Earlier partial walls were linked up in the 3rd century B.C. but there was not a complete Great Wall until the restoration in the 16th century under the Ming Dynasty.

Photo: Annette Juliano

menace of the nomad tribes in the north, which was to be a constant threat throughout Chinese history, sections of defensive wall already built by three of the former kingdoms were strengthened, joined, and extended to form a single wall along the northern frontier, one of the most ambitious construction projects ever undertaken by any civilization. Some subsequent dynasties also built walls, but the Great Wall which we see today, and which once reached from Southwest Gansu to Southern Manchuria, a distance of 1,400 miles, was built mainly in the Ming period (1368–1644).

Unhampered by any respect for the past and eager to impose logical uniformity over the whole country, as already indicated in the matters of law and taxation, the Qin emperor proceeded to standardize weights and measures and to adopt a single coinage, of round copper coins with a square central hole, which remained standard right up to modern times. This replaced a number of more cumbrous forms which had been current in different areas in Zhou times (see p. 28). The written script was now also standardized in form, as was the track width between the wheels of carts. The last was by no means a minor matter in the friable loess soil of north China, where cart ruts become so worn down that the whole unpaved road surface may disappear below the level of the surrounding land. Differing axle widths had hitherto necessitated the transfer of goods between vehicles at the borders of the former states.

But it was in the matter of thought that the policy of standardization provoked most opposition, smoldering beneath the surface at the time but vented by the literati in subsequent dynasties in lasting bitterness against the Qin regime. In order to make a clean sweep, wipe out the past, and undo loyalties to the former states, the chief minister Li Si drew up in 213 B.C. a rescript from Qin Shi Huang Di ordering all books save those on the practical subjects of agriculture, divination, and medicine to be burned. Scholars who disobeyed the injunction were to be executed. Some, in fact, were said to have been buried alive.

With the powerful army he had built up, Qin Shi Huang Di not only secured his boundaries to the north but extended them far to the south. Prior to their conquest of China the Qin had already attacked and gained territory in Sichuan to the southwest. The armies now pushed south as far as Hanoi. They secured the coast around the modern Canton and gained possession of the regions near Fuzhou and Guilin.

In thus consolidating his rule and extending the frontiers of China to almost their present position, the first Qin emperor had shown demonic energy and been phenomenally successful. But the more centralized the empire became, the more vulnerable it was to weakness at the center. This weakness surfaced when the First Emperor died in 210 B.C. He was at the time, ironically, on a trip to the eastern regions to seek the aid of Daoist magicians in securing the elixir of immortality. Li Si and the chief eunuch, Zhao Gao, kept his death secret until they had returned to the capital and put on the throne as Second Emperor a younger son who, they felt, would be amenable to their own ambitions. But they fell out among themselves, Li Si was elimi-

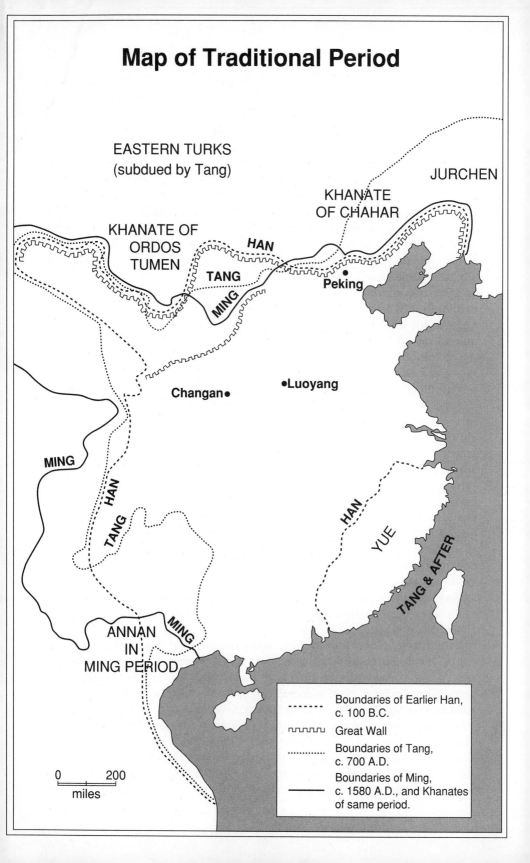

Map of Traditional Period

EASTERN TURKS
(subdued by Tang)

JURCHEN

KHANATE
OF CHAHAR

KHANATE OF
ORDOS
TUMEN

HAN

TANG

MING

Peking

MING

HAN

TANG

Changan

Luoyang

HAN

YUE

TANG & AFTER

ANNAN
IN
MING PERIOD

MING

0   200
miles

Boundaries of Earlier Han,
c. 100 B.C.

Great Wall

Boundaries of Tang,
c. 700 A.D.

Boundaries of Ming,
c. 1580 A.D., and Khanates
of same period.

nated, and when the Third Emperor came to the throne he had Zhao Gao killed. The Qin dynasty, in spite of its strength, could not survive this decimation of its leadership. When faced with popular rebellion, it fell in ruins in 206 B.C. The First Emperor had boasted it would last for ten thousand generations, but in fact all was over in fifteen years.

Qin Shi Huang Di, the First Emperor, had a bad press from the Confucian historians and in actuality was in many ways a ruthless tyrant. Countless thousands, for example, died during the construction of the Great Wall. But he laid down the main lines upon which the empire subsequently developed. In particular he produced a unified and centralized realm which remained the Chinese ideal for empire. Through his sponsoring of Legalism he influenced the whole future Chinese conception of law. Law in this view was to be in no sense the enshrining of custom—he had destroyed hereditary rights and customs—nor simply a means of settling disputes, nor an expression of the common will, for the will of the ruled meant little.

> Excluding all divergent interpretation, [the law was] the means of a hierarchical division of individuals in its function as a general scale of worthiness and unworthiness, merit and demerit. It [was] at the same time the all-powerful instrument which enabled the activities of all to be oriented in the direction most favorable to the power of the State and to public tranquility.*

Qin Shi Huang Di summed up his conception of his own achievement when he had the following words engraved on a stele:

> I have brought order to the mass of beings and have submitted acts and realities to the test: everything has the name which is appropriate to it.†

The promulgation of uniform rules and objective criteria was to put an end forever to doubt, division, and conflict. But in one respect, which Mencius had long before declared essential, the Qin dynasty had failed: It no longer commanded the support and confidence of the people and thus had given evidence of its loss of the Mandate of Heaven.

THE HAN DYNASTY

Popular opposition to the rule of Qin broke out in the form of revolts in central China in 209 B.C. At the same time aristocratic opposition, which had never been entirely stifled, revived in a reconstituted Chu kingdom under Xiang Yu. His lieutenant, Liu Bang, succeeded in defeating the third and last Qin emperor in the valley of the Wei in 206 and then turned against his master, Xiang Yu, and defeated him. Liu Bang soon acquired sufficient territory

---

*Gernet, *Le Monde Chinois,* p. 79. Translation by present author
†Ibid., p. 77.

and power to declare himself emperor, under the name Gao Zu ("High Progenitor"), of a new dynasty, the Han, which was to rule China for the next four centuries.

Earlier Han Period (206 B.C.–A.D. 8)

Gao Zu (202–195 B.C.) was in origin a man of the people and kept his bluff countryman's style to the end, even in the midst of court life. He had the peasant's shrewd sense of the possible and the practical, and he operated on the basis of the philosopher Xunzi's saying: "The prince is the boat; the common people are the water. The water can support the boat, or the water can capsize the boat." He had no intention of being capsized and so moved forward with deliberation, choosing his assistants carefully and rewarding them well. He made it a point to abolish the stern laws of the Qin and to restrain his army from looting. Firm and generally just, he could also be generous and understanding of the needs of the ordinary man. He was by no means averse to the pleasures of women and wine. He prided himself on being direct, even rude, and found that these common traits gave his leadership a certain appeal.

Gao Zu, however, in turning away from Qin legalism and absolutism, had no mind to return to the Zhou system of regional semi-independent rulers. He spent his reign consolidating his centralized power both by diplomacy and by force.

At first some compromise was necessary, and those who had aided his victory were rewarded with kingdoms lying beyond the central area of his own fifteen commanderies. Gradually, however, he arranged that title to these kingdoms would be held only by members of his own imperial family. Maps and tax registers compiled by Qin officials in the preceding dynasty were of help in organizing the new administration. Impatient though Gao Zu was of the niceties of official behavior, he recognized the need for order and dignity, so he had a special form of court procedure drawn up along Confucian lines and even had a list of ancestors for himself composed to fit his new exalted station. Confucian learning was revived, and Confucian theories of the requirements of justice and consideration of the people on the part of the ruler seem to have been respected by the new emperor. His youngest brother, Liu Jiao, was himself a noted Confucian scholar.

The transition from camp to court cannot have been an easy one for Gao Zu to make, for he had once been a bandit chief and then a successful general. One of his envoys, on returning from a mission to the far south of China, quoted passages from the Book of Odes and the History to Gao Zu during an audience. Gao Zu said, "I got the empire on horseback; why should I bother with the Odes or History?" The envoy replied, "You got it on horseback, but can you rule it from horseback?"

The combination of determination and flexibility found in Gao Zu and his immediate successors served to consolidate the empire and set it upon the

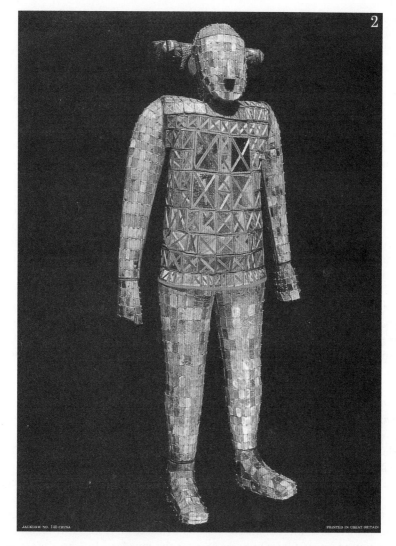

Jade Burial Suit of Princess Tou Wan.

Found in a rock-cut tomb in Hebei province and dating from the Han Dynasty (206 B.C.–A.D. 221). The suit was made from 2,156 pieces of thin jade fastened together with fine gold wire.

Robert Harding Associates

general lines it was to follow in the succeeding centuries. The power of the old aristocracy under the Zhou was gone forever. The doctrinaire theories of totalitarian rule and cruelty in their execution which had obtained under Qin were for the most part abandoned. But the benefits of standardization and centralization which had come with Qin were retained. Thus an era of confidence, stability, and prosperity was ushered in which has made Chinese ever since refer to themselves with pride as "sons of Han."

Yet the new peace and security was not won easily or immediately. The balance between the regional control necessary to establish law and order widely, on the one hand, and the urge toward centralism, on the other, has always been a delicate one in Chinese history. We have seen that the Early Han government granted some independence to peripheral areas without ever intending that they should remain independent. A few kingdoms and certain marquisates were continued in name until the end of the dynasty, but none had more than the appearance of power after 154 B.C. A more serious threat to the central government lay in the power and ambition of Gao Zu's widow, the empress Lu, who was the effective ruler through the agency of her male relatives while a child emperor was on the throne. But on her death in 180 B.C., officials who had remained loyal to the memory of Gao Zu and his policies virtually exterminated the Lu family at the capital. The threat of disruption and factionalism posed by the families of empresses was especially serious later on during the decline of the Han dynasty, and it recurred at intervals in later dynasties.

Such were the internal threats to the establishment of Han rule, but the external threats were no less severe. These threats came as usual from the north, for much of Chinese history is occupied with the incursion of nomads from the steppes and with the Chinese defense and counterattacks. The wealth accumulated in the settled, agricultural lands of north China proved time and again a powerful temptation to these comparatively poor and restless herdsmen. The mobility given them by their hardy Mongolian ponies enabled them to conduct swift, predatory raids and also made them hard to capture as they melted away before a Chinese retaliatory attack. On the other hand they were often divided by tribal feuds and could do little damage in small bands.

At this point the nomad nation of the Xiong-nu (a people of Turkish origin known in the West as the Huns) was united under vigorous leaders and began in Shanxi in 201 B.C. a series of attacks, which forced the Chinese to move for a time south of the Great Wall and brought the Xiong-nu in 166 B.C. very close to the capital of Changan itself. Since Gao Zu in the early stages was preoccupied with the consolidation of his dynasty, he resorted to a stratagem often repeated later, the attempt to buy off the invaders. In Gao Zu's case the inducement offered—and accepted—was the marriage of a Chinese princess to the son of the Xiong-nu "emperor," along with gifts of silk, liquor, rice, and copper money.

The reigns of Gao Zu's successors were comparatively short, but with the accession of the sixth Han emperor, Wu Di, the "Martial Emperor,"* who ruled for fifty-four years (141–87 B.C..), China entered upon a period of confident military expansion which extended her frontiers almost to their

---

* Emperors were given auspicious reign names, such as Wu, "Martial," or Guang Wu, "Shining Martial." This name may be prefaced by the name of the dynasty, as here: Han. Di, or occasionally Huang Di, is a title, meaning "Emperor."

modern position, with the exception of a large section of coastal territory opposite Taiwan. Han Wu Di was by any reckoning one of the most dynamic in the long roll of Chinese emperors. Able and fiercely ambitious, he set a new style of personal control of the governmental process. For the regular officials he substituted in practice a body of Palace Writers, through whom he issued a stream of edicts and orders covering every department of civil and military affairs. The writers in turn controlled which of the multitude of documents (the government of China depended more upon written materials than any other government in the ancient world) should reach the emperor's desk. The power of the Palace Writers may be gauged from the fact that their Intendant was at the same time commander in chief of the army. Yet they remained the servants of Wu Di, for he exercised personal supervision in every department. The obvious dangers of this highly centralized system were mitigated somewhat by the fact that Wu Di was in many ways an enlightened ruler. He encouraged the revival of Confucian studies and was energetic in recruiting the best available scholarly talent for his administration. In this connection he issued a famous announcement:

HEROS WANTED! A PROCLAMATION

Exceptional work demands exceptional men. A bolting or a kicking horse may eventually become a most valuable animal. A man who is the object of the world's detestation may live to accomplish great things. As with the intractable horse, so with the infatuated man;—it is simply a question of training.

We therefore command the various district officials to search for men of brilliant and exceptional talents, to be OUR generals, OUR ministers, and OUR envoys to distant States.*

But the recommendation of qualified applicants for office by existing officials was not enough. The Han dynasty practice of recruitment marks a transition between the early appointment of officials from among the aristocratic families and the later fully developed system of selection by competitive examination, which did not come into full operation until the Tang dynasty (A.D. 618–907). Under the Han a call for recommendations was sent out at intervals, and the resulting candidates were given a written examination at court. The Grand Master of Ceremonies graded the papers and submitted the results to the emperor, who made his own selection. The students at the Imperial University were given annual examinations, and appointments to official posts were made by the emperor from both categories of aspirants.

For all Han Wu Di's attempts to find able men for the imperial administration, he cannot have been an easy master to serve. Of seven chancellors who held office between 121 and 88 B.C., all but one died or were disgraced during their tenure. He was equally hard on the generals, who carried out arduous

*Translated by Giles, *Gems of Chinese Literature,* p. 76.

and often thankless duties in the desert campaigns of the far northwest. Yet Wu Di received respect and loyalty, for general morale, patriotism, and self-confidence ran high during his long reign. He was something of a scholar and wrote poetry which still sounds a universal note of personal feeling.

On the Death of Li Fu-ren

> The sound of her silk skirt has stopped.
> On the marble pavement dust grows.
> Her empty room is cold and still.
> Fallen leaves are piled against the doors. . . .
> How can I bring my aching heart to rest?*

In spite of the rising cultural level of the Han period, the leaders in public life were subject to superstition and the will-o'-the-wisps of magic which were a mark of the age. An ingenious slave at the court of Wu Di gave out that he could cause the Daoist Immortals to appear. He was promoted to a position of honor and wealth and even given the emperor's daughter as wife. When his promises brought no result, he departed "to seek teachers." However, the emperor's agents found that he did not visit any teachers, so he was disgraced and executed. A famous scholar at court, Dong Fangsuo, was more fortunate. He was discovered to have drunk a potion of an elixir of immortality prepared for the emperor. Wu Di was furious and ordered him to be killed, to which Dong Fangsuo, with admirable presence of mind, saved himself by replying, "If the elixir was genuine, your Majesty can do me no harm; if it was not, what harm have I done?"

By far the most important achievement of the reign of Wu Di was the expansion of Chinese power and of the boundaries of territory under Chinese control, and this must now be considered in somewhat more detail. The expansion took place in three directions, to the northwest, the northeast, and the south. The first Han emperor, Gao Zu, as we have seen, faced the problem—even then no new one—of the nomads of the steppes. The Xiong-nu had provided strong anti-Chinese leadership in a regional confederacy of tribes. Some Chinese court opinion was against accommodation and compromise on the grounds that gifts to the Xiong-nu leaders increased not only their wealth but also their power of opposition. On the other hand, the Chinese foreign policy of the doves had been able to turn treaties of peace with the nomads to advantage in the following way. Tribal hostages sent to the Chinese court as guarantees of good behavior were not only magnificently entertained but given a Chinese education and even posts on the palace staff. Thus after their return home they tended to promote friendship with China and gave opportunities for Chinese intervention in local politics when required.

*Waley's translation.

In pursuance of Han Wu Di's aggressive foreign policy, one of his ablest generals, Zhang Qian, volunteered to intervene in tribal affairs in the northwest by trying to secure an alliance with the Yuezhi against their traditional enemies, the Xiong-nu. Zhang Qian set out in 139 B.C. with only 100 men as a bodyguard and was promptly captured by the Xiong-nu. He was kept prisoner for ten years, but when the vigilance of his captors lapsed, he escaped with some of his men and the Xiong-nu wife he had married while a prisoner. With extraordinary courage and loyalty to orders, not to mention the supreme self-confidence of the Han, he turned not eastward to China but westward on his original mission. He found after months of travel that the Yuezhi, an Indo-European-speaking people, had left the Ili Valley for Ferghana. He finally caught up with them in the northern part of Afghanistan called Bactria. They were unwilling to return east and become involved again in the toils of steppe warfare, although Zhang Qian spent a year in their midst in a fruitless effort to persuade them. They subsequently attacked north India and founded the Kushan empire. But the importance to China of Zhang Qian's bold venture was that the Chinese for the first time became aware of the western world beyond their boundaries. Even though the power of the Macedonian successor kingdoms of Alexander the Great (d. 323 B.C.) in the region was by this time minimal, contacts with the world of Parthia, Greece, and Rome had been maintained. Zhang Qian thus reentered China in 126 B.C.—with his Xiong-nu wife and one survivor of his bodyguard—bringing entirely new information to the Chinese court. In 115 B.C. he was again sent west, visiting Ferghana and Sogdiana. He obtained further facts about these regions and found great possibilities for trade with China, particularly in the demand for silk.

Meanwhile, intense military activity was being carried on in all three directions by the generals of Han Wu Di and his immediate successors. Large armies were constantly sent out. In 133 B.C. a force of no less than 300,000 with cavalry launched an attack on the Xiong-nu. Altogether in the eighty years between 136 and 56 B.C. there were twenty-five major expeditions, fourteen to the northwest and west, three to the northeast (Manchuria and Korea), and eight to the south. The southern expeditions were relatively easier, but those in the arid northwest, with long and precarious supply routes and against determined and practiced enemies, occasioned enormous loss of life. Twenty commanderies were set up between 130 and 95 B.C. in the frontier areas. Garrisons were stationed to guard the military routes, and in Wu Di's time alone two million Chinese were sent to colonize the northwest. Even China's vast resources, it is clear, were being overstrained. But by 119 B.C. the Xiong-nu power was reduced, and in 52 B.C. the southern branch of that nation submitted completely to China, while the northern branch ceased to be so great a menace.

Two of the numerous expeditions to the northwest are worthy of special note. In 102 B.C. a general, Li Guang-li, succeeded in bringing back from Ferghana a few specimens of the much-prized great horses of that region, along with 3,000 others of inferior breed. The Ferghana horses immediately became a status symbol and continued to be so regarded in China through subsequent dynasties (see Frontispiece). And three years later another general, Li Ling, with 5,000 Chinese infantry, defeated 30,000 cavalry by a new tactic. In the front of his line he placed infantry armed with shields and pikes, while behind them were archers with powerful crossbows, some multiple-firing, shooting several bolts at a time. Against this formation the nomad cavalry charged in vain. This was in contrast to the Parthian victory over the Romans at Carrhae in 54 B.C. when mounted archers defeated the Romans, the best infantry of their day. But Li Ling was not reinforced, and he had to surrender when his supply of arrows and bolts gave out. He was disgraced by the tyrannical Wu Di, and when Sima Qian, the famous historian, ventured to intervene on the general's behalf, Wu Di meted out to the scholar the barbarous punishment of castration.

Turning now to the northeast, the Han military objective here was to outflank the Xiong-nu, whose leadership had been acknowledged by the peoples of eastern Mongolia and Manchuria. A Chinese commandery was established in Manchuria in 128 B.C. The north and center of Korea were conquered by 106 B.C. and several commanderies were set up, the most important of which was Lak Lang. Archaeological remains of this period of Chinese rule in Korea show a remarkable degree of refinement and luxury.

Zhang Qian had found in Bactria that the Indians had Chinese silk of a type emanating from Sichuan in southwest China. Wu Di was thus disposed to think a way might exist to link Sichuan with India for trade purposes. In fact the terrain over the direct route is impassable, and the silk probably reached India via northwest China and the Silk Road. But the idea of a direct link with India was in part the origin of Wu Di's efforts to explore south China and reduce it all to obedience. Little was known of the geography of the south in early Han times. An alert official from the capital was offered in the city of Canton a mulberry fruit dessert, which he knew was not a local product. He connected it with a type of mulberry grown in Sichuan, and this led to the discovery by the Han government of the west-to-east route already in operation by the tribal peoples using the West River system. If a route from Sichuan to India could be found, trade could flow all the way from the ocean at Canton to the western regions. In any event a major campaign was mounted in 111 B.C., and the southern region of China, called Nan Yue, was conquered by six armies, some forces proceeding by sea, some directly south, and some by the new Sichuan–West River route. Canton was taken, and the provinces of Guangdong, Guangxi, and Tongking in Indochina all became part of the empire.

The army became organized and developed in Han times to a degree not known before. A garrison was kept on duty at the capital, Changan. Expeditionary forces were dispatched for particular campaigns as required. And a permanent defense of the Great Wall and other frontier posts was maintained. Military efficiency was brought to a high standard on the Great Wall. This famous structure consisted in Han times of brick towers or command posts at intervals, usually within sight of one another, connected by earthworks, with a few gates where guards carefully inspected passports and all incoming and outgoing traffic for contraband. (The later Ming dynasty wall with stone facing and crenellated ramparts was much more elaborate.) Signals using smoke, fire, and red and blue flags were exchanged between posts on a precisely timed schedule as well as in emergency. Mail was regularly delivered, and accounts and store records kept. Trained police dogs were employed. Soldiers manufactured arrows, made bricks, and kept the wall in repair. The wall was extended in Han times to the border at Dunhuang, where the two branches of the Silk Road parted to cross the Gobi desert from oasis to oasis and join again at Kashgar to continue the vast distance to the west. The supply problem along military routes was partially met by government-sponsored farms, where colonies of veterans were located, very much in the Roman fashion. Conscripts and even criminals released from jail were used for the unpopular garrison duty on the wall. But in the Later Han period the garrison consisted more of veterans and mercenaries. The mercenary forces were for the most part paid from funds raised by a tax imposed in lieu of compulsory military service.

The expansionist policy of the Earlier Han dynasty and the great public works they undertook proved a severe drain on the treasury. Han Wu Di endeavored to overcome this problem by a variety of fiscal measures. He revived government monopolies in iron, salt, and copper coinage and introduced a monopoly in liquor. He put into operation a system of "leveling," in which the government bought grain in periods of abundance, stored it, and sold it again in periods or localities of dearth. The main object was to make a profit for the state, although the measure was also of assistance to the populace by helping to stabilize prices. Wu Di levied special taxes on ships and wagons, sold official government ranks to the wealthy, and exacted "gifts" from prominent persons. He issued "deerskin certificates," which he compelled certain nobles to buy at the cost of 400,000 copper coins. He also debased the currency to some extent, setting a dangerous precedent for his successors on the throne.

These fiscal devices were moderately successful for the time being, but the most stubborn problem of all proved to be landholding and the related tax. The population was growing, which meant less land for each individual peasant. At the same time the great landowning families were increasing the extent of their holdings, and these were often almost free of tax. Thus the tax base was narrowed, as in Heian Japan at a later date, and the remaining peasants were paying a disproportionate share. Constant legislative efforts were made to remedy this situation by limiting the area of landholdings of the great and so restoring the government's protection, and hence control, of the peasantry, which had been the strength of the Han dynasty in its earlier days. But these efforts were largely unavailing, and private estates continued to grow. In spite of the centralized power of the dynasty, they seemed no more able to halt this trend than the Gracchi brothers and their successors in Rome were able to prevent the usurpation of state lands by senators and wealthy knights. The circumstances were different, but the reasons were the same; in each case a comparatively few entrenched landowners, the court officials in China and the senators in Rome, not the emperor (after Wu Di) or the Roman people, controlled the daily operation of the government.

The political interaction between emperor and officials in Han times forms a paradigm for much of later Chinese history, when the pattern was repeated in varying forms, for an autocratic system does not eliminate the human activity of politics but only alters its manifestation. The autocratic tendencies of Wu Di's handling of affairs were, if anything, beneficial so long as an emperor was as strong and able as he. But after his death in 87 B.C. a general, He Guang, established a virtual dictatorship under Wu Di's successor and secured a number of the principal offices for his own relatives. The factions which arose surrounding palace favorites, powerful eunuchs, and especially the male relatives of the empresses were fatal to orderly government. Wu Di had arrived at a simple solution to the problem of relatives, for when he chose his heir apparent, he had the empress mother executed, but his successors did not put this cruel safeguard into operation. Owing to a combination of the above factors the power of the house of Han rapidly declined, and in A.D. 9 a member of the powerful Wang family, Wang Mang, already a high official and nephew of an empress, seized the throne and attempted to found a new dynasty.

Wang Mang (A.D. 9–23), a strong Confucianist, revived what he supposed to be the titles and institutions of the Zhou dynasty, but his economic reforms were radical. He reinstituted the "leveling" system, introduced agricultural loans, and manipulated the currency. He proposed an extreme solution for the land problem by "nationalizing" the land and redistributing it to peasants. Private slaves, less than 1 percent of the population, were likewise to be government-owned. But this attempt ran into inevitable opposition from the landowners. Nor could any successful way of redistributing confiscated land be found. A peasant revolt broke out in A.D. 17 in Shandong under a vigorous woman leader known as Mother Lu. When neglect of the dikes and heavy rains caused a major shift in the lower course of the Yellow River and consequent disastrous floods, the revolt spread to the central plains. The rebels, making up their faces to look like demons and adopting religious symbols, became known as the Red Eyebrows and set a precedent, often repeated in later Chinese history, of a genuine popular movement arising in times of stress under the aegis of religion. The combination of the highest and lowest classes in opposition to the new regime proved too much for Wang Mang, and he was defeated and killed in A.D. 23. His reputation has suffered from the simple fact that he did not succeed in founding a new dynasty and thus was branded by orthodox historians as a usurper.

Later Han Period (A.D. 23–221)

The new ruler who restored the Han was himself a member of the original Liu imperial family and was given the title Guang Wu Di, "Shining Martial Emperor" (A.D. 25–57). A strong leader, he reduced the Red Eyebrows revolt and freed many who had fallen into slavery during the troubles. The wars had eliminated many of the aristocrats and large landholders, which had the effect of improving the tax yield. The new emperor, starting afresh, did not have so many officials and dependents at court to maintain. The treasury recovered, and under his firm rule a measure of stability was restored. The Wei River irrigation system had suffered, and the old capital, Changan, had been heavily damaged. Moreover, the Later Han emperors, in spite of what has been said, were compelled to depend to a great extent upon the landowning class, whose center of gravity lay farther east. For all these reasons Guang Wu Di shifted his seat from Changan farther east to Luoyang and founded what is known as the Later or Eastern Han dynasty.

The second emperor, now with a firmer base, turned his attention to regaining control over Central Asia. His agent was one of the greatest of Chinese generals, Ban Chao. The high point of Chinese power earlier in Central Asia and the northwest had been in 59 B.C., when a Protector General of the Western Regions had been appointed. But the post, and along with it Chinese control, had lapsed during the troubles associated with the end of the Earlier Han. Ban Chao, beginning in A.D. 73, used both diplomatic and military means to reassert Chinese dominance and in 91 was made Protector General of the Western Regions, by which time he was able to control the whole Tarim basin from his headquarters on the northern edge at Kucha. He had been briefly recalled in 76 for political reasons, but he was able to persuade the emperor that he would only require a small cadre of Chinese officers and men of experience to organize loyal local forces against still-unreduced states. This policy, patiently carried out over seventeen years, was extremely successful, and Ban Chao himself was held in high regard by many tribes for his statesmanlike qualities.

In Ban Chao's greatest expedition he led an army of 70,000 men across the Tian Shan mountains to the Caspian Sea, or almost to the borders of Europe, without encountering any serious opposition. After covering this prodigious distance, some 3,800 miles from Luoyang, he sent a representative to Parthia, Mesopotamia, and the Roman empire, then (A.D. 97) ruled by the emperor Nerva. The envoy reported on Parthia as a country producing excellent soldiers and then was directed on the caravan route to the head of the Persian Gulf. Deterred by a sailor's tale that those who set sail on the Persian Gulf and Indian Ocean might need from three months to two years for the voyage and that many, because of some property of the sea, died of longing for their homeland, the envoy gave up the attempt to reach the Roman world. It is probable that the Parthians did all they could to prevent any link-up between the powerful Chinese and their own traditional enemies, the Romans. Besides, the silk trade was profitable for all who could remain as middlemen, including not least the Parthians. But from the information brought back by Ban Chao, who returned to China in A.D. 102, and from Greek merchant traders who visited China in A.D. 166 and 226, it is evident that the Chinese knew more about Rome than the

Romans knew about China. The dynastic histories of the Later Han and subsequent shorter dynasties contain these statements in their summary accounts:

> The people of Ta Ts'in (Rome) have historians and interpreters for foreign languages as the Han have. The walls of their cities are built of stone. They cut their hair short, wear embroidered garments, and ride in very small chariots. Their rulers only govern for a short time and are chosen from among the most worthy men. When things go badly they are changed. [An anachronism at this point, referring to the consuls under the Republic—C.P.F.] The people of Ta Ts'in are big men. . . . They dress differently from the Chinese. Their country produces gold and silver, all kinds of precious goods, amber, glass and giant eggs (ostrich eggs). From China by way of An Hsi (Parthia) they obtain silk which they re-spin into fine gauze. The conjurers of Ta Ts'in (Syrians?) are the best in the world. They can eat fire and play with many balls. The Ta Ts'in are honest. Prices are fixed and grain is always cheap. The granaries and public treasury are always full. The people of An Hsi prevent them communicating with us by land, also the roads are infested with lions so that one must travel in caravan and with military escort. The Ta Ts'in first sent envoys to us (in 166 A.D.). Since then their merchants have come frequently to Jih Nan (Tongking).*

This may be sketchy, but it is basically correct. The Roman ignorance of China, on the other hand, was profound. The Romans connected China with little else but silk, to the extent that the adjective *sericus,* "Chinese," from the noun *Seres,* comes by transference to mean "silken" (*sericos pulvillos,* little silken cushions, Horace, *Epodes,* 8:15). Horace mentions the Chinese in various widely separated geographical contexts, associated with Parthia, Bactria, and the River Don in present-day Russia. Admittedly, he was writing poetry, not exact geography. Moreover he enjoyed the witticism of unlikely contrasts. But the impression remains that he and his readers were extremely vague, not to say confused, on the location of China and ignorant of its customs. The most egregious geographical error concerning the Chinese comes from the writer Lucan, who was executed by Nero in A.D. 66. Lucan places the Chinese at the sources of the Nile and makes them neighbors of the Ethiopians.

The two great empires of China and Rome thus touched through the silk trade but never really met. What evidence there is of contact is tenuous and indicates only minimal interchange. Two Antonine coins were found at Phnam, a port in the Mekong delta which was a thriving entrepôt for overseas trade in the Han dynasty, but this does not prove the presence of Romans there. In 42 B.C. a Chinese force in the former Hellenistic kingdom of Sogdiana defeated a group of the Xiong-nu and some foreign troops who were possibly captive Roman soldiers. Paintings of the battle were incorporated in a Chinese report to the emperor; this was a practice in Roman triumphs but never a Chinese custom. A city existed in China itself after 79 B.C. called Li

*Quoted in C. P. Fitzgerald, *China: A Short Cultural History,* p. 195.

Farmhouse of the Han dynasty, first to second century A.D.

The L-shaped house and courtyard are viewed from the rear. A human figure looks out from the upper window, and another is sleeping in the cool of the window downstairs. The tiled roofs of house and wall have continued down history with little change. This and the ceramic figures from the Tang dynasty (pages 90 and 95) show tomb figurines (*ming-qi,* "articles of the spirit," or of "the unseen world") buried with the dead.

Collection of Mr. and Mrs. Ezekiel Schloss, Photo: Keith Scott Morton

Jian. This is the Chinese term for Alexandria, and the methods of Chinese nomenclature would indicate that this city was populated by persons from Alexandria in the Roman world. Apart from these minor instances, the Greco-Roman world and China and her satellites existed as separate entities, each considering themselves the center of the civilized world. Interchange between Europe and East Asia would begin in a very small way in the medieval period but not become culturally significant until the nineteenth century.

Returning to the progress of events in the Later Han period, the reigns of the first three emperors up to A.D. 88 were marked by internal solidarity and outward expansion, or rather re-expansion. Thereafter, however, problems increased and decline set in. The northern border situation exhibited interesting differences from that of the Earlier Han. The semisedentary tribes, influenced by Chinese civilization, formed a buffer region which protected China proper. There were no major incursions from the independent warrior peoples farther north and west. Trouble arose rather from those tribes incorporated under the Earlier Han into China itself. Some were ex-nomads while others were mountaineers of Tibetan background. Both groups felt themselves exploited by Chinese officialdom. China in her "civilizing" capacity was always trying to change dependent kingdoms into so-called "military territories" and then into ordinary "administrative circuits" like those of the rest of China. If the newcomers could be turned into farmers, they could be taxed, conscripted into the army, and made to contribute their one month per year corvée, or compulsory labor service. Those who remembered the freedom of a former nomadic life (and forgot its hardships) resented this whole process, the more so as they saw their more aggressive cousins beyond the bounds of the empire being given valuable presents to pay them to keep the peace. (Enormous amounts were expended in this way; 8,000 rolls of silk in 51 B.C. had risen to 30,000 by 1 B.C.; of 10,000,000,000 cash [or copper coins] in government receipts, about a third was expended on this "foreign aid" diplomacy.) Thus, not surprisingly, the exploited ex-nomads within the empire were frequently in rebellion.

This unrest and the withdrawal of former frontier colonies gave rise to the migration of many peasants, who took refuge and employment with the large landowners. The landowners became wealthier and more of a power in the state than ever. Guang Wu Di himself, before becoming emperor, possessed a vast territory surrounded by a wall with gates. It had its own market and a private army to defend it. Irrigation, stock rearing, and fish breeding were practiced on such estates, giving them almost complete economic independence in troubled times.

If the only important factors in the makeup of Later Han society had been the landowner officials and the vast mass of the peasantry, the situation might have remained as stable as it was in the first three reigns. But the eunuchs at court rose to power as bitter rivals of the officials and in A.D. 135 were granted the right to adopt sons. This gave these unfortunates from a lower class in society an incentive to found families and pass on wealth and power. It would be a useful study in the new discipline of psychohistory to examine how the sexual deprivation of court eunuchs, often entered upon voluntarily for career reasons, inflamed their ambition and increased the bitterness with which they fought the privileged officials for riches, rank, and a place in the sun.

A group of landowner officials developed a plot against the eunuchs in A.D. 167, but this was unmasked and the members degraded from office and sent into exile. The landed families had their country estates and local power bases, upon which they normally felt secure. But major agrarian revolts in A.D. 184 threatened them in the countryside, and the peasants, without any official political status, proved able to menace the whole state system by sheer weight of numbers and military force. In this situation the eunuchs made a temporary comeback but were decisively defeated in 189 by strong-arm action on the part of a general of the Imperial Guard, who had over 2,000 of them massacred.

The agrarian crisis of A.D. 184 was similar to but more severe than that of the Red Eyebrows revolt which hastened the end of Wang Mang's short interlude of rule. Bands of wandering peasants already on the move were vastly increased as the result of floods in the lower Yellow River basin. These desperate people found a focus and a purpose in a Daoist-led movement known as the Yellow Turbans. Since there was no place in an autocratic state for dissident movements to express themselves in political form, on this and many subsequent occasions of crisis, general discontent and opposition gathered under a religious aegis. The Yellow Turbans rebellion was led by the patriarch of a Daoist sect known as the Taiping, one Zhang Jiao, aided by his two brothers. This leader was evidently a charismatic figure, felt to have healing gifts as well as the power of military command. Since epidemics had broken out in the wake of the floods, his power to heal attracted many followers. The connotation of the sect title, Taiping, "great peace," was one of a golden age, where men would all be equal, live at peace, and share all worldly goods. The Yellow Turban communities thus spent considerable time in religious observances, fasts of purification, and the public confession of sins. These religious gatherings included collective trances, aided by music and incessant prostrations. The communal hysteria thus induced sometimes ended in orgies in which men and women "mingled their breaths" (he qi).

When the Yellow Turbans moved into open revolt in 184, there were soon 360,000 under arms, and by 188 the rebellion had spread from Shandong in the east to Shanxi in the west of north China. At the same time another rebellion along similar lines broke out in 190 and established for a time an independent state in the southern part of Shaanxi and in Sichuan. They were given the name Five Pecks of Rice Band from the amount of rice members were required to contribute to the common coffers. They abolished private property, instituted free distribution of grain to travelers, and built "inns of equality" where travelers could obtain free meals. They encouraged members to atone for their sins by working on the maintenance of the roads. The last is a most interesting variant on the usual government-enforced corvée, now undertaken by the peasants with a degree of free will but under a religious sanction. Atonement seems to have been a strong incentive, since these sects believed that illness was the result of sin. Although the Five Pecks of Rice center was in the west of China, it is perhaps worth noting that Shandong and the northeast coastal area, so prominent over a long period in the enthusiasms of Daoist magic and the Yellow Turban rebellion, was also the region in which, prior to the Communist regime, millenarian and fundamentalist sects of Christians took their most extreme forms.

These rebellions seriously weakened the Later Han dynasty, already debilitated by factions at court, for three great families allied to empresses had dominated affairs from A.D. 88 to 144. The end came through the rivalry of generals to whose hands wide powers had been entrusted in order to cope with the peasant rebellions. Dong Zhuo sacked and burned the capital in 190, which entailed the loss of the Imperial Library and the Han archives. His excessive cruelties caused his assassination, and ultimate power in the north became vested in the famous general Cao-Cao, adopted son of a eunuch. The empire then fell apart into three natural geographical divisions, Cao-Cao ruling the kingdom of Wei in the north, Liu Bei the kingdom of Shu-Han in Sichuan in the west, and Sun Chuan the south and lower Yangzi valley in a kingdom called Wu. Thus began the era of the Three Kingdoms (A.D. 220–280) and a long period when the unified empire was no more than a dream.

Culture in the Han Period

The vast time scale of Chinese history and the apparently steady sequence of dynasties give a false impression of smooth flow. In truth the revolution wrought by the Qin and Han dynasties was so great that the feudal age of Confucius and the Warring States was a distant memory to the scholars of Han, separated by a great gulf from their own times. They attributed the unity of their own empire to the rule of the early Zhou, and the size of contemporary Chinese territory to the domains of Zhou, which in fact Zhou never possessed. This set a distorted pattern for the interpretation of Chinese history which persisted until modern times and is only now being gradually corrected.

After the Legalism of Qin, the Han emperors restored Confucianism, although retaining many useful autocratic features of Legalism which suited their centralized rule. They appointed specialists in the Five Classics, now regarded as Confucian works, and they made a distinctive Confucian virtue, filial piety, one of the criteria for appointing officials. Classical Confucian studies received more and more attention and reached their summit in Later Han, when in A.D. 175 the text of the Classics was officially engraved on stele at the capital.

Yet the Confucianism thus restored was by no means identical with the original article. The terse, and thus mysterious, style of the original writings and the great veneration in which they were held encouraged scholars to seek and unfold the hidden meanings which they felt must be there. The principles by which Dong Zhongshu (?179–104 B.C.) and others interpreted the ancient texts were derived from the early philosophy of nature, the complementary alternating forces of *yin* and *yang*, dark and light, female and male, which maintain the balance of the cosmos, and which had been a thought pattern of the Chinese before any philosophical schools came into being (see p. 39).

The changes and alternation in nature were elaborated into successive circular victories of the Five Elements: earth, wood, metal, fire, and water. Thus, earth was moved by wood, wood cut by metal, metal melted by fire, fire quenched by water, and water overcome by the mass of earth, only to start the cycle again. The Han interpreters, again drawing upon earlier speculation, extended this sequence by correspondences with the points of the compass, colors, the cyclic characters used for periods in the calendar, and even with

Rubbing from stone relief carving, Wu family shrine. Later Han dynasty, first to second century A.D.

Lower register: Food preparation.
Middle register: Feast and entertainers on right.
Upper register: Tales of filial piety. The second figure from right pretends the beating from his mother's stick (third from right) was a hard one, and the fourth figure, Lao Lai Ze, is playing with toys, in both instances to make their parents feel young again.

The Metropolitan Museum of Art

dynasties. Thus, fire (red) was the sign of Zhou, defeated by water (black), the sign of Qin, and water in turn defeated by earth (yellow), the symbol of Han. The correspondences and sequences were tied in to another ancient symbol, that of the eight trigrams, a pattern of solid and broken lines. (The eight trigrams were further developed in the sixty-four hexagrams, or six-line series.) Strange and farfetched as some of these speculations may appear to Westerners, they do not strike the Chinese in the same way, since they attempt to explain the world in terms of symbols from a venerated past which appear to the Chinese to have universal validity. Dong Zhungshu sought to place Confucian principles in a cosmic setting and to relate them to the workings of the universe as he saw it. In particular he stressed the idea that the emperor's authority came from Heaven. In this way he gave a theoretical solidity to Confucian state philosophy which lasted many centuries beyond his time.

The Chinese have never felt that to hold one belief it is necessary to exclude others, and the Han period was marked by a broad eclecticism. Although Confucianism enjoyed new favor and imperial support, Daoism also was a potent factor in the thought of the age. It had influenced the emperor Wu Di, as we have seen. It impressed the father of the noted historian Sima Qian and was preferred above all other philosophies by the empress of Wen Di and the emperor Hui Di. One of Daoism's undoubted appeals was its claim that the body could be preserved and life prolonged by means of different techniques, by alchemy, gymnastic exercises, diet, sexual practices, and respiratory control. The secrets of eternal life and of the way to make gold were known to the Happy Immortals, who dwelt in the Islands of the Blessed in the eastern sea, and might perhaps be revealed to special initiates. Everything living on these islands was white, and the palaces and temples were of silver and gold. Ideas such as these were expounded in a book of Han date, the *Huainanzi,* which, in explaining the more purely philosophic concepts of Laozi and Zhuangzi (pages 38 ff.) in a supernatural manner, contributed to the turning of Daoist philosophy into Daoist religion. The rise of Daoist religion at this time received further impetus from the popular movements such as the Yellow Turbans and Five Pecks of Rice rebellions, for here were to be found a church organization with a burning faith in a utopian society to come, as well as a popular cult and a stress on moral teaching.

The matter of textual criticism and interpretation also occupied the Han scholars. The rather recondite differences between the schools of the Old Text and the New Text might be passed over in a brief outline such as this, were it not that the differences extended beyond matters of text and were perpetuated in various forms right down to the nineteenth century. A descendant of Confucius claimed to have found an old copy of the *Book of Documents (Shu Jing)* in the walls of the sage's house. This and other materials which turned up were written in the ancient pre-Qin-dynasty script. The majority of the Confucian classics, so intensively studied during Han, had, on the other hand, been passed down orally and recorded in the new script. As indicated, disagreements between the schools which arose in this way went beyond the question of correct readings and split over interpretation, the "new text" enthusiasts emphasizing hidden meanings and supposed connections with cosmology and divination, while the supporters of the "old text" stressed the moral and ritual elements in the original tradition and adopted a rationalistic rather than a mystical attitude. Fortunately all Chinese scholars, then and since, were careful to preserve the texts without alteration and separate from the interpretative commentaries.

Although it is evident that the Han thinkers were breaking new ground in their approach to the meaning of the universe and man's life in it, it is not for philosophy but for historical writing that their age is chiefly famous. Sima Qian (c. 145–85 B.C.), who lived in the reign of the great emperor Han Wu Di, began on foundations laid by his father, Sima Tan, and carried on the work, *The Historical Records (Shi Ji),* from the earliest times down to his own day. It was intended as a universal history but in fact is a history of China, which was legitimately regarded by the author as the center of the world known to him.

The novelty and sweep of his work cannot be sufficiently emphasized, for all that had gone before had been merely annals, and Sima Qian began the writing of history. He arranges, he reflects, and he brings out meaning and significance. With a remarkable power of synthesis he considers the essence of China's history from the point of view of politics and morals. At this early stage in the world's historical writing, three features which modern historiography reckons important appear already in Sima Qian's work: a precision in dating which he inherited from the earlier annalists, a careful reproduction of the exact texts of important documents, and a skilled use of oral material in stories, anecdotes, records of diplomatic conversations, and the like. His prose is concise and discards literary devices to a degree unusual in Chinese prose, as being unsuited to straight historical narrative. He covers a wide range, giving an account of each emperor's reign (with the exception of the reign of Wu Di, an account which was probably too critical to be published) in the first section, the Basic Annals. In the second he writes essays on music, the calendar, astrology, rivers and canals, economics, and other topics; in the third he presents biographies of many major and minor characters in history. Sima Qian, who traveled widely in China and had access to the Imperial Library and archives, explained something of his motives and purpose in a letter to a friend, Ren Shaoqing:

> Those like Tso Ch'iu, who was blind, or Sun Tzu, who had no feet, could never hold office, so they retired to compose books in order to set forth their thoughts and indignation, handing down their theoretical writings in order to show to posterity who they were. I too have ventured not to be modest but have entrusted myself to my useless writings. I have gathered up and brought together the old traditions of the world which were scattered and lost. I have examined the deeds and events of the past and investigated the principles behind their success and failure, their rise and decay, in one hundred and thirty chapters. I wished to examine into all that concerns heaven and man, to penetrate the changes of the past and present, completing all as the work of one family. But before I had finished my rough manuscript, I met with this calamity [castration]. It is because I regretted that it had not been completed that I submitted to the extreme penalty without rancor. When I have truly completed this work, I shall deposit it in the Famous Mountain. If it may be handed down to men who will appreciate it, and penetrate to the villages and great cities, then though I should suffer a thousand mutilations, what regret should I have? Such matters as these may be discussed with a wise man, but it is difficult to explain them to ordinary people.*

Sima Qian's work set a standard for all subsequent Chinese historical writing. It was followed by the *History of the [Earlier] Han (Han Shu)*, by the Ban family. Begun by Ban Biao, the book was carried on by his son Ban

---

*Translated by Burton Watson.

Gu, who wrote the bulk of the work, and finished by his daughter Ban Zhao, one of the most famous of China's few women writers. Another son of this remarkable family was Ban Chao, protector general of the Western Regions. This history in its turn became the model for the subsequent dynastic histories of China, each dynasty composing an official account of the events of the previous one.

In other Han literature the most distinctive type is the *fu*, which has sometimes been classed as poetry, sometimes as rhythmic prose, owing to the fact that meter and length of line are irregular. In these descriptive pieces, highly colored, elaborate in style, and exhibiting the favorite Chinese form of balanced, parallel phrases, the themes revolve around the court: palaces, capitals, beloved landscapes, the hunt, and court amusements. Popular taste was also represented and penetrated the upper circles of Han society in the form of peasant songs, dances, and musical instruments, some coming from Central Asia in the wake of the extensive contacts with the nomads, contacts which were peaceful as well as warlike.

The folk style was skillfully employed by the poet Mei Sheng, whose use of the five-foot meter set a pattern for much of later verse. This poem, filled with the longing of love, has a certain fresh and direct quality:

The animal motif in Chinese art, showing Scythian or Nomad influence.

A plaque of gilt bronze from Inner Mongolia, first century A.D., this has the rather unusual theme of a horse with wings.

The Metropolitan Museum of Art, Fletcher Fund, 1924

The warm sunshine of spring;
The orchids in full bloom.
When winter breaks upon us,
Their flowers will still be there.

From spring to winter time,
Every day and hour,
The old pain springs inside me,
My heart's wound burns.

It seems my love is standing
On the clouds of Heaven's tent,
And a whole wide world
Yawns between us.

I wander in the moonlight
In the shade of cypress trees,
And in between my sighs I think
Of her I never can forget.

I don't believe a man alive
Can understand the shudder in my heart.
The thoughts swell up inside—
My reason's going to crack.

As evidence of the interchange with distant Central Asian peoples, the following poem by a Chinese princess, Xi-chun, sent for reasons of state by the emperor Wu Di to be married to a chief of the Wu-sun in the Ili Valley, carries a note of desperate longing for home:

My family has married me off,
Alas! and sent me far,

To the strange land of the Wu-sun.
I'm now, woe is me, the king's wife.

I live in a tent, and a house wall
Have I exchanged for—felt.

My food is only meat;
Koumiss they give me to drink with it.

O, my heart burns since they sent me here;
I can only think of my home, over and over.

Could I but be a yellow crane,
Fast would I fly back to my own kingdom!

It is quite evident that Han was a many-sided age of considerable sophistication. Technology and invention did not lag behind. The Elder Pliny writes in A.D. 39 of the high quality of the iron manufactured by the "Seres," the Chinese. Steel was made from the second century B.C. onward. The water mill is mentioned in Wang Mang's time at the beginning of the Christian era. The Han had a well-designed wheelbarrow with a low center of gravity and capable of carrying 150 kilograms, over 300 pounds. They had water clocks, sundials, and astronomical instruments. An armillary sphere built in A.D. 124 was soon afterward attached to a daily revolving mechanism controlled by a water clock. Two Han mathematical books have survived, which include examples of calculations in land surveying, taxation, and architectural measurements. The contemporary preoccupation with omens and portents had useful spin-off effects in the scientific field. The first seismograph, said to be able to indicate the direction of the quake, was constructed in A.D. 132, since earth movements had significance as signs of the derangement of nature in evil times. From 28 B.C., systematic records of sunspots, likewise aberrations in nature, were kept, which have proved useful to modern scientists.

6

OUTSIDERS, GENERALS, AND ECCENTRICS

The Six Dynasties Period: A.D. 222–589

During the third century A.D., a gentleman of somewhat dissolute appearance was seen driving about the streets of Luoyang in a small cart drawn by two deer. He was followed by two servants, one with a wine flask and goblet, the other carrying a spade. When asked the purpose of the spade, the second servant replied that if his master dropped dead, he had instructions to bury him on the spot. The gentleman was Liu Ling, one of a coterie called the Seven Sages of the Bamboo Grove. He was, of course, making a point in his own eccentric way. The meaning of the wine flask was obvious, but the point driven home by the spade was a peculiarly Chinese one: that the elaborate Confucian ritual surrounding death, and other things in life, was nonsense and against Nature. To one who took things as they came and enjoyed himself in a mildly inebriated way, the affairs of this world appeared as so much "duckweed on a river."

This hedonistic attitude, deliberately adopted by some scholars such as the Seven Sages, who held free-ranging Daoist philosophical debates known as "pure discussions" (qing-tan), was a far cry from the conventional morality of the Confucian scholar officials which obtained throughout most of Chinese history. It was one by-product of an age of barbarian invasions and extreme political confusion. During this period of three and a half centuries, the longest time of political disunity in China's history, the reaction of many thinking men was one of complete withdrawal from public life. Thus the period is often dismissed or hurried over in the histories. It was nevertheless a time when fresh vigor was injected into society by new blood from beyond China's borders. New ventures in thought and religion, and even in administration, introduced in the Six Dynasties period are now being seen as anticipations or models for the great flowering of culture and society when the Chinese empire became unified once more under the Sui and Tang dynasties.

SUMMARY OF EVENTS

The power shifts among leaders, many of them non-Chinese, and their ephemeral dynasties in the north and south during the Six Dynasties are exceedingly complicated. The main outline of events may be summarized as follows. The Three Kingdoms which emerged at the breakup of the Later Han dynasty dominated the scene from 220 until the 260s—280 in the case of Wu in the south. All three at first were able to expand, the Wei kingdom in the north moving into Korea, Shu-Han in the southwest conquering some surrounding aboriginal tribes, and Wu in the south enlarging its territory as far as Vietnam. Wei annexed its neighbor, Shu-Han, in 263, and soon afterward a general from Wei announced a new dynasty, the Jin, which conquered the third kingdom, Wu, in 280 and briefly united China again. Thereafter a distinct division opened up between north China and south China, which persisted until the end of the era in 589.

The history of the north is marked for a hundred years by many invasions by the "barbarians," some more, some less sinicized. The Sixteen Kingdoms were won and lost by five nations. The Xiong-nu, Jie and Qianbei came from the steppes and spoke languages allied to Turkish, Mongol and Tungusic; the other two, the Qiang and the Di, were mountaineers and spoke languages similar to Tibetan and Tangut. The next phase in the north was important for cultural reasons to which we shall return, and power was held by the Northern Wei dynasty (386–534; to be distinguished from the Wei kingdom of Cao-Cao among the Three Kingdoms, which is sometimes known as the Cao-Wei). Four unimportant and subdivided successor states close the period in the north.

In the south the dominant class consisted of the Chinese aristocrats, many of whom had migrated southward as the fierce tribal leaders moved in and took over their northern homeland. Indeed, over the whole period from the third to the fifth century, those of Chinese descent in the region south of the Yangzi greatly increased in numbers, conquering and supplanting the aboriginal tribes. This movement of people, affecting the whole future of China, is an example of the importance of the period under review, regardless of its political disunity. The rise of the great independent manors, which we have observed at the end of Han, was continued, and the manpower they required was provided by fleeing peasants from the north or conquered southerners. From among the aristocratic families arose the generals who became emperors of the succession of dynasties based upon the southern capital, Nanjing (Nanking).

The Six Dynasties of the south which gave their name to the period were the Wu, the Eastern Jin, the Liu Song, the Southern Qi, the Liang, and the Chen. Only a few words need be said about them individually.

The Eastern Jin were a continuation in the south from 317 to 420 of the Jin (or Western Jin) already mentioned as uniting the country for a short time. They were successful in conquering Sichuan, which gave them access to Central Asia. The kingdom suffered a rebellion in the year 400, led by a member of the Five Pecks of Rice Band who recruited sailors, fishermen, and pirates along the south coast to his cause. The general who put down the rebellion, in a pattern familiar at this time, took advantage of his position to seize power at Nanjing, but he in turn was defeated by a rival who founded the Liu Song dynasty (420–479).

The Liu Song encountered difficulty both from their own aristocrats who clung to their privileges and from attacks by the Northern Wei, and they succumbed, giving way to the Southern Qi (479–502). Commercial enterprise under this dynasty made great advances. As under the Liu Song the general bias was antiaristocratic, but, when this went too far, a massacre of nobles provoked resistance which ended this short-lived dynasty.

The Liang dynasty (502–557) provided a slight respite of peace and prosperity owing to the long reign of its founder, Liang Wu Di (502–549). Meanwhile an important economic change was taking place, which had its parallel at a later point in medieval Europe: Trade and commerce were steadily growing, and the dominance of the self-sufficient country manor with its all-powerful overlord was declining. During the first half of the sixth century in China, the cities of the Yangzi and Canton in the south were increasing in importance. Liang dynasty records reveal the presence and activity of a growing number of merchants, not only Chinese but also Southeast Asian, Indian, and Persian. The foundations were being laid for the vast commercial expansion of south China and its overseas trade during later dynasties. The culture of the Liang was stimulated by Buddhism, of which the emperor Liang Wu Di was an ardent patron. But there was a new military development, which also had its European parallel at a much later date: The rise of mercenary armies under the command of condottieri who made a trade of war threatened the Liang dynasty and the great aristocrats who had enjoyed a place in the sun for so long.

The Liang gave way to the Chen dynasty (557–589), the last of the divided dynasties before Sui reunited China. The troubles attendant on the decline of the Liang had resulted in the loss of Sichuan and the western territories. Chen was too weak to defend itself against a combination of enemies and fell to the Sui in 589.

LITERATURE OF THE THREE KINGDOMS ERA

These kaleidoscopic political changes took place at the summit and must be recorded, if only to keep the framework of Chinese history in order and provide reference points in dynasties for those who wish to go further in the study of Chinese art, philosophy, or literature. But the underlying changes slowly taking place in culture and society during this disturbed period are of more importance. The study of social history has awakened us to the fact that there are often two angles from which the events of any given era should be viewed. The basic angle is the purely factual one: What was it that actually happened? But in the long run the more important angle may be the imaginary one: What did those who lived after the events *suppose* happened? Through what spectacles did they view the events? For that is what determines future history.

The Three Kingdoms era at the beginning of the period we are considering offers a good example of this double angle. There was in fact little to choose between the three generals—one might almost call them desperadoes—who from motives of personal aggrandizement carved out their separate spheres of control. Betrayal and bloodshed marked their progress. But subsequent generations of Chinese have looked back to the Three Kingdoms era as a time of adventure and chivalry. The realist Chinese, who are not as a rule given to glorifying war, have reveled in the daring feats and hairbreadth escapes of this period. Just as Shakespeare drew upon a fund of battle tales from the Wars of the Roses and the Japanese No plays dwelt upon the heroism of the Gempei Wars, so the Chinese authors of later drama and of the famous novel, *The Romance of the Three Kingdoms,* found a rich mine of themes in this period of warfare and changing fortunes. The adventures which brought misery at the time became more romantic as they receded into the mists of the past. Cao-Cao was cast as a villain, while Liu Bei of Shu-Han, claiming to carry on the traditions of the great Han dynasty, was the hero. Every Chinese is familiar with the stratagems of his loyal general, Zhuge Liang, and with the exploits of Guan Yu, who became deified as Guan Di, the God of War. However, contrary to the classical cult of Ares or Mars, Guan Di is reverenced by the common people as the god who prevents war.

The essays of the scholars, as opposed to the tales of the people, tend at this time to be a literature of escape, to speak of the abandonment of the burdens of office and a return to the solace of Nature, as this universally appealing extract from the early fifth century indicates. The classical and slightly pedantic style of the translation by Herbert A. Giles, first professor of Chinese at Cambridge University, suitably reflects the original, in which Tao Yuanming is consciously savoring the simple joys in a scholarly way.

Home Again!

Homewards I bend my steps. My fields, my gardens are choked with weeds: should I not go? My soul has led a bondsman's life: why should I remain to pine? . . .

Lightly, lightly speeds my boat along, my garments fluttering to the gentle breeze. I enquire my route as I go. I grudge the slowness of the dawning day. From afar I descry my old home, and joyfully press onwards in my haste. The servants rush forth to meet me: my children cluster at the gate. The place is a wilderness: but there is the old pine-tree and my chrysanthemums. I take the little ones by the hand, and pass in. Wine is brought in full bottles, and I pour out in brimming cups. I gaze out at my favourite branches. I loll against the window in my newfound freedom. I look at the sweet children on my knee.

And now I take my pleasure in my garden. There is a gate, but it is rarely opened. I lean on my staff as I wander about or sit down to rest. I raise my head and contemplate the lovely scene. Clouds rise, unwilling, from the bottom of the hills: the weary bird seeks its nest again. Shadows vanish, but still I linger round my lonely pine. Home once more! I'll have no friendships to distract me hence. The times are out of joint for me; and what have I to seek from men? In the pure enjoyment of the family circle I will pass my days, cheering my idle hours with lute and book. My husbandmen will tell me when spring-time is nigh, and when there will be work in the furrowed fields. Thither I shall repair by cart or by boat, through the deep gorge, over the dizzy cliff, trees bursting merrily into leaf, the streamlet swelling from its tiny source. Glad is this renewal of life in due season: but for me, I rejoice that my journey is over. Ah, how short a time it is that we are here! Why then not set our hearts at rest, ceasing to trouble whether we remain or go? What boots it to wear out the soul with anxious thoughts? I want not wealth: I want not power: heaven is beyond my hopes. Then let me stroll through the bright hours as they pass, in my garden among my flowers; or I will mount the hill and sing my song, or weave my verse beside the limpid brook. Thus will I work out my allotted span, content with the appointments of Fate, my spirit free from care.*

BUDDHISM

We have seen that Daoism provided a channel for that other, more romantic side of Chinese human nature which was not satisfied by the pedestrian code of Confucianism. Although the full range of developed Confucianism did take account of the spiritual aspirations of man, in much of its practice it was confined to an ethical handbook for the scholar official and had little message and no solace for the common peasant or small merchant, whom it counseled to behave well and keep to his subordinate position. Daoism in its turn divided into a rarefied philosophy for speculative minds, on the one hand, and a popular cult of superstition and magic with no challenge to higher living, on the other. The time was thus ripe, one may cautiously generalize, for the introduction of Buddhism, a foreign religion, which hereafter forms the third of the three great religions or ways of thought of the Chinese.

If the soil of Chinese society had not been so violently harrowed by the wars of the period succeeding the Han, and so altered by barbarian invasion, it is doubtful whether the new religion would have found lodgment and taken root. Buddhism in its original form, springing from the soil of India, is utterly alien to Chinese modes of thought. It is highly speculative and abstruse. It involves an escape from social responsibility and denies family obligations through its monastic ideal. The Hindu notion of *karma,* the series of acts which determine character—and thus destiny—through an everlasting

*Tao Yuanming (A.D. 365–427), translated by Giles, *Gems of Chinese Literature,* pp. 103–04.

sequence of reincarnations, is not native to the Chinese mind, though it was ultimately admitted to both Chinese and Japanese thought.

Buddhism, nevertheless, was welcomed, was adopted widely in China, and had a profound influence upon subsequent history, although the religion itself underwent significant changes in the process. Buddhism appealed to the Chinese because it supplied the religious lack already noted. It offered a profound philosophy and a coherent explanation of life and the universe, taking into account facets of human suffering and destiny upon which Chinese philosophy heretofore had had nothing to say. It was accompanied by a moving ritual and an art and iconography which has never been surpassed and rarely equaled in the portrayal of spiritual qualities. It offered a spiritual challenge and peace of mind, monastic retreat in disturbed times, and a kind of magic appeal to simple souls who could not grasp its more advanced ideas. It was an organized religion with something for everyone.

The historic Buddha, known as Sakyamuni, founder of the religion about 500 B.C., was a prince of Magadha in modern Nepal in the Himalayan foothills. The tradition of Buddhism was at first purely oral, and it is not easy to distinguish early fact from later accretions in the establishment of his beliefs and teaching. Certain of the historic Buddha's experiences seem to have been put into easily memorable form, such as his encounter with four forms of suffering—poverty in a beggar, pain in the cries of a woman in childbirth, sickness, and death in the form of a corpse—as the young prince went out of the four gates of the palace on four successive days, in spite of his father's attempts to keep him within its sheltered walls. Moved by these experiences to go upon a spiritual quest, the prince left his wife and young son and joined a band of ascetics. He entered upon a period of rigorous fasting but came to feel that self-inflicted suffering was not the way to the answer he sought. Retiring to the jungle for meditation, a traditional Hindu method of seeking total privacy, Sakyamuni sat down under a bo tree and vowed he would not leave until he had attained the truth. His temptations were represented in later art by seductive maidens wheeling around his head to divert him from his quest, and the sympathy of Nature represented by earthquakes and portents accompanying his struggle. At length his quest was rewarded, and he attained enlightenment and thus became Buddha, "the enlightened one." It is to be noted that no dependence upon a personal god was involved and that his experience seems to have been in the nature of a psychological breakthrough, in which he arrived at an intuitive understanding of suffering and of life as a whole. The experience was accompanied by a profound sense of release and well-being. He expressed his new insights in sermons in the deer park at Benares, and disciples, including some from the band of ascetics, are said soon to have gathered around him.

The essense of Buddha's early teaching was summarized in the Four Noble Truths: that life is suffering, that the cause of suffering is desire, that the answer is to quench desire, and that the way to this end is by the Eightfold Path, a pattern of right living and thinking. Specifically, his followers vowed not to kill, steal, lie, drink, or become unchaste. Monastic orders for men and women were soon set up. The Three Precious Things were said to be the Buddha, the Dharma (the Law or Way), and the Sangha (the Monastic Order).

The spread of Buddhism in India was promoted by a number of factors, among them a sense of brotherhood in the absence of caste and a stress on the Middle Way between self-indulgence and extreme asceticism. A high point in the fortunes of Buddhism was reached in the reign of its great patron, the emperor Asoka, in the third century B.C. The new religion gradually spread to Ceylon, Southeast Asia, and south China. In A.D. 100 the Kushan empire in the northwest was strongly Buddhist, and from this base the religion traveled by the agency of traders and missionaries through much of Central Asia. The region of Afghanistan and northwest India had been affected by Greek influence from the time of Alexander the Great (early fourth century B.C.), and traces of this influence may be seen in the features and garments of Buddhist images in the early centuries of our era, one of the great ages of Buddhist iconography, whose effect in turn extended as far as China.

Buddhism made its entry into China very slowly, coming to the south by sea and to the northwest by land. There is a tradition that the Han emperor Ming Di, in response to a dream, sent to India for images and scriptures, and that translation of the scriptures into Chinese then began at the capital, Luoyang. However that may be, there is reliable evidence, at least, of a community of Buddhists in northern Jiangsu in 65 A.D. enjoying the protection of the brother of this same emperor, Ming Di. Buddhism in China, however, was at this stage confined to a few at court. It made no wide appeal until about the time of the Northern Wei dynasty (386–534). Two social factors now made this wider acceptance possible. The opposition of Confucian literati to an alien belief was inoperative because they were no longer in power, and the "barbarian" rulers in the north were ready to welcome the new faith. At the same time the common people embraced a religion promising an answer to suffering and some comfort in a time of constant civil strife. A corresponding welcome to Buddhism was accorded in the south a little later by the emperor Liang Wu Di in the early sixth century, as already mentioned.

Buddhism became established in China in its Mahayana form. The split between Hinayana, the Lesser Vehicle (also known as Theravada, the Way of the Elders) and Mahayana, the Greater Vehicle, had already taken place some centuries earlier in India. Buddhism is practiced today as Theravada in the southern branch, in Ceylon, Burma, Thailand and elsewhere in Southeast Asia, while the northern branch in China, Japan, Korea, Mongolia, and Tibet adheres to various sects of Mahayana Buddhism. The differences are significant. Theravada keeps closer to the original Buddhism, but Mahayana has developed the worship of a whole series of deities, the Buddha in various manifestations as Bodhisattvas or Enlightened Existences. One is

Amitabha (Chinese, O-mi-to Fo), the compassionate savior of the Western Paradise. Another is Maitreya (Mi-lo Fo) corresponding to the Messiah, the Buddha who is to come. A third is Avalokitesvara (Guan Yin), literally, in Chinese, "he who regards the cry" of the unfortunate, and depicted later as Goddess of Mercy. The original divinity here represented by the Sanskrit name is a male figure, but it becomes in the course of time a female deity, a mother figure, who is set to face not the fortunate quarter of the south, as emperors do, but the cold and inhospitable north to lend her ear to the needy.

    The term Bodhisattva as understood religiously enshrines the idea of renunciation for the sake of others. These Buddha figures were ready for entry into Nirvana, a release from the cycle of rebirth and suffering and a merging with the All-Soul, as a drop of water loses its identity in the ocean; but they vowed to turn back to the world and not accept their own salvation until all sentient beings, humans and animals, had been saved.

Maitreya Buddha. Gilt-bronze figure, A.D. 536, Northern Wei/Western Wei dynasty.

Some of the finest Buddhist iconography belongs to the Northern Wei period. The elaborate background nimbus and the flowing robes impart both dignity and grace to this figure of "the Buddha who is to come," a Messiah personality. The face and hands together express inner, contemplative calm and outgoing compassion.

The Museum of the University of Pennsylvania

It will be seen that in these descriptions a transference of terms has come about—from Buddha to Bodhisattva, a savior; from enlightenment in the original experience to something approaching salvation; and from what to the practical man is the negative idea of Nirvana, literally a snuffing out, as of a candle, to the positive bliss and reward of the Western Paradise. Corresponding to Paradise there are the punishments of the Buddhist Hell, realistically represented in some Chinese temples by crude plaster figures undergoing vivid forms of torture. These adaptations of Buddhism had begun before the doctrine reached China, but the pragmatic tendencies of the Chinese, and indeed of the Japanese also, carried them further as the faith developed and ramified into various sects. At the same time it is important to recollect that much of the original Indian legacy of Buddhism in its highest form remained active in Chinese and Japanese practice—the discipline, the compassion, the profound philosophical and psychological insight, an intuitive understanding and limited acceptance of the world, the stress on meditation and contemplation, and the making of one's soul, a process furthered, curiously enough, in the course of ridding oneself of the burden of the individual ego.

The early tradition, as mentioned, had been entirely oral, but about the first century B.C. a large body of scriptures began to accumulate. These came to be known collectively as the Three Baskets or Tripitaka, consisting of the Vinayas, rules for monasteries; the Sutras, discourses attributed to the Buddha; and the Abhidhammas, or scholastic developments of doctrine. The solid base established by Buddhism in the various countries of Asia was undoubtedly owing to the fact that the new religion had by this time a literary foundation. This was particularly important in China, where the written word was held in such regard. The early missionaries and pilgrims therefore devoted a great deal of their time to the difficult task of translation. The Chinese language is singularly unfitted to transliterate foreign names. Further, while the language is rich in vocabulary and the expression of nuances, the ideas and technical terms of Buddhism with its Hindu origins formed an immense obstacle to the smooth transfer of the doctrine into an intelligible Chinese which was acceptable to the scholars. The enormous size of the corpus of Buddhist scriptures also required endless patience in the work of translation. Among numerous translators who labored at the task over several centuries, one of the most famous was Kumarajiva, who was brought from Central Asia to China in the late fourth century and directed a team of scholars who produced Chinese versions of ninety-eight scriptures.

In due course, Chinese Buddhists made pilgrimages to the sacred land of India to collect manuscripts and images and visit the well-known shrines. Fa Xian spent about fifteen years on a journey to India through Central Asia from 399 to 414. Two centuries later Xuan Zang made a pilgrimage lasting from 629 to 645, becoming a friend of the great Indian ruler Harsha and leaving a valuable account of his travels in his "Record of the Western Regions." Both men spent much time on their return in translating the Buddhist works they had brought back with them. Their careful annotations of their travels, along with notes by visiting Greeks in other periods, provide many facts and dates not otherwise recorded in Indian history, since the Hindu world view sets little store by the historical process as a whole. China thus made some contribution to Indian civilization while receiving the treasure of Buddhism, but immense geographical barriers have severely limited contact between the two great cultures of South and East Asia.

7

THE FLOWERING OF CHINESE CIVILIZATION

Sui Dynasty: 589–618
Tang Dynasty: 618–907

In the University of Pennsylvania Museum there is a famous stone bas-relief from the tomb of Tang Tai Zong, second emperor of Tang, one of the greatest dynasties in Chinese, if not in world, history. It depicts the emperor's favorite charger, attended by a foreign groom from Central Asia with heavy robe, felt boots, and quiver. The horse is solid, with stout chest and firmly planted legs. Its handsome head has a patient and pensive eye. The reins lie idly over a saddle cloth, stirrup, and saddle very similar to those used today, and the mane and tail are elaborately dressed. The groom's head almost touches the horse's as he tightens the breast strap; the two obviously have an understanding. The composition is symbolic, for the horse may be said to represent the military power which made the vast Tang expansion of empire possible, and the groom to represent the foreign influences which made Tang civilization one of the most open, cosmopolitan, and fruitful periods in China's history. The quiet, realistic, but sumptuous style of the sculpture gives some indication of the confident, aristocratic quality of Tang art.

THE SUI DYNASTY

The Tang emperors had a short-lived but effective dynasty preceding them, the Sui, which formed a unified foundation upon which the Tang could build. The Sui counted but two emperors, the second of whom is given a bad character in the traditional histories, as being the last of a dynasty due for replacement. But in fact the reigns of both Sui emperors and those of early Tang show a constructive continuity. Under the Sui the Great Wall was extended and palaces erected at Changan and Luoyang. Most important of all, Chinese control began to be reasserted in Central Asia. The colonization of south China carried out during the Six Dynasties era had brought economic and cultural prosperity to the Yangzi region, which had only been a distant frontier during Han. The Sui were able to expand their power into this fertile area, which gave them a stronger base for the creation of wider political unification.

The Sui were great canal builders, and by 605 the first Grand Canal had been dug, connecting the capital, Changan, to Yangzhou on the Yangzi River. This served to bring rice from the rich southern plains to supply the armies and the government in the north, and in the process to aid in the unification of the country. (The main line of the Grand Canal was extended to Peking by the Mongol dynasty in the thirteenth century). From the Sui period on the Yangzi became the economic and cultural heartland for the great dynasties, even though most of these still had their capitals in the north.

THE TANG DYNASTY

Reverses in Korea and peasant insurrections nearer home prepared the way for a successful takeover by the Li family, aristocrats from the northwest who had past connections with the "barbarians." Supported by Turkish allies, they took Changan and founded the Tang dynasty in 618. The father became first emperor under the title Gao Zu, "High Progenitor," to be succeeded by his son, the real instigator of the adventure, in 626 as Tai Zong, "Grand Ancestor."

The Li ancestry is an indicator of those factors which made possible the military conquests in Central Asia upon which Tang greatness was founded. The leadership during early Tang, sharply contrasted with that of later Tang and Song, was drawn from the old families of China's northwest. Imbued with an army tradition, they were men of action, stock breeders and lovers of horses, who were open to contacts with the nomads of the steppes, to whom many of them were linked by ancestry. These families supplied the officer corps, the cavalry decisive in Central Asian warfare, and the members of the elite palace guards. They were supported in the ranks by large numbers of *fu-bing,* or militiamen, who were used as infantry, as frontier guards, supporting troops, messengers, foraging parties, and so forth. The militia at an earlier point had been confined to families specializing in the practice of arms, but the system under Tang was extended to the whole of the peasantry as a part of their tax obligation. The Tang also used military colonies of families whose men combined soldiering with farming and were placed in strategic posts on the frontier. Finally, the Tang depended heavily on sinicized nomad troops, who formed excellent cavalry, and allies such as the Uighur tribes, who threw over their connection with the western Turkish confederation and became loyal supporters of the Tang for a long period.

Fortified by a confident spirit and supported by a military system such as the foregoing, the emperors Tai Zong (626–649) and Gao Zong (649–683) were able to defeat the eastern Turkish empire, to reduce the Tarim basin to Chinese control, to make Tibet a dependency, and even to interfere successfully in Indian affairs. Chinese power was pushed beyond the Pamirs and

Lady playing polo. Tang dynasty, seventh to ninth century.

The aristocratic pastime of polo was introduced into China from Persia and Central Asia, and women as well as men played it with enthusiasm. The artist has frozen a moment of fast action. The horse's head is stretched out at full gallop, and the rider sits with confidence, holding the reins with her right hand and the polo stick with her left.

Collection of Mr. and Mrs. Ezekiel Schloss
Photo: Keith Scott Morton

suzerainty established over the Oxus valley and modern Afghanistan. In 657 the western Turkish empire (note that modern Turkey is not the same area) fell to a combination of Tang Chinese and Uighurs. The Koreans had fought off Sui and then early Tang attacks, but the whole of their country was finally brought under Chinese overlordship in 668 with the kingdom of Silla, a Chinese ally, as the dominant local power. North Vietnam, under the name Annan, or "Pacify the South," became one of the Tang military and administrative protectorates.

Without the horse, mobility across the vast distances of Central Asia would have been impossible. The Tang breed, as in the magnificent glazed funerary figures which are favorite collectors' items (see frontispiece), was produced by crossing horses nearer home with races from the Oxus region and the Middle East and was taller and more slender than the small and tough Mongolian pony upon which the later Mongol conquerors were to depend.

The upper classes in Tang were passionately devoted to equestrian pursuits, and the game of polo, imported from Iran, was a fashion at the capital, Changan. Even ladies from the court played the game. The government established stud farms for military purposes, and the number of mounts increased rapidly, from 5,000 at the beginning of the dynasty to 700,000 fifty years later. During later Tang the situation deteriorated with the wholesale carrying off of the stud horses by a Tibetan invasion in 763. The state had then to buy 30,000 mares from private owners for the imperial stables. The Uighurs were given the privilege of official horse-trading for the state in return for their military aid against the Tibetans, but they are said to have swindled the Chinese government by supplying inferior stallions. (Later during the Ming dynasty a regular trade was carried on in which Chinese tea was exchanged for nomad horses.)

Interaction with Other Cultures

The interchange with Central Asia was, of course, by no means confined to dealing in horses. The physical means for maintaining contact and receiving influences from abroad were numerous, provided by merchant caravans, tribute missions from dependent states, Buddhist pilgrims, and official embassies. The vital point was that the open-minded attitude which appreciated foreign cultures was also present in early Tang to a degree never repeated in later centuries. The fashion at this time among the upper classes was to welcome enthusiastically Central Asian, Indian, Persian, and other foreign elements in art, clothing, ornament, music, dances, and cuisine. Interesting evidence for this trend is to be found in the objects, including musical instruments, pottery, and metalwork of early Tang date and non-Chinese origin, still preserved in the Shosoin, a treasury presented to the Todaiji temple in Nara by the widow of a Japanese emperor in 756.

The position of women in society improved during the Tang dynasty. Young widows were permitted to remarry, and divorce was easier than before. Women acquired better protection and had certain rights to the retention of property. It is probable that interaction with other cultures in Central Asia contributed to this improvement for women, especially in property rights. But after Tang the male domination favored by Confucianism seeped back into Chinese society.

As concrete evidence for the existence of foreign religions during Tang there is the stele erected at Changan in 781, recording in Chinese and Syriac some facts about the Nestorian Church in China. A Christian bishop, Nestorius (died c. 451), had been condemned for heresy, though his differences with the orthodox faith were slight. His followers founded the Nestorian Church, with a strong base in Iran in the fifth and sixth centuries. Missionary efforts established Nestorian settlements in Arabia, India (the Malabar coast), and Turkestan. The faith maintained itself in Mongolia and

Dancer. Sui dynasty, late sixth century A.D.

This is a professional, part Turkic in origin, probably from Kucha, an oasis city in Central Asia. Her swaying figure is set off by long sleeves and scarf, bird-wing type of headdress, fitted bodice, and long, full skirt. Musicians and dance troupes from regions to the west of China were fashionable in Sui and Tang times. The Chinese who employed them ascribed to them the free morals which settled civilizations tend to attribute to foreigners.

Collection of Mr. and Mrs. Ezekiel Schloss
Photo: Keith Scott Morton

Bronze mirror. Tang dynasty, seventh to ninth century.

The boss in the center is pierced to carry a silk holding cord, and the reverse is the polished mirror surface. The 5-inch diameter is filled, but not overfilled, with cheerful and exquisite bird and flower designs.

The Newark Museum Collection

Central Asia for several centuries. It was introduced into China in 631 by a Persian named Olopan (also spelled Alopen), and imperial permission was later granted for preaching and the erection of churches. Adherents of Zoroastrianism (or Mazdaism) and Manichaeism were also to be found in China in Tang times. The great religious persecution of 841–45, which severely weakened Buddhism, brought an end to the first two of these religious groups, namely the adherents of Nestorius and Zoroaster. Manichaeism, Judaism and Islam, however, continued to survive in China.

The Japanese, Koreans, peoples of Central and Southeast Asia, and elsewhere were in their turn receiving cultural influences from the brilliant Tang court and incorporating them in their own lifestyles; the traffic was out as well as in. Foreign visitors must have been immensely impressed with the display and the sheer extent of Tang power, wealth, and sophistication. They would see, for instance, imperial progresses, when the emperor went on tours of inspection, to show the flag as well as to check on the conduct of regional officials. He would be accompanied by regiments of mounted palace guards, high officials with their own staffs, a large harem with accompanying eunuchs and servants, gold and silver plate, porcelain, priceless rugs, tapestries, and all the accoutrements of the imperial court. The processions of men, women, carts, and carriages often took several days to pass a given spot. The Japanese, notably, sent to China many embassies, including monks and scholars in their personnel, over a long period from 607 to 838, in order to discover and adopt what they thought suitable in Chinese calligraphy, art, Buddhist and Confucian thought, and administrative and legal procedures.* The debt of the Koreans to China, beginning in the third century B.C. and continuing strongly through Han and Tang, was even greater.

Among the products and inventions exported to the West during the Tang period were two without which the existence of the modern world as we know it is inconceivable; namely, paper and printing. The long time lag in transmission may be seen from the accompanying table. It is possible that the invention of printing from movable type was arrived at independently in fifteenth-century Europe. But the Chinese had been printing from woodblocks since at least the beginning of the eighth century and from movable type since the eleventh. There is no doubt at all that the invention of paper traveled westward from China, where it had been in use since the second century A.D. It was thought at one time that rag paper was a European invention, but it has been established for some time now that the early papers in China, going back to at least the fourth century and probably to the second, were made of rag, much like the best paper we know today.

It is evident that in the political sphere also the Tang Chinese had contacts with the world which lay to the west of them. These were numerous and

*See W. Scott Morton, *Japan: Its History and Culture,* pp. 17ff.

Stages in the Invention and Use of Paper and Printing
(Based on Carter and Goodrich, *The Invention of Printing and Its Spread Westward*)

PAPER		PRINTING	
		255 B.C.	Seals first mentioned
		100 B.C.	Ink made from lampblack
A.D. 105	Invention of paper by a court eunuch, Marquis Cai Lun	A.D. 175	Standard text of the Classics cut in stone and rubbings soon made therefrom
C. 105	Earliest extant paper, found at Kharakhoto in Ningxia, northwest China		
250–300	Paper of this date found in Niya, Turkestan		
650	Earliest importation and use in Samarkand	600–700	Earliest use of inked seals, red cinnabar on paper
		680–750	True block printing: Buddhist scroll printed from woodblocks, discovered in 1966 at temple in Kyongju, South Korea
706	In Mecca	700–800	Large Daoist seals made of wood
		835	First mention of printing in literature
		868	Earliest complete printed book, *Diamond Sutra,* at Dunhuang
C. 800	In Egypt	800–900	Experimentation in Buddhist monasteries: seals, rubbings, Buddha stamps, stencils, and textile prints
C. 950	In Spain		
		1030	Movable type appeared in China: wood, porcelain and copper used
C. 1100	At Constantinople	1436–37	Gutenberg of Mainz, first European to print with movable type cast in molds
1154	In Sicily		
1228	In Germany and, at approximately the same time, Italy		
1309	In England		
1346	In Holland		

Notes: Carter and Goodrich give 768–70, the printing of 1 million Buddhist charms in Sanskrit and Chinese by order of a Japanese empress, as the first example of extant block printing. The South Korean scroll was discovered subsequent to the latest edition of the Carter and Goodrich book.

Knowledge of paper manufacture in the West is ascribed by Carter and Goodrich and others to Chinese prisoners from the Battle of Talas in 751 teaching the process to their Arab captors. But Gernet (*Le Monde Chinois,* page 250) states that Chinese paper makers, along with other artisans, were installed southwest of Baghdad and in Samarkand at the time of the Arab conquest, i.e., seventh and very early eighth century.

Carter and Goodrich remark that the invention of printing in the West dates from the use of movable type, but in China from the use of woodblocks, cut a complete page or two pages at a time. Movable type is not so practical in China, where the number of separate characters is so enormous. China seems also to have invented movable type four centuries before Gutenberg, but the great printing on which the renaissance of the Song was based was from wooden blocks.

of varying degrees of importance to China. Some of them have been mentioned. One further example may be given, of minor political significance but interesting in its geographical range. Peroz, last of the Sassanian dynasty of Persia, asked help of the Tang emperor in 661 against the onslaughts of the Umayyad Muslim caliphate. Perhaps surprisingly, a response was forthcoming, and a Chinese force went as far west as Ctesiphon on the Tigris and placed Peroz back on his throne. The unfortunate monarch, however, was again driven out and, with an honorary palace title from the emperor, finally made his home in China. The Tang court later made an alliance with the Abbasid caliphate directed against Tibetan attacks in Central Asia at the end of the eighth century.

The Civil Service

After this rapid overview of external influences and affairs in the Tang era, it is time to resume consideration of the internal situation. The early consolidation of the dynasty and its remarkable military expansion under Tai Zong and Gao Zong were succeeded by what is regarded as the golden age of Tang culture under Xuan Zong (712–756), also known as Ming Huang ("Enlightened Emperor"). But in between, China was ruled by a woman, the empress Wu. An impressive personality but ruthless in her search for power, she had been a concubine of both Tai Zong and Gao Zong. Upon the latter's death in 683, she had hundreds of her opponents and possible rivals slaughtered, including many of the Li imperial family. She was an ardent Buddhist and probably had behind-the-scenes support of the Buddhist church when she took the unprecedented step of having herself declared emperor in 690, the only woman ever to do so. In the wider context of the Tang dynasty, her reign is of importance as promoting the selection of officials for the imperial bureaucracy by competitive examination. Her motives in this came less from a disinterested concern for scholarship than from an anxiety to reduce the power of the old military aristocracy of the northwest, which during early Tang had wielded major political influence. The literati entering these public examinations became a new gentry class and from the Tang era onward formed, in spite of many vicissitudes, the backbone of China's ruling class.

The Han dynasty had already employed examinations as a means to the selection of officials for the imperial service, but only in addition to recommendation, patronage, and almost automatic entry for sons of high dignitaries. The examination system was perfected and generally applied during Tang, and with various changes it remained the road to office until the end of the empire in 1911. The Sui had set up examinations and government schools to train the candidates; the Tang continued and expanded the system, including prefectural schools in addition to those at the capital. The examinations were administered by the Ministry of Rites under different categories, such as *xiu-cai,* "flowering talent," dealing with political problems; *jin-shi,*

Examination halls with 7,500 cells, Canton, about 1873.

Candidates after being searched were sealed into these cells, sometimes for several days, to complete their papers for the civil service examinations. The rewards in power and wealth were considerable for the few who passed.

Library of Congress

"presented scholar" (i.e., presented to the emperor), covering a wide range of literary studies; and examinations in classics, mathematics, law, and calligraphy. (The last three were considered to be skills of lesser importance.) In the end the *jin-shi* degree in literature became the outstanding one. The entrants in Tang were mainly those who had passed through the government schools. For those who were successful in the first examinations and thus considered qualified to bear responsibility, the Ministry of Personnel conducted another series of tests, both written and oral, to determine actual appointment to office.

The remarkable quality of administration and the stability of the Chinese state over a period of many centuries may be set down to the credit of this competitive system. It was a serious attempt to recruit an elite corps for the government based not upon birth or wealth, as in so many other societies, but upon brains and character. We shall reassess some of the weaknesses of the system at the time when the empire was drawing to its close, but on the whole it may be said that the intellectual effort required of aspirants to office was matched in the realm of character, at least theoretically and often in practice, by the Confucian emphasis on morals. It has been pointed out that a general education in the literature of the classics prepared both Chinese and British imperial officials for a generally successful and fair-minded rule. But it is not always stressed, or indeed remembered, that in the heyday of classical educa-

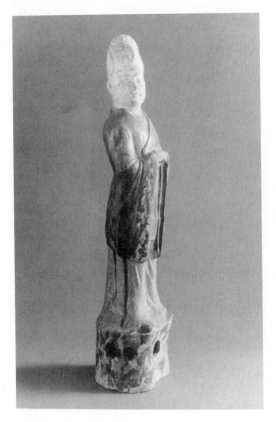

Official. Tang dynasty, seventh to ninth century.

The set of the mouth and eyes, the turn of the head, and the hands emerging from the heavy sleeves of the official robe all indicate the bureaucrat who has power and intends to use it. Mr. Schloss points out that he is even standing on a rock formation to appear more impressive. The bird on his head-dress is a symbol of rank.

Collection of Mr. and Mrs. Ezekiel
Schloss
Photo: Keith Scott Morton

tion in both these regimes, the object was not the mere acquisition of knowledge, but knowledge for the sake of character in the hope of attaining wisdom. The young aspirant for office in China received an education in classics written with a distinct didactic aim. The schoolboy at Westminster School read the Greeks and Romans and the Bible, not merely to excel intellectually but to imitate the best, Socrates and Cicero, and avoid the worst, Nero and Commodus (with even more important lessons from the Bible, though these were haphazardly applied). Then both young men, the Chinese and the British, were thrown out at an early age, to govern and control the lives of thousands with the confidence that their general education, without benefit of any specialized study, would fit them to do a good job.

Poetry

When the empress Wu was over eighty she was overthrown in a palace coup. Power was soon seized by Xuan Zong, and his long and brilliant reign began. Chinese control in Central Asia was to a great extent restored, as the Uighur allies, who had been opposed to empress Wu, returned to their allegiance to the house of Tang. But it is for cultural rather than military glories that Xuan Zong's reign is remembered.

The city of Changan made a superb setting for the life of the court and the metropolis of the nation. The palace was at the north end facing south in the great grid plan of the city. The offices and administrative buildings were grouped to the south of the palace in the government quarter and not placed at random, as in the Han capital. Broad, treeshaded avenues ran down and across the remainder of the area within the great city walls. East and west sectors were evenly divided, with a vast market served by canal transportation installed for each sector. The city blocks had their own internal walls and were closed down at curfew every night to increase security. The whole plan was symmetrically conceived to match the balanced forces of the cosmos.

Among the many achievements of Tang, the Chinese themselves consider its poetry as the most valued. The emperor Xuan Zong was himself a poet, musician, and something of an actor. No less than 2,300 authors are included in the complete corpus of Tang verse. The most famous, such as Li Bo (see illustration, page 109, Du Fu, Wang Wei, and Gao Shi, during Xuan Zong's reign, and Bo Juyi and Yuan Zhen shortly afterward, were remembered chiefly as poets. They were all of the scholar-gentry class and most held official posts. Their poems made an appeal far beyond their own coterie, for they were sung as ballads by the *chanteuses,* or singing-girl courtesans, and passed from mouth to mouth in the smart circles of the capital and the provinces, and even among the common people. Wang Wei was also renowned as a landscape painter.

The poems of the era were known as *shi,* one among several genres of Chinese poetry, and they conformed to strict classical rules of word parallelism, rhyme, and meter. They were short, lyric pieces, some long enough to be styled narrative poems; but China never developed the epic style. Chinese verse is a poetry of mood, strongly allusive and depending on an intimate knowledge of the literature and legends of the past. Nature is never far away, and references are constantly made to flower and mountain, river and cloud, bird and beast, though rarely to the sea, for the Chinese are a land-loving people. The themes are sometimes slight, though treated with intentionally brief glimpses of profundity. The serious themes tend to be treated with apparent lightness, for the poet likes to wear, at least on the surface, a self-deprecatory air. Arthur Waley, in his delightful introduction to the book *A Hundred and Seventy Chinese Poems,* points out that, far from recommending himself as a hero and a lover in the Western manner, the Chinese poet is a "neat and tranquil figure," not ashamed to write a poem called "Alarm at Entering the Gorges." He recommends himself rather as a friend than as a lover, and poems of sadness at friends' parting are numerous.

Yet every generalization about China and the Chinese must be qualified. Some tender love poems appear in almost every age of Chinese literature. There are a thousand others, but here is part of one:

A Song of Pure Happiness

Her robe is a cloud, her face a flower;
Her balcony, glimmering with the bright spring dew,
Is either the tip of earth's Jade Mountain
Or a moon-edged roof of paradise.

There's a perfume stealing moist from a shaft of red blossom,
And a mist, through the heart, from the magic Hill of Wu—
The palaces of China have never known such beauty—
Not even Flying Swallow with all her glittering garments.*

Most men, even high officials, had the countryside in their background;
here is a temporary townsman in search of the country again, his thoughts of
Nature suffused with religion:

A Buddhist Retreat Behind Broken-Mountain Temple

In the pure morning, near the old temple,
Where early sunlight points the tree-tops,
My path has wound, through a sheltered hollow
Of boughs and flowers, to a Buddhist retreat.
Here birds are alive with mountain-light,
And the mind of man touches peace in a pool,
And a thousand sounds are quieted
By the breathing of a temple bell.†

The present-day authorities in China, at first apparently inclined to reject
the traditional literature, have now singled out for commendation poets with a
social concern. Bo Juyi wrote a memorial to the emperor in 809 concerning
prisoners held indefinitely in a local jail. But he went further; he wrote a ballad
to arouse public opinion:

Song and Dance

In Ch'ang-an the year draws to its close;
A great snow fills the Royal Domain.
And through the storm, on their way back from Court,
In reds and purples the dukes and barons ride.
They can enjoy the beauty of wind and snow;
To the rich they do not mean hunger and cold.
At a grand entry coaches and riders press;
Candles are lit in the Tower of Dance and Song.
Delighted guests pack knee to knee;
Heated with wine they throw off their double furs.

*Li Bo, translated by Kiang and Bynner.
†Chang Jian, translated by Kiang and Bynner.

The host is high in the Board of Punishments;
The chief guest comes from the Ministry of Justice.
It was broad daylight when the drinking and music began;
Midnight has come, and still the feast goes on.
What do they care that at Wen-hsiang tonight
In the town gaol prisoners are freezing to death?*

Some of the lapidary phrases of the Tang poets are unforgettable—"the years are bounding by 'like a hoop rolled down hill'" (Waley). Or the last line from this extract by Bo Zhuyi on his famous friend Yuan Zhen:

We did not go up together for Examination;
We were not serving in the same Department of State.
The bond that joined us lay deeper than outward things;
The rivers of our souls spring from the same well!†

The modest air and deceptive lightness of tone, not to hide but to help to control deep feeling, come out in two poems of Bo Juyi on the death after two days' illness of Golden Bells, his only child, a girl of three, perhaps two by Western reckoning:

Girls are a burden, but if one has no son
It is strange how fond one can grow, even of a girl!
. . . The clothes she was wearing are still hanging on the pegs;
The rest of her medicine is still at the side of her bed.
I bore her coffin down the long village street;
I watched them heap the small mound on her grave.
Do not tell me it is only a mile away;
What lies between us is all Eternity.‡

And then, three years later:

Ruined and ill—a man of two score;
Pretty and guileless—a little girl of three.
Not a boy—but still better than nothing:
To soothe one's feeling—from time to time a kiss!
There came a day—they suddenly took her from me;
Her soul's shadow wandered I know not where.
And when I remember how just at the time she died
She lisped strange sounds, beginning to learn to talk,
Then I know that the ties of flesh and blood
Only bind us to a load of grief and sorrow.

*Bo Zhuyi, translated by Waley.
†Ibid.
‡Ibid.

At last, by thinking of the time before she was born,
By thought and reason I drove the pain away.
Since my heart forgot her, many days have passed
And three times winter has changed to spring.
This morning, for a little, the old grief came back,
Because, in the road, I met her foster-nurse.[†]

Poetry and history come together in the personal destiny of the emperor Xuan Zong, for a romance and a tragedy of his own, which became the subject of a famous poem, accompanied one of the decisive historical events of the Tang dynasty, the rebellion of An Lushan, which in the end proved to mark a turning point in Chinese history. As a military career came to be less highly regarded by the new literati than it had been by the old aristocrats, there was a dangerous tendency to depend upon foreign-born generals for major military commands. An Lushan was one such. Of Sogdian and Turkish parentage, he had succeeded in gaining control of three military districts north of the capital, instead of the normal one, and in ingratiating himself with the emperor. Xuan Zong in his sixties had fallen in love with a famous beauty, Yang Guifei, the concubine of one of his sons. An Lushan was good company, and both the emperor and his favorite were amused by this stout and uninhibited character, who seemed harmless enough. Yang Guifei adopted him as her son, and it was rumored he was her lover. But at the death of the powerful chief minister Li Linfu, An Lushan appeared as the rival of Yang Guifei's cousin, Yang Guozhung, for that post. He failed to secure the position and, when he was ready, dropped all disguise and in 755 marched on the capital in open revolt. The emperor was forced to flee, but before he had gone far, his guards mutinied and refused to proceed until he got rid of his favorite. He was compelled in humiliation and despair to consent to her being strangled. An Lushan was later killed by his own son and the rebellion ultimately suppressed after eight years of fighting, considerable loss of life, and a disastrous fall in the prestige of the government. The whole incident became the subject of the poem by Bo Juyi *The Everlasting Remorse,* in which the ghost of Yang Guifei appears to the emperor.

The combination of the rebellion, fiscal difficulties, and the defeat in 751 of the Korean general commanding Chinese forces against the Arabs at the Battle of Talas (see notes to table, p. 87 resulted in a considerable diminution of Tang power. The dynasty continued for another 150 years and witnessed a return to economic strength, but it never recovered its earlier verve or that vital central control over its own generals which had marked the earlier years.

[†]Ibid.

Economic Growth

One of the chief differences between early and late Tang, or the years preceding and following the rebellion of An Lushan, lay in the sphere of economics and taxation. Stress has been laid on the military and cultural achievements of the dynasty, but the first would have been impossible and the second unlikely without that period of more than a century prior to the rebellion when there was a favorable balance in the treasury. Sound tax foundations had been laid in Northern Wei and continued in Sui by what was called the "equal field" system, which the Tang authorities refined and developed. The system was based upon the traditional conception of government control of persons rather than of property. Taxes in kind and compulsory labor were assessed per capita and not per acre. But in order to enable the peasants to pay these dues and to prevent their being absorbed into the estates of large landowners and thus lost to the government, each man and his wife were assigned an average of 100 *mou,* or about 13.5 acres, with additional amounts according to the ages of family members. Only one-fifth of the allotment could be held permanently, usually as a mulberry orchard for silk culture; the remainder of the land had to be returned to the government in case of death or exceeding the given

Merchant. Tang dynasty, seventh to ninth century.

This Khorezmian from northern Iran has a bolt of cloth or a rug under his arm. His features are not Chinese. Of all the foreign commercial groups in China, the Persians were at this time the largest.

Collection of Mr. and Mrs. Ezekiel
Schloss
Photo: Keith Scott Morton

age limit. The tax to be paid by each individual was in triple form: a stipulated amount of grain; a stipulated amount of silk or hemp cloth, floss or fiber; and twenty days' corvée, compulsory labor for the central government, and certain other days for local government. Some peasants were liable for military service without pay, but these were granted exemption from other dues. "Rank lands" and sometimes special imperial grants of land were given to officials, and the expenses of local government were met from "office lands." The pattern of the main amount of land being government-owned, and small plots privately owned, reappears under the present Communist regime.

The system was complex. It depended on an accurate census and a careful land survey. It is known that these were completed. A useful table of equivalences was also worked out, where a certain weight of silver and measures of grain, silk cloth, and silk floss were all equated in value with the standard string of 1,000 cash. The system seems to have functioned moderately well, at least for a time. Difficulties in keeping an accurate record of changes in family status, with births and deaths constantly occurring, added to the peasants' well-known aversion to relinquishing any land whatever, undoubtedly made reassignment of land and tax a major problem. Under Xuan Zong there were difficulties of this kind, and the government was faced with fiscal pressures arising from increased expenditure as well as decline in tax income. A decisive change, long in the making, finally came in 780 when direct taxes, no longer per capita, were levied on the land itself, based on acreage and yield. At the same time commercial taxes became more profitable, owing to the growth of trade and industry. It was these new taxes, as well as government monopolies and the growth of the economy south of the Yangzi River, shortly to be discussed, which made the recovery of the treasury possible after the disastrous period of the An Lushan rebellion.

The Han had instituted government monopolies in salt, iron, and liquor. The salt and liquor monopolies were now revived and one in tea was added. Tea, originally a medicine, became generally used as a beverage during Tang, and the government profit from the monopoly increased significantly. The tea merchants who sold to the monopoly were incidentally responsible in the early 800s for a new financial device, the exchange note, or "flying money." On delivery of their consignments of tea at the capital they received a note of money owing to them, which they could exchange at home for goods, less a proportion for the government tax. By the end of the century merchant enterprises, pawnshops, and money changers were using negotiable certificates of deposit to avoid the awkward carrying of heavy currency. These certificates were the forerunners of bank notes. The first actual paper currency issued by the state is traceable to Sichuan in 1024.

The greatest single economic growth factor during Tang was the increase in the agricultural population in the lower Yangzi River basin, both along the river itself and in the fertile lands beyond. Along with the rise in population went an improvement in the yield of the rice paddies. Formerly the rice had grown and been harvested in the fields where it was planted. Now the shoots were grown in nursery plots and planted out in the flooded paddy fields, an immense but profitable labor. At the same time better, early maturing strains of rice were developed. The resulting improvements in yield were dramatic. Moreover, the canals built under Sui and Tang linking the Yangzi with the Wei and Yellow River valleys made it possible, even when northern conditions of agriculture were poor, to bring in enough rice to support the court and the armies based on the capital.

These great economic changes benefited the south and significantly altered the balance in China as between the north and the south. They increased the resources available to the country as a whole. And they enabled the Tang dynasty to survive for a further period after the great rebellion. But there were other factors at work, and it would be erroneous to suppose that the Tang government was always the beneficiary of the new conditions in society. The rebellion was a portent, for it presaged the rise of independent military commanders and mercenary armies. This was a potent factor for change in the West also, at a later date, and was accompanied in China, as in the West, by a rise in urbanization and an increasing dependence upon a money economy. The military districts had to be increased in number in late Tang to cope with internal disorders, and this strengthened the persistent menace of regionalism in Chinese history and decreased the power of the central government.

Famines in north China once again gave rise to insurgent bands of desperate peasants, who in this instance roved far and wide over almost all of China by the main routes. They found a leader in one Huang Chao and pillaged the rich cities as far south as Canton, where they massacred the community of foreign merchants in the quarter of the city set aside for their residence. They turned north again and in 881, with a force now grown to some 600,000, sacked the capital, Changan, and after enormous slaughter left it in total ruin. The emperors moved to Luoyang, and the glories of Tang had departed. A former subordinate of Huang Chao began a new dynasty, the Later Liang, at Kaifeng in Henan province in 907. But the intervening period of disunity, known as the Five Dynasties, was in this case much shorter. The techniques for centralization were by now stronger and more sophisticated, and the empire was reunited under the Song dynasty by 960.

8

THE CHINESE ENTER ON THEIR MODERN TIMES

Five Dynasties: 907–960, North China
Ten Kingdoms: 907–970, South China
Song Dynasty: 960–1126
Jin Dynasty (Jürchen): 1126–1234, North China
Southern Song Dynasty: 1127–1279, South China

Han Yu, a prominent Tang official and one of the most admired masters of Chinese prose, thus addressed himself to the throne in the year 819. The subject was the proposed introduction of a relic, a finger bone of Buddha, into the imperial palace.

> Your Majesty's servant would submit that Buddhism is but a cult of the barbarians, and that its spread in China dates only from the later Han dynasty, and that the ancients knew nothing of it.

> [Should the emperor set the bad example of honoring Buddha] by and by young and old, seized with the same enthusiasm, would totally neglect the business of their lives; and should Your Majesty not prohibit it, they would be found flocking to the temples, ready to cut off an arm or slice their bodies as an offering to the God. Thus would our traditions and customs be seriously injured, and ourselves become a laughing-stock on the face of the earth;—truly, no small matter!

> For Buddha was a barbarian. His language was not the language of China; his clothes were of an alien cut. He did not utter the maxims of our ancient rulers, nor conform to the customs which they have handed down. He did not appreciate the bond between prince and minister, the tie between father and son.

> Supposing, indeed, this Buddha had come to our capital in the flesh, under an appointment from his own State, then Your Majesty might have received him with a few words of admonition, bestowing on him a banquet and a suit of clothes, previous to sending him out of the country with an escort of soldiers,

and thereby have avoided any dangerous influence on the minds of the people. But what are the facts? The bone of a man long since dead and decomposed, is to be admitted, forsooth, within the precincts of the Imperial Palace! Confucius said, "Pay all respect to spiritual beings, but keep them at a distance."*

Han Yu's arguments are worth noting. As a rationalist and a humanist he exhibits a marked antipathy to religious enthusiasm. But he is opposed to Buddhism mainly because it is not Chinese, not a part of their own tradition. He and many of his contemporaries had moved away from the early Tang eagerness for things foreign and were turning back to native Chinese sources. Han Yu exhibited this in his own writing, for he aimed to reproduce in simple form what was called "the antique style" (gu-wen). He lived in late Tang times but anticipated much of the culture and attitude of mind which characterized the Song dynasty. Late Tang and Song cannot be divided; together they show China leaving behind her "medieval" and entering her "modern" era.

The chapters of the present work follow the traditional chronological division by dynasties, because these are still in themselves important and because they form a universal framework in all discussions of the separate aspects of Chinese culture, such as art, literature, or economics. Yet unfolding events do not always fall into the dynastic divisions. Thus the men of early Tang belong with those of the Six Dynasties in their contact with the life of the steppes, in their aristocratic and military traditions, and in their openness to non-Chinese influences. The men of late Tang and Song, on the other hand, turned away from the military tradition and from those sports such as hunting, the martial arts, and physical exercise, which go with it. They employed mercenaries, drawn usually from the lowest social class, and thus they came to despise the military as a whole. The leaders of policy gained their official position through scholarship, and it was scholarly values and pursuits which they held in esteem: polite learning, poetry, the fine arts, and belles lettres. It is true that the burgeoning urban civilization of the new era might have given rise to a new governing class and hence new ideals, as it did in the cities and merchant classes of Europe. But this proved not to be the case in China. The scholars were too well entrenched. There was a wider diffusion of wealth and a general rise in the standard of living for all above the basic peasant class. But the scholar officials held onto their leading position—the past was on their side—and the merchants and wealthy landowners tended to become their allies but never their masters. The classes overlapped, since many of the scholar officials derived their wealth from land. And, like Han Yu, they became increasingly contemptuous of things foreign.

Furthermore, the pattern of Chinese civilization laid down in late Tang and especially during the Song dynasty persisted in all its essentials during the remainder of the Chinese empire, through the Ming and Qing dynasties, until the impact of the West in a new and massive form brought inevitable changes.

*Han Yu, translated by Giles, Gems of Chinese Literature, pp. 124, 127.

Changes there were after the Song, for the Mongols and then the Manzhou made violent irruptions into Chinese society. But the changes were from the outside and in a sense ephemeral. The basic Chinese form remained stable, and internal shifts were few. This stability was in itself a major achievement, denoting attainment of the Chinese ideal—a successful balance of forces. But it has unfortunately given the impression of a perpetually static civilization, obscuring the remarkable progress made by the Chinese in social forms, administrative methods, and technological inventions from Neolithic times up to, say, the thirteenth century.

The period following the collapse of Tang comprised the Five Dynasties in the north and the Ten Kingdoms in the south. No attempt need be made here to distinguish the brief duration and location of these regimes. In spite of the divisions between the dynasties, cultural continuity was maintained. They produced overall a rise in bureaucratic centralization and a decline in provincial power that opened the way for the concentration of power at the center in the succeeding Song dynasty.

A Chinese general, Zhao Kuangyin, was sent out in 960 by the last of the Five Dynasties, the Later Zhou, to ward off a new nomad foe from the northeast, the Khitan. But Zhao, with the support of his troops, seized power for himself and succeeded in founding the Song dynasty. Once he had north China under control, the conquest of the south followed in short order. But it was not to be a soldier's empire. In line with late Tang, the new state gave the most important place to officials recruited by examination. The system was regularized and examinations were held every three years at three levels: an examination in the prefecture, an examination at the capital, and an examination in the palace, the last of which largely determined appointment and promotion. The passing rate at the first two levels was usually not more than 10 percent. A recurring criticism of the examination system has been that it favored sons of incumbent officials, who won positions either through patronage, in spite of precautions to the contrary, or through educational opportunities denied to others. This was often the case, but research has revealed the interesting fact that from the mid-twelfth century to the mid-thirteenth over 50 percent of successful candidates came from new families not previously in office.

The scholar officials enjoyed during Song a greater degree of influence than at any other period in Chinese history. They succeeded throughout the dynasty in preventing the rise of imperial relatives and eunuchs to power. Though they were not threatened from outside, there were among themselves strong political feelings, and political parties of conservative and reformist character developed rivalries of some acerbity. The Song chart of government comprised, in brief, a council of high ministers, less than ten in number, who advised the emperor, and three main bodies: a secretariat, under which operated a number of separate ministries and boards; a privy council, which handled chiefly military affairs; and a finance commission, which proved efficient and built up a considerable reserve in the early decades of the dynasty.

This satisfactory situation in the early Song period was, however, counterbalanced by fresh threats from the northern nomads. The Khitan in the northeast, and a mixed people in the northwest, who took the Chinese name Xia, brought considerable pressure to bear upon the Song. These peoples were partly sinicized through long association with their Chinese neighbors, in contrast to the enemies of Han, the Xiong-nu, and the enemies of Tang, the Turkish tribes, or the Mongols to come, all of whom were but little influenced by Chinese civilization prior to their incursions.

The Khitan were a stock-rearing people of Manchuria who expanded rapidly, made Peking one of their capitals, and penetrated as far as Kaifeng in 947. There they overthrew one of the Five Dynasties, the Later Jin, and took the dynastic name Liao, claiming Chinese legitimacy. Their empire at its height asserted control over Korea, north and south Manchuria, and part of north China west to the Ordos region. The Song had regained most of north China but in the Peace of Shanyuan in 1004 had been compelled to pay a large annual tribute to the Khitan of 100,000 ounces of silver and 200,000 rolls of silk. This tribute was raised to even higher figures in 1042. So great was Khitan power that they were in diplomatic contact with Japan in the east and the Abbasid caliphate in the west. Their name, Khitan or Khitai, was used to represent China in Persian and Turkish and is still so used in Russian. It was thus that Marco Polo came to refer to China as Cathay, and it was some time before Europeans, who learned the name China from what they knew of southern maritime trade, discovered that Cathay and China were one and the same.

The Khitan were enfeebled and became less aggressive through Chinese luxurious living, and their empire crumbled in 1125 under pressure from another northern people, the Jürchen. A portion of the Khitan nobility moved west into Central Asia and set up a successful kingdom, which was influenced both by Buddhism and Nestorian Christianity. Their victory over the Seljuk Turks, in one of history's curious byways, may have given rise to the European medieval hope of finding a Christian ally against the Turks in the fabled kingdom of Prester John.

The second source of pressure upon the Song, who were not warlike and had no "barbarian" allies such as the Tang had known, was the Xia, or Xi Xia (Western Xia), a people with Tangut, Uighur, Tibetan, and Chinese elements in the population. They lived on the northwest marches of China, raised horses, sheep, and camels, and engaged in trade. To them also the Song emperors were forced to pay a costly annual tribute of silver, silk, and tea. The Xia were ultimately destroyed by the Mongol Genghis Khan in 1227.

The favorable fiscal balance built up by the Song at the beginning of the dynasty was gradually exhausted, not so much from the demands of tribute as from the expense of maintaining mercenary armies. These considerations of economics and defense gave rise to proposals of reform by certain ministers, among whom the most prominent and the most controversial was Wang Anshi (1021–1086).

Enjoying the support of the emperor, Wang Anshi instituted a number of reform measures which were far-reaching and astonishingly similar to economic control devices employed in the modern world. It is likely, however, that he was motivated by practical and administrative concern for government solvency and efficiency, and not by ideological, "socialist," or purely humanitarian considerations, although no one can state positively what was in the minds of the Song reformers. In order to strengthen the peasant base of the state, Wang set up loans for farmers at 20 percent interest, then considered very reasonable. Sometimes known as the Green Sprouts Act, this enabled farmers to borrow for seed grain in the spring and repay the state after harvest. In case of bad harvest or natural disaster, there was provision for deferment of payments until the next year. Wang instituted price controls and extended credit to small businesses. He rationalized the taxes, which were paid in kind, by selling grain on the spot or exporting it to needy areas, transferring only the proceeds to the capital to save heavy transport costs. He altered the incidence of the land tax, to distinguish between fields of high and low yield, and commuted corvée for money payments. In the area of defense he attempted to enlist the peasants in their own protection by encouraging militia under local gentry leadership, with prizes awarded for archery and drill. In a new move he arranged for farmers to have state-owned horses quartered on their farms, to be used in farm work on the understanding that a member of the household would report for duty with the horse on emergency call to form a cavalry militia.

Wang Anshi was severely criticized by the conservatives for these measures, which would seem to many nowadays as rational and beneficial. Some were new and some were old measures more radically applied. Among his opponents were reputable figures such as the historian Sima Guang (1019–1086) and poet and essayist Su Dongpo (1036–1101). One criticism was that in involving the state in trade right down to the local retail level he was demeaning the emperor by having him "peddle coal and ice like any small merchant." (The age-old official prejudice against merchants must here be borne in mind.)

The opposition was no doubt sparked by the self-interest of moneylenders and landlords who had strong influence with the official class. Some measures, such as the Green Sprouts Act, were sabotaged by dishonest administrators, even though this scheme had been tried out in a pilot project over a limited area and found to work well. But Wang undoubtedly suffered from a certain arrogance of power—he was known as "the bullheaded premier." In any event most of his reforms, instituted in 1069, were abolished on the death of the emperor Shen Zong in 1085.

Not long after this the Liao (Khitan) dynasty was to be swallowed up by a new nomad power, the Jürchen, based farther north on the Sungari River in Manchuria. Sweeping south they made short work of the Liao and overwhelmed the Song capital at Kaifeng in 1126. With their own capital at

Peking they set up a dynasty known as the Jin, or Kin, meaning "gold," possibly derived from the gold-bearing sands of their northern rivers.

This conquest is the reason for the division of the Song dynasty, the second half from 1127 to 1279 being called the Southern Song. The Song court retreated perforce from Kaifeng and set up a new government at Hangzhou. A frontier was drawn at the Huai River valley, and for the most part the Song in the south managed to coexist with the Jin in the north. But there was guerrilla resistance to the Jin in Shandong and periodic forays by both sides. The Song were still involved in heavy military expenditure, not lessened by the outfitting of a war fleet in the twelfth century.

In spite of the repeated blows inflicted upon them by the northern nomads, the Song were comparatively safe in their southern sanctuary, since a profusion of lakes and rivers made large-scale nomad cavalry operations impossible. The Song rice economy prospered, especially after the introduction of southern strains of rice which bore two crops per year. Society exhibited a bewildering richness and diversity with the development of urban life. The cities and towns formed a striking contrast to the strictly controlled life of Tang dynasty Changan, with its state-run markets and its curfew for every separate city block. A pattern of much greater freedom developed at Kaifeng, the Song capital, and was repeated in the Southern Song cities, where markets outside state control grew up just beyond the great gates of cities, to be adopted, as it were, later and included within a further wall. Before long still other markets and amusement quarters arose, and artisans and private enterprises of all kinds were located all over the city at will. Urban life was varied by the arrival from the country of the rich, who lived on their rents in what was now a capitalist and not a manorial society, and by the arrival of the poor, who found jobs as servants, small shopkeepers, and employees in inns, teahouses, cabarets, and innumerable workshops. There were workshops for the manufacture of paper, ceramics, objects in metal, printed books, lacquer ware, and countless articles for use and luxury. Others eked out an existence in the underworld of thieves, swindlers, and prostitutes of both sexes.

A higher standard of living and even a modicum of luxury became possible for many more urban dwellers than before. This was to be seen in more elaborate mansions, rich furnishings, the laying out of beautiful gardens, and the cultivation of haute cuisine. The interchange of goods was facilitated by a vast fleet of boats of all sizes on a network of inland navigation comprising the coasts, harbors, rivers, and lakes of south China.

In a more mobile society, a new rootlessness gave rise to the consciousness of new needs for mutual aid and protection. Thus new human groupings arose, such as merchant corporations and clan associations, many of which arranged for agricultural property to be set aside for the perpetual endowment of charitable foundations for education and the support of indigent members of the clan.

TECHNOLOGY

The inventions to be credited to the Chinese of late Tang and Song are bewildering in their number and complexity. Mention has already been made of paper and printing, which had a long ancestry but came into very general use during Song. To these must be added such specialized devices as a water-operated escapement to a clock drive for an astronomical instrument, where buckets filled at a fixed rate and, releasing themselves by a trip mechanism, broke time into very accurate divisions; and an oil-burning flamethrower, operated by a double piston to give a continuous discharge.

The two main fields of innovation in this era are to be found in ships and firearms. The great seagoing junk of the tenth and eleventh centuries stirred the admiration of experienced Arab sailors and was easily the leader of its time. It had watertight compartments, four decks, four to six masts, and could carry a thousand men. It carried sails of cloth and of matting to enable it to sail both before and close to the wind. Paddleboats were invented with a large stern wheel and as many as twelve additional wheels on each side, operated by manpower through pedals or cranks. They could attain considerable speeds. But the most important innovations were the sternpost rudder and the mariner's compass. The compass in the form of a floating needle (the Chinese reckoned it as pointing south) was first used by geomancers and then adapted to maritime use. It was known in China by at least 990, and mentioned in Europe in 1190, but did not come into much practical use in European ships until 1280.

As to firearms, it is commonly said that the Chinese invented gunpowder but sensibly used it only for fireworks. The latter is unfortunately not the case. Catapults using explosive grenades were successfully employed by the Song against the Jürchen in a battle in 1161. The use of gunpowder as a propulsive force for projectiles seems to have been the subject of experiments as early as 1132. Bamboo or wooden tubes for mortars were used at first, and bronze and iron tubes succeeded them in the Chinese-Mongol wars in 1280. The use of gunpowder as a propellant seems to have reached Europe via the Mongols and the Arabs.

LANDSCAPE PAINTING

The disturbances of Song times did not lessen the interest of the scholar class in cultural pursuits. Indeed, the impetus given in Tang came to completion during Song, particularly in the field of landscape painting. Among the many arts of China—bronze casting, jade carving, sculpture, architecture, the painting of birds and flowers, and the production of masterpieces in ceramics and lacquer—the art of landscape painting came to assume the highest place as the classical art par excellence. In the West the human form was the point of central interest throughout most of history, from the sculpture of the Greeks through medieval and Renaissance paintings of the Holy Family and classical figures to the Dutch interiors and the portraiture of the seventeenth and eighteenth centuries in the French and English schools. Landscape as a major theme emerged comparatively late, in association with the romantic movement. The works of Constable, Turner, and Corot all date from the second half of the eighteenth century. In China it was otherwise. Although Man was the main focus of philosophy, artists from the eighth century or earlier found their inspiration in Nature, and not in one aspect or another but in Nature as a whole. Nature in her various moods of sunshine and mist, in the changing seasons, in the balance of high mountains and low water-courses, not only solaced and uplifted the spirit of the artist but appealed to his mind as a clue to the harmonious working of the universe, its *dao* or Way. For the artist as an artist, whatever his other preoccupations, tended to be a recluse, an individualist and a Daoist. Landscape painting was thus the grandest and most satisfying way to represent Nature as a whole, to feel a sense of communion with Nature and know oneself to be part of an orderly cosmos.

Herein lies the reason for an important difference in the viewpoint and perspective of the painter in Western and in Chinese art. The eye of the Western artist takes in the scene from the level of the average man five or six feet above the ground. The Chinese artist works from a raised viewpoint, on a hillside opposite the scene, as it were, so that he is delivered from too much teasing detail in the foreground and can obtain an overview of the whole. Or it may be said that he has no fixed viewpoint and that his gaze can rove at will, both horizontally and vertically. The idea of multiple or indeterminate perspective seems fanciful until one looks for some time at a Song landscape, such as "Buddhist Temple in the Hills After Rain" by Li Cheng (active c. 940–967). The temple stands on a hill in the middle ground, waterfalls to the left and beyond. Behind it, over a misty valley, two great peaks rise to towering heights. The foreground, merging imperceptibly into the rest of the picture, shows the nearer reaches of the river, a steep bank with gnarled, angular trees, and peasants and courtiers depicted in minute detail eating and drinking in the inn used by pilgrims to the temple. Almost every part of the scene, high and low, is packed with interest and can be viewed with satisfaction from the stance of the artist; yet the picture is a whole.

Li Cheng's composition is in the well-known form of a hanging scroll. But the changing perspective operates also in the horizontal hand scroll, which is designed to be unrolled from right to left and viewed about two feet at a time. An excellent example is a section of a scroll by Xu Daoning (active at the end of the tenth century and beginning of the eleventh), entitled "Fishing in a Mountain Stream." A mountain mass separates two valleys which run directly away from the viewer back into the distant ranges. Each of the valleys may be conveniently seen in succession as a main view. But there is a third valley floor to the left, which forms a scene of its own, skillfully focused by a moderate peak in its center, behind which the valley forks to right and left. Foreground accents are dropped in here and there by dark trees and a few fishing boats on the river, but mountain outlines are intentionally dissolved in wet washes as the picture recedes into the distance, giving an exhilarating sense of vast space.

"Buddhist Temple in the Hills After Rain." Attributed to Li Cheng (died A.D. 967), Early Northern Song dynasty. Ink and slight color on silk.

Landscape painting is the art par excellence of the Chinese. They describe it as *shanshui* ("mountains/water"), and indeed these two elements enter into most of the great pictures. Man and his works are present but subordinate to Nature.

"Fishing in a Mountain Stream." Xu Daoning (Hsü Tao-ning); (died c. A.D. 1066), Northern Song dynasty. Hand scroll, ink on silk, 6 feet 10½ inches long, to be "read" from right to left.

The urban scholar/poet/artist found refreshment in the grandeur of Nature. This refined and sophisticated painting was executed at about the same time as the Bayeux Tapestries. It is an example of Chinese multiple perspective.

Laurence Sickman remarks that

the horizontal scroll form is the culmination of Chinese creative genius in painting. It is the only painting form in the world that brings to the art a true progression through time. As the observer progresses through such a scroll, there is a unique element of the theme unfolding and developing in much the same way, and, incidentally, with much the same mechanics, as a theme is developed in poetry or in Western music. The composition of these scrolls would be impossible with a fixed vanishing point and one-point perspective. There must be multiple vanishing points, the one fading imperceptibly into the next. . . . It is impossible sympathetically to view a landscape scroll without becoming part of it and entering into the artist's world of peaks and streams. Again and again in these landscape scrolls a road or a path appears at the beginning, and we are almost bound to follow it. These roads direct the attention of the spectator and instruct his vision. Now and again he must walk in the foreground, viewing the plains and distant hills; he is led on to the hills themselves, crosses bridges, climbs mountains, rests at high-placed temples; occasionally he may choose between the path and a boat, and often he is led completely out of sight behind a cliff or hill only to emerge again farther along.*

In addition to the question of perspective, a second practical point marks off Chinese from Western art, and this concerns the medium and the consequent technique. Classic Western art works are executed in oils on canvas, whereas Chinese paintings are done by means of water-soluble ink on silk or highly absorbent paper. Colors are, of course, used, but much of the most prized art is done in black and white with delicate variations of gray. Where oil paints are employed, it is possible to paint out a portion of the canvas and redo it in a new version. But with ink and watercolors the stroke once drawn is beyond recall and cannot be altered. The Chinese artist in calligraphy or painting—and the two are considered virtually one—must thus practice again and again, until he has acquired such control over his brush that in the final work he can move with confidence and without error or quiver. For purposes of practice there are stereotyped ways of painting leaves, rocks, grass, bamboos, mountains, pine trees, birds, and hosts of other single items, listed and schematized in the Chinese manner. But once the technique is mastered, the genius of the artist can take off in freedom and in his own personal style. This "takeoff" the Chinese critics compare to the flight of a dragon rising into the clouds. The artist's state of mind is of the utmost importance in attaining this end. He is, as a rule, not painting the portrait of any actual scene. He will visit the mountains and streams and soak himself in the scenery. Then, returning to his study, laying out his brushes, ink, and paper on a clean desk and clearing and composing his own spirit, he will, when the moment is ripe, put down on paper with sure and rapid strokes the ideal composition which exists already in

---

*Sickman and Soper, *The Art and Architecture of China*, p. 108.

his mind. When the dragon flight has been achieved, then the words of a seventeenth-century critic may be true: "The best method is that which has never been a method."

The minds of the great Song artists were affected by philosophical influences emanating from both Daoism and Buddhism. The Daoist view of the totality of Nature has already been touched upon in this connection, but the Daoist stress on emptiness is also of great significance. Non-being is as important as Being in the nature of the Dao. This is illustrated in the *Dao De Jing,* the Classic of the Way and Its Power, by the fact that a common bowl is valuable only because of what is not there, the space inside created by the outside of the bowl, into which the contents—rice, soup, or anything else—may be put. This principle of the positive value of emptiness emerges in painting in the artist's creative use of space. It would be idle to pretend that this idea exists only in China, for all great artists everywhere employ it instinctively in composition. Yet it is a major, conscious feature of all Chinese landscapes, and particularly of later Song painting, where it is used with consummate skill.

After the collapse of Song rule in the north, the first emperor of the Southern Song, Gao Zong, gathered together in the Academy of Painting at Hangzhou on the famed Western Lake as many as he could of the artists who had been members of the earlier Academy. This had been founded by Gao Zong's father, the emperor Hui Zong (reigned 1101–1125), himself a noted

"Li Bo (Li T'ai-po) the poet." Liang Kai, active c. 1200, Southern Song dynasty.

The poet is walking in solitude, reciting poetry. The rest of the scroll is blank, for extraneous decoration would be an impertinence. Extreme economy of line and broad brush strokes for the garment serve to concentrate all the attention on the precise definition of the poet's erudite but charmingly human features. (See pages 91 and 108–111)

The National Museum, Tokyo
Photo: The Zauho Press

"The Five-colored Parakeet Perched on an Apricot Branch." The emperor Hui Zong of the Northern Song dynasty (reigned 1101–25). Hand scroll, color on silk.

This emperor, who during the Northern Song period gathered a number of famous artists in an academy, was himself a well-known painter, unexcelled in his portrayal of birds and flowers.

Museum of Fine Arts, Boston, Maria Antoinette Evans Fund

painter of birds and flowers. Among the most famous members of the new Academy were Ma Yuan (c. 1190–1224) and Xia Gui (c. 1180–1230). Both these artists exhibit to a degree greater than that known in Northern Song this quality of suggestion, of the use of space deliberately left over, inciting the observer to supply from his own imagination what is powerfully absent on the silk before him. "Landscape in Moonlight" by Ma Yuan, for instance, shows a convivial scholar and his servant on a small, flat outcrop of rock in the left bottom corner of the vertical scroll. They are overshadowed by a magnificent, knobbly pine, and behind on the left rises a precipice with a few pines perched precariously upon it. On the right in the valley below is a smaller gnarled tree and a minor upthrust accent of rock needles. But the whole of the top right of the picture is left blank, and is felt to be filled with ghostly moonlight, though the moon itself is nowhere visible. Another picture, Xia Gui's "Landscape in Autumn Storm," goes even further in intentional emptiness. It is not surprising that this picture is in a private collection in Japan, for the Japanese are devoted to their preference for suggestion over statement in all art. Here the leaves are being ripped off a bending tree in a violent wind, and a tiny man under a rain hat struggles over a footbridge to a hut under the tree. The top two thirds of the picture contains little but part of a sloping crag, with a distressed tree upon it, and the hint of a farther mountain peak. The rest must be swirling cloud, for there is nothing to be seen. The effect is awesome, but somehow humanized and tolerable; even, in a curious reverse sense, exalting.

Influence from the Buddhist realm of thought may be seen in the way in which Man is subordinated to Nature in the landscape art of China. Man himself, fishing, riding, drinking in a pavilion, is usually present, or traces of Man, in the form of temples, bridges, or boats, but they are dwarfed in size and importance by the vastness of the natural scene. Man takes part in Nature but does not dominate it, as in the Hebrew tradition, or seek to control it, as in the Western scientific tradition. This is also an aspect of the wholeness of the universal process in Daoism. But it is particularly strong in Buddhism, where Buddha's immanence in all things evokes religious feeling and where man, animals, and even plants and stones are all caught up in one endless chain of being. Every second landscape painting in almost any era could be used to illustrate this, but one by Zhu Ran (active at the end of the tenth century) makes the point with special subtlety. Although it has been titled "Seeking Instruction in the Autumnal Mountains," there is no human figure visible, only the faintly discernible thatch of a rustic monastery nestled in a cleft at the foot of folding hill slopes. Zhu Ran was himself a Buddhist priest.

The more overt influence of Buddhist ideas is to be seen in the famous pair of pictures by Liang Kai (active c. 1200) called "Patriarchs of the Chan (or Zen) Sect." One old man with a snub nose, sketched with extreme economy of line, is squatting down with a heavy knife upraised to trim a length of bamboo for a staff. The three-quarter rear view of the face shows extreme concentration. It is this concentration and single-mindedness which does not simply exhibit but *is* his Zen religion in everyday life, whereby he loses himself and finds the Buddha within. The other old man is doing something quite outrageous by both Confucian and Buddhist standards; he is fuming and stamping and tearing up scriptures, the sacred written word. But then Zen does not depend on scriptures or knowledge or ritual but only on the immediate, incommunicable, individual experience of enlightenment. The vivid strength and spiritual vigor of these pictures is seen in the few heavy lines and sharp angles of the clothing and the gaunt segments of rock and branches which complete the scene. Here everything extraneous has been cut to the minimum and only inwardness is left.

Many great names in this era of masters have been passed over in this brief account—Guan Tong in the mid-tenth century, Dong Yuan at its end, and Fan Guan active from 990 to 1030, all of Northern Song. Li Tang was the most honored of the reassembled academicians in 1138 in Southern Song, and Mu Qi (also known as Fa Chang) was a famous priest and painter of Chan (Zen) themes in the first part of the thirteenth century. One who formed a bridge

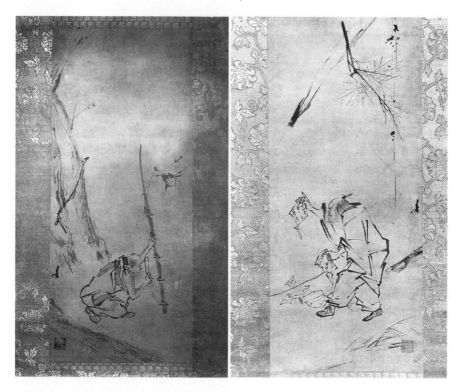

"Patriarchs of the Chan [or Zen] Sect." Liang Kai (active c. 1200), Southern Song dynasty.

Chopping a bamboo (left): "concentration and singlemindedness which does not simply exhibit but *is* his Zen religion in everyday life."

The National Museum, Tokyo
Photo: The Zauho Press

Tearing up Buddhist sutras (right): "doing something quite outrageous by both Confucian and Buddhist standards. . . . But then Zen does not depend on scriptures."

Collection of Takanaru Mitsui, Tokyo

between the Song era and the Yuan dynasty painters was the eccentric all-around gentleman scholar, Mi Fei (1051–1107), friend of the poet Su Dongpo. His free, highly impressionistic style was not acceptable to the Emperor Hui Zong, and none of his works were included in the imperial collection. But his style inspired Ni Zan, an even less traditional artist of the Yuan dynasty. Ni Zan was proud of his "awkwardness"; it was he who replied to a friend's remark that his bamboos did not look like bamboos, "Ah, but a total lack of resemblance is hard to achieve; not everyone can manage it."*

*Ni Zan, quoted in *The Legacy of China*, ed. R. Dawson, p. 205.

"Monk Riding a Mule." Southern Song dynasty, thirteenth century.

The inscription is by a monk known as Wu Zhun (1175–1249), and it is possible he also painted the picture. The feeling is Chan (Zen). The contrast between the soft mane and the delicate, precisely accented legs of the mule, the economy of line, and the sharp features of the unworldly, dreaming monk combine simplicity with sophistication.

Collection of John M. Crawford, Jr.

NEO-CONFUCIANISM

Since new trends and increasing sophistication had become evident in so many areas during the Song era, it is not surprising that philosophy also saw changes of great moment. The trend away from Buddhism and back to the Confucian classics begun by Han Yu continued. But the Confucianism which emerged from the speculations of Zhou Donyi and the Cheng brothers in the second half of the eleventh century was by no means the same as in the days of Confucius and Mencius. The challenge of Indian Buddhist metaphysics and Daoist thought required that some attention be given to a philosophic framework which would serve to explain the world and human nature. There was considerable debate between the various schools of thought, but in the end the comprehensive views of Zhu Xi (1130–1200) prevailed and he became, though not by his own design, the leader of a new orthodoxy, known in the West as Neo-Confucianism.

In the system of Zhu Xi, which depends in part on insights reached earlier by other thinkers, everything in the world was constituted by the interaction of two factors, the *li*, or form of the object, and its *qi*, or matter. (The meaning of the second term is literally "breath" or "ether.") The *li* of all things are summed up in the *tai ji*, or Great Ultimate. The similarity between this theory and Plato's theory of Ideas or Forms is immediately apparent, and the parallel extends to the notion of the Great Ultimate, which is not unlike the Idea of the Good. As to man, the *li* of human nature is common to all and is basically good, but men vary in their exemplification of good or evil according to their *qi*, or physical endowment. "Those who receive a ch'i [*qi*] that is clear are the sages in whom the nature is like a pearl lying in clear cold water. But those who receive a ch'i that is turbid are the foolish and degenerate in whom the nature is like a pearl lying in muddy water."*

There had been a long-continued debate between the realist Confucian school descended from Xunzi, who said human nature was evil, and the idealists depending on Mencius, who maintained it was good. Zhu Xi supported Mencius's view but said the education Mencius recommended must be backed up by *xiu shen*, self-cultivation. This term had also been used before, but Zhu Xi understood it in a particular sense. For him it meant something much deeper than the English word implies, something in the nature of personal commitment. He says the goal should be reached by "the extension of knowledge through the investigation of things" and "attentiveness of mind." Again, "the investigation of things," which sounds either colorless or coldly scientific in English, did not have those connotations in the thinking of Zhu Xi. He says (*zhuan* 46) that the investigation of things "means that we should seek for 'what is above shapes' by 'what is within shapes' [that is, the *li* through the *qi*]. Then "by means of the *li* which he already understands [the student must] proceed further to gain exhaustive knowledge of those [with which he is not familiar]." The Song debt to the religious and psychological elements in Buddhism is clear in Zhu Xi's conclusion to this passage, where he says, "When one has exerted oneself for a long time, finally one morning a complete understanding will open before one. Thereupon there will be a thorough comprehension of all the multitude of things, external or internal, fine or coarse, and every exercise of the mind will be marked by complete enlightenment."†

In 1313, a century after Zhu Xi's death, by a decree of the Yuan dynasty, Zhu Xi's commentaries on the Four Books were made the official standard for the civil service examinations, and thus the man who pressed for the investigation of things became the unwitting originator of an orthodoxy which grew ever tighter and more rigid as time passed. The comparison often made between the two contemporaries, Zhu Xi and Thomas Aquinas, is not inapt. Both had minds capable of vast syntheses; both brought in metaphysical concepts derived from outside sources, in one case from Buddhism, in the other from Aristotle, to complete and fortify a comprehensive framework for ethical or religious ideas coming from an earlier revered master; and both founded orthodoxies which lasted with little change for centuries after their times.

---

*Zhu Xi, *Recorded Sayings*, zhuan 4.
†Zhu Xi, *Commentary on the Great Learning*, chapter 5. (I am indebted in this section for some material and the quotations to Fung Yu-lan, *A Short History of Chinese Philosophy*, translated by Derk Bodde.—Author.)

9

THE MONGOL INTERRUPTION

Yuan Dynasty: 1280–1368

It is said that as a young man Temuchin, later to be known as Genghis Khan, was discussing with his companions the question of the greatest joy in human life. Some proposed hunting or hawking, but Temuchin said, "The greatest joy that a man can know is to conquer his enemies and drive them before him, to ride their horses and deprive them of their possessions, to make their beloved weep, and to embrace their wives and daughters." The territory of the Mongols extended ultimately from Korea to the borders of Hungary, and so great and so universal was the terror they inspired that mothers in medieval Europe hushed their children with the threat, "Be quiet, or the Mongols will come and get you."

The whole of China was included in the vast area of Mongol conquest, and thus, following the Song, there was a brief period of Mongol domination known as the Yuan dynasty. In order to grasp the significance of this extraordinary upthrust of nomad power, it is necessary to go back a few years and examine the career of Genghis Khan (1167–1227), whose genius for leadership and power to unite the normally independent tribes made the Mongol Empire possible.

GENGHIS KHAN

The Mongols depended on their flocks of sheep and herds of horses, the sheep providing warm clothing and felt for the tents as well as meat, and the horses providing transport, leather for armor, and mare's milk for curds and for a fermented drink called koumiss. The Mongols also raised camels for traffic in the desert and oxen to pull their great carts with supplies. They ranged over wide areas from summer pastures on the steppes to mountain valleys for some protection from the winter weather. Although their life was nomadic and largely self-supporting, they did require to keep in touch with settled agricultural neighbors. From these neighbors they acquired through trade or conquest two essential commodities, grain to add to their diet and metal for weapons, aside from luxury items such as tea and silk.

As a people they were highly mobile. All were thoroughly accustomed to the saddle from childhood. They could rapidly erect or dismantle their yurts, or tents, made of felt stretched over a light wand framework. Sometimes the yurts were transported on huge ox wagons just as they were, without being taken down. The papal legate Giovanni de Plano Carpini described these wagons when he visited the camp of Batu Khan near the Volga River. The huge wheels were twenty paces apart and had axles as thick as ships' masts. They were dragged by twenty-two oxen, harnessed in pairs. Batu had twenty-six wives, and each had a large yurt of her own mounted on such a wagon, with 100 to 200 carts in addition for equipment and provisions. Batu's camp was so enormous that it took Carpini over an hour to go from the edge to Batu's headquarters. The results of victory in each campaign tended to increase the number of the leader's wives and the size of his family. One is known to have had forty children, another a hundred.

Temuchin came from a family of hereditary leaders but had to work long and hard to reach a position of power, since his father had been killed when he was a boy. His mother was a Nestorian Christian, a strong and much respected personality. By fighting, diplomacy, and determination, Temuchin increased his standing and wealth, until a great gathering of the tribes in 1206 granted him the title of Genghis Khan, equivalent to "Universal Ruler," and swore loyalty to him.

Genghis Khan remained a true nomad all his days. A number of factors contributed to his rise to power, the chief being his ability to attract and hold his followers, both by fear and favor, and thus build a united Mongol nation out of scattered clans. The Mongol soldiers were already formidable, and he developed the army still further into an invincible force. The iron stirrup, known since the fourth century, provided a firm base for the mounted archer to fire either forward or to the rear, the latter known through the Romans as the famous "Parthian shot." The handy, double-curved, compound bow was a powerful weapon whose arrows could pierce armor and kill at 200 yards. Deceptive tactics were often used, such as a feigned flight of the Mongol center, then a swift turnaround and fresh attack, while concealed cavalry on the flanks closed in and cut off the enemy's retreat.

Such maneuvers executed at high speed required exact coordination, and this was accomplished by an advanced communications system using smoke signals, flares, colored flags, and messengers. Every warrior had spare horses— at least three and as many as eight—which he took with him on the march. Genghis Khan improved the whole system of communications, control, and strict discipline in battle tactics and brought these to a higher level of efficiency than ever before known among the Mongols. He kept his finger on the pulse of tribal politics at all times. At the height of his power his messengers on regular post routes took priority even over Mongol princes. Their horses carried bells to warn of their approach, and at the relay stations the rider leaped onto the fresh mount almost without stopping. He was bandaged about head and body, to withstand the strain of riding, and could half sleep in the saddle. By riding his horses to the point of exhaustion he could cover 300 miles in a day. On one occasion Genghis Khan took a city by the stratagem of retreating two days' journey, leaving his camp and supplies where they were outside the city walls. The besieged came out to loot the camp and were overwhelmed by the Khan, who had brought his whole army back in the hours of one night.

An entirely new feature introduced by Genghis Khan was to have his personal bodyguard function as an officers' training school. He made it an honor for clan chiefs to be allowed to send their sons for enlistment in the Guards. From the Khan's point of view this had the double advantage of providing hostages to guarantee the loyalty of the clans and supplying a pool of highly trained young leaders thoroughly familiar with his methods of warfare and personally devoted to himself. The Guards were given special privileges and a larger share of plunder.

But prowess in war alone would not have secured the Khan's position for so long. Everything he did reflected his intellectual acuteness. He made wise choices for high officers and, in appointing his successor, Ogotai, said that ability to manage men was of more weight than skill in warfare. His personal magnetism and fearless leadership were the original foundation of his power, but he secured his position by a form of judicial structure, the publication of the *Yasa*, or Code of Laws. These laws were on the whole faithfully followed during his lifetime and for a considerable period thereafter.

With Mongolia secured and this war machine at his back, Genghis Khan began the conquest of the Xi Xia on China's northwest border in 1209. The Jin rulers of north China were defeated in 1215 and Peking captured. A famous member of the Khitan royal house, Yeluchucai, is said to have persuaded the Mongol leaders at this point not to destroy the Chinese peasants and their agriculture wholesale, in order to turn north China into pastureland for horses, but instead to reap the benefits of taxing them and using the products of their mines and their industry. Genghis Khan with part of the Mongol horde moved west into Central Asia, and Turkestan was conquered by 1221, including the wealthy cities of Bokhara and Samarkand. He thus laid the foundations of the Mongol empire and arranged before his death in 1227 for it to be divided among the four sons of his chief wife and their descendants.

The momentum was maintained under Ogotai. Merely to enumerate places and dates gives no conception of the vast distances and the problems of command and logistics involved, even allowing for the self-sufficient style of the Mongol troops. Persia was overrun by 1231. Another force under Batu crossed Russia, capturing Moscow and Kiev, and fanned out with demonic energy into Poland, Bohemia, and Hungary in 1241. They were at the gates of Vienna when suddenly and mysteriously they melted away. Batu had been called back at the death of Ogotai to elect a new Great Khan. But no one in

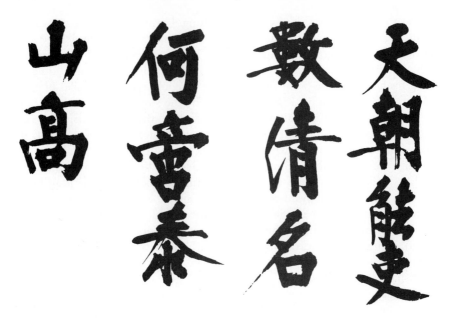

Calligraphy by Yeluchucai (1190–1244).

This scholar, himself of nomad origin but thoroughly sinicized, collaborated with Genghis Khan to the great benefit of the Chinese (see page 117). The boldness, strength, and decisiveness of his writing in this, the *kaishu* style, are immediately apparent.

Collection of John M. Crawford, Jr.

Europe knew when they might return. The forces in Persia, known as the Il-khans, overthrew the Abbasid caliphate of the Muslims with the capture of Baghdad in 1258.

With the help of Chinese and other experts, the Mongols had perfected the art of siege warfare and used great catapults and explosive missiles. But often they did not need to use siege engines, because fear was sufficient to open the gates. They employed psychological warfare of an extreme kind, by letting it be known that if a city surrendered at once, the inhabitants would be spared, but if any resistance were shown, all would be massacred and the city destroyed. The Mongol definition of destruction was to raze a city to the ground so that, if a horseman galloped over the site in the dead of the night, his horse would not stumble on even one brick.

After these conquests the original division of the empire made by Genghis Khan resulted in four great khanates: that of the Great Khan in East Asia, the khanate of Chaghadai in Turkestan, the khanate of Persia under the Il-khans, and the khanate of the Golden Horde based on the Volga River under Batu. The whole empire was held together for about a century, and the individual khanates for varying periods, the longest being that of the Golden Horde, where Batu's descendants ruled south Russia for about 200 years.

KUBLAI KHAN

Meanwhile in East Asia, which mainly concerns us here, Mongol progress was noticeably slower, owing to the watery nature of the terrain in south China and the skillful resistance of the Southern Song. The capture of the city of Xiangyang on the Han River, for example, took the Mongols five years. The leader who engaged in the conquest of China was the famous Kublai Khan (1215–1294), who was made Great Khan in 1260 and took the title of Emperor of China in 1271, calling his dynasty the Yuan, or Original Dynasty. The conquest of the entire country was completed by 1279 with the last disappearance of Song rule in the far south. Mongol attempts at conquest by sea were less successful. An expedition sent against Java was defeated, and two attempts upon Japan failed, partly because of Japanese resistance but mainly because of severe typhoons. Kublai Khan made sure that in China the Mongols would be dominant both in the military and administrative spheres. The chief government posts involving policy were held by Mongols, and in the provinces Mongol governors sometimes had assistants of Muslim origin, for Kublai Khan did not trust the Chinese. The large number of lower posts in the administration and some higher ones were held by Chinese. Clear distinctions were made between three groups in the population—Mongols, other races, and Chinese—and intermarriage between the groups was forbidden. Among the Chinese, those from the north were more acceptable to the Mongols than those from the south, since the north had become accustomed to rulers of nomad origin in the Liao and Jin dynasties, and the Mongols themselves had been among them for a longer time. The Chinese were denied all possession of arms, and the penal code bore down upon them more severely than upon Mongols for similar offenses.

On the other hand Kublai Khan, with an experienced eye to what was useful, adopted and extended a number of Chinese practices which had been in use earlier. He set up translation bureaus to make available the Chinese classics and official dynastic histories in the Mongol language. He created an Imperial Library and issued paper money of universal validity, in contrast to the Song paper currency which had been limited to certain regions and certain periods of time. The capital was moved in 1267 from distant Karakorum to Peking (then known as Yenjing in Chinese, Cambaluc in Mongol), indicating the increased value placed upon China as a Mongol possession. Maritime transport from the Yangzi River estuary around the Shandong coast to Tientsin was developed, while at the same time new construction of the Grand Canal was undertaken, along the lines which would be followed by the later Ming and Qing dynasties.

In trade as in administration, the Mongols regarded non-Chinese favorably and granted opportunities to merchants of Central Asia and the Middle East. Caravans plied along the Silk Road in numbers once again. Thousands in all from the Western regions must have visited or remained in China, some as captives, some as merchants, and others on official embassies. In the first half of the fourteenth century nine embassies from Europe appeared at the Khan's court, and no less than fifteen traveled from China to Europe. In addition to products and processes already mentioned, such as gunpowder, the compass, and printing, many other items filtered west from China, among them playing cards, new knowledge in the field of medicine, and influences in art and design.

Of the many Western visitors to China during the Mongol period only a few names are known, but even a partial list makes interesting reading. The friar Giovanni de Plano Carpini, who reached Karakorum in 1246, has already been mentioned. A Flemish Franciscan, Friar William of Rubruck, was sent by the saintly French king, Louis IX, between 1253 and 1255, and five years later Maffeo and Niccolo Polo, merchants of Venice, made their first journey to China. They brought back a request from Kublai Khan for 100 Christian scholars and technicians, but the request was not met. On the Polos' second trading expedition they were accompanied by Niccolo's son, Marco. An Italian Franciscan, Friar John of Montecorvino, was the most successful representative of the Roman Church in China. He embarked at Hormuz in the Persian Gulf in 1291, was joined for a short time by Friar Odoric of Pordenone, and died as Archbishop of Cambaluc about 1328. There is record of a visit by Friar John of Marignolli, but after that Christianity disappears in China until about 1600 and the arrival of the Jesuits, who had apparently no knowledge of the Franciscans who were there before them.

By far the fullest and most accurate Western account of China in the time of the Mongols is contained in the book written, or rather dictated to a writer, by Marco Polo. The immense influence of this work in stirring the imagination of Europe and stimulating further exploration is well known, although much of it, since proved true, was regarded at the time as the wildest exaggeration. Marco Polo had opportunity to visit many parts of China during his seventeen years in the service of Kublai Khan (from 1275 to 1292). He was immensely impressed by the princely state, the social concern, and the unlimited power of his master. Kublai Khan's life was nothing if not exotic. His koumiss was prepared from the milk of 10,000 pure white mares kept in his stables. Each of his four principal wives maintained a household of up to 10,000 attendants. Thirty or forty concubines annually were selected for the emperor from among 500 girls brought from all over the kingdom. And when he went hunting he traveled in an elephant howdah decorated with gold embroideries inside and tiger skins outside. From this vantage point he watched his huntsmen hawking or slipping trained cheetahs from leather pads on the horses' cruppers to chase and bring down deer and antelope. The Pax Mongolica under Kublai Khan, as Great Khan as well as Emperor of China, extended from the Pacific Ocean through Turkestan and Tibet to Russia and West Asia. The movements of caravans were carefully checked and governors held responsible for their safety. With pardonable exaggeration it was said that "A maiden bearing a nugget of gold on her head could wander safely throughout the realm." Marco Polo could not but be impressed. Medieval Europe was not organized to this extent. But he longed to return to Venice. He was at length given an opportunity by the emperor to conduct a Mongol princess to India to be married. They travelled west by the sea route, and after delivering his charge Marco Polo continued on his journey, landed in the Persian Gulf, and reached home in Venice in 1295.

The cultural aspects of the Yuan dynasty exhibit, as might be expected, popular rather than scholarly trends. The atmosphere was not conducive to creative work among the literati, and satire and protest carried with them an altogether unacceptable risk. An important exception in the scholarly field was in the art of landscape painting, where the subtle and vigorous work of the Song schools was carried on. The Mongols were well disposed toward works of practical benefit, and thus treatises on mathematics, cartography, astronomy, and water conservancy met with favor. Interest in these fields was stimulated by contributions from Persians and scholars from various parts of the Muslim world.

In the popular realm, on the other hand, there was considerable creativity, notably in the theater, in folk tales, and in the beginnings of the Chinese novel

"Fisherman." Wu Zhen (1280–1354). Yuan dynasty.

The Song inspiration in painting was by no means quenched during the short Mongol dynasty. Poetry, painting, and calligraphy, the "Three Perfections," combine in this composition. The poem by the artist himself (translated by Wango Weng):

> West of the village evening rays linger on the red leaves.
> By the shore the faint moon appears among the yellow reeds.
> Lightly stirring the oar, seemingly homeward bound,
> He puts away his fishing pole and fishes no more.

Collection of John M. Crawford, Jr.

in everyday language, which was to witness a great development in later centuries. The anonymity of popular literature made satire more possible, and occasionally hatred of the Mongols and scorn for their foreign henchmen found expression. Plays or operas with several actors on the stage, combining sung parts, musical accompaniment, recitative, and dances, flourished and took root at this time, to continue as highly popular entertainment down to the present day.

Kublai Khan died in 1294. Internal dissension and the growing slackness of the Mongol leaders caused a rapid decline in the efficiency of government. It was a familiar story in Chinese history. There were no less than four emperors in the period 1320–1329. Accompanying the weakness at the center there was a rising opposition to Mongol rule among the Chinese masses, particularly in such oppressed groups as the salt workers, who were virtually slaves of the state. Peasant desperation found expression in secret societies with a strongly religious, even millenarian, cast. The White Lotus, founded under Southern Song, drew many recruits near the end of the Yuan dynasty. This society was ardently Buddhist and vegetarian, and members expressed their protest by refusing to pay their taxes or contribute corvée labor. The White Cloud Society was somewhat similar. The Red Turbans, also founded during Song, played a major part in the rebellions which followed flooding of the Yellow River in 1351. It was these rebellions which in the main caused the final collapse of the Mongol dynasty in 1368.

10

THE RESTORATION AND CONSOLIDATION OF CHINESE RULE

Ming Dynasty: 1368–1644

From beggar to emperor, the rise of Zhu Yuanzhang (1328–1398), founder of the Ming, or Brilliant, dynasty, outdistances most modern success stories on the theme of rags to riches. Son of a landless farm laborer and early left an orphan, Zhu was forced to beg and for a time entered a Buddhist monastery, as much for physical as for spiritual sustenance. But the connection of poor peasants with Buddhism was not merely fortuitous, for they were buoyed up in their desperation by millenarian hopes raised by that religion. Zhu soon left the monastery and organized his own band of rebels in Anhui province. He worked in conjunction with the secret society known as the Red Turbans, whose leader claimed to be an incarnation of Maitreya Buddha, the Messiah of Buddhism. Zhu made rapid progress, capturing Nanjing and by 1364 establishing himself as the major power in central China.

The problems of the Mongol rulers, brought about by their own dissension as well as by inflation and the greed of Mongol and Muslim officials, were compounded by a series of floods and famines in north China. This gave rise to several successful revolts, so that Zhu Yuanzhang was faced with the task of subduing his rivals before he could seize the throne for himself. He was proclaimed emperor in 1368 with the name Hong Wu. He captured Peking in the same year and drove out the last Mongol emperor, but he chose Nanjing as the seat of his government, fortifying that city with the largest urban defense wall in existence, 60 feet high with a 20-mile perimeter. He steadily extended his power, surrounding the Mongol forces in Mongolia itself in 1370, taking Yunnan in 1382, and completing the reconquest of the whole of China by 1387. The Chinese domain included Manchuria up to Shenyang and down to the Yalu River border of Korea. Hami on the western trade route was captured and used as a control base, but no attempt was made to reduce all of Turkestan to obedience. Once the new government was firmly established, an enormous effort was immediately made to restore the economic situation, which at this point, as during most of Chinese history, meant reviving the agricultural yield. Neglected dikes and canals were repaired, and land abandoned during the rebellions was again brought under cultivation. Tax exemption for a number of years was granted as an inducement to peasants to move into the ruined areas—parts of the emperor's own province of Anhui, for instance, had been completely depopulated. Some figures given by Gernet* indicate that the effort was successful, for the amount of land brought back annually into cultivation was almost three times as great in 1379 as it was in 1371. At the same time a major program of tree planting was undertaken, involving among others palms, mulberry, and lacquer trees. To facilitate control of the population, families were divided into occupational classes of hereditary peasants, soldiers, and artisans, under separate administrative systems. But this degree of regulation could not be maintained, and the poor tended more and more to pass under the control of the rich in the operations of the free market.

The conventional picture of the dead hand of rigid mandarin bureaucracy, always looking to the past and stubbornly opposed to any change, which foreigners derive from a narrow consideration of the late Qing period in the nineteenth century, is not borne out by the history of the Ming or of several earlier creative periods in Han, Tang, or Song. One is struck in these periods not only by the degree of innovation but by the logic and courage of the attempts to think out basic administrative solutions to tough economic problems with which the modern world, with vastly improved electronic aids, is still manifestly struggling. Certainly the peasants suffered. The landlords inevitably tended to become extortioners. The laws of supply and demand have always been harsh and no respecter of persons. China's rivers required unremitting conservation, century after century, if they were to benefit and not to annihilate the surrounding population. But insufficient attention has been directed to the care, subtlety, and occasional brilliance of the policies of the central government in eras when it appears to have acted in an enlightened and highly responsible manner, as under the rule of Hong Wu.

Hong Wu retained the broad outlines of the government system of previous dynasties: the Six Ministries, the army staff, and the bureau of the Censorate. The Censorate had a staff at the capital to prevent abuses and even, on occasion, to warn the emperor against certain courses of action. It had traveling censors in the provinces to investigate the conduct of magistrates and receive complaints. This advanced Chinese system of securing justice and efficiency was, however, robbed of some, though by no means all, of its effectiveness by the fact that the censors were often young officials, belonged to the regular civil service, and were inadequately protected against damage to their later careers from superiors whom they had criticized. Furthermore, Hong Wu's style of government tended toward per-

---

*Le Monde Chinois, p. 342.

sonal control. He became suspicious, for example, of a man who had helped him gain power, Hu Weiyung. In 1380 Hu was accused of treasonable contacts with Mongols and Japanese and was executed. The affair was a cause célèbre, with no less than 15,000 persons said to be involved. The emperor took occasion to strengthen his direct control of the army and to eliminate the office of prime minister and the body, the Central Chancellery, over which the prime minister presided. The Grand Secretaries, varying in number up to about six, whom Hong Wu installed to assist him in centralized rule, had no political power comparable to that of the former prime minister and chancellery.

Upon the death of Hong Wu in 1398 the throne passed to his grandson, a youth of sixteen. The young emperor's attempt, not unknown at other periods in history, to reduce the power of family members who held military commands was resented by an uncle of experience who was in charge of the Peking frontier area. This uncle, with the aid of his army and support from the palace eunuchs, secured the throne and reigned as Yong Le from 1403 to 1424. His climb to power was costly in military damage to the northern provinces, but the benefits he ultimately conferred upon Ming China as a strong and decisive ruler were considerable. Events and policies such as those seen in the reigns of Hong Wu and Yong Le have given rise to the phrase "Ming despotism" often applied to this dynasty.

The expansion of China's frontiers begun under Hong Wu was continued under Yong Le. The enemies of Mongol descent were now the Oirats to the northwest and the Tatars to the northeast (the latter mispelled "Tartars" by later European writers). Yong Le put his military experience to use, in a manner rarely seen in emperors, and himself took charge of five expeditions into the steppes, defeating the Tatars near Ulan-Bator in 1410 and the Oirats in 1414. But these victories in the nature of things could scarcely be decisive, and three further campaigns were undertaken between 1422 and 1424. The nomads of the steppes, however, did not pose any real threat to China proper during Yong Le's time. At an earlier point in his reign a large expedition captured north Vietman, but Chinese control there could only be maintained until 1427.

Aside from these large-scale campaigns, Yong Le's fame in Chinese history is chiefly linked with the rebuilding of Peking and with the maritime expeditions in the Indian Ocean.

Historians are divided as to the necessity and value of his removal of the Ming capital from Nanjing to Peking. The northern site had the advantage of enabling a closer watch to be kept over the movements of the nomads, but inasmuch as Peking is only forty miles distant from the Nankou Pass in the southern section of the Great Wall, the capital was placed in a highly vulnerable position. More important may be the fact that the northern site sundered the government from contact with and understanding of the vast and increasingly important southern section of the country, its problems, and its reservoir of often brilliant scholar officials.

PEKING AND THE PALACE

There is no question of the greatness of the architectural achievement in the construction of Peking and the palace known as the Forbidden City, begun in 1421. There had been earlier cities on the site, and Kublai Khan's capital of Cambaluc had occupied almost the same position, but the Ming construction was entirely new. The walls of the Ming city stood 40 feet high and extended for 14 miles in a square with nine gates. An outgrowth of the city to the south was later surrounded by a further wall. The Forbidden City, still substantially as it was in Ming times, is a magnificent complex of audience halls, vast courtyards, sumptuous living quarters, pavilions, and ornamental lakes, set on a due north-south axis in the northern center of the city. The style is impressive and majestic, but the contrast of white stone courts, bridges, and plinths with rose-red walls and roofs of imperial-yellow glazed tiles imparts a lightness, sparkle, and brilliance to the whole architectural composition. In spite of the high and heavy roofs, the prevailing lines are horizontal, an effect achieved by the prodigal use of the terrain and the wide and leisured spacing of the buildings. This horizontal effect of the seat of the Son of Heaven, under the overarching dome of the blue sky in north China's dry climate, gives an impression of enormous dignity. To enter such a palace through gate after gate, passing through court after court, flanked by guards and officials in brilliant silks, and finally arriving before the raised throne of the emperor, must have created in the minds of tribute-bearing envoys from distant states an overwhelming sense of awe and majesty. Even the width of the throne itself and the lateral spread of the emperor's robes emphasized the horizontal solidity of the whole imperial structure.

This is in marked contrast to the European emphasis on the vertical line, seen in the tall columns and windows, the heaven-seeking spires of Gothic cathedrals, the towering walls of such fortress churches as Albi or fortress dwellings as the Palais des Papes at Avignon, or Virgil's picture of the Italian towns—*"tot congesta manu praeruptis oppida saxis fluminaque antiquos subterlabentia muros* [so many towns piled up by hand on precipitous rocks and rivers gliding by beneath ancient walls]." No greater architectural contrast could be imagined, and each style represents in vivid concrete form certain basic assumptions about human life.

The European is a pilgrim and a sojourner upon earth. He is called to a high vocation, of religion, of knightly honor, or of worldly success, for which in one form or another he must pray or fight or strive. The American skyscraper is but a further projection of the same world view, while the rocket to the moon is the ultimate in vertical projection, both glorious and absurd.

The Chinese, on the other hand, has arrived; he requires to strive no longer, at least in the overtly ambitious Western sense. If he is emperor, he has not so much gained as been placed by Heaven at the summit of human affairs. The form of the world is known and determined; the golden age is in the past. What is required is the maintenance of balance between the cosmic forces of *yin* and *yang*, a balance expressed in the perfect symmetry of the Forbidden

City in plan, elevation, and scale. (The Japanese, by contrast, have gone over to asymmetry in an attempt to reassert a Zen freedom and individuality over a stifling formalism.) The Chinese are fully aware of the changes and chances of this mortal life, and so they attempt to construct in their palace, as in their polity, something abiding, dignified, solidly based on the ground. They evolve an architecture which will impress both their friends and their foes with its completeness, its inevitability, and its permanence. That the Forbidden City in Peking so perfectly expresses these qualities, as well as that brilliance which was the motto of the dynasty, is no small tribute to the imagination of Yong Le and the Ming architects.

THE MARITIME EXPEDITIONS

It has long been customary to characterize the Chinese as a continental and not a seagoing race. There is truth in this assertion, taken as an average over the whole of Chinese history. Yet it cannot be said of the vital age of Yong Le and the vigorous trade with Southeast Asia which was conducted both before and long after this period. Moreover, the great Chinese maritime expeditions of the early fifteenth century we are considering here cannot have been isolated phenomena, though their ambitious size and range had not been previously known and were not to be repeated subsequently. The large

The Imperial Palace, or Forbidden City, Peking.

The vast scale, horizontal dimension, and formal plan of this grandest of the world's palaces (built mainly in the fifteenth century) take precedence over detail in this picture of a part of the whole scheme. The intimate relation of the buildings with the sky above is symbolic in the dwelling of the Son of Heaven, thought to be at the center point of the universe. The pavilion on Coal Hill in the left distance is where the last Ming emperor hanged himself.

Photo: Annette Juliano

seagoing junks of the great Ming expeditions were some 400 feet in length, but comparable ships had already been constructed in both the Song and Yuan dynasties (see p. 104). The Ming vessels carried compasses, navigated with the aid of accurate sailing instructions, and could make a steady 6 knots with the wind astern. It is probable that ship construction was part of government planning, and that one aim of the planting of 50 million trees in the Nanjing region under Hong Wu's reign was the ultimate provision of timber for shipbuilding.

There were seven major expeditions between 1405 and 1433, six of them during the reign of Yong Le. The admiral in command was a court eunuch from Yunnan called Zheng He (1371–c.1434). His father had made the pilgrimage to Mecca, and Zheng He, as a Muslim, was a suitable choice for expeditions which would visit Southeast Asia, where there were local Muslim rulers, and India, where the Mogul dynasty was already powerful, though not universally in control. Zheng He's prestige, boldness, and wisdom must have made an impression, for he was deified in parts of Southeast Asia, where his worship continued into modern times.

Of the seven expeditions, the first, fourth, and last may be considered to be representative and also to exhibit features of special interest. The first, from 1405–1407, comprised 28,000 men and visited Champa in southeast Vietnam, Java, Sumatra, Malacca, Ceylon, and Calicut on the west coast of south India. The fourth expedition (1413–1415) reached Calicut and Hormuz on the Persian Gulf, while a separate flotilla made a direct crossing from Sumatra to the east coast of Africa at Mogadishu in Somalia, a straight run of some 3,700 miles, and then went on to Aden in Arabia before returning home. It was not until the end of the same fifteenth century that the Portuguese explorers were to attempt ocean crossings of such magnitude. The seventh expedition (1431–1433) called at Champa, Java, Palembang in Sumatra, Malacca, the Malabar coast, and Hormuz, while some ships reached Jedda in the Red Sea, the port for Mecca.

The motives which lay behind these voyages are not entirely clear. The primary one was probably not commercial but concerned politics and international prestige. In all likelihood Yong Le's ambition to assert Chinese power in all directions led him to extend the tribute system to Southeast Asia, Ceylon, and south India. The tribute system was a practice which had developed since Han times, whereby foreign states sent tribute to the Chinese capital in return for political and commercial recognition. The eunuchs and others stood to gain commercially, and the court incidentally acquired some new and exotic gifts such as zebras, ostriches, and giraffes, the last identified with the fabled unicorn of good fortune. The fact that Zheng He intervened in local politics and succession disputes in Sumatra and elsewhere, somewhat after the manner of the French at Pondicherry and the British at Madras in the eighteenth century, may indicate that military and diplomatic reasons figured largely in the instructions he was given. It is said that the fourth expedition gave rise to two embassies to China from the Mameluke rulers of Egypt.

After these spectacular displays of power, the reasons for the sudden cessation of the expeditions are not much more evident than the reasons for their commencement. Doubtless motives of economy predominated, for by 1433 the treasury was becoming depleted and external threats were still present. The official class was in any case opposed to the two elements in the state which profited by these expensive overseas ventures, the eunuchs and the merchants. Trade with the not-too-distant regions of Southeast Asia continued, but the technical achievements of voyages across the open ocean thus begun were not exploited by the Chinese and were left, with fatal consequences, to the upstart European nations.

PORCELAIN

Among the most prized items of the Chinese export trade was porcelain, appropriately called "china" in English, from its country of origin. It was already being exported in Tang times, and large quantities were delivered overseas during Song, in Japan, the Philippines, Southeast Asia, and as far afield as the east coast of Africa, Egypt, and the Persian Gulf. In the Ming period production on a considerable scale was undertaken in factories, notably at Jingdezhen in Jiangxi province. The imperial factories produced exquisite ware, not only for the palace but for purchase by the wealthy and for export. The fine china clay known as gaolin could be heated to a high temperature, when it became extremely hard. Vessels could thus be made with walls thin enough to be almost translucent. Considering the fact that the Chinese had no instruments for the scientific determination of furnace temperatures on the order of 1,300 to 1,500 degrees Celsius, the standards and accuracy in firing, the brilliance and exactness of color in decoration, and even the control of the size of the "crackle" marks in the glaze were astounding performances.

Because of the fame acquired abroad by the Ming cobalt-blue and white designs, the Ming era has become associated in the minds of many with the height of the art of porcelain. But the art has a long history. The dripped glazes of Tang in green, yellow, and rich brown, seen on the famed figures of horses and camels, as well as on bowls and vases; the delicate pale green celadon and *blanc de chine* glazes of the Song on vessels sometimes plain and sometimes lightly incised, and valued by connoisseurs for their extreme restraint; and the brilliant glazes of *sang de boeuf,* apple green, and plum which recur in various eras all attest to the consummate skill and rainbow variety of taste of the Chinese craftsmen and their discerning patrons. One of the most notable though least noticed characteristics of Chinese porcelain is the satisfying nature of the shapes of the various bottles, vases, beakers, and plates. The full bodies, narrow necks—some more, some less elongated—and everted lips of the rims are all subtly different, yet all fulfill an innate desire for solid forms and gentle curves, a desire which all nations share with the Chinese, though few others have been able to execute them so well or so consistently.

A special type known as trade porcelain arose during the Qing to meet the demands of European aristocrats, wealthy merchants, and the like in the seventeenth and early eighteenth centuries. (The process for porcelain manufacture was first used commercially in Europe in 1710 in Meissen, Germany.) In this trade porcelain, Western designs, in many instances a coat of arms, were painted to the customer's order by the Chinese. A piece in the Royal Scottish Museum in Edinburgh showing two figures in kilts has a comic effect, since the kilts of impressionistic tartan are too brief and too broad; but they are not as absurd as the Oriental figures painted by Europeans, in fancy pavilions with little visible means of support, as seen on chinoiserie wallpaper.

THE PHILOSOPHY OF WANG YANGMING

In the intellectual life of the Ming period a strong current running counter to the orthodoxy of Zhu Xi developed under Wang Yangming (1472–1528; also known as Wang Shouren), a fact that belies the common notion that Chinese thought after Zhu Xi was reduced to a monolithic dullness until the impact of Western ideas in the nineteenth century. Where Zhu Xi had believed in learning based on Reason or the Informing Principle, Wang Yangming believed in the Learning of the Mind, an intuitional process; and where Zhu Xi stressed the dualism of Heaven and Man, Wang Yangming saw them as united in one whole. It followed for Wang that the way to advance in understanding of the world was not through discursive knowledge or "the investigation of things" but through the discovery of one's own mind, by a process of meditation and contemplation similar to Buddhist practice.

This philosophy of intuition is known in China as the Lu-Wang school, thus acknowledging as Wang's predecessor an opponent and contemporary of Zhu Xi, Lu Jiuyuan, who denied that *li*, the order of the world and the immanent cause of all things, was a reality exterior to consciousness. Wang Yangming followed this up by stating that knowing and acting were inseparable from each other, and that a "spontaneous understanding" was the best guide for conduct. He based this latter notion on a sentence of Mencius, "What a man knows without reflection, that is spontaneous understanding." Wang Yangming was influenced not only by Lu but also by a group which was even further away from Neo-Confucian orthodoxy. A member of this group was Chen Xianzhang (1428–1500), who refused to take up an official career, became a popular teacher, and, though not a monk, assiduously practiced contemplation, "sitting in a state of quietude" (*jing zo*) after the manner of the Chan (Zen) Buddhists.

Wang Yangming rose to an important level in his official career and sought to apply certain other of his ideas in the social realm. In order to stem rural decline in the face of economic changes and the constant tax demands of officials, he proposed the establishment of agrarian communities under a type of social contract. They would be subject to a leader, but there would be communal accountability for income and expenditure. A sense of common responsibility would be fostered by mutual confession of faults and the public award of praise and blame. It will be noted that a number of these features appear in the current practice of the People's Republic of China. The prevailing temper of the Ming dynasty regarded his views, both philosophical and social, as too idealistic. Wang's thought, however, became very influential in Japan, where it appealed to certain free spirits seeking self-cultivation and development in new directions under the somewhat repressive atmosphere of the Tokugawa regime.

THE JESUIT MISSIONARIES

A Western element now began to be felt in Chinese life at the Ming capital in a manner different from the sporadic and fleeting contacts of earlier times. The Jesuits came to China as propagators of the Christian faith, but their role cannot be understood unless it is recognized that they were also scientific experts and the first overseas consultants.

Francis Xavier, one of the original companions at the Sorbonne of Ignatius Loyola, founder of the Society of Jesus, had landed in Japan in 1549 and after successful work there had, with great courage, attempted to go to the fountainhead of East Asian civilization in China. He died on an island off the south coast but was followed by a considerable number of Jesuits, of whom the most prominent was an Italian priest, Matteo Ricci (1552–1610). Ricci is known to have been in Macao, the Portuguese settlement near Canton, by 1582 and to have lived in Peking, at first briefly, and then permanently, from 1601 until his death in 1610. He and his companions faced great difficulties, since they were identified by the Chinese with rough and lawless European traders at a time when piracy was so prevalent as to be causing embarrassment to the government. Ricci at first adopted Buddhist dress but soon found that the only way to earn the respect of the officials was to observe the customs and manners of a member of the Confucian literati. He had a brilliant mind and became thoroughly conversant with the Chinese classics. The Jesuit fathers took advantage of the fact that certain educated Chinese were extremely interested in Western science and technology. The fathers were thus able gradually to establish themselves in the good graces of the officials in a number of cities on the main south–north route from Macao to Peking. They also penetrated farther inland to the west, to Henan, Shanxi, and even as far as Sichuan. It appears that Ricci ingratiated himself at court by presenting the emperor with a chiming clock. In order to prolong his contacts with the palace, he had the foresight secretly to retain the key, so that he had to be summoned weekly for a period in order to wind the mechanism. (Ricci subsequently became the patron deity of Chinese clockmakers and was worshiped up to the nineteenth century in Shanghai as Bodhisattva Ricci—Li Ma-tu pusa.)

But the interest of Chinese intellectuals in Western science was much more serious than such an anecdote would indicate. Contributions of moment were made by the Jesuits to the Chinese understanding of mathematics, astronomy, and cartography in particular. Three noted converts, Xu Guangqi, Li Zhizao, and Yang Tingyun, all of whom held high official positions, translated works on these subjects from sources in the 7,000 books in Western languages which the fathers brought to Peking. They also wrote Chinese treatises on Christian doctrine and built churches on their own lands. Although the fact was not recognized at the time, Joseph Needham has pointed out that the Chinese views on astronomy were more "modern" than those of the Jesuits. The equatorial coordinates of the Chinese corresponded to the new work being done, unknown to them, by Tycho Brahe (1544–1601) in the West, which would replace the ecliptic coordinates still being used by the Jesuits. And the Chinese notion of stars floating in infinite space was certainly in advance of the Jesuit teaching of the celestial spheres of Ptolemy.

The astronomical calculations of the Jesuit fathers, however, gave new accuracy to the calendar, a matter of great importance in the Chinese view, and their methods in map-making and hydraulics were prized at court. Their activities covered a wide field, for they were instrumental in securing cannons for the imperial forces from Portugal, and they obliged the emperor by landscaping the grounds of the Summer Palace, complete with fountains and buildings in semi-Western style. As an example of the traffic of ideas in the reverse direction, suspension bridges employing iron chains were first constructed in Europe by Johann Fischer von Erlach of Austria in 1741. The famous architect acknowledged that he owed the idea to what he had read about China, where such suspension bridges had been in use since the sixth century.

The influence of the Jesuits continued for nearly 200 years, from the beginnings under Matteo Ricci and his companions in 1600 until near the end of the eighteenth century. There were evident obstacles to the acceptance of Christianity in the rationalist temper of the gentry class. In a sense each side in the exchange was content to be used by the other, the Jesuits willing to contribute knowledge in order to gain a chance to commend their doctrine, and the Chinese willing to permit the Jesuits to remain at court in order that they might profit by the new scientific learning with its valuable practical applications.

The interchange of ideas over such a long period was, however, of some significance, for this was the first continued communication which had ever occurred between intellectuals of the Far East and the West. The Chinese acquired some idea of the nature of Christianity and a clearer idea of world geography and of the scientific knowledge of the West. The intellectual circles of Europe gained an entirely new and more coherent view of China. The reports from the field, assiduously circulated in Europe by Jesuit headquarters in Rome, were written by perceptive men with a thorough knowledge of the Chinese gentry class. In the interests of their work, the fathers were prone to stress the similarities between the best thought of China and Christianity and to represent Confucianism as a preparation for the gospel. Their somewhat glowing reports were interpreted with delight—but in a different sense to that intended—by certain French thinkers as indicating that a sane and rational society could subsist upon an ethical basis without the aid of revealed religion. The truest European appreciation of Confucian values was attained by the philosopher Leibniz (1646–1716), who was considerably influenced by Chinese ideas.

PROBLEMS OF THE LATER MING RULERS

The latter half of the Ming dynasty was seriously affected by the decline in tax income that has been noted in connection with the abandonment of the distant expeditions by sea. The renowned Chinese civil service was much more limited in the number of its personnel than its counterpart in a modern nation, and thus administration at the local level had to be carried on through village headmen and rich farmers. This opened the way to abuses, since there was a marked tendency for the rich men responsible for delivering the tax quota to shift some of their own share onto the poorer households and at the same time to manipulate the charges levied in lieu of compulsory labor. So serious did these abuses become during later Ming times that the peasants of whole villages were absconding rather than submitting to the payment of impossible amounts. The government was thus losing large sums in unpaid taxes. Attempts made after 1522 by government officials in different districts to set the situation to rights were moderately successful and came to be known collectively as the Single-Whip Reform. Simplification and rationalization of a complex and by now chaotic tax structure was the essence of the reform. The varying rates of land tax were reduced from scores to a few, and the categories of payments in lieu of labor service were likewise reduced. In some instances all dues were combined into one payment, and one or two fixed dates were set for collection. The wry humor of the Chinese peasant appears in the name Single-Whip, derived from a punning substitution of the characters for "single whip" for the similar-sounding characters *yi tiao bien,* meaning "combination in one item," or "under one head." These provisions greatly lessened the chances for unscrupulous manipulation and falsification of records by the wealthy at the expense of the poor and of the government. Moreover, taxes were now to be paid in silver, which was easily transported to the capital. Payments were no longer to come through village headmen; they were made direct by farmers into chests placed in front of the local government office and were acknowledged by an official receipt. The life of the Ming dynasty was undoubtedly extended, perhaps by more than a century, through these enlightened if overdue fiscal measures.

The recurrent problem of eunuch control assumed serious proportions once again in Ming times. The emperor Hong Wu had forbidden the eunuchs to take any part in politics or even learn to read and write. But gradually they had come to have access to both power and wealth by several routes. Eunuchs, for example, were put in charge of bodyguards required in the palace and thus acquired some positions of military command. Articles for palace use, whether made in the imperial workshops or coming in as tribute gifts from abroad, passed through the hands of the eunuchs, and this gave opportunities for illicit economic gain. Power and prestige accrued to those of their number who were sent on embassies to India and to Central and Southeast Asia. But the most sinister addition to the power of the eunuch class came from the rise of a secret police under eunuch control and from files on government officials which were kept in the palace.

Perhaps the most disgraceful example occurred in 1449 when a eunuch named Wang Jin persuaded the emperor to undertake an expedition over the Mongolian border simply in order to have the honor of entertaining his master in his own village near the city of Huai Lai. Wang Jin, though entirely without military experience, was placed in command of the expedition. He flew in the face of all cautionary advice and, when confronted with a serious Mongol threat, delayed the Chinese retreat in order to carry out his cherished plan of hospitality. The result was that the Chinese army was completely defeated and the emperor himself made a prisoner.

The later Ming governments were faced with formidable problems. It would be incorrect to say that the emperors were confronted with these difficulties, for they themselves were not infrequently a part of the problem, one even refusing to grant audiences to his chief ministers or to transact any business at all for long periods at a time. In addition to the internal questions already mentioned involving fiscal policies and the power of the eunuchs at court, there were external threats from two directions, the nomads stirring again in the north and the extensive pirate raids being conducted along the coast. A Mongol leader, Altan Khan, became powerful enough to lay siege to Peking in 1550, though he did not take it. He gradually extended his sway through Turkestan to the borders of Tibet and obtained recognition of his powerful position by concluding a treaty with the Ming in 1570. His regime benefited economically by the establishment of two important horse marts on the Chinese side of the frontier.

Piracy on the coast, which had long been endemic, reached serious pro-portions in the 1550s, at about the same time as the threat posed by the nomads. The emperor Hong Wu at the beginning of the dynasty had already been troubled by pirate activity, but his protests to the Japanese authorities produced little result. The shogun Yoshimitsu, the great art patron in the last decades of the fourteenth century, had shown due deference to China in his communications out of respect to a culture he so much admired and had been at pains to promote legitimate trade, known at this time as the tally trade. The Chinese would issue a fixed number of paper tallies which would be distrib-uted in Japan, not without rivalry and dissension, to a number of merchants. When they arrived at the only permitted port, Ningpo, their tallies would be checked against the other half of the paper retained by the Chinese officials. Only those thus authenticated would be allowed to trade. The goods brought in by the Japanese consisted, among other things, of swords in great number and quantities of copper ore and sulfur, the last used in gunpowder. Considerable numbers of Japanese came bearing "tribute," the essential symbolic and deferential preliminary to trading. In course of time the entertainment, gifts, and land transportation costs from port to court for these large Japanese missions became a burden on the Chinese exchequer, and the number of persons involved had to be limited. In the meantime, however, the authority wielded by the Ashikaga shoguns in Japan had declined, and piracy unrestrained had begun again to replace legitimate trade.

In the Chinese records these marauders appear as "Japanese pirates," but in fact men of several nations were taking part, and latterly the majority were actually of Chinese origin. They were also from differing social strata, from the merchant prince Wang Zhi, based on an island south of Japan, to the humble "boat people" of the south China ports, who ferried goods to and from the large pirate junks standing offshore. Occasionally Chinese government officials were implicated in the traffic. It should be borne in mind that there was only a fine line to be drawn between legal and illegal trading in East and Southeast Asia generally, between "pirates" and regular merchants, and that the same persons frequently carried on now one and now the other form of activity. Similar conditions obtained in the West at the same time, for the raids of the Elizabethan adventurers were regarded in a very different light by the courts of England and Spain.

The Ming government attempted to cope with the problem of piracy by building warships, placing them under a single command independent of provincial boundaries, and fortifying strongpoints along the coast. But an area so extensive could not be successfully fortified, and the pirate raids continued and progressively undermined the authority of the dynasty.

A positive force acting to arrest the decline of the Ming appeared among concerned officials in the form of the Dong Lin party, based on the Dong Lin (Eastern Forest) Academy of the Song dynasty. These scholars called for a return to pure Confucian morality, unadulterated by the Buddhist and other elements introduced by Zhu Xi and Wang Yangming. They were vigorous in applying their principles to political life and the administration of affairs and began to have a noticeable reforming influence. However, when they dared to draw attention to the conduct of a notorious eunuch, Wei Zhongxian, they were defeated. Wei in 1626 had many Dong Lin leaders tortured, beaten, or executed, while hundreds of others were deprived of office. Spontaneous popular protests arose over these acts against respected officials, but in vain.

The Ming dynasty was forfeiting the public support essential even to an autocratic regime. Rebellions in the classic pattern began to break out. A general known as the Yellow Tiger ravaged parts of north China and ended by capturing the southwestern province of Sichuan and ruling it by the most ruthless methods. A more significant rebellion was that of Li Zicheng, who took the lead among bandits rendered desperate by a famine in the northwest in 1628. Li became master of three provinces by 1643. He captured Peking in 1644 and there found that the last Ming emperor had hung himself in a summerhouse on Coal Hill behind his palace (see illustration p. 127). This was the end of the brilliant Ming dynasty, but the dragon throne was not to pass into the possession of the rebel general Li. Instead it was to be occupied once more by the chief of a people from beyond the Great Wall. The Manzhou (Manchu) were to provide the last dynasty in the long roll call of the Chinese empire.

11

THE MANZHOU: SUMMIT AND DECLINE OF THE EMPIRE

Qing Dynasty: 1644–1911

The Chinese were past masters of the art of divide and rule. But when a Jürchen tribal leader of genius arose in Manchuria, the policy boomeranged and they lost their empire, only to gain it back again by making the tribesmen more Chinese than themselves. This extraordinary drama of the Qing dynasty moved to its tragic climax when the empire, more generally cultured and apparently more powerful than it had ever been, suddenly crumbled in the face of internal rebellion and the external pressure of foreign powers.

In order to understand the Qing dynastic period, its strengths and weaknesses, it is necessary to go back and look at the origins of the people known first as the Jürchen tribes and later as the Manzhou (Manchu). The country they inhabited has been called "the Canada of Asia." It is rich in natural resources, with wide, fertile plains, mineral deposits, and abundant timber in the mountains to the north and east. Today the plains produce soya beans, millet, and other hardy grains in great quantity. The southern region was under Chinese jurisdiction in Han times and was being increasingly settled in the Ming period by Chinese immigrant farmers coming by sea and land, mainly from Shandong province. The speech of the countryside still shows marked traces of the Shandong accent. This region, known as Liaodong, "east of the Liao River," was marked off from Mongolia and the warlike, nomadic hunting tribes to north and east by a "palisade" of earth and willow trees and was governed as a part of Shandong province.

In order to protect this valuable agricultural investment and to safeguard access to their ancient dependency of Korea, the Chinese had recourse to the same device of the commandery (*wei*) which had stood them in good stead on the Mongolian border. The commanderies consisted of local tribes enrolled as Chinese military regiments officered by their own leaders under a hereditary chieftain. The prestige of the Chinese empire was such that a number of these chiefs were glad to accept offices, titles, and seals from the emperor and to send tribute missions to Peking. By thus attaching them severally to himself, the emperor hoped to divide them from each other and to form a series of buffer states on his border. The process was somewhat similar to the method employed by the Hanoverian government in London in "pacifying" the Scottish Highlands in the eighteenth century, where the traditional enmity of the Campbells and the Macdonalds was exploited to the benefit of the crown. The first Jürchen commandery was established at Jianzhou, northeast of Liaodong, in 1403, and others rapidly followed. In the next fifty years the Chinese had cause for anxiety, for there were movements of revolt and warfare from the Yi kingdom in Korea, from certain Mongol tribes, and especially from the Oirats. Although the Jürchen tribes took advantage of this unrest to plunder, the Chinese in the main retained control of the region.

NURHACI

The situation altered drastically, however, with the rise to power of a gifted Jürchen leader, Nurhaci (1559–1626). He moved slowly. Accepting confirmation by the Chinese as leader of his clan, he increased his power at home by disposing of enemies under the acceptable excuse of a blood feud. He cemented alliances with other tribes by marriage and erected a strong castle in the northeast as his base of operations. While maintaining good relations with the Ming court—he received the complimentary title of "Dragon-Tiger General"—Nurhaci over a thirty-year period succeeded in uniting the principal Jürchen tribes. He built at the same time an economic foundation for his nascent state by successful trading in minerals, furs, pearls, and especially ginseng, a root much in demand for restoring youth and increasing sexual powers.

Nurhaci is to be distinguished from other, less successful tribal chieftains by his notable achievements in military structure and in administration, by means of which he began the process of turning a loose coalition of tribes into an organized state. The army consisted of companies of 300 grouped in larger units called banners (*qi*), distinguished by the color of their flags. There were originally four Manzhou banners, then eight, followed by eight Mongol and eight Chinese banners, which formed an effective force of almost 170,000 men by the time the Manzhou invaded China. Although the name "banner" was applied to contingents in the earlier Chinese commanderies, Nurhaci introduced important changes when he evolved his own banner system. His leaders were not the hereditary chiefs but officers appointed by himself, and members of the banners did not hold land all in one region; nor did they fight as a unit. When an expeditionary force was required, it was made up of drafts from different banners. These provisions virtually eliminated the danger of tribal defections or disobedience.

Nurhaci and his successors were well aware of the advantages of Chinese administration. Advisers and even generals were chosen from among the large

Chinese population of southern Manchuria. Nurhaci himself saw to the development of a system of writing using an adapted Mongolian script. Stone monuments and tablets erected after the full establishment of the Qing dynasty carry inscriptions in this Manzhou script as well as in Mongolian and Chinese. The possession of a script enabled Nurhaci not only to keep records and improve routine administration but also to have the Confucian classics translated as a basis for ordered government and social cohesion.

In 1618 Nurhaci moved into the open and attacked the Ming, capturing Fushun in Liaodong in that year and Liaoyang and Shenyang in 1621. Shenyang was renamed Mukden and made the capital of a new dynasty, to which Nurhaci had set up a claim some years earlier under the title Late Jin.

When Nurhaci died in 1626 he was succeeded by his eighth son, Abahai (1592–1643), who instituted the standard Chinese Six Ministries for the government in Mukden and appointed as Grand Secretary a prominent Chinese official, Fan Wen cheng. Fan was a prize for the Manzhou. An ancestor of his had been a well-known statesman in the Song dynasty, and he himself had been captured by Nurhaci and had then collaborated with him. He was not atypical, for many Chinese of northern origin were quite prepared to work under the Manzhou. Abahai united the main area of Manchuria under his rule by 1642; the Amur region in the far north was brought in by 1644. Abahai's death in 1643 did not prove a setback to the mounting ambitions of the Manzhou, for his six-year-old son was fortunate in having as regent a loyal uncle, Dorgon, who carried on the tradition of the bold and determined yet wise and realistic rule of his immediate predecessors.

The Ming at this point were in no condition to offer strong resistance to any attempt to supplant them. Their finances were low, there was widespread disorder, and the armies in the north charged with defending Peking were demoralized. Even so, Dorgon might not have launched an attack but for one circumstance, for he knew that a child ruler made a poor rallying point for a people emerging from tribalism. The circumstance was that the Manzhou were invited into China by a Ming general, Wu Sangui, who was supposed to be defending the frontier. In the chaotic conditions prevailing at the end of the Ming period, as at the end of other dynasties, there was more than one rebellion afoot, and another general, Li Zicheng, was aiming at taking over power at the capital. Faced with this threat in 1644 the Ming emperor called upon Wu Sangui to help. Wu at this point felt that his own forces were not sufficient and secured valuable allies by opening the pass at Shanhaiguan to the vigorous "barbarians." He was too late to save the dynasty, for meanwhile time had run out for the emperor. Li entered Peking at the head of his troops and, as we have seen, found that the emperor had taken his own life.

It may have seemed that the Manzhou came to help Wu, but once in Peking they showed no disposition to depart and in fact stayed for nearly 300 years. Li was soon evicted from Peking and, after a long retreat, was ignominiously killed a year later by two peasants who offered his head to the pursuing

Rice paddies and tea shrubs in the hills of Jiangxi, southeast China. Photographed by Underwood and Underwood in 1902, the last decade of the Qing dynasty.

The Chinese in the foreground is wearing the queue, as required by the Manzhou rulers. Painstaking maintenance of dikes between the fields is needed in order to retain standing water for the rice plants. The hillsides are utilized for growing the tea bushes in the hot, moist climate of south China.

Library of Congress

general. The Manzhou from the first benefited in their political style from the fact that they had already become familiar in Manchuria with Chinese institutions. The offices in the main ministries at the capital were equally divided between Manzhou and Chinese, and the provinces were governed cooperatively by a Manzhou governor general and a Chinese governor.

The lower classes were not treated so well. Chinese men were compelled to wear the queue, or pigtail, and mixed marriages at all levels of society were forbidden. Manchuria was to be reserved as a special area sacred to Manzhou of pure blood, and Chinese were not allowed to settle there. During the early years of the new dynasty, Manzhou enclaves were set up in north China, where the farming was done by Chinese slaves, who could actually be bought and sold. But the experiment was seen by the Manzhou themselves to be unsuccessful. Production was scanty, and it was difficult to prevent slaves from absconding and becoming lost in the general population. The Manzhou found, as the Mongols before them in a different context had found, that you could do better by taxing free farmers. By 1685 no new enclosures were being made. And when it came to agrarian taxes, those levied by the Manzhou were lighter than the taxes demanded by most of the other dynasties.

Although the new dynasty, named the Qing, was ruling in north China, it was some decades before the south came fully under its control. Wu Sangui was collaborating with the Qing, and incidentally drawing considerable funds from Peking, but he was also pursuing his own ambitions. He drove the Ming supporters from one province to another and defeated a Ming prince in Burma in 1662. (The last Ming empress was converted to Christianity by the Jesuits.) Finally Wu, with his base in the southwest, made a bid for complete independence in 1673 and was joined by two other Chinese generals in the south in the Revolt of the Three Feudatories. It took the Qing forces until 1681 to suppress this rebellion. The last stronghold of Ming sympathizers was Taiwan (Formosa). Guo Xingye, the name Europeanized as Koxinga, was a power on the Fujian coast. Allied with the last of the Ming, he attempted unsuccessfully to secure Japanese help for them. He then seized Taiwan from the Dutch. From this base he revived the pirate menace to the south China coast and supported the Revolt of the Three Feudatories. The Dutch fleet, however, joined up with the Qing forces in the suppression. With this assistance Taiwan was captured from Guo Xingye in 1683 and became a part of Fujian province. The Qing emperors were at last established as the rulers of all China. The last phase of the conquest, however, was costly for the inhabitants of the seacoast, since they were forced to move ten miles inland and their coastal towns and villages were burned. The aim of the dynasty in this measure was, of course, to deny the rebels and pirates any support or supplies, but the anti-maritime frame of mind exhibited here by the central authorities rendered them less fitted than ever to cope with the overseas rivals from the West who would soon harass them.

KANG XI

The Qing dynasty thus took some time to establish itself, but, once established, it enjoyed a long middle period of stability and prosperity. This was due in part to the occurrence of two exceptionally long reigns in close succession, that of Kang Xi* (1654–1722) who ruled for over sixty years, from 1661 until

---

*Strictly speaking, these and other emperors should be referred to as "the Kang Xi emperor" and so forth, since the Chinese characters are not personal names but designate the year period of the emperor's reign. However, the simplified form is widely used.

his death, and that of Qian Long, whose reign, from 1736 to 1795, was almost as long. Both emperors and their advisers devoted a great deal of attention to China's northern and western frontiers, and both reigns witnessed an expansion of the empire, until in Qian Long's time it reached proportions unknown before or since. Diplomatic and military means were employed by the Qing, and the religion of Lamaism also played a large part in the outcome. The chief example of the effect of Lamaism on the politics of the northern and western regions was the victory of the Yellow Sect, under the fifth Dalai Lama, over their Red Sect rivals. This Dalai Lama visited Peking in 1652, bearing tribute. He was well treated, exempted from the customary prostration before the emperor, and given the usual gold symbols of authority as a tributary ruler within the Chinese sphere.

This visit took place just before Kang Xi's time, but Kang Xi himself commanded a large Chinese force which penetrated as far as Urga in Outer Mongolia and defeated a powerful khan of the Western Mongols. The mounted nomads whose fighting skills had dominated the steppes for so long were now doomed to decline, for in this battle the Chinese employed artillery with deadly effect. Under the later great emperor Qian Long, several expeditions were sent farther west beyond the Altai Mountains to the Ili River region between 1755 and 1759. The Qing thus succeeded finally in controlling all of Chinese Turkestan. They planted colonies of political prisoners in the region and placed it under a military governor.

Kang Xi by no means confined himself to the pursuit of military achievements. A brilliant ruler, a scholar and an all-around personality, he enjoyed hunting in the manner of his ancestors and built a summer palace for the purpose at Rehol, north of Peking. Hunting was more than a sport, since with a veritable army of beaters coordinating their efforts to round up the quarry, it served also as a war game and had been extensively so used by the Mongols. Kang Xi made it a point to go on inspection tours in south China, which had the double advantage of keeping him in touch with that reservoir of first-rate scholar officials and of enabling him to check on the conservancy of the Yellow and Huai rivers in the north and on the vital Grand Canal artery which brought tribute rice from the south. Most important of all, he had a genuine love of scholarship and succeeded in attracting to his side some of the best Chinese literati of the time. A small group was attached to his personal study, and they and wider committees of scholars collaborated in works to which he wrote prefaces. Thus there appeared under Kang Xi's patronage the great dictionary of some 40,000 characters, a collection devoted to calligraphy and painting, an extensive treatise of geography, and a complete edition of the works of Zhu Xi. The vast encyclopedia, *Tu Shu Ji Cheng,* begun in the seventeenth century, was published in 1728.

In his capacity as moral leader of the nation, Kang Xi published in 1670 the *Sacred Edict,* an amplification of earlier imperial maxims of the fourteenth century, which exhorted the people to be filial and thrifty, to value scholarship and avoid unorthodoxy, and to respect the law and pay their taxes. This edict was to be brought to the attention of the populace twice a month by the officials and gentry. The wording of the edict provides a good illustration of the division between the rulers and the ruled and of the lofty, paternalistic attitude of the Chinese government toward its people, which was based on a genuine moral concern but was before long to strike foreign governments as arrogant and anachronistic. (It can be argued that the attitude of the present government has not greatly altered.)

Kang Xi's interest in astronomy, cartography, and other branches of science led to continued imperial patronage of the Jesuit fathers at the court of Peking. Unfortunately for the Christian cause, inter-order rivalry developed with the arrival of Franciscans and Dominicans in some of the port cities. The European tradition of these orders of friars had been to make a direct appeal in popular terms to the mass of the people, and this practice they carried on in China. The contrast which they drew between heathen and Christian rites was in black and white, uncomplicated by any of the subtle interpretation whereby the Jesuits sought to enlist the support of the Chinese literati. The friars, for example, condemned ancestor worship out of hand, whereas the Jesuits justified it as permissible respect and different from the worship of the Supreme Being. The Rites Controversy, as it was called, reached a climax over a point which need not have been major: namely, what the most suitable translation for the name of God was, the terms used in the Chinese classics, *Tian,* Heaven, or *Shang Di,* the Ruler on High, favored by the Jesuits, or, alternatively, a new term, *Tian Zhu,* Lord of Heaven, favored by the other side. The Jesuits in Peking secured support from the emperor Kang Xi, which angered the Pope as an interference in the realm of Christian belief. A papal bull, *Ex Illa Die,* was issued in 1715, which in turn angered Kang Xi, who considered himself the competent authority where questions of language and religion within China were in dispute. Papal legates attempted compromises, but Kang Xi's successor in 1724 finally added a sentence to the Sacred Edict branding Christianity as a heterodox sect. Some missionaries were expelled, a number outside Peking were persecuted, and the practice of Christianity declined. Exceptions were made for Jesuits at the court in Peking. Brother Giuseppe Castiglione was appointed court painter, and he and others laid out the gardens and constructed buildings and fountains on a lavish scale for the famous Summer Palace near Peking.

Kang Xi died in 1722, after a long and brilliant reign, and was succeeded by one of his twenty surviving sons, Yong Zheng (1723–1736), who reached the Dragon Throne with the backing of military force. He concentrated still greater power under the emperor's personal control, reorganizing the inner group of ministers and transmitting orders to the provinces only through his own edicts, although the proposals might come from the Six Ministries of the government. This centralization of authority increased the load of work which the emperor had to carry, but Yong Zheng maintained a steady devotion to duty and was rarely absent at the dawn audience. (The word *chao* in Chinese means "dawn," "court audience" (held at dawn), and, by transference, "dynasty.")

QIAN LONG

Yong Zheng was succeeded in turn by his son, the emperor known as Qian Long (1736–1795), who carried on the tradition of an autocratic but hard-working and morally concerned ruler. Qian Long's interest in scholarship was as genuine as that of his grandfather, and under his patronage the vast collection known as the Four Treasuries was completed in 1789. Seven sets of 36,000 volumes containing 3,450 entire works were completed under the four categories into which the Chinese were accustomed to divide their literature: classics *(jing)*, history *(shi)*, philosophy *(zhe)*, and belles lettres *(ji)*. The bibliographical catalog published in the collection listed no less than 10,230 works, including those which were reproduced in their entirety. One may assume that this enormous expenditure of effort served several purposes besides reflecting the personal literary interests of the emperor, for it enhanced the prestige of the Manzhou dynasty, employed a large number of Chinese scholars, and convinced the general body of literati that the foreign dynasty bore the genuine stamp of civilized gentlemen and thus was worthy of their support. This emphasis on scholarship was only one factor, but an important one, in the causes which contributed to the impressive stability of the empire under the three great emperors, Kang Xi, Yong Zheng, and Qian Long. As Gernet remarks:

> *Tout devait contribuer à calmer l'amertume des patriotes les plus intransigeants: la relative douceur des moeurs politiques, l'adoption par les empereurs eux-mêmes et par l'aristocratie mandchoue de la culture chinoise, l'expansion de l'Empire au dehors, la paix intérieure et la prospérité générale.* *

> [Everything was designed to contribute toward assuaging the resentment of the most unyielding patriots: the relative gentleness of political manners, the adoption of Chinese culture by the emperors themselves and by the Manzhou aristocracy, the outward expansion of the Empire, its internal peace, and its general prosperity.]

All the cultural achievements of earlier dynasties were treasured under the Qing dynasty emperors and were either imitated or further developed. There is much truth in the common statement that fresh and original creative impulses were lacking in the artistic life of the Qing. Imitation, elaboration, and decoration run riot, for example, are to be seen in ceramics, but works of pure and exquisite taste also abound. In general, however, simple monochrome porcelains are overshadowed by large vases, often of square shape, with complex pictures and designs, against brilliant backgrounds of rose, yellow, green, blue, and black, categorized as *famille rose, jaune, verte,* and so forth.

---

* *Le Monde Chinois,* p. 415. Translation by W. Scott Morton.

In literature also the stress was on reproduction more than upon original-ity, save in one field, that of the novel. The Chinese novel developed as a true literary form during the Ming and Qing dynasties, but it took its origins from a long line of rich oral sources. The popular taste for odysseys and stories of travel and adventure is insatiable and worldwide. Thus in China one of the great favorites of all time is the novel *Xi You Ji,* "The Record of a Journey to the West." It is a humorous and delightful *Pilgrim's Progress,* loosely based on the actual pilgrimage in the seventh century A.D. of a Chinese monk, Xuan Zang, to the original home of Buddhism in India. Since this and other novels were written in less than classical language, the authors out of fear for their scholarly reputation often preferred to remain anonymous. But in this case the authorship can be ascribed with some confidence to the scholar official Wu Cheng'en, who lived from ?1500 to 1582.

The story may be regarded from one point of view as an allegory trans-posed down one step in the scale of universal life, in which a monkey emerges almost disciplined enough to become a human being, just as a human being should aspire to becoming a saint or a Buddha. But most read the book purely for its entertainment value.

The first part relates the adventures and prowess of the hero, Monkey, who by virtue of his enlightenment has acquired magic powers, such as the ability to jump 108,000 *li* (a *li* is one third of a mile) in one bound and the capacity to summon aid when in a tight spot by plucking out one of his own hairs, chewing it up, and spitting out the pieces, which immediately turn into an army of monkeys. By these and other means Monkey, who is a mischievous and boastful but sympathetic character, defeats all the forces the Jade Emperor sends against him. He is finally curbed by Buddha and given a constructive task, to fetch scriptures from India and bring them to China, one of the actual objectives of Xuan Zang's historic journey. Descriptions of Monkey's numer-ous adventures on his journey occupy the remainder of the novel.

In his assigned task Monkey is aided by a faithful white horse and by a pig with a history. "I am not really a pig at all," he said. "I was a marshal of the hosts of Heaven, but one day I got a bit drunk and misbehaved with the God-dess of the Moon." This light, familiar, and colloquial tone pervades the book. For instance, Guan Yin, Goddess of Mercy in Heaven, asks, "How are you people down below getting on?" And Buddha says to the Bodhisattvas around him, "You stay quietly here in the Hall of the Law, and don't relax your yoga postures. I've got to go and deal with this creature [Monkey] who is making trouble at the Taoist court." Yet this irreverence, which is tolerated and enjoyed even by Chinese who are also capable of serious worship, has nothing of bitterness or cynicism in it. It pokes fun at the pretensions of religion with-out resorting to the acid satire of a Voltaire. In the pragmatic Chinese manner, the heavenly beings reproduce exactly the bureaucracy known on earth. The Dragon King of the Eastern Sea has dragon children, shrimp soldiers and crab generals, whitebait guardsmen and eel porters. Occasionally a double shaft of irony is directed against both religion and civil administration, as when the monkey rank-and-file comment on the long-distance leaping powers of their leader, saying that "he is in luck. If he learns this trick, he will be able to carry dispatches, deliver letters, take round circulars—one way or another he will always be able to pick up a living!"*

"The Record of a Journey to the West" is only one of a series of famous Chinese novels which appeared comparatively late in the history of Chinese literature, but still much earlier than the comparable genre in the West. (Although I have chosen to discuss novels under the Qing dynasty, it should be noted that the *Xi You Ji* and others belong in date of composition to the Ming, the previous dynasty.) All of the novels can be broadly characterized either as historical romances or novels of social manners. All depend heavily on an ancient tradition of popular storytellers in the marketplaces and teahouses. This dependence carries two consequences: first, that the long, sprawling novels are strong in fascinating detail but weak in unified plot, and, second, that the authors are rather to be described as collectors, editors, and rewriters of earlier material. Yet this description itself requires qualification, for in writing up the folk material the authors imprint on it a clear and consistent individual literary style.

Although certain of the following attributions of authorship and date are still controversial, a summary of a few of the best-known novels may be given as follows:

"The Romance of the Three Kingdoms" *(San Guo Zhi)* by Luo Guanzhong	c. 1330–1400
"The Water Margin" *(Shui Hu Zhuan)* (also known as "All Men Are Brothers") by Luo Guanzhong possibly from material put together by Shi Naian	c. 1330–1400
"The Record of a Journey to the West" *(Xi You Ji)* by Wu Cheng'en	?1500–1582
"Golden Lotus" (or "Gold Vase Plum") *(Jin Ping Mei)* by Xiao-xiao Sheng ("A Laughing, Laughing Scholar")	End sixteenth century
"The Dream of the Red Chamber" *(Hong Lou Meng)* by Cao Xueqin	?1724–1764

The last two novels in this list are individual creations in which the writers resemble more closely the Western concept of an original author. There appear to be autobiographical elements in the second of these, "The Dream of the Red Chamber."

The novels show marked contrasts to classical and official writing in style and language, as already noted. The contrast in tone and content is even more marked. The novels cater to the popular appetite for deeds of daring and brag-

---

Monkey, translated by Waley, p. 26.

gadocio, for the image of the Robin Hood rebel fighting a corrupt regime, and for the glitter of merchant wealth and high life. Written from the point of view of the people, they are not without malicious delight at the occasional discomfiture of the evil rich or wayward mandarin officials. They go in for untrammeled descriptions of pleasure which at times are frankly pornographic. The ribald passages, however, take their place in a general setting of minute and fascinating descriptions of social manners, including domestic life, plural marriage, legal battles, street scenes, wedding and funeral customs, and so forth, almost indefinitely.

12

THE IMPACT OF THE WEST IN THE NINETEENTH AND EARLY TWENTIETH CENTURIES

China and Europe had known of each other's existence in a nebulous way for centuries. A thin line of commerce had extended between them along the Silk Road through Central Asia from Roman times. Marco Polo and a few other intrepid travelers had carried news in both directions. The Jesuits of the seventeenth century at the court of Peking had broadened and deepened the currents of mutual recognition and respect. But it was not until the nineteenth century that the Western world began to make itself felt in China to any marked degree.

To some extent the influence was mutual, but the effect of the West upon China was in the end much more devastating than any influence in the other direction. In the early nineteenth century the significance of the Western impact was not at all evident to the leaders of China, who thought that the barbarians could be contained and controlled by the time-honored methods which China had long employed. But the force of the impact was cumulative and different in kind as well as degree from the older, more limited interaction. The situation from the Chinese point of view gradually got altogether out of hand.

THE BRITISH EAST INDIA COMPANY

Many European nations and the United States were involved in this commercial and cultural invasion of China, but Great Britain was in the forefront and set the pace. The British instrument was a peculiar one, an empire within an empire, the British East India Company, founded under charter of Queen Elizabeth I in 1600. The nature of the company is little understood, since it was unlike any other organization before or since, save perhaps its contemporaries, the Dutch East India Company and La Compagnie des Indes Orientales (founded in 1602 and 1664 respectively).

The original title of the British joint-stock company was "The Governor and Merchants of London Trading into the East Indies," but in course of time it came to resemble a government as much as a merchant company, not only building ships and stocking them with goods for sale but arming those ships with guns, maintaining an army staffed by its own officers to defend the company's interests on sea and land, acquiring the right to levy taxes in India, and keeping law and order in foreign lands where local control was weak. J. R. Seeley's epigram about the English seeming "to have conquered and peopled half the world in a fit of absence of mind" is especially relevant to the East India Company, for it soon found itself conquering and holding territory overseas, making treaties with oriental governments, administering justice, maintaining harbors, channels, and coastal defenses—in fact, affecting the lives of millions in the hinterlands of its trading posts whom it had no authority to rule and indeed no original intention of ruling.

The anomalies, not to say illegalities,* of British rule in India and British interference in China were due in part to the fact that the Western powers were all operating with one eye on the Orient and one on their rivals in Europe. Philip II's ban on the sale of oriental goods to Protestants in 1598 provoked the Dutch into voyages to obtain a share of the spice trade for themselves. The Dutch, in drastically raising the price of pepper from three shillings to eight shillings a pound, in turn provoked the British into forming their own company for commerce with the East. British advances in India were then further stimulated by rivalry with the French. And once launched upon the venture, the London merchants were nothing if not enterprising and thorough.

The activities of the British East India Company in India during the seventeenth and early eighteenth centuries are beyond the scope of this book. But by the late seventeenth century the company had begun trade with Canton. The East Indiamen built in the Thames dockyards were impressive vessels for their day, often technically in advance of the men-of-war being constructed for the Royal Navy. They ranged in the eighteenth century from 750 to 1,250 or more tons, with deep holds for cargo, three masts, flush decks for seaworthiness, and mounting up to fifty-four guns for protection. They had to be solidly constructed to undertake voyages of two years for the round trip, yet even so had only a life of four voyages or eight to ten years. After 1780, when the underwater timbers were fitted with copper sheathing, their average life was extended to twelve to fourteen years. The profits on each voyage were thus considerable to make this rate of replacement possible.

The object of each voyage was safety, not speed, for the monopoly over the London market held by the company meant that there was no competition to be outdistanced. An average day's run, with speed reduced at night, was

---

*One of the foundations of British rule in India was the *diwani* of Bengal, the right officially granted by the Mogul emperor to collect taxes in that province. But British governors subsequently extended their jurisdiction without authority.

only about 50 miles, a speed of 2 knots. After 1813, however, when the monopoly on the India trade was in part relaxed, speed became more important. There is note of a sailing time of 109 days from Canton to the Thames, 15,000 miles, giving 137 miles per day or 5.7 knots throughout the voyage. From 1813 on, it appears the spread of canvas was no longer shortened at night.

The company established a "factory," the trading post of a factor, or agent, in Canton in 1699. Company ships had already begun to take part in the so-called "junk trade" with Southeast Asia ("junk" is a Malayan word for ship), conducted by Chinese merchants and operating out of Ningpo, Amoy, and Canton. Canton soon became the chief entrepôt for the English trade, which dealt in such articles as silk, porcelain, lacquer, fans, rhubarb, musk, and "tutenag," an alloy similar to zinc. Before long, however, tea became the principal article of trade, and the demand in England rose steeply. In spite of conservative objections to this new and insidious drink, the popularity of tea did much to deliver the lower classes in Britain from the use of cheap gin, whose harmful effects are so vividly displayed in Hogarth's prints.

The figure for tea exports to Europe in 1720 was about 12,700 chests per annum, the major amount going to the London market. A marked increase took place between 1760 and 1770, and by 1830 the figure had reached 360,000 chests a year. In 1803 the tea imported into England was worth over £14 million sterling. Dr. Samuel Johnson must have been in the forefront of those who popularized the drinking of tea, for Boswell remarks, "I suppose no person ever enjoyed with more relish the infusion of that fragrant leaf than Johnson. The quantities which he drank of it at all hours were so great, that his nerves must have been uncommonly strong not to have been extremely relaxed by such an intemperate use of it." The year was 1756.

The Canton system of trade was conducted along lines which suited Chinese ideas. The Chinese restricted trade to that port in order to control it. This was a variation on the "tribute system" mentioned elsewhere as China's mode of conducting foreign relations. (See page 128.) Only *hong* merchants, those in an officially appointed and limited Chinese guild of less than a dozen members, could trade with the foreigners, and each foreign merchant had to be guaranteed by a member of the *hong*. The Chinese had to meet large and fluctuating demands for fees and "presents" from the mandarin officials in Canton, a circumstance which altered the price of tea and gave rise to discontent among the foreign traders. On the whole, however, the tea trade was conducted amicably and honorably on both sides, the more so as the profits were high in both directions.

The better brands, Congou and Souchong, were sold wholesale in London about 1800 for 2 shillings 10 pence to 6 shillings 10 pence per pound, but the most expensive teas would retail at 16 to 18 shillings per pound. The high value of tea serves to explain its careful storage in beautifully made tea caddies of hardwood with elaborate brass locks. The common people were also able to afford tea in small quantities of a brand known as

Bohea, selling for less than 2 shillings 6 pence a pound, in which tea leaves were mixed with some leaves from other plants, such as sloe, liquorice, or even ash and elder.

Precautions had to be taken by tea inspectors in Canton and London to guard against fraud—such as treating old tea with Prussian blue to make it look fresh. But if fraud was detected, the Chinese merchant would usually be prepared, without written contract and on the word of a gentleman, to replace the whole "chop," or consignment, without demur. The wealthy East India Company merchants kept up some style in their factory, dining in the leisurely eighteenth-century manner with crystal, silver plate, and ornamental candelabra. The memoirs of a young cadet, William Hickey, provide glimpses of entertainments given by the *hong* merchant Pankeekwa during which the Chinese put on a play. The common language on these occasions was pidgin English, a corruption of "business" English. Such diversions were no doubt greatly welcomed by the foreigners to relieve the tedium of their lives, for Chinese regulations did not allow them to bring their wives to China, forbade them to enter the gates of Canton, and compelled them to live an isolated life on an island.

Tea was normally paid for in silver, and this in the course of time gave rise to problems. The balance of trade being unfavorable to Britain, there was a constant search for commodities which could be successfully imported into China to offset the drain of silver. Among the goods known to have been sold to the *hong* merchants in 1800 were raw cotton from Bombay and piece goods from Madras, woolens from England, and tin from the county of Cornwall. But the most profitable item was opium from Bengal, and this high-value, low-bulk commodity assumed second place after raw cotton in the import trade. The opium was grown by the company in India, sold at auction to private merchants known as "country traders," and brought to Canton in their ships. The company then reentered the picture, for the country traders used the company's financial services to transmit their profits to London by buying company bills of exchange. The silver currency thus realized by the company in Canton was used in turn to purchase tea.

Both the company directors and the *hong* merchants were on the whole well content with the Canton system as just outlined, which was in effect a part of the old and well-tried mercantilist trade. But by the late eighteenth century the Industrial Revolution and the growing textile industry of the English Midlands were causing pressures for the abolition of monopoly in India and the expansion of free trade everywhere. The British government responded to these pressures by seeking to put the China trade on a basis more in conformity with new international custom as understood in Europe. The government incidentally had a considerable financial interest in the prosperity of the tea trade, for it levied a 100-percent duty on tea. Once the governments entered the act, the whole scene altered. The old ease of merchant-to-merchant contact on a purely profit basis was gone, and questions of national pride and the use of force began to predominate.

In 1793 Lord Macartney was sent as an official ambassador from George III to the emperor Qian Long, with a guard of soldiers and a large consignment of valuable presents. He was to request the opening of more ports such as Tientsin, an island depot for warehousing and ship repair, and especially a regular tariff of fixed customs dues and handling fees. He refused to perform the full *kowtow*, or prostration, before the emperor and was allowed to go down on one knee in the manner of an Englishman before a sovereign. His gifts were interpreted by the Chinese as tribute; George III doubtless felt it galling to be complimented on his "respectful submission." Macartney was told that the Chinese empire was not in any need of English goods; in fact, that the Canton trade could not be expanded or altered in any way. A subsequent embassy by Lord Amherst in 1816 fared no better.

Meanwhile the Canton trade was undergoing change on its own from within. The "country trade" was increasing in volume and importance relative to the company trade, and the "country traders," each on his own, were less concerned with policy and more with profit. Trade in opium increased in proportions alarming to the Chinese authorities: forty-fold from the late eighteenth century to the year 1838 (and at an equally steep rate thereafter, until it reached almost ninety-six times the eighteenth-century figure by 1873). In spite of constant official bans, smuggling of the drug spread widely for sale to lower government servants, soldiers, and even highly placed officials. Smuggling operations were extensive, and foreign traders began delivering opium at points along the coast north of the Canton estuary. An item as valuable as opium naturally increased that corruption in official circles which was already threatening the stability of the Manzhou dynasty. To this intolerably evil situation was added a further economic factor: the rise in the ratio of copper to silver in the Chinese currency. Taxes had to be paid in silver *taels*, and opium paid for in silver. Instead of 1,000 copper cash being required to make up one *tael*, the rate had risen to 1,800 or 2,000 cash to a *tael*. The Chinese were acutely aware of silver going out of the country to pay for opium and less aware of it coming in as exchange for tea. After 1830 there was a true net loss of silver leaving China, and the general alarm caused the Peking government at length to take stronger action.

This action consisted in the appointment to Canton in 1839 of a respected and incorruptible official, Lin Zexu, as commissioner, with overriding powers and orders to stop the importation and consumption of opium. Lin took strong and largely successful action against Chinese smugglers and opium traders. He also addressed two letters to Queen Victoria on the subject of opium, on the strength of some study he had made of Western practices in international law.

> The ways of God are without partiality; it is not permissible to injure another in order to profit oneself. . . .

> It appears that this particular form of poison [opium] is illegally prepared by scoundrels in the tributary tribes of your honourable country and in the

devilregions under your jurisdiction; but of course it is neither prepared nor sold by your sovereign orders. Further . . . that you do not allow your own people to smoke, under severe penalties for disobedience, evidently knowing what a curse it is and therefore strictly prohibiting the practice. But better still than forbidding people to smoke, would it not be to forbid the sale and also the preparation of opium? Surely this would be the method of purifying at the fountain-head. Not to smoke yourselves, but yet to dare to prepare and sell to and beguile the foolish masses of the Inner Land—this is to protect one's own life while leading others to death, to gather profit for oneself while bringing injury upon others. Such behaviour is repugnant to the feelings of human beings, and is not tolerated by the ways of God. . . . Our divine House controls the myriad nations by a spiritual majesty which is unfathomable; do not say that you were not warned in time! And on receipt of this letter, make haste to reply, stating the measures which have been adopted at all seaports for cutting off the supply. Do not falsely colour the matter nor procrastinate! Anxiously waiting; anxiously hoping.

2nd moon of the 19th year of Tao Kuang (1839).*

It is surely one of the supreme ironies of history that this irrefutable moral and religious appeal was addressed completely in vain to a queen who, of all the long roll of English sovereigns, prided herself the most upon her Christian convictions and moral principles. Queen Victoria probably never even saw the letters. The British government at this point decided it would do nothing about the supply or smuggling of opium.

Lin was determined to get control of the opium trade at the source and kept 350 foreign traders strictly confined and without Chinese servants for six weeks, until the British surrendered their stock of 20,000 chests of opium, which Lin then publicly destroyed. The British retreated to Macao and later to the island of Hongkong, from where they carried on trading operations, supplying the opium smugglers up the coast and securing cargoes of tea with the help of American firms as intermediaries.

The Chinese authorities had repeatedly refused to deal directly with the British government official, Captain Charles Elliot, superintendent of trade at Canton. They insisted that all negotiations, in line with the ancient tribute system, be conducted through a *hong* merchant. Lin's treatment of the foreign community, which to us appears morally justified, was in the nineteenth century construed as arrogant and led finally to hostilities. A British force was sent out, well equipped with armed steamships of shallow draft suitable for operations in estuaries and harbors, and during the years 1840–1842 established control over numerous ports from Canton to Shanghai. The British captured Chusan Island near Shanghai and began negotiations with the imperial government at a point off Tientsin, felt by the Chinese to be dangerously near the capital at Peking. Lin, for all his efforts, was considered to have failed in his

---

*Lin Zexu, translated in Giles, *Gems of Chinese Literature,* pp. 265–68.

objective of dealing with the foreigners and was temporarily disgraced, though subsequently reinstated in favor.

British efforts were intensified in 1841. There was little unity in the Chinese resistance. Secret societies supported smuggling operations, and mobs looted in the wake of British victories. The Manzhou dynasty felt it was losing control of its own subjects and gave in to the foreign enemy in order to maintain some semblance of authority and stability at home. The Treaty of Nanking concluded this strange and scattered war in August 1842 on terms highly favorable to Britain: the opening of five ports to trade (Canton, Amoy, Fuzhou, Ningpo, and Shanghai), the abolition of the Canton *hong* monopoly system, the institution of a fixed customs tariff of about 5 percent, and a large indemnity. No mention was made of opium, and the trade continued to flourish. Britain had led the way in forcibly changing the relations of China with the rest of the world, but other foreign nations immediately benefited by extracting the same conditions from China. Each treaty of a foreign power with China contained the "most favored nation" clause, which meant that any right given, even at a later date, to another power would automatically accrue to the signatory also.

One main cause of the war of 1839–1842, protection of the opium trade, makes this probably the least defensible war Britain has ever fought. But it would be an oversimplification to suppose that opium was the only issue at stake. The fluctuating exactions of the Canton officials, usually known as "squeeze," have already been mentioned as an irritant. In former days, monopoly on both the Chinese and British sides had been an accepted fact of life, but now new concepts of the desirability of international free trade were in the air. Widely divergent ideas of law and legal procedure formed a gulf between Chinese and British; these were not superficial but based upon different philosophies of life and views of society. The Chinese view was communal, the British individual. The Chinese official, who was administrator and sole judge in his district, was supposed to rule by example. Anyone accused of an offense or of any conduct outside the customary norms was assumed to have overstepped the mark in some way and to be guilty until he could establish his innocence. He could be imprisoned at the magistrate's pleasure and examined under torture. The British system operated through enactments and case law, presuming innocence until individual guilt was proven. A case in point was the dispute over the killing of a Chinese, Lin Weixi, by a party of English sailors in a drunken brawl in the summer of 1839. Captain Elliot held an official inquiry but could not fix the blame on any individual. He refused to hand over anyone to the Chinese authorities as a symbolic culprit. He also adhered to the existing British custom of not recognizing the competence of Chinese courts in disputes between British subjects and Chinese. Finally, the two sides differed in their approach to diplomatic representation, the Chinese trying to adhere to the tribute system based on the superiority of China, while the British tacitly assumed that the way to conduct international business was by exchange of plenipotentiaries between sovereign states which were all technically and by

"Foochow [Fuzhou]. Pagoda Anchorage." Pencil sketch from the diary of Private Allen Walter Bronson, U.S. Marine Corps, during the cruise of the USS *Alaska* on the Asiatic Station, 1870–73.

Note the British flag in this picture, the U.S. flag in the picture of Niuchuang (following). The *Alaska* must have touched at a number of ports that had just been opened up as a result of the Opium Wars. Niuchuang is in Manchuria and Fuzhou in south China.

U.S. Defense Department Photo (Marine Corps Museum)

protocol of equal status, although in fact the differences caused by the realities of power were always present.

The elements of Greek tragedy on a continental scale were thus present in the impact of the West upon China in the nineteenth century. It was not so much a matter of direct conflict as of two mutually incompatible views of life and society passing one another by without any contact, like ships in the night. The British made little attempt to comprehend the Chinese way of thinking, and the Chinese, compelled by *force majeure* to accept the Western viewpoint in practice, accumulated a sense of bitter resentment which has persisted over a century until the present day. Each side felt they and they only represented civilization, and each found examples proving their point conclusively, the British in the "barbarity" of Chinese law, and the Chinese in the burning and looting of the Summer Palace by British and French troops which was to take place in 1860. The incompetence of Chinese courts was erected into a principle and the Chinese forced to accept it by the incorporation of "extraterritoriality" in the series of foreign treaties, beginning with the Supplementary Treaty of the Bogue in 1843. Cases involving foreign nationals alone or foreign nationals and Chinese were to be decided by the consul concerned, according to the law

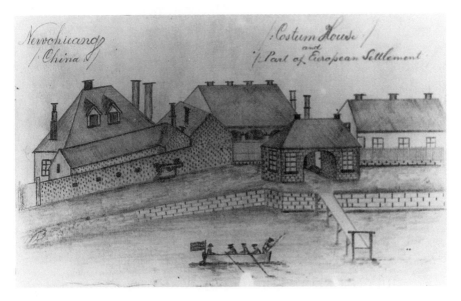

"Newchuang (Niuchuang), China: Costum [sic] House and Part of European Settlement." Pencil sketch also from the diary of Private Allen Walter Bronson, U.S. Marine
Corps, during the cruise of the USS *Alaska*, 1870–1873.

The ordinary man's view of China at that date did not extend much beyond the foreign sections of the port cities.

U.S. Defense Department Photo (Marine Corps Museum)

of his country. They were to be adjudicated on consular ground or in an international settlement leased from China, which was essentially "outside the territory" of China proper. When all factors are considered, there is in the end no
doubt that Great Britain, followed by the other Western powers, was guilty of
aggression and took every advantage of China's unpreparedness and weakness.

The years following 1842 were decisive in establishing the ascendency of
foreign modes of conducting trade, law, and diplomacy in China. The culmination of the process of extracting rights from China under the "unequal
treaties" came with the Anglo-French War of 1856–1860, sometimes called
the Second Opium War. The excuses for war this time were only slight, but the
underlying object was to ensure once and for all that the Chinese empire could
be counted on to conduct negotiations with other nations along accepted
Western lines. A Chinese-owned river vessel, the *Arrow*, was registered in
Hongkong and therefore flew the Union Jack. Chinese police had boarded the
ship and hauled down the flag, an insult for which the determined governor
general of Canton refused to offer apology to the equally determined British
consul, Harry Parkes. A French missionary, Father Chapdelaine, had been tortured and executed. Britain bombarded Canton and, when that proved ineffective, captured it outright in 1858. Lord Elgin from Britain and Baron Gros
from France proceeded in force to Tientsin and there extracted the right to

place ministers of their respective countries on a permanent basis of diplomatic equality at Peking. A year later, however, the Chinese court refused ratification of this Treaty of Tientsin, and the ministers found their way to Peking barred. Moreover, four British gunboats were sunk by gunfire from the Dagu forts near Tientsin. In 1860 the British and French returned in overwhelming force. The emperor and his court fled northward to Rehol, and Prince Gong, the emperor's brother, was compelled to ratify the treaty, to which a higher indemnity was now attached. The priceless treasures of the Summer Palace were looted, and the buildings erected there under the guidance of the Jesuits were put to the flames as an act of vengeance. Ten further ports were opened to foreign trade, and the right of travel and residence in the interior of China given to missionaries and traders.

REBELLION

During the later phases of these harassing problems of foreign relations, the Qing dynasty was seriously threatened by a large-scale revolt, the Taiping Rebellion, which lasted from 1850 to 1864. It may be considered both a symptom and a cause of further dynastic decline. Peasant discontent had frequently in China's past gathered and been fomented under the aegis of religion. Desperation found outlet in messianic hopes, and religious observances provided a rallying point for the disaffected in a monolithic state which permitted no political party organization. Thus the Yellow Turbans, in the Han dynasty, and the White Lotus, traceable from the twelfth to the nineteenth centuries, were anti-dynastic secret societies under Daoist and Buddhist auspices respectively. The *Taiping Tianguo* (Heavenly Kingdom of Great Peace) was distinctive in that it owed its origin to Christian ideas, though these were only partially adopted. The name Heavenly Kingdom reflected the New Testament, although in fact Old Testament ideas predominated in the resulting structure, while Great Peace was a utopian notion of a time of justice and purity which had found expression under the same name in the Han and Tang dynasties.

The founder of this remarkable movement was a disappointed scholar, Hong Xiuchuan (1813–1864), who had had contact with an American missionary, Issachar J. Roberts. During an illness Hong had seen visions and subsequently interpreted these along Christian lines suggested by some tracts he had in his house. He felt called as the Younger Brother of Jesus Christ to save the Chinese people from their plight, which was the work of the devil. The movement, first called *Bai Shang Di Hui* (Worship God Society) would scarcely have succeeded had there not been to hand a means to power in the form of militia bands, which arose for the maintenance of local law and order where central control was weak, as in the province of Guangxi in south China at this time. To these bands could be added desperate men who were unemployed. Changing patterns of trade brought about by the new foreign commerce at the treaty ports made for economic distress among large numbers in the eastern part of the province where Hong was spreading his message. His combination of religious fervor and anti-Manzhou incitement appealed to boatmen and coolies out of work, miners, charcoal burners, and poor peasants who were often reduced to becoming bandits. The converts, who in three years numbered 30,000, received occasional support from members of secret societies who were even more anti-Manzhou, and the movement became organized along military lines. The members abandoned the queue, which was a sign of subservience to the Manzhou (they were known as "long-haired bandits"), held goods in common, and organized the equal distribution of land. Under what the founder claimed to be a theocracy, the members lived by puritan standards in which chastity was demanded of men and women, divided into separate bands. There was complete equality for women, who were organized into regiments for war and squads for labor just as the men were. Concubinage and foot binding were forbidden, as was the use of alcohol, tobacco, and opium.

In 1851 Hong changed the title from Worship God Society to Heavenly Kingdom of Great Peace and announced himself as Heavenly King (Tian Wang) with five other kings to assist him. One of these, Yang Xiuqing, a capable general and organizer, was appointed commander in chief. In 1852 the rebel army moved north, turned down the Yangzi River, and the next year captured Nanjing, which thenceforward formed the base of operations. The Taipings were extraordinarily successful. Government troops were at first quite ineffective, and the dynasty was in an embarrassing position because of the disruption of transport north from the rich Yangzi basin and the serious loss of tax income. Taipings were to be found at one period or another in all but two of the provinces of China and gained possession, though not all at the same time, of six hundred walled cities. The loss of life consequent upon the revolt was aggravated by a disastrous natural occurrence, floods caused by the alteration of course of the Yellow River in finding its way to the sea to the north instead of the south of the Shandong Peninsula. The process began in 1855, but the new riverbed was not finally brought under control until 1870.

A Taiping expedition north of Nanjing was defeated in Shandong in 1855. Gradually the military tide began to turn in favor of the reigning dynasty. The credit for this should go not so much to the central government as to the provincial leaders and the local scholar gentry, in particular to three great names, all of whom had a decisive influence upon later history: Zeng Guofan (1811–1872), who recaptured Wuchang in 1854 and took a fleet down the Yangzi to threaten Nanjing; Zuo Zongtang (1812–1885); and Li Hongzhang (1823–1901), a protégé of Zeng. All three commanders cooperated in a systematic reconquest of the central area of China held most strongly by the rebels. All three used various combinations of Western guns, ships, and troop-training methods with success. There were other factors in the eventual defeat of the Taipings. Their philosophy alienated the gentry, and thus the rebels lacked skilled manpower to set up civil administration in the wake of their conquests. The middle landowners were alarmed by the forcible redistribution of farmland. The Taiping armies lacked mobility since they had no cavalry. The Western powers, at first watching the struggle from the sidelines, came out for the dynasty in 1862 when they felt Shanghai was threatened. A mixed Chinese and foreign force under the leadership of F. T. Ward of Salem, Massachusetts, and then of Major Charles George Gordon (subsequently governor general of the Sudan) was recruited for the defense of the Shanghai hinterland and became known as the Ever Victorious Army. Perhaps most serious of all there was dissension among the kings, who, in contrast to the rank and file, kept harems and much of the apparatus of luxury and power. Corruption and rivalry ended in murder plots and counterplots. In July 1864 the *coup de grâce* was dealt the Heavenly Kingdom through the hard-won capture of Nanjing by Zeng Guofan's younger brother. Hong Xiuchuan took poison, and a great experiment ended.

The present leaders of the People's Republic of China have taken a favorable view of the Taiping Rebellion, and indeed there are similarities between it and the modern Communist movement: the aim of an ideal social order, a powerful force of soldier farmers, a strict ideological stand, anti-Confucian tendencies, an admiration of discipline, and a sense of purpose and higher destiny reaching down to the rank and file in a manner rarely seen in traditional China.

There were other revolts going on at the same time as the Taiping Rebellion. The Nian Rebellion (1853–1868) in the north China plain was touched off by the Taiping northern expedition, but the two rebellions never succeeded in coordinating their efforts fully. The Nian (meaning "bands") made use of fortified villages and cavalry mobility to build up an area of power virtually independent of the dynasty, but they acted in a piecemeal fashion and lacked central direction. Zeng Guofan, and later Li Hongzhang, managed to surround the rebel strongholds and suppress the Nian Rebellion in 1868. A Muslim rebellion in the northwest ran from 1868 to 1873, while in the southwest other Muslims were in revolt from 1856 until 1873.

THE EARLY MODERNIZATION OF CHINA

When the fires of all these rebellions were extinguished, it may be imagined with what relief the reestablishment of dynastic control was welcomed by the scholar class throughout the empire. The new era of internal peace beginning in the 1860s was sufficiently notable to be given a title drawn from the name of the reigning emperor, the Tong Zhi Restoration. This restoration took the form of a revitalizing of Confucian principles, and its very success complicated and probably delayed the modernization of China in the latter part of the nineteenth century. The antecedents of the Tong Zhi Restoration included two new intellectual trends which had been building up over a period. From the late seventeenth century the "new text" school had criticized the orthodox "old text" of the classics (see page 66), had claimed to find earlier and more authentic versions, and had produced entirely new interpretations. This was not a merely academic matter, for the new interpretations of the classics were applied to contemporary politics in a critical manner and served to break open the closed circle of standard and sterile Neo-Confucian orthodoxy of the Song period which had dominated the political scene. The second new trend appeared in the early nineteenth century and is known as the school of "statecraft." Some of the more intelligent and forward-looking of the scholar officials, faced with corruption, rebellion, and the problem of dynastic decline, attempted, still entirely upon a Confucian basis, to apply thought and reason in a fresh way to the practical problems of administration.

Wei Yuan (1794–1857) was an influential writer on geographical and historical subjects who was active in both the "new text" and "statecraft" movements. He had practical experience in the First Opium War and the suppression of the Taiping Rebellion, and his illustrated book on overseas countries had considerable influence in both China and Japan. Commissioner Lin Zexu, Zeng Guofan, and Li Hongzhang were all identified with the school of "statecraft," and all sought to apply its principles to cope with the new and pressing problem of foreign aggression. At the point of early crisis, the First Opium War, Wei Yuan had stressed an old Chinese strategic principle, "Use barbarians to control barbarians," and he had also recommended the use of Western arms and military methods to contain and suppress widespread rebellion. Thus the application of "statecraft" resulted in the recognition of the value of Western technology but at the same time confirmed its proponents in their belief in the superiority of Chinese culture and the Confucian way of life. The call was for "self-strengthening," by which was meant the use of all valid means, including Western weapons and devices, to maintain the Chinese empire in its existing form. With the comparative success of the Tong Zhi Restoration there seemed to be no reason to alter the empire's fundamental assumptions. This idea was summed up in the last decade of the century in the widely current epigram, "Chinese learning for substance (or essence, t'i); Western learning for use (or application, yong)." Wholesale, radical modernization or Westernization was thus never seriously entertained as an aim among the leaders of China in the nineteenth century.

At the same time considerable progress was made in several areas, the technical sphere not least, during the last forty years of the century. Significant pioneering examples of Western technology are associated with the career of Li Hongzhang, and these may be taken as typical of a continuing movement.

Li and his patron Zeng Guofan at first bought overseas arms for their troops and then established arsenals for Chinese production at Xuzhou, Nanjing, and other centers. These smaller establishments were superseded in 1865 by the large Jiangnan Arsenal located at Shanghai. This factory, one of the largest of its kind in the world, produced not only arms and ammunition but also machine tools and the first Chinese-built steamship. Zuo Zongtang set up another arsenal and a navy yard at Fuzhou with the cooperation of the French. Li moved into the sphere of civilian industry and commerce with the floating of the China Merchants' Steam Navigation Company in 1872, which bought out the American firm of Russell and Company and successfully rivaled the

British firms of Jardine, Matheson and Butterfield and Swire in river and coastal steamer service. The functioning of the firm was in a traditional Chinese mode, "government supervision and merchant operation." This had advantages, such as the guarantee of government contracts for the conveyance of tribute rice, but also disadvantages, such as unwillingness to take risks for development, and the quick dissemination of profits instead of ploughing a proportion back into the business. It was lack of official foresight on the last count which enabled the British firms in the end to regain their ascendancy in the shipping trade, in spite of good early direction of the China Merchants line by the British-trained manager, Tong Jingsing.

Li Hongzhang was stationed in Tientsin as governor general of the capital province from 1870 to 1895, and this enabled him to develop with some degree of stability several industrial enterprises in the north. A coal mine with modern machinery at Kaiping produced coal for the shipping line, and a rail-

A back street in Peking, 1860.

The covered cart on the extreme right, typical of north China, is standing outside an inn whose sign indicates that overnight lodging and meals are provided. The wooden lattice windows, such as those on the left were commonly backed with translucent paper, which lets in some of the light and keeps out some of the cold. Temperatures in the Peking winter drop well below zero degrees Fahrenheit.

Library of Congress

way distributed coal and other goods to Tientsin, Shanhaiguan at the Manchurian border, and Peking. Railway development was slow, but telegraph lines, also initiated by Li and extended by provincial authorities, provided 34,000 miles of communication between many of the main cities by 1900. Cotton mills made a late start, but by 1894 five were in operation.

Telegraph links proved troublesome and expensive at first. Thinking they disturbed the "spirits of wind and water"—and indeed childhood memories do conjure up nameless mysteries connected with the humming of the wires—the farmers simply cut the poles down. The resale value of copper wire may have reinforced this purifying zeal; in any case, the government had for some time to provide soldiers to guard the telegraph lines.

The Western impact on China has been stressed in this chapter because of its ultimate effect on China's development and because of its intrinsic interest to the Western reader. But it should be borne in mind that this impact had very little effect on the average Chinese in any village or town in the interior during most of the nineteenth century. Life in the traditional style was still the norm for peasant, merchant, and official alike. It was only after about 1865 that the influence of the West began to be felt at all widely through the gradual spread of Western trade goods, travel, and the residence of missionaries and others in the interior, and the hesitant moves toward modernization being made by a few leading authorities such as Li Hongzhang.

Certain groups and individuals can be identified through whom Western influences were mediated to the Chinese. One of the most significant was the efficient organization known as the Maritime Customs Service. In order to prevent evasions and irregularities in the collection of customs dues at Shanghai, the British consul, Rutherford Alcock, made an amicable arrangement in 1853 with the responsible Chinese official to have a foreign inspector check the collections, control the foreign merchants, and remit the dues to the Chinese authorities. An ambitious young Britisher, H. N. Lay, was appointed as foreign inspector and by 1861 had taken part in the formation of a full-fledged customs service, of which he was made inspector general. Lay was also instrumental in securing from British shipyards a fleet of eight gunboats for the Chinese government, but it was discovered that he had planned to have all orders from the Chinese authorities to the flotilla commander transferred through himself. This fact and his high-handed conduct in the customs service clearly made him an unsuitable choice for the highest customs post, and he was replaced in 1863 by Robert Hart (1835–1911), who had already been a foreign inspector of customs at Canton.

Hart by contrast saw himself and his foreign staff as servants of the Chinese government, and throughout his life (he served until 1908) he set an example of hard work and scrupulous fairness. By 1875 the foreigners in the service numbered over four hundred, the majority being British. The morale of the service as a whole was high, and the large numbers of Chinese employed received a good technical training and a thorough acquaintance with Western business methods in their best form. The Maritime Customs Service performed numerous tasks beyond the collection of dues. These included duties normally associated with a coast guard service, such as the dredging of channels, charting of waterways, provision of lighthouses, buoys, and wharf and harbor facilities, and financial management of a somewhat complicated nature. Although financial matters were handled with commendable honesty, the power of the foreign-directed customs service represented an encroachment on Chinese sovereignty, since foreign loans and indemnities owing to foreign countries were frequently by treaty made a first charge on the customs revenue, only the balance being payable to the Chinese government. After the crushing indemnity demanded following the Boxer Rebellion (225 million ounces of silver paid between 1902 and 1910, in addition to numerous earlier indemnities), the total maritime customs revenues were actually insufficient, and salt tax and other internal taxes also had to be paid over to meet foreign requirements. All these arrangements were deeply resented by patriotic Chinese. By using the customs network and by bringing in private systems, Hart set up a postal service in 1896, which became a fully independent post office in 1911. The court placed a great deal of trust in Sir Robert Hart, as he later became, and consulted him on many matters involving foreign relations.

The second group to familiarize the Chinese with Western methods were the traders. Among early well-known British firms (some of them already mentioned) were Jardine, Matheson, still operating in Hongkong; Butterfield and Swire; Dent and Company; and the Hongkong and Shanghai Banking Corporation, formed in 1865. The most famous American firm was Russell and Company, which became the China Merchants' Steam Navigation Company and ran a successful river service on the Yangzi from Shanghai to Hankou. From the Chinese viewpoint the key person in each of these enterprises was not the foreign director but the senior Chinese known by the Portuguese title of "comprador." The comprador hired and fired the Chinese staff and acted as their guarantor, from the educated clerks and translators in the office to the guards and coolies in the "godowns" (warehouses). He made sales arrangements with the Chinese market in city and hinterland and acted as go-between in a multitude of ways where the foreign world of commerce and the society of China, so odd and unpredictable to the Westerner, came into contact. He thus received unrivaled training and experience enabling him to go into this new type of business on his own. He also made an important contribution to mutual understanding across a difficult cultural boundary line. Existent Chinese business skills, augmented by the presence of the new compradors and their clerks, made it unnecessary and unprofitable for Western firms to set up many branches in the interior. Their head offices in the port cities were able to operate through a distribution network which was soon manned entirely by Chinese.

The third and most widespread agent of change was the Christian church and its missionaries. The Roman Catholics began the nineteenth century with a comparatively large number of scattered adherents, perhaps between 150,000 and 200,000, remaining from the earlier days of missions in China.

The Protestants began work with the coming of the first missionary, Robert Morrison, who was sent by the London Missionary Society and arrived in Canton in 1807. He maintained his position by acting as a translator for the East India Company and worked on the production of Christian literature. He compiled the first Chinese-English dictionary and translated the Bible into Chinese. A colleague sent to support him was not allowed to stay and retreated to the British port of Malacca to work among overseas Chinese. The earliest group from the United States was the American Board (Congregationalist), but soon there were numerous churches represented, from Britain, America, and the continent of Europe. Protestant missionaries in China numbered under 200 in 1864 but had increased to about 1,300 by 1890. Full communicants of the Protestant churches were only 55,000 in 1893 but by 1914 were reckoned at over 250,000. The Roman Catholic membership increased rapidly, multiplying seven times in the century between 1812 and 1912 and reaching 1.4 million by the latter date. Numbers only tell part of the tale. Calculations were made in different ways, by individuals among Protestants, by all members of a household among Catholics. Referring for a moment to a later date, the total number of all Christian church members in China by the 1930s was only about 1 percent of the population, but the influence of Christianity among the leaders was greater than the figure would indicate, since the ratio of those of the Christian faith listed in the Chinese equivalent of *Who's Who* was 16 percent.

The whole subject of missionary work and religious propaganda has become a controversial one, owing to a major shift in world public opinion in the last forty years and the present greater respect for national heritages. Omission of the topic is, however, impossible even in a short cultural history of China. Recently, serious objective study has been undertaken of the historical contribution of missionaries in China and of the reactions of the Chinese, positive and negative, to their presence. Some of the salient factors may be summarized. Prior to 1900 the majority of the Protestant churches operated in or near the port cities, whereas the Roman Catholics and a strong evangelical Protestant body, the China Inland Mission founded by Hudson Taylor, were to be found deep in the interior. There the risks of war, riot, and famine were much greater, and missionaries had sometimes to be rescued and removed by gunboat or by contingents of foreign troops. France in particular made a point of championing the Catholic missionaries in China, but even Hudson Taylor, mobbed near Yangzhou, was the recipient of help from four gunboats sent by Rutherford Alcock, British consul at Shanghai, to insist on the dismissal of local officials for negligence. The unpopular umbrella of extraterritorial privilege was sometimes extended to cover not only foreign missionaries but also their Chinese converts. It was hard for the foreigners, especially in the early days, to distinguish between genuine converts and "rice Christians," those who came into the church for what they could get out of it. In this way quite unwarranted foreign help was occasionally given to undeserving Chinese who used mission support in their disputes with local officials, but instances such as these were the exception rather than the rule. The right to ownership of land and buildings in the interior, extended to foreigners by the Treaty of Tientsin in 1858, gave rise to numerous difficulties. Indemnities exacted from China for incidents involving missionaries and the local Chinese population between 1862 and 1869 amounted to the large sum of 400,000 ounces of silver.

There were also, however, a number of positive factors to be found in the coming of the churches to China. Missionary schools and later universities, such as Yenjing University in Peking and its associated Harvard-Yenjing Institute, made a notable contribution to Chinese education, not only in knowledge of the West but in raising standards for modern education. Schools for girls in China, as in many other countries, were pioneered by the churches. Hospitals open to all, the training of doctors and nurses and the promotion of public health, technical training in engineering and agriculture, the advancement of science, as in the famous Jesuit center at Zikawei near Shanghai, the setting up of orphanages and institutions for the blind and the insane—all these at one period or another from the mid-nineteenth century until World War II were recognized contributions of the Christian church.

Quite apart from the social benefits of Christianity, a number of Chinese found in the faith itself a religious appeal which was missing in the contemporary scene. Confucianism seemed less and less adequate as the empire declined before their eyes and was succeeded by a warlord era, popular Daoism was hopelessly superstitious, and Buddhism, in itself a profound religion, was not held in high esteem in China in the later centuries and had not been reinterpreted in the light of modern thought to the extent that Christianity had been. The mainstream Christian churches had a distinct appeal to certain Chinese in that they presented a faith and way of life which had relevance to the contemporary world, which was not iconoclastic but represented the fulfillment of certain Chinese ideals, and which took account of national aspirations. Chinese Christians played a significant part in the Republican Revolution of 1911. The missionaries gradually succeeded in disassociating themselves from dependence on consular aid and from identification with the policies of their respective foreign governments. Not enough was done to present Christianity in an oriental rather than a Western dress in music, architecture, and the arts, but devolution of authority and financial management to indigenous control, a practice now insisted upon in every country, was already well begun in China by the 1930s.

Timothy Richard (1832–1919) and the Christian Literature Society made available from the end of the nineteenth century not only religious but secular knowledge. The determination of Christians that the Bible should be available to the people in their own tongue resulted in an important indirect contribution to modern Chinese culture. The use of colloquial written language in translations of the Bible marked the first successful major departure from the classical literary language accessible only to scholars (the language of the Chinese novel of the Ming and Qing eras is in a separate category), and contributed not a little to the Chinese literary renaissance associated with the scholar Hu Shi and others from 1915 on. All newspapers, magazines, and books in China now use only colloquial written Chinese *(bai hua wen)*. In this respect the Chinese Bible may be distantly compared for its effect upon language to the famous King James or Authorized Version of the Bible of 1611 on the English language.

The very success of these examples of the social outreach of the Christian church in China engendered hostility among the scholar-gentry class. They felt that the territory of their privileges and age-old obligations to promote schools, orphanages, famine relief, and other community services was being seriously invaded. Certain of them put out pamphlets containing scurrilous charges against missionaries and Chinese Christians, such as accusations that orphan children received by nuns were being starved or killed and their hearts used for purposes of sorcery or even their eyes for camera lenses. The nuns' custom of giving a small cash reward to finders of unwanted children unfortunately lent color to the charge that the children were being "bought."

A convent orphanage was involved in one major incident, the Tientsin Massacre of 1870. Incited by rumors of witchcraft, a crowd of Chinese demonstrators led by a local official advanced upon the orphanage. The French consul, who was present, lost his head and ordered his guards to fire. The angry crowd then attacked and destroyed the orphanage, killing twenty foreigners, including the consul and ten nuns. France demanded the execution of eighteen Chinese, a mission of apology, and a large indemnity. It was curious to note that, on a recent visit of the writer to Canton, rumors of the mistreatment of orphans by missionaries were still circulating and were repeated with every appearance of conviction by an intelligent government interpreter in the People's Republic today.

The last group of note in the interaction between China and the West were the botanists. The first English collector was a surgeon, James Cuningham, who lived in China from 1698 to 1708. Chinese plants, along with other things Chinese, became fashionable; the naturalist Sir Joseph Banks took to his English garden the Chinese monthly rose, ancestor of all modern tea roses, the tree peony, and the chrysanthemum. (The last had been known to the Dutch earlier but all the strains brought to Holland had died.) Following the First Opium War, the Scottish botanist Robert Fortune was sent to China specifically for botanical purposes and introduced into England anemones, forsythias, rhododendrons, and umbrella pines, among many other plants. Clematis, asters, and azaleas followed. A Chinese wistaria planted in Chiswick in 1818 was still blooming profusely over a century later. And in the early twentieth century one of the greatest of all botanical explorers, E. H. Wilson, made a thorough study of the vast botanical riches of west China. The traffic was not all one-way, for Western botanists not only took plants out of China but brought knowledge and training to a new generation of Chinese botanical scholars, who were thus able to build afresh upon a long tradition of botanical records, illustrations, and experiments in China's past.

THE END OF THE EMPIRE

We now approach the final phase in the downfall of the Manzhou dynasty and of the Chinese empire as an institution. This took place in the two decades from the early 1890s to the year 1911 and contained a repeat of the main nineteenth-century pattern of foreign attack and internal rebellion. The debacle was made more complete by the fact that the center of power in the court at Peking was to a great extent out of touch with reality. Comprehension of the rest of the world and measures to meet the radically new situation were to be found among certain regional leaders, whose efforts at modernization have been touched upon. The court contained a few who read the signs of the times, such as Prince Gong, brother of the Emperor Xian Feng (reigned 1851–1862), but the majority of his fellow Manzhou and many of the Chinese officials were both blind and reactionary. Too many persons, including the eunuchs and palace officials, had too big a stake in the continuation of the status quo.

The leader of the forces of reaction was that formidable personality, the empress dowager Cixi (1835–1908). She began her palace life as a minor concubine at the age of sixteen but rose to prominence as the mother of the emperor Xian Feng's only son and became coregent for this son, the emperor

Prince Gong (Kung).

Very few principal court figures or high officials were photographed in the early 1870s, when this picture was taken. The Manzhou prince, shown in informal dress, was the most progressive of the imperial family, but here he seems to brood uncertainly over China's future.

Photo: J. Thomson, London, 1873; Stuart Collection, Rare Book Division, The New York Public Library, Astor, Lenox and Tilden Foundations

Tong Zhi, when Xian Feng died. She had a remarkably acute political instinct, a ruthless streak, few scruples, and an inordinate love of wealth and power. Passionately fond of theatrical performances, she indulged this whim in the company of two different palace eunuchs, who in succession became powerful and rich through her patronage to the detriment of the state and the disgust of the officials. Although Cixi had little grasp of the nature of the Western impact on China, her political sense caused her to see the value of the efforts of Prince Gong to steer a wise course in implementing the foreign treaties, and of Li Hongzhang in his adoption of many aspects of Western technology.

Prince Gong had had to act as head of state when the court fled Peking at the time of the Anglo-French War in 1860, and he had been compelled to acquiesce in the demand for the permanent residence of foreign diplomats at the capital. In order to handle the resulting business of foreign relations, he had been instrumental in setting up the Zong-li Yamen, or Office for General Affairs, in 1861. This body, with rapid access to the throne and named in this intentionally vague way, was an ad hoc creation, designed not to disturb the pattern of the traditional Chinese government ministries yet to deal with the troublesome foreigners expeditiously and quietly at the top level of the administration. Although the empress dowager respected Prince Gong's contribution, the two did not see eye to eye. French victories in the Sino-French War of 1883–1885, fought over the control of Vietnam, gave the empress dowager an excuse to dismiss Prince Gong, and she arranged in 1884 for him to be succeeded in charge of the Office for General Affairs by a more pliant official, Prince Chun.

The difficulties attending international relations, even twenty years after the institution of the Office for General Affairs, may be deduced from some casual remarks of one of the members, Weng Tonghe, a distinguished official, imperial tutor, and president of the Board of Revenue. Weng attended a New Year reception for the diplomatic corps and confided to his diary the opinion that they were like "a confused flock of geese and ducks." After taking part in negotiating railway and mining concessions, he said the foreigners were "greedy like wolves and stubborn like goats—truly not of our kind!"[*] He felt he was "associating with dogs and swine—a misfortune in a man's life."[†] It is therefore small wonder that the Qing government was in turn hard put to it to find officials willing to go abroad as diplomatic representatives of China.

The young emperor, Tong Zhi, was completely dominated by his overpowering mother. He led a dissolute life, in which Cixi is rumored to have encouraged him in order to serve her own ends. In any event he died at the age of nineteen and was succeeded by the Emperor Guangxu (reigned 1875–1908). The elevation of this emperor as a four-year-old boy was patently engineered by Cixi, for this enabled her once more to enjoy the role of coregent. She was in no way deterred by the fact that he was her nephew and not

---

[*]Quoted in Immanuel C. Y. Hsü, *Readings in Modern Chinese History*, p. 323.
[†]Ibid.

of the correct generation; the new occupant of the throne should have belonged to the generation below that of the late emperor, in order to satisfy the requirements of ancestor worship.

The cooperation of Li Hongzhang with the empress dowager was much closer than that of Prince Gong. He had been the hero at the time of the suppression of the Taiping Rebellion, and he had continued to earn the gratitude of the court for his ability to make the best bargains possible with the foreigners. He seemed able to use Western inventions to advantage while remaining loyal to the dynasty and in particular to the empress dowager. The progress of the Chinese navy provides a good example of Li's strength and weakness. There were four separate fleets, based at Canton, Fuzhou, Shanghai, and Tientsin. The Beiyang fleet at Tientsin, of which Li was commissioner, received the greatest financial support and was much the most powerful. But about 1890 the funds began to dry up. Encouraged by her eunuch favorite, Cixi was building a new and magnificent Summer Palace outside Peking, for which naval funds were appropriated with Li Hongzhang's connivance. The only boat involved was a marble one which never moved from the edge of the ornamental lake. No additions or replacements were made to the Beiyang fleet.

At this point Japan struck. The first Sino-Japanese war of 1894–1895 was the beginning of a series of encroachments on China's traditional tributary state, Korea, and on the territory of China herself, encroachments which were to become ever more serious until the end of World War II. And Japan's crucial victories in her early years of empire were won at sea. The origins of the conflict of 1894 were complicated and involved a pro-Japanese modernizing party and a pro-Chinese conservative one at the Korean court. During the summer large numbers of troops from Japan and some from China were sent into Korea, and on August 1 the Japanese compelled the Korean regent to declare war on China. The Japanese were soon in control of south Korea and the capital, Seoul. They captured Pyongyang in the north in September. The Chinese pinned their hopes on the Beiyang fleet, which moved into action off the mouth of the Yalu River. Foreign opinion expected China to be victorious at sea, since her total naval strength was greater, but only the Beiyang contingent was committed to the Yalu River battle. China held superiority in size of ships and caliber of guns. Japan's advantages lay in the speed of her vessels, the rapidity of their fire, but above all in the quality of her men in tactics and training. The Chinese admiral, a protégé of Li Hongzhang, had more show than substance. It is said he could not communicate with the British gunnery officer on his flagship; the language barrier became of less importance when the bridge was hit by a shell fired by their own side and both men became casualties. The Japanese steamed around the Chinese fleet and inflicted severe damage while incurring only light losses themselves. They forced the remaining Chinese ships to flee to Weihaiwei in Shandong, where they were later destroyed. Port Arthur in Manchuria was captured from the landward direction in the same manner as Singapore in World War II, since in both naval bases all gun emplacements were aimed toward the sea.

The aging Li Hongzhang was compelled to sue for peace on behalf of China and at length met with the Japanese plenipotentiary, Ito Hirobumi, at Shimonoseki in the spring of 1895. Li was wounded in an assassination attempt, and the Japanese in embarrassment reduced the terms. They were severe enough: recognition of the independence of Korea (Japan annexed the country outright in 1910); the cession of Taiwan, the Pescadores, and the Liaodong peninsula in south Manchuria; a commercial treaty of great advantage to Japan; the opening of more ports; and a heavy indemnity. Russia, Germany, and France combined to force Japan to give up her demand for the Liaodong peninsula in exchange for a larger indemnity. The Japanese were understandably incensed when Russia followed up by increasing her own pressures for railway concessions in Manchuria.

The war of 1894–1895 was a spectacular proving ground for the modernizing efforts of both China and Japan and, as such, was watched closely by many other interested parties. China had actually invested greater sums in naval and military development and built up her weapons technology to a greater extent and at a slightly earlier period. But if an overall comparison is made for the second half of the nineteenth century, Japan emerges as the stronger nation by reason of such comparisons as follow. Japan had the advantage of strong government direction and central planning, while China's efforts were conducted with varying success by regional authorities with little support and no coordination from the Manzhou court at the center. Japan's modernization was deliberate, China's reluctant. Japan's students profited by their training; China's, while equally intelligent, were often hampered by official equivocation and incompetence. Financially Japan tightened her belt, taxed her farmers, made a united national effort, and so remained comparatively free of the load of foreign indebtedness and retained her independence. China was overwhelmed by the burden of indemnities and the repayment of overseas loans. Finally, Japan, served by a remarkable group of young samurai-turned-statesmen, grasped at an early stage the vital principle that with the Western bag of tools goes a way of life, which must be understood as a whole, even if it is not uncritically adopted. A modern army and navy as protection for a modern state presupposes the underpinning not only of a well-rounded industrial complex but also of a set of ideas in education, law, and administration which will be viable in the common world of international relations. China, by contrast, for all her size, potential strength, and intellectual brilliance, stumbled onto the scene, modernizing piecemeal, with no unified, enthusiastic leadership or any coordinated policy.

China's humiliating defeat in Korea in 1895 spread shock waves among reformers and conservatives alike. By the spring of 1898, as foreign powers exacted territorial concessions, an atmosphere of crisis emerged at the capital. Self-strengthening in the sense of gradual industrialization had been going on in the earlier decades, but now, with the new sense of urgency, a more radical reformer, Kang Youwei (1858–1927), and others saw their opportunity. The empress dowager having gone into retirement in 1889, the reformers gained access to the emperor Guangxu and persuaded him to promulgate a series of far-reaching reforms in a brief period called the Hundred Days Reform from June to September 1898. These included overhaul of the official examination system, with the introduction of practical subjects; the creation of modern schools; the planned abolition of sinecures, bureaucratic waste, and corruption; the introduction of Western military training; the advocacy of a free press; the adoption of an annual budget; and improvements in agriculture, roads, and railways. It was an ambitious scheme. Much of it, however desirable, could exist only on paper, since adequate support in official opinion, preparation, and finance was lacking. Kang Youwei had ideas of a socialist utopia which went far beyond the reforms listed and which were only published in 1935 after his death—including the abolition of separate nations, private property, and family, the last to be effected through communal dormitories, restaurants, and nurseries, with temporary and changing cohabitation for one year as a replacement for marriage. The leader of the party of more moderate reform was Zhang Zhidong, whose aims were a revival of Confucianism once again, reforms in education to include traditional Chinese and Western learning, and progress in industrialization. Upon the last subject Zhang's own achievements in promoting mining, iron, steel, and weapons manufacture gave him some title to speak. Opposition gathered to the reform measures promulgated by the emperor at Kang Youwei's instigation. Then in September 1898 the empress dowager, when she judged the moment ripe, came out of retirement and with dramatic suddenness had the emperor seized and six of the reformers executed. The two principals, Kang Youwei and Liang Qichao, barely managed to escape to Japan. The Hundred Days were over almost before they had begun.

Forcible suppression of reform at the top did not cure the worsening malaise of the land as a whole. Rebellion was again stirring under the banner of the Righteous and Harmonious Fists (*I Ho Chuan*), usually known as the Boxers. The strange title enshrined a very ancient belief, that by calisthenic exercises the ascendancy of mind over matter could be established. By undergoing training in a traditional form of shadow-boxing, an athletic ballet with swift, complex movements and an elaborate pattern of held pauses, accompanied by the use of magic charms and trances, the devotees were taught they could be victorious and that even foreign rifle bullets would bounce harmlessly off them. The wide extent of this rebellion shows to what a minute degree modern ideas had spread among the Chinese peasantry and indeed among higher circles by the year 1898. As in former rebellions, flood and famine conditions rendered many peasants desperate. But there were new factors. The sale of imported cloth and kerosene oil and the increased use of steamers and railways instead of boatmen and porters had led to unemployment. Fear that railway and telegraph construction was offending local gods and spirits was an element in rising discontent, and resentment against missionaries and Chinese Christians became a dominant feature of the rebellion. Conservative Manzhou and Chinese at court sympathized with these latter aims of the Boxers; their

support, and ultimately that of the empress dowager herself, turned the movement from being anti-dynastic to being purely anti-foreign. Beginning in
Shandong in 1898, the Boxers spread over north China, attacking railways,
factories, and shops which sold foreign goods. They killed missionaries and
Chinese converts, the latter in large numbers.

Shandong was a province which had been a cradle of revolution earlier in
Chinese history; it was also a place where foreign aggression had been particularly noticeable, for the Germans had secured the port of Jiaozhou and the
concession for a railway, while the British used Weihaiwei for a naval base. The
Manzhou governor of the province, Yu-xian, encouraged the Boxers, but
when foreign objections caused him to be removed, the new governor, Yuan
Shikai, reversed this policy and drove the rebels out of the province altogether.
The equivocal attitude of the court is to be seen in the fact that Yu-xian was
soon appointed to be governor of Shanxi, where later he was officially present
at the execution of forty-six foreigners, mainly missionaries.

In June of 1900 the struggle became more bitter. In Peking itself Christians were massacred and buildings burned, the foreign settlements in
Tientsin were besieged, a foreign naval force seized the Dagu forts on the
river there, and a land force on its way to Peking was attacked not by rebels
but by imperial troops and forced to retreat. On June 20 the German minister in Peking, Baron Klemens von Ketteler, was shot and killed, and the next
day the court declared war on the foreign powers. At this point the Boxers,
backed by imperial troops, besieged the Legation Quarter. There was considerable hardship owing to lack of food and a number of casualties, among
them Chinese Christians who had been brought to the quarter for protection. There were divided counsels among the Chinese, for the legations were
not heavily bombarded. There was even a short truce, during which the
empress dowager sought to observe a form of politeness by sending in a present of fruit to the besieged diplomatic corps. A larger international force,
half of whom were Japanese, was quickly prepared under the command of a
German field marshal, Count Alfred von Waldersee, and was able to defeat
the Boxers and the imperial regiments. On August 14 they relieved the legations in Peking through the Water Gate, a low entrance passing beneath the
city wall.

It was thanks to certain leading officials outside Peking—Li Hongzhang,
now governor of Guangdong and Guangxi, among others—that the situation
had not deteriorated even further and involved the whole country instead of
mainly the north. These men simply ignored the court's declaration of war and
maintained a neutral relationship with the foreign powers. The court had fled
to Xian in the west, but before her departure the empress dowager, prompted
by sheer cruelty, had arranged for one of the emperor's favorites, the Pearl
Concubine, to be drowned in a well.

Von Waldersee was dissuaded from pursuing the empress dowager and the
hapless emperor. Instead he sent his troops to many north China cities to
make an example of the rebels, but it is not to be supposed anyone troubled

The Meridian Gate of the Forbidden City, Peking.

This formidable entrance barred the way to anyone not privileged to have access to the Imperial Palace. Here the Bengal Lancers escort the Supreme Commander of the Allied Forces, Count Alfred von Waldersee, as he enters the palace after the suppression of the Boxer Rebellion in 1900.

Library of Congress

very much to find out who were or were not rebels. In these cities, in Peking, and in the Forbidden City palace itself, the looting and raping were horrific. Heavy terms were imposed upon China: an indemnity equivalent to over $330 million, payable with interest over forty years, the execution of Yu-xian and nine other leading officials, the right of foreigners to occupy garrison posts on the Tientsin–Peking railway (a precedent to be claimed on a large scale later by Japan), and the canceling of the civil service examinations in certain northern cities as a punishment for the official class. The examinations were not given again in north China, and the whole system came to an end in 1905. But the worst result was not written into the terms of any agreement; it was the virtual occupation of Manchuria by the Russians. This in turn alarmed and provoked the Japanese and led to the Russo-Japanese War of 1904–1905. This was a foreign quarrel fought on Chinese soil but decided at sea in the battle of Tsushima Strait, as had been the Sino-Japanese War by the naval battle off the Yalu River. The Japanese victory, which surprised the world—the first victory of an Asian over a European power—was to have momentous consequences for China.

In the wake of the Boxer Rebellion it became more obvious than ever that reforms were necessary, and much of the program begun and undone in the Hundred Days of 1898 was enacted in separate parts between 1901 and 1910: the creation of modern ministries in the government, reform of education at the same time as the abolition of the civil service examinations, publication of an annual budget from 1908, the creation of provincial assemblies, and the issue of a new code of law.

Nevertheless, the Manzhou dynasty—and with it the imperial system, which had lasted for over 2,000 years—was coming to an inevitable end. The personality holding the dynasty together, "the old Buddha," Cixi, died in 1908. One day before her death the emperor Guangxu had passed away, presumably poisoned on Cixi's orders, her final revenge for the reforms of 1898. She had arranged once more for a boy emperor, the three-year old Pu Yi. But his occupation of the throne was to be short, for the revolution broke out and the Republic was founded on the "Double Tenth," October 10, 1911, the tenth day of the tenth month.

13

THE REPUBLICAN REVOLUTION

1900–1949

Chinese history even in modern times has its full share of melodrama. A Chinese man of about thirty years of age was walking along a street in London in the year 1896 when without warning a door opened and several men sprang out, pinioned the passer-by, and dragged him into what proved to be the London legation of Qing-dynasty China. Preparations were begun to charter a special ship to take the prisoner back to China to be beheaded. But the prisoner, Sun Yat-sen (1866–1925), managed, through an English employee of the legation, to smuggle a note to Dr. James Cantlie, his former medical professor in Hongkong. Dr. Cantlie obtained publicity for the case in the London *Times,* and the Foreign Office intervened. The Chinese legation was forced after twelve days to release Sun, who found that the incident had made him something of a hero and increased financial support for his cause, the overthrow of the Qing dynasty.

SUN YAT-SEN, "FATHER OF THE REPUBLIC"

Sun Yat-sen (or Sun Wen), born near Canton in 1866, was unlike any Chinese leader before or after his time. He spent much of his life abroad and had no power base in China. Yet today he is revered by Nationalists and Communists alike. He was a man of ideas, a professional revolutionary with an uncanny sense of the coming mood of the times, who could rally men to a cause. Perhaps it was because he had no army behind him until the very end of his life, not even a local group of solid supporters, that he was elevated in retrospect to the position of Father of the Republic. Not a political boss or a warlord but a "pure" revolutionary, Sun could serve as a symbol in his lifetime and still more after his death.

At the age of twelve Sun Yat-sen went to live with his brother in Hawaii, attended a Church of England school there, and became a Christian. He received a medical training in Hongkong and for a short time practiced medicine in Macao, but he could not obtain a license from the Portuguese authorities. He made an approach to Li Hongzhang in 1885, hinting that he could help in the work of reform, but was ignored.

Sun then turned in the direction of revolution rather than reform. In 1894 he formed the Revive China Society *(Xing Zhong Hui)*, a revolutionary secret society with branches in China and abroad, and in the next year staged a plot to seize the buildings of the provincial government in Canton. The plot failed and Sun fled to Japan, which proved for him a refuge and a stimulus both then and in days to come.

The Japan of the Meiji era, beginning in 1868, was in the first flush of enthusiasm for Western thought and technology. Chinese students with similar ideas could reach Japan more easily than they could the source countries of Europe and America, and they could study there more inexpensively. Some notable Chinese figures were there, translating foreign works, writing, debating, diagnosing China's plight. An early leader and by far the most brilliant writer was Liang Qichao (1873–1929), who had escaped to Japan after the suppression of the Hundred Days Reform of 1898. Liang had been trained in classical learning but had also absorbed Western ideas and gained some editor-

Sun Yat-sen, also known as Sun Wen (1866–1925).

Sun Yat-sen was trained as a doctor in Hongkong and affected by Christian and Western influences. He became a full-time revolutionary and was known as the "Father of the Republic." His widow, a sister of Mme. Jiang Jieshi (Chiang Kai-shek), joined the Chinese Communist Party.

ial experience under Timothy Richard of the Christian Literature Society. He edited a newspaper advocating reform in Changsha, the first city in China other than the ports to introduce such innovations as street lighting, steam river transport, and modern subjects in college. Liang was a prolific writer and also edited several journals at different times. Many of the new journals were ephemeral, but they were filled with the heady wine of startling and controversial ideas. They circulated widely not only among Chinese students of all ages in Japan but on the mainland of China itself. In his articles and books, Liang kept stressing that the old polite way of tolerance and a modest posture had caused China to be shamelessly exploited by foreigners. Now the need was for competition, struggle, determination, and a new nationalism—in fact, for nothing less than the creation of a new type of man, a theme taken up later in more far-reaching form by Mao Zedong.

Another influential writer in Sun Yat-sen's time was Yan Fu (1853–1921), who from an education in classical Chinese literature had gone on to the arsenal at Fuzhou for technical training. He was attached to the Royal Navy in Great Britain and took up the study of English law and administration. This varied background enabled him to become one of the most successful translators and interpreters of current Western thought. Among the books which made him famous were his translations of Thomas Huxley's *Evolution and Ethics,* Adam Smith's *The Wealth of Nations,* Herbert Spencer's *The Study of Sociology,* and works by John Stuart Mill and Montesquieu. Both Liang Qichao and Yan Fu thus contributed to an emphasis on Social Darwinism, the struggle for existence and the survival of the fittest as applied to nations as well as individuals.

The strangest Chinese author then in Japan was a contemporary of Yan Fu, Lin Shu (1852–1924). Possessed of a prodigious memory and literary facility, Lin would listen to a literal Chinese translation of a foreign novel given section by section by a friend or subordinate and then write out a translation or, more often, a free adaptation of the story in elegant classical Chinese. He thus "translated" over 160 works of Defoe, Dickens, Dumas, Victor Hugo, Sir Walter Scott, Cervantes, Ibsen, and others.

In such a milieu Sun Yat-sen promoted the cause of the overthrow of the Manzhou dynasty and the founding of a republic. He traveled and spoke ceaselessly, seeking funds and support among overseas Chinese and others in America, in Britain—anywhere. It was on one of these trips that the Chinese legation incident in London took place. At first the viewpoint of Liang Qichao, advocating reform under a constitutional monarchy, drew most adherents. But in the end Sun's more radical insistence upon revolution and a complete break with the past proved to have a greater appeal.

While in Japan, Sun formulated the famous Three People's Principles (*san min zhu yi*) which were his political platform: People's Nationalism, People's Democracy, and People's Livelihood. In the circumstances the principle of Nationalism had naturally a strong anti-foreign bias, but this could not be placed in the forefront when foreign support was being solicited. Nationalism in practice and as understood by Sun himself was directed both against the

Manzhou dynasty and against foreign imperialism. Sun's writing on the subject reveals a sensitive Chinese self-criticism and at the same time an animus toward the West.

> What is the standing of our nation in the world? In comparison with other nations we have the greatest population and the oldest culture, of four thousand years' duration. We ought to be advancing in line with the nations of Europe and America. But the Chinese people have only family and clan groups; there is no national spirit. Consequently, in spite of four hundred million people gathered together in one China, we are in fact but a *sheet of loose sand* [my italics]. We are the poorest and weakest state in the world, occupying the lowest position in international affairs; the rest of mankind is the carving knife and the serving dish, while we are the fish and the meat. Our position is now extremely perilous.*

The principle of Democracy was to be secured by a constitution embodying five powers.

> If we now want to combine the best from China and the best from other countries and guard against all kinds of abuse in the future, we must take the three Western governmental powers—the executive, legislative and judicial; add to them the old Chinese powers of examination and censorship and make a finished wall, a quintuple-power government. Such a government will be the most complete and the finest in the world, and a state with such a government will indeed be of the people, by the people and for the people.†

Sun quotes with approval Mencius's saying, "Heaven sees as the people see, Heaven hears as the people hear."

The import of the third principle, the People's Livelihood, is less clear and more controversial. Historians stress the fact that, although the principle is sometimes described as socialism, it was not seen by Sun in the Marxist sense but rather derived from an American, Henry George. George had an urban-centered notion of a single tax on land designed to inhibit speculation by taking into account the *future* increment in the value of land. Sun is said to have favored some such tax system to curb excess profits on land, and not to have envisaged its wholesale redistribution. But he was concerned with the peasants and their food supply.

> What are the real conditions among Chinese farmers? Although China does not have great landowners, yet nine out of ten farmers do not own their own fields. Most of the farming land is in the possession of landlords who do not do the cultivating themselves. . . . We must immediately use government and law to remedy this grave situation. Unless we

---

*Sun Yat-sen, *San Min Chu I: The Three Principles of the People*, quoted in Hsü, *Readings in Modern Chinese History*, p. 410.
†Ibid., p. 420.

can solve the agrarian problem, there will be no solution for the livelihood problem. Of the food produced in the fields, sixty percent, according to our latest rural surveys, goes to the landlord, while only forty percent goes to the farmer. If this unjust state of affairs continues, when the
farmers become intelligent, who will still be willing to toil and suffer in
the fields? . . . If we apply the People's Livelihood principle we must
make the aim of food production not profit but the provision of sustenance for all the people. . . . The fundamental difference, then, between
the Principle of Livelihood and capitalism is this: capitalism makes profit
its sole aim, while the Principle of Livelihood makes the nurture of the
people its aim. With such a noble principle we can destroy the old, evil
capitalistic system.*

In fact, much of what Sun propounded remained in the realm of theory.
He himself was never in a strong enough position to make any redistribution
of land. And when Jiang Jieshi (Chiang Kai-shek) came to power as Sun's successor, he became dependent on the right wing of the Nationalist party and
did not attempt any land reform either.

Returning now to the main events which preceded the Revolution, Sun
Yat-sen, a Japanese supporter, and another Chinese revolutionary, Huang
Xing, combined forces to form a fairly successful new body, the *Tong Meng
Hui*, United League, in Tokyo in 1905. Sun and Huang, in pursuance of their
revolutionary aims, went to Hanoi and from there fomented several uprisings
in south China. Although none of these early attempts was individually successful, all helped to undermine confidence in the dynasty. The most
significant point was that subversive influences were spreading among the government troops.

It was an army revolt which finally sparked the Republican Revolution,
and ironically this took place when Sun Yat-sen was once again out of the
country. Revolutionary groups formed in Shanghai and Hankou evolved a
scheme to stage an outbreak in Hankou. The plot was discovered, so the
rebels immediately advanced their timetable, and some troops in Wuchang, the
city across the river from Hankou, came out in open revolt on October 10,
1911. The Manzhou governor general and the military commander fled. Very
little violence accompanied the revolution. It seemed as though there was a
general feeling that the sands had run out for the Manzhou dynasty and that
China could only recover and progress along new lines. What exactly these
lines were to be was not quickly or easily determined. Within two months of
the Double Tenth, celebrated as the beginning of the revolution, cities and
provinces in the center, south, and northwest of China had declared their
independence of the dynasty and had loosely organized under army officers,
members of the Tong Meng Hui, and leaders of the provincial assemblies, created in 1909 as a Qing measure of constitutional reform.

*Ibid., pp. 425–26.

Sun Yat-sen was in the United States when he heard of the Wuchang revolt. He did not return at once but went to London to try to arrange a loan. When he arrived back in China, he was offered and accepted the post of provisional president of the Chinese Republic and was inaugurated on January 1, 1912, in Nanjing. He had the semblance but knew he had not the reality of power. As successor to the Tong Meng Hui, an open party was formed in 1912 known as the *Guo Min Dang* (National People's Party), usually contracted as KMT from its former spelling, *Kuo Min Tang*.

In the meantime the Qing government had turned to the only man with sufficient authority and an army behind him, the former official Yuan Shikai, who stood in the modern military tradition of Zeng Guofan and Li Hongzhang. Yuan did not work wholeheartedly for the dynasty or, it proved later, for the Republic, but he was the only figure at the moment able to maintain law and order. He was in a position to bargain between the opposing forces of the court in Peking and the new provisional government in Nanjing. In the event, a settlement was arranged whereby the emperor Xuantong, also known as Pu Yi, age six, resigned in February 1912, bringing the dynasty and empire to an end, while Sun also resigned as provisional president, allowing Yuan Shikai to occupy that office and, it was hoped, put his power at the disposal of the new republic. Yuan, however, was a military man with no interest in democracy. He was inaugurated as president in Peking, which became the capital of the provisional government, with Yuan's henchmen in the principal cabinet posts. Yuan permitted and took part in political corruption and played fast and loose with the new constitution. A bicameral parliament was elected in 1913, but Song Jiaoren, leader of the winning party, the KMT, was shot, and the parliament became a mere shadow. By 1915 Yuan was made president for life, but then he became involved in the serious crisis of the Twenty-One Demands presented by Japan, which will be dealt with in the next section. In spite of this he went on with plans to become emperor and found a new dynasty. But opposition from Liang Qichao and from generals in south China gathered strength, and Yuan was checked. He died in June 1916. The physical cause was uremia, but the real reason was probably injured pride and thwarted ambition. He had no sense of the spirit of the times and not the faintest idea of the meaning of democracy.

THE WARLORD PERIOD

There now ensues a period in the history of modern China, up to about 1927, which is most confused and which must have been to all idealist reformers among the Chinese one of near despair. It is sometimes called the Warlord Period, but in addition to the semi-independent military commanders known as warlords there were other elements in the mix, such as the power of Japan, the growing influence of students and intellectuals, and the rise of the Chinese Communist Party under the influence of Russia. The period was brought to an end by the triumph of the KMT.

The warlords were a relic of the past in its worst aspects, a phenomenon of regionalism which had emerged before in the troughs of confusion between dynasties, when central purpose and therefore central control was weak. The new feature about the warlords was that they now were the possessors of modern weapons, which united them with their suppliers, the Western powers, and gave them command of money and resources.

The rising power and imperial ambitions of Japan were the dominant foreign mark of this period. Japan was heir to the aggression of the Western powers in the nineteenth century. It defeated China in Korea in 1895. Its part in providing 50 percent of the relief force at the time of the Boxer siege of the legations was much more significant than is commonly realized, for it gave Japan the assurance of being accepted by the West; it had been received into the club of modern nations, distinguished, unfortunately, by their possession of effective armed forces. Japan defeated Russia in Manchuria in 1905, the first Asian power to bring off such a victory. Japan sought to fall heir to Germany's holdings in Shandong without success; it did succeed in stepping into Russia's place in Manchuria. In 1931 Japan staged the Mukden Incident and founded the puppet state of Manzhouguo in 1932, a rich Manchurian region which formed the training ground and base for the armies Japan loosed against China in 1937. Japan went on to conquer most of the Asian Pacific area and only lost its supreme gamble as a world power by running headlong into total defeat in 1945. It is an extraordinary record for fifty years' expansion. And it is no wonder that perceptive Chinese in the decade 1910–1920 looked at Japan, saw ahead, and feared the worst.

BEGINNINGS OF THE CHINESE COMMUNIST PARTY

Intellectuals, writers, and university professors often feel ineffectual on the stage of history, especially when faced with crass and self-seeking warlords. Similarly, the beginnings of the Chinese Communist Party in 1921 and the years following represented so little in the way of numbers and influence as to seem ludicrous. But the leadership of intellectuals and students, their effect upon a new public opinion in China, and the later growth of the Communist movement proved to be the wave of the future.

To attempt a simple summary of complex relationships, one might say that the republican Nationalists under Sun Yat-sen and Jiang Jieshi (Chiang Kai-shek) succeeded, with Communist help, in overcoming or neutralizing the warlords (cynics would say by adopting them into the family). Students and intellectuals gave a new drive to patriotism. As many of them turned to Marxism, they shaped the future of China from the peasant base up. The threat and the reality of Japanese power meanwhile spurred patriotism and national self-consciousness, unified resistance, hampered the Nationalists, and indirectly aided the Communists in their rise to power.

The specific events which show these trends in operation begin with Japan's declaration of war on Germany at the very beginning of World War I. The Japanese proceeded immediately to capture the port of Qinqdao in Shandong and to take over the German interests in that province. They followed this up the next year by presenting to Yuan Shikai the Twenty-One Demands, in five sections. These included recognition of the cession of German rights in Shandong to Japan, the right to hold land in and exploit the mineral wealth of south Manchuria, and joint Sino-Japanese operation of the large Han-ye-ping Iron Company in central China. The fifth group of demands went even further by proposing joint police control of key places in China, the right to provide advisers and weapons for the Chinese army, and the sole privilege of mining, railway, and harbor development in Fujian province. If agreement had been given to this last set of demands, it would have meant the end of Chinese independence and sovereignty within her own country. Yuan Shikai, long an opponent of Japan, took the precaution of leaking to the world press the content of these demands. In spite of their preoccupation with fighting the war, on which Japan had no doubt banked, the Western powers saw that Japan had here exceeded all bounds, and they asked for information. Only the United States sent an actual complaint to Japan concerning American interests and the infringement of Chinese sovereignty, but when Yuan was forced to accede to the demands, the fifth group was omitted. Anti-Japanese feeling all over China intensified.

The Chinese warlords in the first quarter of the twentieth century had all begun their military training under Yuan Shikai or were in some way connected with him. They were all in the same need of money to pay and equip their armies as he was. There were a number of ways to raise cash, but the method which yielded most in a short time was a foreign loan. In order to be able to offer a consortium of foreign banks the required guarantees, it was necessary for the warlord to be able to show that he represented by way of effective power the official government of China, or at least that he could command sufficient returns on customs duties and salt tax to meet the interest on the loan. Hence a man with an army, such as Yuan, could secure a loan where Sun Yat-sen, whatever title he claimed, could not. Yuan in fact obtained a loan in 1913 from a consortium of German, English, French, Japanese, and Russian banks amounting to £25 million sterling (about $100 million). A first charge of £4 million was withheld, and for the £21 million Yuan received, almost £68 million including interest was to be repaid over a period extending to 1960. It was scarcely a good bargain for the Chinese people. Moreover, no person or group proposing a reduction of foreign privileges in China could hope to secure a loan. The warlords were thus unable to be anywhere in the van of progress or reform where the independence of China was the desired end.

The warlords had other means of raising money besides loans or the regular taxes and balance left in customs and salt revenues after foreign interest was paid. Some extracted from the people taxes several years in advance. If such a leader was defeated and driven out, his successor would demand taxes afresh. Some started again the highly profitable growing of opium, although the drug had been largely suppressed and the incoming British traffic ceased in 1917. Most warlords allowed their armies to live off the land, by pillage and looting, with all the accompanying mistreatment of peasant families. Since constant feuding frequently brought commerce to a standstill, the people in many areas sank to a new low in poverty and misery.

After the death of Yuan Shikai in 1916, some semblance of order was continued by the government in Peking with Duan Qirui as premier. Duan was dependent on the Japanese and secured the Nishihara loans from them. His rule was interrupted in 1917 by the incursion of a general, Zhang Xun, who captured Peking and set up a Manzhou Restoration, declaring the boy Pu Yi, who was living in seclusion in the Forbidden City, to be emperor once again. General Zhang also wore a queue and required all his troops to do likewise as a sign of loyalty to the Manzhou. The restoration lasted twelve days. Duan, back in power, discovered resistance in the parliament and announced there would be a new election. A considerable number of members then pulled out and joined Sun Yat-sen in Canton, where a rival government was set up.

The real power in the north was held by the Northern Army, but here too a split developed. On one side was the Anfu clique, including Duan Qirui, on the other the Zhili clique led by a warlord from central China, Wu Peifu. The makeweight between them was one of the most powerful of the warlords, Zhang Zuolin, from Manchuria. He at first took the side of the Anfu clique but in 1920 changed over and captured Peking in company with the Zhili group. However, Zhang fell out with Wu Peifu and once again looked for new allies. He found them in Duan Qirui, who emerged from "retirement"; in Sun Yat-sen, who hoped for the unification of China; and in the backing of the Japanese, who regarded Wu Peifu as a foe because he was favorable to British interests in central China. This seemed a strong combination, but in 1922 Zhang Zuolin's forces were unexpectedly and totally defeated, and he was compelled to retreat ignominiously to his Manchurian lair, promising never to come south of the Great Wall again.

During these chaotic moves in a pointless chess game, a new factor, student power, entered politics in China in the May Fourth Movement. On that date in 1919 a mass meeting of 3,000 at the Tiananmen, Gate of Heavenly Peace, in Peking was held to protest the terms of the Versailles Treaty and the aggressive policy of Japan. It was also a protest against the Anfu clique then in control of the northern government. The students had discovered that Japan, which had seized Shandong and presented the notorious Twenty-One Demands, had also secured in 1917 secret agreements from Britain, France, and Italy that Japan would retain Shandong at the time of the peace treaty. The treaty itself came out in the same terms. The United States was involved, though less directly. The Lansing-Ishii agreement of 1917 had openly recognized that Japan's "territorial propinquity" to China gave her "special interests" in that country. This was suitably indefinite as a statement, but it did not sound well in China in the year 1919. One reason all the Western powers were so ready to favor Japan was that they considered her the best ally to counter Bolshevik Russia. Worst of all, the students found out that in 1918 the Peking government itself had secretly sold out and confirmed Japan's rights to Shandong.

The demonstration on May 4, 1919, got out of hand. Shouts were heard of "Cancel the Twenty-One Demands! Down with Japan! Down with power politics!" Rioting began, and the house of the Minister of Communications was set on fire. Lenin's words had a clear appeal: "The League of Nations is nothing but an insurance policy in which the victors mutually guarantee each other their prey." The Peking government reacted with ruthless force, in course of which thirty-two students were sent to jail. The government was astonished at the nationwide reaction. Telegrams from all over the country poured in. Vociferous support was given to the students by merchants, the newspapers, Sun Yat-sen, and the Canton government. Students in other cities boycotted Japanese goods and then closed down schools and universities. In Tientsin a student newspaper edited by Zhou Enlai took up the cause. In June, as the unrest continued, the police imprisoned over eleven hundred students and used Peking University as a jail. Women students joined the men in the streets. Shanghai merchants closed their shops in sympathy, and workers went on strike in Shanghai factories. Sailors and railwaymen refused to work. Nothing like it had ever happened in China before. Now the financiers took notice. They warned the government that, unless it gave in, the country would face economic collapse. At length the government reversed its stand and instructed the Chinese delegates at Versailles to walk out without signing the peace treaty. They set the imprisoned students at liberty and dropped the three pro-Japanese officials from the government. Finally the cabinet as a whole resigned. It was a triumph for the new nationalism, championed by the students.

The importance of Peking National University (*Beida,* short for *Beijing daxue*) in all this can scarcely be overemphasized, for "May Fourth" came to stand not only for a political and nationalistic but also for a cultural movement of which Peking University was the hub. The chancellor, Cai Yuanpei, himself a writer on philosophy who had studied in Berlin and Leipzig, brought to the university some brilliant men of great variety, among them the dean of letters, Chen Duxiu (1879–1942). Chen collaborated with Hu Shi in promoting the colloquial written style, already mentioned, and published an influential journal, *La Nouvelle Jeunesse (Xin Qing Nian),* which attacked the outmoded nature and harmful effects of Confucianism and gave a forum to radical and other Western ideas. Li Dazhao, the university librarian, was a frequent contributor to the journal, and both Chen and he were founding members of the Chinese Communist Party. Mao Zedong worked for a time in the library, and Li was a dominant influence in Mao's early life. Following the May Fourth incident, Hu Shi, who had studied at Cornell and Columbia universities, arranged for his teacher, John Dewey, to spend two years lecturing in China on education and the theory of pragmatism. About the same time the lectures of Bertrand Russell, the mathematician and logician, had an enormous influence on young Chinese intellectuals.

This period produced other notable crusading figures in the field of literature, all pointing to change, often violent change—men such as Lu Xun, novelist, polemicist, translator of Gogol and of East European and Japanese works, who poured the vials of his satire on the Confucianism of the past; Wang Guowei, who in 1905 had made the works of Nietzsche and Schopenhauer known in China; Ding Ling, a woman writer, whose gothic novels expressed the current sense of hopelessness and revolt; Mao Dun, who edited *Short Story* magazine and was himself a novelist of repute; and Ba Jin, who went to Paris in 1922, became an anarchist, and formed his nom de plume from Chinese syllables of his favorite authors' names, Bakunin and Kropotkin.

The political activists and the pure scholars in the May Fourth Movement had at first been indistinguishable, but in the course of time men such as Chen Duxiu and Li Dazhao took the road of practical politics, while Hu Shi drew back from ideological extremes and said that reform must come "drop by drop." Guo Moruo, who in a sense took up the role of Hu Shi in theorizing on the place of literature in society, was one of the early converts to Marxism. Its simple explanation of China's ills as being due to capitalist, imperialist exploitation from abroad and the feudalism of warlords at home appealed to him. He therefore felt literature could find no higher calling than to serve society; it could and should provide a sharp weapon of propaganda for the socialist revolution.

COOPERATION WITH THE SOVIET UNION

The problem of Shandong, which had given rise to all the turmoil of May 4, 1919, hung in the air for a period. Then it was settled in the context of a wider agreement, the Washington Conference of 1921–1922. Japanese statesmen, at this point slightly less bellicose, were willing to accept certain new arrangements in the Pacific. The naval agreement limiting capital ships gave Japan a ratio of 3 to 5 for Great Britain and 5 for the United States, but at the same time it gave Japan further security in the matter of naval bases in the Pacific. A bilateral treaty between Japan and China then returned Shandong to Chinese control, and a Nine Power Treaty was signed in 1922 embodying the American-sponsored principle of the Open Door to trade for all in China, accompanied by respect for Chinese territorial integrity. China's young leadership, however, was more impressed by the offer of Soviet Russia in 1918 (confirmed in 1920) to give up all privileges acquired by Czarist Russia under the nineteenth-century unequal treaties. The fact that the Soviets were in no position to enforce or profit by these treaties did not affect the new popularity of Russia in Chinese eyes.

In 1920 Gregory Voitinsky, an agent of the Communist International (Comintern), came to Peking, went on to Shanghai, and there set up a news agency and center for the dissemination of literature. Some Communist study groups were started, the one in Hunan being led by Mao Zedong, and in 1921 twelve delegates from these groups met for what is reckoned as the First Party Congress in Shanghai. Voitinsky's successor, a Dutchman, Maring (Sneevliet), was present at the meetings, as was Mao Zedong. Chen Duxiu and Li Dazhao could not be there. In spite of the greatest precautions, the delegates just escaped a raid by the Shanghai police and finished their deliberations in a boat on a lake in Zhejiang province. Chen Duxiu was elected secretary general. The membership of the Chinese Communist Party is said to have been 50 at the start in 1921 and to have grown in the two succeeding years to 120, then 432.

During the disturbed warlord era, affairs in Canton and the south had been no more stable than in the north. We have seen that Sun Yat-sen had gathered around him in 1917 certain self-exiled parliamentarians from the north, but the southern warlords whose support he required had proved fickle, and Sun had been forced to retreat to the safety of Shanghai. He had made attempts to find allies in the north, but with no permanent success. After the May Fourth Movement, which he supported, Sun had been in and out of Canton in 1920–1922; he was even elected president of the Republic in the south in 1921. But then a change took place, for he found an important ally in Soviet Russia. The Russians were vitally interested in supplanting the great powers anywhere in the world, and East Asia was a fruitful field. Certain Chinese leaders such as Sun, for their part, were eager to learn more about methods of revolution, and the Russians with their recent experience of the 1917 Revolution were the world's experts. A Russian agent, Adolf Joffe, had approached Sun in Japan and a preliminary decision to collaborate had been made. That the Russians were actively seeking a toehold in China is evidenced by the fact that they had already approached the warlord Wu Peifu on account of his army; they pronounced him militarily strong but without sufficient political consciousness.

In the summer of 1923, Sun sent his loyal lieutenant and (later) brother-in-law, Jiang Jieshi (1888–1975), to Moscow for a period of training with the Red Army. Jiang had already received a military education in Japan, where he had first met Sun, but was now to study Soviet methods, in particular how the Red Army and the Communist Party functioned together. The KMT was accepted as a member at Comintern meetings and two Russian advisers were sent to Canton, Mikhail Borodin as political and Galen as military counselor. An alliance favored by Moscow was then formed between the KMT and the Chinese Communist Party, abbreviated hereafter as CCP. At the Second CCP Congress Maring had proposed that their members join the KMT, and at the Third Congress this was agreed, over Chen Duxiu's dissent. By this decision Communists were to apply individually for KMT membership, which they did, but the Communist Party would retain its separate identity. In actuality Communists could not by party rules act individually, so they held caucus meetings all the time to decide their party line on current decisions, thus in effect forming a party within the KMT party. This was to lead, as one might without difficulty predict, to trouble later on.

The KMT was then tightened and reorganized on the Soviet model. With Borodin making the main contribution and Sun Yat-sen and Wang Jingwei collaborating, the party was centralized under strict bureaucratic control, which made it all-powerful over every civilian and military department. Again with the aid of the Soviet advisers, the Huangpu (Whampoa) Military Academy was set up near Canton, and Jiang Jieshi became its first commandant. There was a conscious effort to instill in the new leaders of the army a spirit of patriotism and integrity, as opposed to the selfish and senseless struggles of the warlords. With these hopeful signs the KMT leadership prepared to carry out what had for some time been an aim of Sun Yat-sen and undertake an expedition northward which would unify the country at last. But before that, Sun was to make one more diplomatic effort. There had been another reversal of fortune in Peking and Feng Yuxiang, the "Christian general" of peasant origin, had overturned the other northern warlords and captured the city in 1924. Sun went north to seek an alliance with Feng but never came back. He died in Peking on March 12, 1925, and became a national hero, posthumously admired by all.

Jiang Jieshi (Chiang Kai-shek; 1888–1975).

Jiang succeeded Sun Yat-sen as leader of the National People's Party (KMT). His usual title, Generalissimo, derives from his conquest or winning over of the warlord generals during his establishment of the Nationalist government. He continued in power in Taiwan from 1949 until his death in 1975.

THE NORTHERN EXPEDITION

In July of 1926 the joint Northern Expedition of the KMT and the CCP was ready to move off from Canton under the command of Jiang Jieshi. One army group out of six was made up of personnel recruited by the KMT; the other five were reconstituted warlord forces. Only one regiment was composed of Communist-controlled troops, but the main contribution of the CCP was the advance network of propaganda agents for whose training the Communists had been mainly responsible. The activity of Mao Zedong in Hunan, his native province, between August 1926 and May 1927 is a good example of the new phenomenon—the excitation and the effective channeling of peasant discontent. Mao reported that two million peasants alone were organized by the CCP in peasant associations. They demanded the lowering of rents and then rose in sporadic rebellion against their landlords. The Northern Expedition did not encounter much serious resistance and reached the Yangzi valley by the end of the year. Wuhan (the compound city on the middle Yangzi whose name is composed of the first syllables of Wuchang and Hankou) was captured, and the KMT government moved thither from Canton on January 1, 1927. The Wuhan government was increasingly dominated by the KMT left wing under the leadership of Wang Jingwei, who had recently returned from Europe. Jiang Jieshi had been marching north with another column and now set up his headquarters at Nanchang, far to the southeast of Wuhan, and there was a pause in the action. Forces commanded by Jiang then moved into the lower Yangzi valley and obtained control of it during February and March. Feeling had been running high in Shanghai ever since an incident on May 30, 1925, when strikers had been fired on by British and Japanese troops. As the KMT armies now approached Shanghai, a Communist-led uprising of workers broke out, and this greatly facilitated Jiang's capture of the city.

Then came Jiang Jieshi's sudden break with the Communists on April 12, 1927. Swiftly and secretly at dawn he moved against the labor unions and their organizers in Shanghai. Three hundred were killed, including many leading Communists. Others escaped and went underground. Jiang thus joined forces with the KMT right wing, and a conflict with the Communists which had long been latent came out into the open. Jiang had been suspicious of the Communist leadership as early as March 1926, when he dissolved a successful Hongkong Strike Committee and had a number of Communists prominent within the KMT dismissed from their posts. He suspected that the CCP was primarily interested in the world aims of the Communist International and only secondarily in the national goals of the KMT for China.

Jiang Jieshi made Nanjing the capital of his Nationalist regime and was thus in obvious conflict with the left wing of his own party under Wang Jingwei in Wuhan. They accused Jiang of "reactionary acts," "crimes and outrages," "massacre of the people," and "oppression of the Party" and condemned him to be "expelled from the Party [that is, the KMT] and dismissed from all his posts." Jiang, however, had certain evident advantages in this domestic dispute; not only was he in command of the main armed forces but he had secured a $3 million loan from Chinese financiers in Shanghai, which rendered him less dependent on the USSR. (He had himself been in a brokerage firm in Shanghai for ten years at an earlier period of his life.) He was also looked upon favorably by foreign firms in Shanghai and Hongkong because of his suppression of the workers' uprising which threatened the stability of commerce. So Jiang paid little attention to the fulminations from Wuhan.

At this point Feng Yuxiang entered the picture again. He had returned from a visit to Russia armed with Soviet military aid and had supported the Nationalist cause in central China against two warlord factions, those of Wu Peifu and of the Zhangs, father and son, from Manchuria. After the victory he was in a position to support either branch of the KMT, and he threw his weight on the side of Jiang Jieshi. The left-wing branch at Wuhan was now also becoming disillusioned with its Communist allies. Disquieting news had come from Peking. In a raid on the Soviet embassy there on April 6, Zhang Zuolin's police seized documents which were alleged to show that the Russian government was involved within China in activities of a revolutionary nature which could be described as subversive. Twenty Chinese, including Li Dazhao, were discovered inside the embassy and removed, to be subsequently strangled.

Then in June, Wang Jingwei was shown a telegram from Stalin to M. N. Roy, an Indian Comintern agent recently sent to China. The telegram stated among other things that the KMT leadership should be rendered more active by the introduction of workers and peasants. Later, more urgent Soviet instructions recommended that workers and peasants be armed and the "agrarian revolution" developed. This dictation of policy—and a policy, moreover, which would have lost the KMT its middleclass support—was too much for even the left wing, and they veered sharply right. Stalin had seriously misread the Chinese situation. The Communists were expelled from the Wuhan section of the KMT also. Borodin, M. N. Roy, and others, including Sun Yat-sen's widow, escaped to Russia. Some of the Chinese Communist leaders tried to organize uprisings in response to urgent demands from Moscow: Lin Biao at Nanchang, Mao Zedong among the peasants in Hunan—the Autumn Harvest Uprisings—but without success. The Nationalist troops soon put an end to all these attempts. Mao Zedong was dismissed from the Politburo for the failure of the uprisings and took refuge in the Jinggang Mountains on the Hunan-Jiangxi border in southeast China. It was now the summer of the eventful year 1927.

The main object of the Northern Expedition was to reduce the separate warlord regimes under one Nationalist banner. All was not plain sailing. Zhang Zuolin and his allies prevented the Nationalists from extending their power north of the Yangzi. Certain of Jiang Jieshi's lieutenants were insisting that he become reconciled with the Wuhan branch of the KMT. To facilitate reconciliation, Jiang resigned from his posts and took some time off in Japan. The armed forces of Zhang's faction and the KMT swayed back and forth. Wang

Jingwei made his base in Canton but was there severely discredited by a desperate and last-ditch effort at revolt by the Communists, the Canton commune. These city uprisings were all undertaken on orders from Moscow, following the orthodox Marxist-Leninist line that the urban proletariat would be the leaders of the revolution. Warlord troops were brought in, and Canton was recaptured in five days. When the Communists were being rounded up, some were recognized by the red stains left by the sashes they had hastily removed. Six thousand were killed. The Communists were soon dislodged from Canton, but all signs pointed to the need for one strong man to lead the KMT and the country. Jiang Jieshi, as he had shrewdly calculated, was asked to return. He entered upon the final phase of unification. Zhang Zuolin was forced to retreat northward. Intended aid from a Japanese landing in Shandong boomeranged, because Chinese nationalist sentiment was strong enough by now to make the Japanese a liability to Zhang. For their part, with cynical realism, the Japanese abandoned Zhang Zuolin, their protégé during the many years since he had started his career as a Manchurian bandit; they actually blew up the train in which Zhang was retreating to Mukden in June 1928. By October 28, 1928, the KMT under Jiang Jieshi's undisputed leadership was in control of virtually the whole of China from the capital at Nanjing.

THE NATIONALIST DECADE 1928–1937

The writing of history is as subject to the swings of fashion as any other human activity, and present-day assessments of the work of Jiang Jieshi and the Nationalists tend to be low. This is due to several causes: for one, the undoubted achievements of the People's Republic of China lead to undue credence being given to their simplistic and overcritical judgment of the pre-1949 period; for another, the unpopularity of the China lobby in contemporary America has obscured the positive aspects of the Jiang regime. But those who were resident in the China of the 1930s remember the relief and enthusiasm with which Jiang Jieshi was welcomed, by contrast with the grim period which went before; support for Jiang was widespread. The Nationalist decade started with high hopes and achieved a great deal. The later unquestioned decline of idealism and rise of selfish opportunism in the KMT during and after World War II has left a strong impression upon the minds of those with little first-hand acquaintance with the magnitude of China's problems. The attack by Japan and the coming of World War II set an ineluctable term to the short period of ten years at Jiang's disposal for reconstruction after the settlement of 1928. The primary objects of bringing an end to the warlord chaos and of setting up a modern state were by and large accomplished.

Jiang and his critics parted company on the question of priorities. Jiang, accustomed by temperament and training to trust to military solutions, felt that unification of the country under his rule must take precedence over resistance to Japan, and so he fought the Communists with fanatical zeal. He was involved in a further tragic contradiction, for by turning against the Communists in 1927 and refusing to depend on the left, he came to depend unduly on the right and thus never reached the point of implementing any land reform to improve the miserable lot of the Chinese peasant. The KMT was an urban-based movement from which the bankers, moneylenders, and landlords stood to gain the most.

In spite of pressing financial problems, the Nationalist government was able to improve the fiscal situation. T. V. Song (Soong), Jiang's brother-in-law, was made manager of the Central Bank of China in Canton, one of four major government banks, and then he became finance minister. He recovered for China the right to set her own tariff of duties, which yielded a higher customs revenue. He reformed the tax structure and took successful measures to stabilize the currency. At the same time a disproportionate amount of the revenue, on occasion as much as a third, went to pay interest on the national debt, and many officials received unduly high returns on government bonds, even up to 40 percent when discount and interest were reckoned.

Highway construction linked many cities and opened up remote areas. Less was done on railways, but the completion of the Wuchang–Canton line in 1936 meant that a railroad now went all the way from Peking to Hongkong. The Chinese National Airways Corporation was set up in 1930. After disastrous floods in the Yangzi valley, which claimed 100,000 lives, a large conservancy scheme was completed in 1932. An irrigation project benefited the province of Shaanxi, but it was only a drop in the bucket after a famine in 1929–1931 which affected 20 million people in nine of the northern provinces. In spite of considerable efforts in education and modernization, China could not be altered in a day. There were many anachronisms and anomalies. Surviving warlords were growing opium in outlying areas. The northwest province of Gansu had a multitude of taxes which severely oppressed the poor. And the central government kept an army of five million men under arms and spent up to 80 percent of its revenue on military expenditure.

The government did little to improve conditions for the farmer, but some pioneering work was done in rural reconstruction by the YMCA and other Christian bodies. Dr. James Y. C. Yen received recognition and help from the Rockefeller Foundation for his project in north China for mass education for peasant farmers. The work expanded to include agronomy, marketing, and farmers' cooperatives. The China International Famine Relief Commission collected $50 million for river conservancy, sinking wells, and building roads as well as distributing food. Among a multitude of instances of cultural advance in this period, one may single out the archaeological excavations of the Shang dynasty site at Anyang, the foundation of the League of Left-Wing Writers in 1930 (indicative of the fact that the KMT was far from running a totalitarian state), the publication of Guo Moruo's *Researches on Ancient Chinese Society* in 1932, and the founding of the Chinese Chemical Society and the Chinese Mathematical Society in 1933 and 1935 respectively. Biochemical studies in China attained an international level of recognition by 1938.

Jiang Jieshi's good relations with the Western powers and particularly with America were aided by his marriage to Meiling Song, which took place during his self-imposed brief retirement from politics and visit to Japan in late 1927. He divorced his first wife, who had borne him two sons. Miss Song, an elegant and intelligent woman, belonged to a Chinese business family in Shanghai and had been educated in the United States. Her eldest sister was married to H. H. Kung, a prominent banker, and another sister was the widow of Sun Yat-sen. Her brother, T. V. Song, has already been mentioned as finance minister. There was justification for ironic references to "the Song dynasty." The Song family was Christian, and Jiang Jieshi was baptized into the Methodist Church at the time of his marriage. The requirements of politics and the necessity of maintaining a generally Confucian image, in addition perhaps to his own inclinations, meant that Jiang did not make much of his Christian profession in public. Mme. Jiang was of inestimable help to him in maintaining contacts with the United States and in drawing the attention of the American public to the modernizing efforts of the New China.

Apparently stirred by the success of the Communist propaganda arm, Jiang Jieshi launched in February 1934 what was known as the New Life Movement, an updating of traditional Confucian morality combined with modern hygiene. Discipline was to replace laziness and the *suibien*, lackadaisical, doing-what-I-like attitude; cleanliness, hygiene, an alert mind in a healthy body were to be stressed instead of the dirt and superstition which had characterized the old days. The ways of common people in the West were held up as an example, but the values inculcated by the New Life Movement did not need to be derived from the West, for they were all there in Confucianism truly understood. After 1936 Mme. Jiang took a greater part in promoting the movement, and a reformer with missionary experience, George Shepherd, was put in charge of it. After the movement had made a strong start, Jiang himself admitted that it did not continue at the same pace. It was sponsored and directed entirely from above through the KMT Party and the state apparatus. It tended to tell the people what to do but to make little change in the conduct of the officials. It smacked of the officer on the parade ground and had only a limited influence. But it was seriously conceived as a means to making a new type of citizen, and features of its discipline and hygiene have been more successfully carried out over a longer period by the present People's Republic.

The political and military events of the Nationalist decade revolved around the twin problems of the Communists and the Japanese. Jiang Jieshi was well aware that the Japanese were threatening in the north, but he thought he could deal with the internal Communist menace first. He made five separate attempts between 1930 and 1934 to encircle and capture the position Mao had set up in the Jinggang mountains in the south. Here Mao was joined by Zhu De and Lin Biao, each of whom brought some forces with him. Later still the Central Committee of the CCP along with Zhou Enlai were forced to leave Shanghai, and they too arrived in the southern stronghold. Resources were poor, life was extremely hard, and the peasants were at first apathetic. Mao and the other leaders developed guerrilla tactics here which were of the greatest usefulness later on. "The enemy advances, we retreat; the enemy halts, we harass; the enemy tires, we attack; the enemy retreats, we pursue."

Jiang's first two encirclement campaigns were unsuccessful. He himself took charge during part of the third campaign in the summer of 1931. A battle was fought in September at Gaoxing with great losses on both sides. Jiang claimed it as a victory and the Communists moved their base to Ruijin in south Jiangxi, but the Red Army was by no means wiped out. A fourth effort was made in the spring of 1933 with 250,000 government troops, but it too was a failure. By this time other Chinese soviets had been set up in Hubei, Hunan, Sichuan, and Shaanxi provinces. Finally a fifth campaign was undertaken on a very large scale with some 700,000 troops (opposed by 150,000 of the Red Army), and the crucial aid of General Hans von Seeckt of the German High Command, whom Jiang Jieshi had secured from Hitler. The campaign began in October 1933 and was based on a systematic plan of surrounding and slowly strangling economically the Communist-controlled area by means of pillboxes, forts, and checkpoints on all the roads. After a year the hard-pressed Communist command decided to make a break from the trap, and, in the autumn of 1934, 90,000 men escaped in five separate groups and joined up again to begin the famous Long March. (Some authorities place the number at the start of the march as high as 130,000.)

THE LONG MARCH

The Long March by any reckoning ranks as one of the great military exploits and as a fantastic example of human endurance. Those on the march covered 6,000 miles in just over a year, crossed twenty-four rivers and eighteen mountain ranges, five of them under permanent snow. They passed through twelve provinces and occupied sixty-two cities. By the end their numbers had been reduced to about 30,000 (some say less), the losses being accounted for not only by casualties in fighting both provincial and KMT forces but also by those who dropped off or were intentionally left behind to organize revolution in towns and villages en route. There were fifteen pitched battles and a skirmish of some sort almost daily. Perhaps the most remarkable statistic in moving this large body of men is the fact that, counting out prolonged rest periods, the average distance covered on marching days was nearly 24 miles per day.

At first the purpose was escape from capture, and the line of march shows many twists and turns in south China. But in January 1935 the army took a break and a rest in Zunyi, Guizhou province, and Mao Zedong pressed for holding a conference. His bold conception, "Go north to fight the Japanese," won the day, and Mao attained leadership as the new chairman of the Politburo. In addition to the propaganda value throughout China of an anti-Japanese slogan, the move north had the additional advantages of linking up with the existing Shaanxi Soviet and of placing the Red Army and the Party leadership in an area in the northwest where they could more easily make contact with the USSR. But to reach Shaanxi on foot was a task of almost unimaginable difficulty. Mao's force went south, then west into Yunnan, and then took the northerly direction. (Another leader, Zhang Guotao, with whom Mao had frequently disagreed, took the 4th Army north by another route.) Mao's column at length crossed the Gold Sand River far into the west China mountains in May 1935. It took them eight days and nights to make the crossing in small boats. They were now comparatively free from KMT pursuit but had to contend with formidable obstacles of nature. When they reached the Dadu River there was only one available suspension bridge, from which the planks had been removed, which was guarded by a blockhouse at the far end. Twenty volunteers, armed with swords and hand grenades and covered by machine-gun fire, swarmed along the chains, overcame the garrison, and replaced the planks on the bridge to enable the army to cross.

The worst natural barrier, the Grasslands, remained—scores of miles of swamp consisting of evil-smelling mud with patches of matted grass. The area, subject to rain, hail, and constant wind, was bitter cold at night. To avoid being lost by sinking into the mud, the men had to sleep half sitting up, back to back in pairs. Losses here were considerable, but the force made its way over further mountains and through two enemy lines to join the 15th Red Army Corps in safety by October 20, 1935. On its alternate route, Zhang Guotao's 4th Army suffered heavy losses, for which his strategy was blamed. Tried in 1937 and sent for "rectification study," he ended by going over to the KMT.

The CCP then entrenched itself in the remote and comparatively safe region in the northwest around Paoan and, later, Yanan. The philosophy, ideological discussion, guerrilla methods, and training hammered out in Yanan are a part of Communist and Chinese history and will be touched on in the next chapter.

Meanwhile, the Japanese menace became more pressing than ever. The complex reasons for Japan's imperial expansion and the history of its progress fall outside the scope of this book;* a brief summary of the stages of expansion has been given earlier in this chapter. The CCP was well aware of the danger, for the conclusion of the Long March fell midway in time between Japan's creation of the puppet state of Manzhouguo in 1932 and its full-scale attack on China in 1937.

The shadows cast by the Rising Sun were more clearly seen in north China than anywhere else. Inner Mongolia was falling into the Japanese orbit. Zhang Xueliang, son and heir of Zhang Zuolin, had been appointed by Jiang Jieshi as Deputy Commander in Chief of Bandit Suppression, which meant in plain language that he was to fight the Communists. He was much more concerned about Manchuria, his family's homeland, now under the Japanese. And

*See W. Scott Morton, *Japan: Its History and Culture,* chapters 14 and 15.

his troops had been affected by Communist thinking to a degree quite unsuspected by Jiang Jieshi. Therefore, when Jiang arrived in Xian to coordinate a further anti-Communist campaign, he was arrested by Zhang Xueliang and his soldiers in what became known as the Xian coup. Its suddenness came as a severe shock to the Nanjing government. Jiang was presented with the demand that he call off the attack on the CCP and join forces with all Chinese in an all-out effort against the encroachment of Japan. Some wanted to kill Jiang forthwith. His bargaining counter was that he alone was the main rallying point for Chinese loyalties in most of the country. Zhou Enlai, representing the CCP in the negotiations, realized this and put forward the then-Comintern line of a united front against imperialism, which fell in with Zhang Xueliang's proposal. In face of this coalition, and with belated realization of the strength of similar demands for a hard line against Japan that had already arisen in Canton and Shanghai, Jiang Jieshi reluctantly agreed to the terms of Zhang and the CCP and was released on Christmas Day, 1936. Zhang Xueliang accompanied him to Nanjing and for his pains was promptly condemned to imprisonment and then close surveillance in Nanjing and later in Taiwan.

WAR WITH JAPAN AND WORLD WAR II

The date of the outbreak of World War II varies with one's habitat. Americans usually reckon it from December 7, 1941, the date of the attack on Pearl Harbor. But for Europeans the war began in 1939, and for the Chinese in 1937. There is clear evidence that Japan's strengthening of her Guandong Army in Manzhouguo was a precaution against Russian ambitions in the Far East. It is true that Russia maintained in her eastern provinces a larger number of troops than Japan had in Manzhouguo, and that the Russians had superior armored support. It is true also that there were border clashes and trials of strength between Japan and Russia, at Zhanggufeng on the Soviet-Korea-China border in 1938 and on a larger scale near Nomonhan in Outer Mongolia the next year. In both these engagements Russia had the upper hand. But it is difficult to believe that Japan's actions in north China were simply to secure her rear while getting ready to defend herself against Russia. Japan also seems to have had deliberate designs on China, although she would have liked to take a bite at a time. Some of the difficulty in assessing Japanese policy stems from the fact that the Japanese themselves did not always know what their policy was. The army and navy from the 1930s to Pearl Harbor were often working at cross purposes and on different plans. The Foreign Ministry was not always informed by either service of its secret war plans. Big business had invested a considerable amount in Manzhouguo and did not receive a very satisfying return. A determined Chinese boycott of Japanese goods in protest against the seizure of Manchuria had proved very successful, and Japanese exports had markedly declined. And the super-patriotic younger officers of the Guandong Army on the mainland tended to run ahead of their superiors on the Imperial General Staff in Tokyo. It is thus not always clear at any given point in Japan's thrust into China how much was deliberate policy and how much on-the-spot improvisation.

The Japanese army had managed to create an East Hebei Autonomous Regime between the Shanhaiguan border and Peking. They hoped to go farther and lop off the five northern provinces, Hebei, Shandong, Shanxi, Chahar, and Suiyuan, and make them into another puppet state. The spark that set off the war seemed small enough at first. Japanese forces carrying out maneuvers near Peking on July 7, 1937 seemed as though they were trailing their coats. When they demanded to search a small town, shots were exchanged at the Marco Polo bridge. Both sides had an interest in settling the affair, but while negotiations went on, other clashes broke out. The Nanjing government stood firm, and the Japanese then launched a full-scale assault. Troops were sent in waves from Manzhouguo, and bombers roared over the north China cities. The Japanese navy, not to be outdone, bombarded Shanghai, where the Chinese put up strong resistance. It was clear that Japan could not limit the war to north China; China had displayed a determination the Japanese did not expect.

Chinese troops had inflicted heavy losses on the Japanese on one or two occasions, but the Japanese had better equipment and training. With the advice of his German staff officers, Jiang Jieshi decided to avoid pitched battles and use the vast area of China to gain time. He felt certain that ultimately Japan would embroil herself with other enemies who would then come to China's aid.

In October 1937 the Chinese government moved inland, at first to Hankou and then beyond the protecting Yangzi gorges all the way to Chongqing in Sichuan, which remained its seat throughout the war. Shanghai was taken. With zeal and determination, workers, students, and businessmen dismantled the factories, machinery and all, and transported them piece by piece in carts, on boats, and on the backs of men far into the interior. University libraries and equipment were similarly salvaged on the great trek into Free China.

The Japanese took possession of the principal cities and fanned out over the main transport routes, but they never controlled all the intervening rural districts. Nanjing fell in December of 1937, the first year of the war. The Japanese officers had given the men carte blanche in order to try to break the Chinese will to resist, but the city became the scene of such horrible rape, murder, and looting that even the Japanese High Command was alarmed at the total breakdown of discipline. Hankou and Canton were captured by October 1938. In November, Prime Minister Fumimaro Konoye said that China was virtually defeated and that Japan was instituting her "New Order in East Asia," which would become a "Co-Prosperity Sphere" for all. The Japanese had already set up a puppet "Provisional Government of China" in December 1937 in Peking. The end of 1938 saw the completion of the first stage of the war: the rapid occupation by the Japanese army of all the urban centers in the plains up to the western mountain barriers. The KMT was in control of the southwest and the CCP of the northwest. There was also considerable Communist-led guerrilla activity in the provinces of Henan, Zhejiang, Shandong, and elsewhere in between lines of Japanese control. There were various types of guerrilla action: the overwhelming of small Japanese garrisons guarding railway stations; allowing a truck convoy to pass a certain spot and, when the Japanese had grown less vigilant, ambushing it on the return journey; exploding a hand grenade under a city wall and killing off by sniper fire the Japanese officers who rushed to the wall head to survey the damage; acquiring intelligence from friendly peasants in villages where political organization and cooperation had been thoroughly established and elementary training given; coordinating guerrilla movements from a central CCP headquarters by means of mobile radio posts manned by students. The guerrillas had few regular sources of weapons supply but managed to maintain themselves from captured Japanese matériel.

This guerrilla activity continued through the second phase of the war, 1939–1941, when there was little change in the combatants' positions but a good deal of political maneuvering. Wang Jingwei, pessimistic about China's chances, accepted the post of premier in a Japanese-sponsored government which was set up in 1940 in Nanjing. Chongqing suffered constantly under Japanese bombing attacks, and its people held out with considerable bravery in dugouts and cliff shelters. Jiang Jieshi could not easily strike back at the Japanese, and the war became a stalemate. But the united front with the CCP had disintegrated, and Jiang actually employed troops to limit the area in the northwest which was directly controlled by the Communists. Although each guerrilla action was so small as to be a mere pinprick, the combination of a multitude of these over a period of years made itself felt and began to bleed away the Japanese military effort. The government in Tokyo was embarrassed by the unending drag of the "China Incident," the greatest undeclared war of modern times.

Americans may have had a bad conscience, but for the sake of business they went on supplying Japan from 1937 through 1940 with scrap iron and petroleum for her military effort. It was a shortsighted policy. Finally, in January 1941, the U.S. government placed an embargo on the export of scrap iron to Japan. It was aware that events were taking a serious turn, for in December of 1940, a year before Pearl Harbor, both the American and British governments warned their nonessential nationals to evacuate East Asia. On July 2, 1941, the Imperial High Command decided not to wait for any further resolution to the China Incident, or else to solve it by a greater gamble, and took the resolve to expand the war into Indochina. Part of their objective was to reach the sources of oil in the Dutch East Indies. On July 26 the United States, carrying out its threat to retaliate if the Japanese moved the war to the south, blocked the export of petroleum products to Japan and froze all Japanese assets in the States. The Imperial Navy depended heavily on imported oil, and in September the decision was taken in Japan to go to war with the United States and Great Britain in the Pacific. With the attacks on Pearl Harbor and Manila and the sinking of two British capital ships off Singapore, the war with China, now immeasurably enlarged, entered its third and final phase. Jiang Jieshi had found the powerful allies for whom he had been waiting.

Yet the last phase of the war was for the Chinese a sad and frustrating one. The coming of allies did not alter the geographical or the political facts in China. Jiang understood military buildup of the orthodox kind (five million men under arms in the Chongqing phase) and was a master of political bargaining, but he had few new ideas and profoundly mistrusted any policy of arming peasants for guerrilla warfare. He had never had anything to do with peasants at first hand, while the Communists had gained invaluable experience in knowing their thoughts, harnessing their abilities, and raising their political consciousness.

Inflation was the main problem of the beleaguered KMT government in the southwest. In 1944 the Chinese yuan was worth only 1/500 of its value before the war in 1937. The ranks of poverty and misery were swelled by the middle class and the civil servants, who had sold all they possessed and were reduced to the most desperate straits. Everyone who could peddle any influence was driven to do so, and graft and corruption of all kinds were rampant. Resentment against the government and wealthy officials grew more and more bitter. The presence of Allied war supplies, trucks, gasoline, radios, and weapons, brought in first by the Burma Road and then flown in "over the hump" of impassable mountains from India, made corruption in Chongqing all the worse.

Japan suffered the atom bomb attacks, and surrendered on August 14, 1945. But relief and new hope were is sight. Immediately disagreement arose in China concerning those entitled to receive Japanese surrenders of men and equipment. Jiang Jieshi claimed the sole right, while the CCP, to whom equipment was vital for the struggle they intended to continue, went ahead receiving matériel in the areas they controlled. Generals Joseph Stilwell and Albert C. Wedemeyer had been chiefs of staff to Jiang Jieshi and had attempted without much success to influence him. Now a still more distinguished American, General George C. Marshall, was sent at the end of 1945 to try to work out a coalition or some form of agreement between the KMT and the CCP. A cease-fire was with difficulty arranged in January 1946. Meanwhile the Americans helped the Nationalists transport troops back into the main cities of China to reestablish control over the country. The government returned to Nanjing, and China was recognized internationally as a great power with a major share in the victory over Japan. The United States had supplied China with aid worth $1.5 billion during the course of the war and, in the years after, from 1945 to 1948, provided $2 billion more. It was now in the anomalous position of trying to be the honest broker between the two sides, yet supplying one and not the other with massive aid. The KMT preponderance in weapons and supplies was enormous. But the Nationalist garrisons in the cities were on the defensive and guarded their resources instead of taking prompt and needed action to reassert control.

Military forces were hampered by rivalry with each other and by Jiang Jieshi's own unwillingness to delegate authority over strategy. As inflation soared, both civilians and the military became increasingly demoralized, and desertions to the CCP mounted. Prices multiplied 45 times in the first seven months of 1948, and in August of that year one U.S. dollar was equivalent to twelve million Chinese yuan. The CCP, sensing the mood of many leaders and intellectuals, outwardly welcomed the idea of coalition government, but the KMT would have nothing to do with it and repressed any who made such a suggestion.

The military showdown in this protracted and costly civil war took place in two theaters. In Manchuria the KMT secured the main cities, but the retreating Russians, while packing off to Russia a large amount of valuable machinery, handed over supplies to the CCP forces where possible, and at times delayed their departure (they had only been in the war for eight days) in order to ensure Japanese surrenders to the Communists and not to the KMT. The climax to the civil war in the northeast came with the surrender of over 300,000 Nationalist troops to the CCP in Manchuria in October 1948.

The second great battle was a roundup in the Huai River basin in north-central China. The CCP, by their control of the rural areas and by recapturing and using the railways, managed to surround a large number of Jiang Jieshi's available divisions, 66 out of 200 in the end. The KMT superiority in arms dwindled through desertions and Communist captures. In the end over half a million men were lost in December 1948, and of these probably more than two thirds gave themselves up. The Jiang Jieshi regime was finished on the mainland. In April 1949 the Communists penetrated south of the Yangzi. Shanghai fell in May, and Canton in October. Distant Chongqing was captured in November, and in December 1949 Jiang Jieshi and his government fled to Taiwan.

The last American ambassador, Dr. Leighton Stuart, had been president of Yenjing University and had spent a lifetime in the service of China. As negotiator he had tried every means to bring the two sides together, but without success. He now appealed to former students to stay on and try to influence the new China. This was interpreted by the CCP as an invitation to subversion from within. When Dr. Stuart left China he was vilified in the Chinese press. A succession of highly qualified and sympathetic Americans had done their best to bring about a reconciliation, but the fact was that it had never been in their power to do so. The gulf was too great, and the disagreement about both the ends and the means of the continuing Chinese revolution too fundamental, to permit of any but the most radical solution within China itself.

14

THE COMMUNIST REVOLUTION

1949–1965

One of the best pictures of Mao Zedong (1893–1976) shows him alone, in profile, striding along the street in Beijing (Peking) on a gray day in the early years of the People's Republic. In the background are a bronze lion of old China, a luxurious official limousine made in Russia, and the bare trees of winter. Mao is wearing, and filling out well, the plain jacket buttoned up to the neck, trousers, and soft cap with visor which became associated with his name. His hands behind his back, head set with determination, and eyes looking slightly upward, he is ploughing forward, calm, unhurried, but clear as to where he is headed. No one in the picture is paying any particular attention to him.

MAO ZEDONG

The Chinese people saw in Mao someone they could trust. He had an everyday common-man touch. He came from an upper peasant background, worked hard in the fields, studied China's past, wrote in a fairly good calligraphic hand, and used to compose poems on the grueling Long March. He had been for so long so fully accepted as the ideological leader that he could afford to seem to treat lightly the orthodox statements of the Communist Party, yet he was an absolutely convinced Marxist. He had an utter ruthlessness where necessary, beyond that of Jiang Jieshi and probably even of Napoleon, though that is not a quality to be quantified. Yet he won victories and disarmed opponents by occasionally—not often—admitting mistakes.

Mao found out early in his life how much could be accomplished by solid determination. When he was ten years old, his father once criticized him in front of strangers as being "lazy and gluttonous." He quarreled furiously with his father and carried out his threat to leave home. His mother brought him back and effected a reconciliation, in the course of which the boy apologized to his father. On another occasion he was beaten at the small school of his tutor and ran away, planning to go to a neighboring town. He became lost and wandered for three days in the hills before he was found and brought home. This has happened in other families, but it was interesting that Mao called it a "strike" and that he felt the strike had been successful, for he was not treated so severely either at home or at school thereafter.

Mao was self-educated after secondary school, which he completed when much older than his classmates. The chief influences in his early life and young adulthood were probably a teacher, Yang Changji, who had spent ten years in Japan and Britain; the Marxism both of Li Dazhao, whom he assisted in the library of Beijing University, and of Chen Duxiu, professor and editor of *La Nouvelle Jeunesse;* Mao's own omnivorous reading ("like a vegetable garden to an ox") of news and of political economy, philosophy, classic Chinese novels, sociology, and revolutionary literature; and his life among the peasants of Hunan and the analysis of their condition which he wrote up in 1926–1927.

His knowledge of the peasants and the loyal support of Zhu De and his nascent Red Army enabled Mao to develop guerrilla mobilization of peasant forces in the Jiangxi Soviet area from 1928 to 1934. He pursued a line independent of the official leadership of the CCP, then under control of the so-called Returned Students. These were younger men who, with the agent Pavel Mif, came back from Russia to the headquarters in Shanghai with the cachet of Soviet training. Shanghai became too hot, and this Central Committee with Zhou Enlai joined Mao and Zhu at Ruijin in Jiangxi in 1932. There was no proletariat of urban industrial workers in the mountains for the Returned Stu-

Mao Zedong (Mao Tse-tung).

An unusually cheerful and relaxed portrait of the Chairman. Trusted by the rank and file of the Communist Party, Mao could occasionally take a debonair attitude in trying to make the Party hacks place the spirit above the letter of Communist doctrine.

Xinhua News Agency

dents to promote or to rely on. Mao continued with the organization of the peasants and the fight for survival against Jiang Jieshi's attacks, although he never denied the importance of the industrial proletariat in Marxist theory. On the Long March the Party was perforce out of all contact by radio or otherwise with Moscow, and Mao rose to the supreme position at the Zunyi conference en route, as we have seen. He rose because of his Chinese experience and not through any Comintern appointment from Moscow. He was challenged but never ousted from the leadership from that point on.

When the Long March was over, Yanan became the scene of intensive training of Army and Party cadres, and those principles were worked out in the realities of the Chinese situation which would enable the takeover in 1949 to work as smoothly as it did and would determine the broad lines of CCP policy from then on. In the Red Army officers and men received equal pay. Soldiers were allowed to express their ideas, but there were always Party members among them in the ranks, usually in the proportion of one out of every four men. Corporal punishment was abolished. Mao insisted that guerrilla tactics alone were not enough, that secure bases must be built up, and that working out from these bases it was the noncombatant function of the Army to spread political propaganda and organize the peasant masses. To do this the soldiers had to respect the peasants and help them with their farming. In Yanan the soldiers made shoes and knitted gloves. Women leaders dressed like men— "Why should we look like women?" Though a majority of Communists in the area were comparatively youthful, Yanan was reported to be "sexless." Contrary to the usual experience with resident troops, rape of peasant women was practically unknown. Everyone was expected to work hard. Now that Yanan is a shrine to the modern generation of Chinese, the rooms where Mao Zedong worked are shown to the public, including the place where he wrote the "Essay on Protracted War" in 1938. For the first two days he is said not to have slept at all, and he was working so hard, the story goes, that he was not conscious that his shoes were smoldering in contact with the stove until they burned through to his toes.

In Yanan in 1942 Mao placed special emphasis on intensive training periods to "correct unorthodox tendencies," first in the thought of Party members, then in their speaking and writing, and lastly in their relations with each other and with others beyond the Party. The methods of training and retraining were to become classic means to be expanded to the whole of China later. They resemble in certain ways the early Methodist class meetings of the days of John Wesley; like him, Mao aimed at nothing less than the creation of a new type of man. In small groups and with religious fervor members criticized themselves and each other and uncovered their motives. Then in public meetings they confessed their guilt and made clear their repentance, cleansed state, and new resolves.

It is often a matter of convenient shorthand to attribute all leadership to Mao Zedong himself, but this conveys a false impression. Mao acted within the leadership circle of the Party, and the decisions under Party discipline were joint ones. Yet Mao Zedong did play an important role, and he was elevated to the position of a sage in retrospect partly because of his mastery of the pungent phrase and his constant realization that he had to speak in the simplest possible way to the ordinary man and woman. "Political power comes from the barrel of a gun." "A revolution is not the same as inviting people to dinner . . . or doing fancy needlework." And of the united front with the KMT to fight Japan during the Yanan days, he used an old Chinese saying, "Each dreaming his own dreams while sleeping in the same bed." He made frequent use of Chinese proverbs and folk sayings: "lifting a rock and dropping it on one's own foot," "the frog in the well who thinks he sees the whole sky."

Yanan was a place for consolidation and training but also a base for action, first in winning over the peasants of the surrounding area and, after 1937, in fighting the Japanese. The Shanxi-Hebei-Chahar Border Region Government was the result of action both local and emanating from Yanan, while the Japanese were in control of most of north China. Then the guerrillas moved out east from Yanan across the Yellow River, into the great north China plain, and farther east into Shandong, using the route along the provincial border between Hebei and Henan. In this, as in southeast China before the Long March, they were following an old practice of peasant rebellions, which found the safest bases or operating areas to be those on the boundary between two provinces, where neither provincial governor wanted to take the trouble or the responsibility for bandit suppression. When the Communist-directed guerrillas reached their fullest effectiveness in the later stages of the war against Japan, they were in control of areas of China north of the Yangzi River whose inhabitants totaled 90 million.

THE TAKEOVER

Thus, when the civil war ended in 1949 with the victory of the CCP, the takeover of the country as a whole was rendered much easier. The question which puzzles many is how the Chinese people, with deep roots in tradition and a strong sense of family, could accept with such apparent ease the coming of the alien philosophy of communism. The answers to this question touch upon many facets of the national character and are hard to summarize.

One feature was sheer war weariness, which is not surprising when one considers the agonies of the declining Manzhou dynasty, the chaos and suffering of the warlord era, and the grave divisions of the Nationalist phase, despite some real gains in unity and stability. This was followed by the aggression of Japan and then four years of civil war. Peace at any price is a phrase with a pejorative meaning in the West, but in China's circumstances it is readily understandable.

The discipline and helpfulness shown by the Red Army, now called the People's Liberation Army, or PLA, was a second reason for the acceptance of the CCP government. In spite of the usual view of soldiers as little better than bandits, the contrast with the traditional and especially with the warlord armies was so marked as to create a very favorable image of the new regime. These men said "please" and "thank you," paid for what they took for supplies, and had strict instructions not to commandeer even a needle from a civilian home. The government at first took a soft line with the propertied classes, with certain exceptions in areas where land reform was put into operation before the takeover. Glowing promises were made concerning the new day of benefits for all which was dawning with the coming of the Communist power.

Apart from this element of propaganda, there was a greater similarity between the new Communist and the old Confucian order than is commonly realized by those little acquainted with the traditional inner dynamics of Chinese rule. The Chinese had always had various and sometimes clashing views on many subjects but expressed differences openly on matters concerning the government only on rare occasions. There was a state orthodoxy and experts, who were the officials old or new, put in place to guard the orthodoxy and administer the country in accordance with it. It was the duty of the ruled to obey the rulers and within the allowed framework to carry on their lives and their production in their own way. When the Communists came to power, few guessed how penetrating and all-embracing would be the interference of the rulers with the private life of every citizen, but the framework was somewhat the same. Then there was an undoubted positive element in the Marxist interpretation of history, which, after the decades of conflicting views, appealed to the intellectuals. Here was a Western philosophy of history—and the West was by now intellectually respectable—which seemed to fit the facts as the Chinese saw them, or wished to see them, in their own experience. The inevitable decline of capitalism, the self-defeating nature of imperialism, and the certain rise of a socialism whose egalitarian ideals coincided with an ancient messianic strain recurring at intervals in China's past (see page 157—all these seemed to have enough basis in fact to be believed. There is nothing so reassuring as the feeling that history is on your side.

"The world is progressing, the future is bright and *no one can change this general trend of history* [my italics]. We should carry on constant propaganda among the people on the facts of world progress and the bright future ahead so that they will build their confidence in victory."*

When the CCP took over control of China, the first form of government was the People's Political Consultative Council set up in September 1949 with 662 delegates. This was in theory a coalition government, and some non-Communists were given important official posts. But in the controlling committee of 56 persons, 31 were members of the CCP. The Premier was Zhou Enlai. To ensure a rapid exercise of control, the country was divided into six regions, each under a bureau with military and political authority. Most of the existing administrators at the local and some higher levels were retained in their jobs.

*Mao Zedong, *On the Chungking Negotiations,* in *Selected Works,* vol. IV, p. 59.

LAND REFORM

One of the first tasks of the new government was land reform, the redistribution of land confiscated from landlords and given to the poorer peasants. This process had been begun in the Jiangxi Soviet, carried on in north China, and intensified after 1947. The Agrarian Law of 1950 made land reform the rule for the whole of China, and the process was largely complete by the first months of 1953, a gigantic undertaking. A small cadre would find out who in a given village were the worst "enemies of the people." (The word "cadre" *[ganbu]* may refer to a group of Communists with some training, as here, or to an individual.) They would gather all the persons in the village and encourage them in "struggle meetings" to denounce those who had exploited them. When hatred had erupted or been worked up, certain of the most grasping landlords and richest farmers would be paraded before a People's Court, accused, and condemned, some to execution, which the people would be compelled to witness, and some to reeducation and rehabilitation by labor. Peasant associations were set up, which arranged the classification of land by productivity, the confiscation, and the redistribution to those designated to receive it. The first two classes, landlords who lived on rents and rich peasants who tilled part and leased part of their land, would have some or all of their land taken. Middle peasants were usually left their own holdings, which they were already farming. The lowest two classes, poor peasants and landless farm laborers, received a new allotment. The number of the accused whose land was confiscated would be different in different districts and usually proportional to the amount of land required in that area to provide a minimal amount for the poor peasants and farm laborers. The average distributed share was just over one third of an acre, and in heavily populated districts about half that amount.

It was a time of terror. A French observer in 1951 wrote of the "shouts of the crowd *'sha! sha!'* [kill! kill!], the screams of those stoned or beaten to death broadcast at every street corner all day long. No one could escape."* The labor camps had a fearsome work program. The American Federation of Labor estimate, drawing on Communist figures, was that two million died in five years under abuses of the slave labor system. An escaped slave laborer reported in 1952 that more than half the men died from exposure, undernourishment, disease, and overwork on the Chongqing–Chengdu Railway.

Many farmers in the countryside and merchants in the towns, to whom attention was given later, committed suicide rather than face constant struggle meetings. It is estimated that one and a half million persons were executed during the land reform movement. Li Li-san of the Politburo gave this figure publicly, and a British doctor, resident at the time in central China and known to this author, arrived at the same figure from calculations he made, admittedly extrapolating from numbers killed in the area of which he had personal knowledge. The terror drew to a close in 1953. Thought control continued.

*R. L. Walker, *China Under Communism: The First Five Years* (Mystic, Conn.: Verry, 1956), p. 219.

The objectives of land reform were to improve the lot of the poor and make them feel they had a stake in the country and a loyalty to the new government. In many though by no means all cases, the victims had in the past shown greed and cruelty in their dealings with the peasants. But the objectives of land reform also included information and control. The CCP by means of the cadres obtained an insight into conditions in every part of China and useful lists of enemies of the people. By implicating the local population in the "judicial" process and the killings, control through fear was quickly established. Those most enthusiastic in carrying out Communist principles, particularly among youth, were also revealed to the Party and could thereafter be enlisted and trained.

THOUGHT REFORM

The most intensive efforts were made by drives and campaigns to move the whole of China off one psychological base and onto another. The "four olds" were to be abandoned: "old ideas, habits, customs, and culture." Sustained supervision and persuasion were needed. "Individual small peasants, if not organized and guided, will spontaneously take the capitalist path" said a *People's Daily* editorial in October 1953.

The Three-Anti *(san-fan)* campaign was instituted in October 1951 and was intended to eliminate corruption, waste, and "bureaucratism" among officials, many of whom were not Communist by conviction. The Five-Anti *(wu-fan)* campaign which followed helped to expose among businessmen and the bourgeoisie bribery, tax defaulting, stealing state property, cheating in all forms, and benefiting by state economic secrets. This second campaign gave the government a large measure of control over private businesses (450,000 firms are said to have been examined) and produced the equivalent of over $1 billion, as well as gains in standards of public honesty which distinguished the PRC, particularly in its early years.

Every segment of society was included in reform. For intellectuals there was the Thought Reform movement of September 1951. They were expected to sever all links with the bourgeois world at home and abroad. Six thousand five hundred professors took courses directed by Professor Ai Siqi, a leader in the application of Chinese Communist thought, although previously not too highly regarded professionally by his colleagues. For Chinese in the Christian churches there was the Three-Self movement: self-government, self-support, and self-propagation. The natural, patriotic, and indeed necessary desire for independence was pushed further by the authorities, and leading churchmen were encouraged to denounce the cultural imperialism of their former overseas colleagues in a manner and to a degree which bore little relation to the facts. Art and literature were to be regarded henceforth as instruments in the class struggle. At first the tendency was to discard all of China's past heritage as belonging to the "feudal" period and hence of no value. But very soon the results of reconsideration began to surface, and certain authors were commended as having taken the part of the people against their masters. We are too near the events of the time to attempt any final appraisal of contemporary authors and artists in the People's Republic, but so far little of lasting artistic merit seems to have been produced. The CCP leaders consider that this is of far less importance than the pressing reorientation of the whole society.

As the decade of the 1950s progressed, it was possible to reduce the emphasis on fear and increase the use of methods of persuasion. Some of these were copied from Russia. The People's Republic has been free of the wholesale purges and liquidation of leading figures which marked the Stalin regime in the USSR. But the methods of persuasion included severe psychological pressures on individuals, which were justified by the CCP as necessary to turn the thinking of the entire country around. The system of self-criticism, and criticism by others in small groups, was adopted as standard in the retraining process in which thousands, then millions, were involved. Cut off from family and familiar surroundings, these persons were set to read and memorize such texts as Liu Shaoqi's *How to Be a Good Communist*. Long hours and hard work produced fatigue, tension, and uncertainty. There was always the lurking threat of being taken away to a labor battalion. Extreme language of praise and blame was used to paint the two sides in the struggle for "liberation" in tones of total white or black. Life was serious and humor decadent. Romantic love was a mark of bourgeois mentality. Friend and foe were to be distinguished on the basis of class, but anyone of any class could become one of "the people" by a change of heart—and only "the people" had rights. Confessions had to be written and rewritten and recited in public before the group. Feelings of guilt, shame, and "face" were used as manipulative devices in brainwashing (the literal translation of *xi-nao*). Silence was no defense; everyone had, sooner or later, to take part. When the confession was finally accepted, the individual experienced an enormous sense of relief and cleansing. He or she came to associate this new "liberation" with the Communist way of life and with service to the people. Emotions, sentiments, individual plans—all were to find their place only in the battle for a new society. These highly intensive methods of persuasion were effective in raising trained cadres, winning over enemies, extracting confessions, and gaining control of the masses. But by 1953 there had been a plethora of "drives," and under the slogan "The Five Too Many" these were reduced. One railway freight yard official in Tientsin was said to have attended seventeen meetings in five days occupying seven hours' time per day.

KOREA

Although the Chinese government was deeply involved in internal changes, it did not fail to devote attention to affairs on its borders. The attack of North Korea on South Korea in June 1950 was made possible by the supply of Russian arms. It does not appear to have been instigated by China. However, when the United Nations forces crossed the 38th parallel, the Chinese responded in October by sending in "volunteers" in large numbers to aid North Korea. When President Harry S. Truman had dispatched the large American contingent which formed the backbone of the UN force, he had also ordered the U.S. Seventh Fleet to isolate Taiwan and prevent the Communists and the Nationalists from invading each other's territory, thus blocking an attempt on Taiwan which it was suspected the PRC had planned at this point. Although the war in Korea ended in a draw with the truce of 1951, its conclusion was hailed in China as something of a victory. (Truce talks went on slowly at Panmunjom and an armistice was finally signed in July 1953.) Patriotic Chinese, especially among the liberal intellectuals, were impressed by their country's performance. Korea had been traditionally a dangerous back door into China, and now the Chinese had for the first time in the modern period been able to fight foreign nations to a standstill and halt their advance on Manchuria, with its valuable resources and comparatively modern industry. In the same year as China's defense of North Korea (1950), Chinese troops were sent into Tibet and within twelve months had "liberated" that country, which had traditional ties with China but which deeply resented this interference.

THE CONSTITUTION

It will be evident that the CCP now felt itself to be in control of the situation. The Constitution of 1954 did not radically alter the government arrangements but enhanced the power of the central organs and gave less scope to non-Communists. The six regional bureaus were discontinued. (They were reinstated in 1960.) The National People's Congress met for the first time in 1954, and under it were People's Representative Congresses down to the village level. On the principle of "democratic centralism," congresses were elected at the local level, and each of these in turn voted to send a certain small number of their members up to the congress of the level above. Thus the system was representative and "democratic" upward in a limited sense. But the policy came downward from the top—"centralism." Its application was discussed, but it could not be altered. The congresses gave those in command a feel for public opinion and transmitted their requirements and goals for local action. A great deal of initiative and feeling of participation, new in China, was developed at the grass-roots level.

The real power lay with the Communist Party, whose officials also held government posts in a parallel system. The Party's Central Committee had 187 members (1962 figure), the Politburo 25, and its Standing Committee 7. Beneath these again were district and local Party committees corresponding to the government's congress structure. As a means of enlisting the energies of all, and directing their thinking and action, there were mass organizations for Women, Youth, Cooperative Workers, and so on. The New Democratic Youth League had twelve million members in 1954 of ages fourteen to twenty-five, and the Children's Pioneer Corps eight million, ages nine to fourteen. The children were taught the Five Loves—for fatherland, people, labor, science, and public property. Beneficial results in cheerful public responsibility are to be seen in China today. It is to be noted that love for parents was not on the list. Every citizen in the land met for discussion, planning, "struggle," and inspiration in one or more ongoing groups in these mass organizations and in street, neighborhood, factory, village, or professional groups. By no means all were admitted to membership of the Communist Party, considered a high privilege. The Communist Party membership was:

1921	57
1927	58,000
1945	1,211,000
1949	4,488,000
1961	17,000,000
1989	48,000,000

Figures from Reischauer, Fairbank, and Craig, *East Asia: The Modern Transformation*, p. 877, except for 1989 and 1921.

As soon as the civil war was over and the CCP had gained control, Mao Zedong went on a visit to Moscow in December 1949. He signed a thirty-year Sino-Soviet Alliance for defense against Japan and any ally associated with Japan. The ally clause clearly referred to the United States. The USSR extended military aid to China and arranged joint development of mines in Xinjiang province. Technicians came to China in considerable numbers, while Chinese students were received in Russia for training. The Chinese, however, had to pay for all aid received.

China became more independent of Russia after the death of Stalin in 1953. Russia then relinquished joint control of the railways in Manchuria and, two years later, turned over the Port Arthur naval base to the Chinese without requiring compensation in return. A combination of factors led to estrangement between the PRC and the USSR: increasing nationalism on both sides, the problems of a very long common land frontier, the Chinese sensitivity to any potential threat to their nuclear installations in Xinjiang and above all the ideological split which began about 1956 and grew steadily wider. The nature of the split is an important topic, but its detailed treatment would take us too far afield. The essence of it seems to be contained in the mild word "revisionism." The Chinese felt they were keeping the true Marxist-Leninist faith, while Russia, by de-Stalinization, a soft line toward the West, prominence given to technocrats over revolutionaries, stress on consumer goods, and similar policies, had betrayed the cause. The Russians with no warning withdrew their technicians from China in 1960, and by 1963 the two countries were exchanging insults and competing for the leadership of the Communist world.

ECONOMICS

The Chinese Communist government tackled the problem of inflation with determination at the very beginning of its period of rule. The government took control of the banks and the system of credit, set up six national trading corporations to help bring consumer prices into line, and greatly improved the efficiency of tax collection. The country's main asset was the increased productivity of the people under a more stable and energetic government. But stringent measures had also to be used, such as increased fines, rationing, forced loans, and the sale of government bonds sometimes under pressure. Inflation was no longer a threat by the middle of the year 1950.

The decade of the 1950s proved crucial to the emerging new China. Problems had constantly to be faced, some arising from nature (the floods and crop failures of 1953–1954), others from overboldness or poor planning, such as the Great Leap Forward of 1958. But when the decade ended, astounding advances in agriculture and industry had been registered.

The First Five-Year Plan

In order to pay for Russian aid, which was of enormous benefit to China, and in order to finance the establishment of heavy industry, China did what Japan had done nearly a hundred years before. The maximum returns had to be extracted from China's basic source, agriculture. The Party decided, in a manner entirely different from that of the Meiji statesmen, on the collectivization of farmland, but on a gradual basis, which might avoid the calamitous experience Russia had had in a similar venture. The first step was to form mutual-aid teams, in which implements, animals, and labor were pooled. Then the authorities set up cooperatives, which bought the land from the peasant owners who had in many cases so recently acquired it. The cooperatives sold or loaned seed, purchased the crop, fixed prices, sold fertilizer, and controlled the whole agricultural process. This in turn yielded a higher proportion of grain for government use. The plan was announced in 1953, and large numbers of cadres were used to get it adopted. By May of 1956, 90 percent of the farmers were said to be in cooperatives.

A similar process was going on in industry. By October 1952 nationalization extended to about 80 percent of the heavy industry, and 40 percent of the light industry; the government operated all of the railways and about 60 percent of the steamships plying the home waters; it controlled 90 percent of all loans and deposits through the People's Bank; finally State trading companies were responsible for about 90 percent of imports and exports, for about half of the wholesale trade and for about 30 percent of the retail trade.*

The first Five-Year Plan ran from 1953 to 1957 but required administrative preparation and the training of personnel. Its goals were therefore not

*Ibid., pp. 106–07.

announced until midway through the period. The support of the educated class was obviously necessary if these sweeping changes in agriculture and the rapid promotion of industry were to succeed. Both restraints and inducements were employed to secure greater cooperation from able men. In 1956 a campaign against "rightists" was launched, and at the same time promises made to improve working conditions for trained leaders, including more opportunity for research and time for themselves. The authorities, feeling confident at this point about the acceptance of the regime and desiring to improve performance, invited criticism of the bureaucrats and the cadres. To popularize the drives and campaigns, each one had a pithy phrase or a slogan. This one operated under a phrase from the classics: "Let a hundred flowers bloom together, let the hundred schools of thought contend." The results surprised if they did not overwhelm the Party. Complaints and criticisms poured in, and by May 1957 critics were being severely repressed. The idea had never been to call in question the authority of the Party or the validity of its aims.

The unity of the CCP leadership had been well preserved through the years since 1934, partly no doubt because of the shared experiences of the bitter Long March and the formative Yanan period. Such differences as there were had been well hidden from the outside world. But politics and disagreement over ways and means, if not ends, are to be found in all human affairs, and the aftermath of the Hundred Flowers showed that there were two opposing views within the Party. It was not the substance but the pace of change which appears to have been in question. Mao Zedong, Liu Shaoqi, and those supporting them initiated in 1958 the Great Leap Forward, which by a mighty effort of the will of the Chinese people was to bring in the socialist society.

THE GREAT LEAP FORWARD

The Great Leap Forward had the announced aim of overtaking Britain in steel production in fifteen years. One objective was to support the investment in heavy industry by using the spare energies of farmers and townspeople in a vast decentralized network of small-scale production. In particular, scrap iron was to be melted down in "backyard furnaces." But in a short time the scrap ran out. The iron and steel produced in the small furnaces was of inferior quality and did not hold up in use. Critical controls of purity and temperature probably could not be maintained. The plan to use the vast manpower and will of China to make up for technical lacks ran into trouble over the facts of metallurgy.

In the field of agriculture, collectivization was forced onward from the cooperative to the much larger commune, of which 26,000 were created, averaging 5,000 households and about 10,000 acres each. The commune was a self-sufficient entity embracing not only agriculture but education, industry, and the functions of local government. Men and women were in some communes housed in separate dormitories and families only allowed to be together at certain times. Children were cared for in nurseries while mothers worked. The small private plots, fruit trees, and mulberry trees which had been permitted in private ownership heretofore were done away with.

The 1958 weather conditions and harvest were good, and it seemed as though considerable success was attending the new scheme. But resistance developed among peasants to this totally regimented existence without benefit of family. The agricultural plan was running into difficulties over the facts of human life. Moreover, it appeared that the reports for 1958 had been wildly exaggerated. Grain production had really been 250 million tons, not 375 million as claimed. Steel had reached 8 million tons output, not 11 million. Zhou Enlai admitted the errors, and targets for the next year were revised downward. The commune as the main rural unit remained but it was divided into production brigades and production teams. The production team corresponded roughly to the old-style village and was a manageable and familiar human unit. Domestic life in homes was restored, and private plots, trees, and the right to keep and sell a few hens and a piglet or two was given back to the people. Nurseries continued to be widely used in order to enable women to work outside the home.

The political aftermath of the Great Leap Forward in the inner circles of the Party is not easy to assess. Mao Zedong retired as Chief of State in 1958, to be succeeded by Liu Shaoqi, but remained on as Chairman of the Party. He spent a period in Shanghai and is said to have been in poor health for a time in the early 1960s. The economic and social aftermath of the Great Leap among the people generally was serious enough to make it perfectly clear that some gross errors and miscalculations had been made. Their effect was felt for three or more years. Three bad harvests followed the good one of 1958. Many had insufficient food, though serious famine was averted. Industry declined. Workers in field and factory showed signs of being overworked and dispirited. The top leadership developed a more cautious and realistic approach. They gave a higher priority to the needs of agriculture and revised the style of the communes, as indicated. Party bureaucrats, theoreticians, professors, and many others from the cities and towns were sent to the countryside (*xia fang,* "downward transfer") "to learn from the masses," to be renewed—and put in their place—by manual labor. This policy was continued, for Mao had an almost mystical feeling for the ultimate wisdom of the masses.

FOREIGN AFFAIRS

Some of China's military activities beyond its own borders have been touched upon (pp. 207–208), but it was active also in diplomatic affairs. The leading, and for years almost the only, Chinese Communist expert on foreign affairs was the veteran Zhou Enlai. Zhou saw Africa as "ripe for revolution" and visited it at least eight times. Some attempts at intervention in Africa's new states were unsuccessful, and the ousting of Nkrumah from Ghana set back the

Zhou Enlai (Chou En-lai).

"Sheer capacity, integrity, and experience: Is it fanciful to imagine that Zhou's sophistication and adroitness in handling foreign affairs stemmed in part from his familiarity as a student with Tokyo and Paris?"

Xinhua News Agency

Communist cause. But the aid to Tanzania in the building of the railway from the coast to the interior, and the friendly relations established by the Chinese technicians and workers, made an impression all over Africa. Considerable efforts were made to spread communism among the large number of Chinese in Indonesia and among the Indonesians themselves. But a planned coup d'état was ruthlessly suppressed by the Indonesian military, who were strongly Muslim and anti-Communist. Yet since the 1960s China has had some success in its efforts to represent itself as the champion of the third world nations and as an example of how to emerge as a great power from a dependent and underdeveloped position.

15

THE CULTURAL REVOLUTION

1966–1979

Unquestionably the major event of the 1960s in China was the Great Proletarian Cultural Revolution *(wu-chan jieji wen-hua da ge-ming)*. It is a long, clumsy title, but each word counts, for it was strongly egalitarian, intended to appeal to the masses over the heads of the Party officials, and it was cultural in the Communist sense of altering the values of society. That it was great may be seen from the fact that it shook the Party and the country to their foundations, closed schools and universities, slowed production, and virtually shut down all diplomatic activity. It lasted in a virulent form for about two years, and in milder form for at least eighteen months more. Mao appeared to think it ideologically worthwhile, though for a period the revolution was almost out of control. The basic values of the Cultural Revolution, however, were sustained until Mao's death in 1976. The Party itself later assessed it as a disaster.

THE GREAT PROLETARIAN CULTURAL REVOLUTION

The opening shot was fired when Jiang Qing, Mao's wife, wrote an article in the summer of 1966 criticizing a popular play as having made veiled threats against Chairman Mao's ideological line. The agitation by student youth began in Peking in August. An early account reaching the West gave a clue to the aim of the upheaval—"to bypass the Communist Party apparatus and force the hierarchy's political foes into submission"—and to its methods—"Mao's opponents criticized before a mass rally [1,500,000 Red Guards]."* Bands of students with apparently true spontaneity, but also with Chairman Mao's support, published their views and their demands on wall

* *The New York Times,* October 20, 1966.

posters and demonstrated in large numbers, using red armbands indicating themselves as Red Guards. Opposition began to center on Liu Shaoqi, who had actually been designated as number two in the Party hierarchy and Mao's probable successor. Liu was criticized as being too pragmatic and moderate, and as deceiving the people by taking the capitalist road. The background to these charges lay in Mao's own belief in the necessity of continuing revolution, in his feeling that Party functionaries were settling down to make careers of their jobs, like mandarins of old, and that the youth of China needed to experience something akin to the "revolutionary dynamism" their predecessors had known on the Long March. Mao took an enormous risk in attempting not merely to reform but to bypass the whole structure of Party committees from top to bottom.

In February 1967 his veteran companion Zhu De was attacked for having opposed a plan of Chairman Mao and Defense Minister Lin Biao "to strengthen defenses along the Soviet border." Zhu De was said to be "attempting to glorify the Soviet Union and to make us relax our guard and precautions against that country." But in the same month a change took place; the army by then was being called on to curb the pro-Maoist faction, and in March the government cautioned the Red Guards against "the dangers of anarchy." Students from universities and schools were being given free railways passes and were pouring into Peking and the other cities in huge numbers. For them it was a "revolutionary experience." But they were splitting into factions over ideology, tearing down each other's posters, and outdoing one another in claims to be of the true Maoist faith.

Lin Biao, who had issued "the little red book" of quotations from Chairman Mao for army use—now reprinted in millions of copies for the students—did not find it a simple matter, it seems, to call in the army to quell disturbances. There were reports of pro- and anti-Mao divisions in the army itself, particularly in outlying areas such as Xinjiang and north Manchuria. In March 1967, which was a crucial time in the progress of the Cultural Revolution, Zhou Enlai was called upon to conduct the daily affairs of the government. This was seen by some in the West as evidence of a softer line but probably did not indicate a major change of policy. The vast bulk of the army remained obedient to the commands of the government, which was still controlled by Mao Zedong and his main supporters, who were listed in the spring of 1967 as Lin Biao; Gang Sheng, a Politburo member; Chen Boda, long a close associate of Mao; and Jiang Qing, Mao's wife.

After more than a year of the Cultural Revolution, China was still in a very disturbed state. Factions were reported as clashing in many of the provinces, especially in the south, in September 1967—as in Guangdong, Guizhou, Zhejiang, Yunnan, Jiangsu, Inner Mongolia, and to a lesser degree in Hunan, Henan, and Shandong. By March 1969, over two and a half years from the beginning of the revolution, there was a government-directed drive to see that all schools were opened and factionalism stamped out. The schools were supposed to have begun full operation a year before, but most did not.

Universities were not reopened until September 1970, a four-year interval. Liu Shaoqi, the Chief of State and former Deputy Chairman of the Party, was not liquidated but was kept under house arrest. A meeting of the Central Committee of the CCP in December 1968 ousted him from all his government and Party posts, an action that normally requires a two-thirds majority vote. This majority was attained by including in the meeting nonmembers who had been given "full rights," including voting rights. That Liu Shaoqui's expulsion had taken so long to achieve indicates the political strength of his supporters. Once expelled, however, Liu was treated abominably. In spite of having authored the once-classic instruction book, *How to Be a Good Communist,* Liu was subjected to calumny, to ceaseless interrogations and physical abuse in prison, and was refused medical care, all factors which contributed to his death in 1969. He was posthumously reinstated by the Party in 1980. But Liu was not the only prominent Communist Party member to become a victim of the Cultural Revolution. When the long-postponed Ninth Congress of the CCP convened in April 1969, two-thirds of the Central Committee's old membership of ninety were missing.

People who were considered "intellectuals" had come under special attack during the Cultural Revolution. Opposition to them actually had begun long before, particularly during the Anti-Rightist Campaign of 1957. But their situation became much worse during the Cultural Revolution when the revolution's leaders promoted an attack on the Four Olds—old customs, old habits, old culture, and old thinking. Any contact with Western education, Western businessmen, or Western missionaries was ample cause for suspicion. The Red Guards were left to interpret and to carry out this general mandate against the Four Olds, and they did so with vicious determination. Thousands of scholars and professional persons were literally beaten to death. Many others committed suicide, sometimes after having tried to stave off Red Guard attacks by destroying their art collections or libraries. Thousands more were condemned to years of imprisonment, often in solitary confinement. The May Seventh Cadre Schools, which were essentially hard-labor camps, subjected millions to exhausting farm work, meager rations, the incessant study of Mao's works, and constant public self-examinations and confessions.

The extreme behavior of the Red Guards, most of them of high school age, rebelling against their parents, teachers, and even local Party officials, has been attributed to their own frustration and sense of powerlessness, built up over years of being reined in and spied upon, prevented from contact with the opposite sex, and force-fed an education comprised of propaganda studies and exhortations on the necessity for revolutionary sacrifice.

Despite its draconian excesses, however, the immense egalitarian effort of the Cultural Revolution did help to eliminate some of the old contrasts and rivalries between town and country, rich and poor—but at the cost of years of work and hard-won progress. In place of the former Party committees, a triple control system was instituted at all levels in the provinces, districts, schools, communes and factories. The system consisted of representatives from the

Army, the more responsible Red Guards, and the "peasants and workers." Among this last category, rehabilitated Party committee members could be and were included.

ADMISSION TO THE UN

Great Britain had recognized the People's Republic of China soon after its inception, but that action had not brought any noticeable benefit to Britain. The United States had consistently led the opposition to the admission of mainland China to the United Nations. Then in 1971, President Richard M. Nixon, in a move widely felt to be sensible and statesmanlike, publicly altered his own stand on China and prepared to pay an official visit to Peking in the near future.

On August 2 the United States announced it would support action in the fall meeting of the UN General Assembly to seat the PRC, but at the same time said it opposed the expulsion of Nationalist China from that body. The UN debate on the question opened on October 18. On October 25, a resolution to expel the Republic of China and give the Chinese seat to the People's Republic of China, sponsored by Albania and twenty other minor nations, was approved in a historic vote of 76 for, 35 against, with 17 abstentions. The overwhelming majority for the PRC seemed to come as something of a surprise to the United States delegation.

President Nixon's visit to China, thoroughly prepared for by Secretary of State Henry A. Kissinger and American China experts, took place in February 1972 amid much publicity and unprecedented television coverage. In this instance, personal summit diplomacy did serve a useful purpose in creating a new climate of opinion worldwide and influencing favorably the attitudes of the people of China and the United States toward one another after many years of isolation. A joint communiqué issued in Shanghai at the end of the visit pledged both countries to resume normal diplomatic relations as soon as this could be arranged. U.S. authorities were clear that this implied significant changes of some kind in their relations with Taiwan, although it was left open at this point exactly what these would be. In March, Great Britain proceeded from its earlier recognition of the PRC to full diplomatic relations on the basis of acknowledging that Taiwan was a "province of China."

THE CAMPAIGN AGAINST LIN BIAO AND CONFUCIUS

Meanwhile, in 1971, shock waves were disturbing the inner leadership group of the Communist Party. Mao Zedong had dispensed with one possible successor, Liu Shaoqi, at the time of the Cultural Revolution. He had designated in his place Lin Biao, Marshal of the People's Liberation Army, who had been a longtime aide. Then, to the consternation of everyone within and without China, it was reported that Lin Biao had plotted against Mao Zedong and been found out. It was further reported that, in endeavoring to escape to Russia along with his wife, son, and several leaders of the Army, he had been killed when his plane crashed in Mongolia on September 13, 1971. The exact details of the episode have never been established. Mao Zedong needed the Army to limit the chaos produced by the Cultural Revolution, but he was dissatisfied with the purges and long investigations of veteran party cadres being conducted by the Army. He began removing supporters of Lin Biao within the Army *before* Lin's alleged plot came to light.

But whatever the truth of the matter, the downfall of Lin Biao required some justification, and the position of the Party needed strengthening. In 1973 an intensive "Campaign against Lin Biao and Confucius" was launched. To criticize a military figure of the present in conjunction with a philosopher from the distant past may seem strange. But in the PRC, history, philosophy, ideology and politics are one, and are used together to drive home a lesson. Moreover, the lesson must be in stark and simple terms which a peasant can understand, since the mass line is what is ultimately important.

According to an article in the Party publication *Da Gong Bu,* Confucius was criticized for only "pretending" to be loyal to his sovereign and standing for morality for all, but in reality supporting the exploiting aristocratic class. So it was claimed to be with Lin Biao, who pretended to support Chairman Mao with "the little red book" of the *Sayings,* but who was actually working for private ends against Mao and the Revolution.

ECONOMIC GAINS

The National People's Congress, meeting in January 1975 for the first time in ten years, passed new regulations in a Constitutional Charter, which included: the right of farmers in communes to maintain private plots for "sideline production" (an activity that was not new, but was now clearly recognized); the right of factory workers to perform limited work for themselves, provided they did not hire employees; and the right to engage in demonstrations and strikes. These regulations reflected the influence of Zhou Enlai and a more moderate group in the leadership.

Zhou was able to report gains of 51 percent in agricultural yields during the decade 1964–1974 and a doubling of industrial output in the same period. The beginning of oil drilling and distribution showed very promising results. But at the same time there was considerable social unrest. Factional strife among workers and even sabotage were reported in Jiangxi province, and there were labor troubles in Hunan and northern Manchuria. In the midsummer of 1975 labor unrest in Hangzhou was severe enough to require the presence of 10,000 troops to maintain order.

On the political front, Zhou Enlai was able in 1973 to secure the rehabilitation and appointment as Deputy Premier of his protege, Deng Xiaoping, who had been purged in the Cultural Revolution in spite of having held the office of Secretary-General of the CCP.

DEATH OF ZHOU ENLAI

Zhou gave to the Congress the aim of "comprehensive modernization of agriculture, industry, national defense, and science and technology before the end of the twentieth century," which, he said, "would place China in the front rank of the world." But when the Congress disbanded, Zhou Enlai had only a year to live. He had had heart trouble in 1974, and on January 8, 1976, he died of cancer at the age of seventy-eight.

Born of a gentry, and not a worker, family in 1898, Zhou Enlai attended a Christian Middle School in Tientsin and began to study Marxism at the university. He spent some time in Japan and then, as a student in Paris, joined a Young Communist group at the same time as Li Lisan. On returning to China he was put in charge of political indoctrination at the Huangpu (Whampoa) Military Academy at the time of joint action of the CCP and the KMT. Active in the unsuccessful period of Communist city uprisings, he survived when the Li Lisan line was condemned by the Comintern (which had insisted on it in the first place). Later Zhou joined Mao Zedong in the Jiangxi Soviet in 1931 and went through the hardships of the Long March in 1934.

Zhou was prominent in the top leadership of the Party continuously from 1949. A superb and charming negotiator, he took a notable part in 1954 at Geneva in the settlement of Indochina after the defeat of the French. The next year saw the significant meeting of the Bandung Conference, when twenty-nine Asian and African states met for the first time without any of the great white powers being present. Zhou Enlai was recognized as a leader when he and Jawaharlal Nehru promulgated the five points for peaceful coexistence which Zhou had previously worked out. Of all the Communist leaders, Zhou was the most knowledgeable by far concerning the world outside China. He was Foreign Minister of the PRC from 1949 to 1958 and Premier from the foundation of the state in 1949 until his death. In all the ups and downs of politics, Zhou showed a remarkable ability to survive, even during the Cultural Revolution, but this was due less to any trimming of his beliefs than to sheer capacity, integrity, and experience. He became virtually indispensable to the conduct of his country's business, at least in foreign affairs. He was involved in the split with Russia in 1961 and the approach to the United States in 1972.

Zhou's influence was felt even after his death. At the Qing Ming spring festival commemorating the dead, wreaths were laid in his memory in Tiananmen Square on April 5, 1976. (He had died in January.) The wreaths were removed, apparently by government order; more wreaths appeared, and a riot broke out. In an unprecedented scene 30,000 persons broke loose, burned a government building, and were only brought under control when the militia was called out. Blame for the riot was laid at the door of Deng Xiaoping, and two days later he was ousted for the second time in his life, deprived of all his posts but allowed to retain his Party membership. Acting Premier Hua Guofeng was raised to the second position in the hierarchy as Premier in place of Zhou Enlai, immediately below Mao Zedong. This probably represented a compromise between the radical and moderate factions. Still, the death of Zhou Enlai was like the loosening of a linchpin. Serious vibrations were set up in the functioning of the state machine.

DEATH OF MAO ZEDONG

Nineteen-seventy-six was a fateful year. Zhu De, another veteran of the Long March and the greatest general in the history of the PRC, died on July 6. The Great Helmsman, Mao Zedong himself, after contesting every inch of the way in a series of illnesses, had to give up the struggle and died on September 9 at the age of eighty-two. Even allowing for the excessive adulation and the myriad portraits of the Chairman, promoted as a symbol of unity and a center of coherence, Mao Zedong had truly written his epitaph in the entire history of the People's Republic from its beginning. He had been the one above all others to recognize the importance and the potential of the Chinese peasant, that immemorial and unchanging figure, and, in spite of Marxist-Leninist doctrine about the industrial worker, to insist that the peasant would make the Chinese revolution succeed. Mao was based in China's past. He was fond of the traditional novels, especially *The Water Margin* (also known as *All Men Are Brothers*), written in the fourteenth century. His immense charismatic power depended in part on his felicitous use of pithy phrases and common metaphors drawn from the life of the people. His poems and his calligraphy make evident his debt to the cultural heritage of the past. Yet it goes without saying that he, perhaps more than any other contemporary world statesman, looked to the future. In his bold attempt to create a new type of man, in his faith in science and industrial development, which grew out of his thorough grounding in Marxist doctrine, he set China on a new course into the future.*

THE PURGE OF THE GANG OF FOUR

Although propaganda requirements and the national need for a father figure exalted Mao Zedong to a supreme position, collective leadership has still been the norm through most of PRC history. But the back-and-forth tug of politics is an inevitable human reality, even in a state which stresses solidarity. And if Zhou's death worked the linchpin loose, at Mao's death it fell out, as indeed he had feared it would. The business of the country continued and the basis of the Communist ideology remained in position, but a fundamental policy rift came clearly into the open.

In early October, less than a month after Mao's death, over thirty radical leaders were purged, in the Chinese, not the Stalinist, sense: that is, they were arrested and deposed from their offices but not killed. Chief among them were Jiang Qing, Mao's widow and an initiator of the Cultural Revolution; Wang Hungwen, a Shanghai radical and deputy chairman of the Party; Zhang Chunjiao, a vice-premier; Yao Wenyuan, another Shanghai radical; and Mao Yuanxin, a leader in the Manchurian province of Liaoning and a nephew of

*But see p. 227, reassessment of Mao.

Mao Zedong. All but the last were later designated "The Gang of Four," and to their machinations were attributed all manner of faults and calamities. The primary accusations at the beginning included attempts to forge Mao's will (or sections of it), to make up instructions and attribute them to Mao, and even to hire a gunman to fire on Hua Guofeng as he traveled in an automobile. It was reported early in November that 30,000 militiamen had been called up in Shanghai two days after the arrests, but that plans for a coup d'état had been given up a few days later, when it was discovered that the moderate Party members who had ordered the arrests were clearly dominant at the capital. The serious nature of the rift in the Party can be deduced from the fact that actual fighting occurred over the ousting of the Gang of Four, particularly in the central provinces of China, where much of the agricultural wealth is concentrated. Reports of unrest continued from December 1976 to June 1977. Troops had to be called out in January, and so-called "foes of the government" were executed in March.

As we have seen, Deng Xiaoping had been disgraced for the second time in early 1976, but this time his exile from power was not nearly so prolonged as the earlier period of five years, for by January 1977 posters appeared calling for his rehabilitation, and by July it was an accomplished fact. Early the next year his supporters were being accorded positions of real influence, and in February Deng was formally granted clearance of all responsibility for the occurrence of the riots at the time of the death of Zhou Enlai.

Before Deng could rise to the summit of affairs it was necessary, as always in a system where orthodoxy is vital, to wipe the slate of the past completely clean. The action was taken just before the convening of the National People's Congress on February 26, 1978. (This body, the nominal legislature, is to be distinguished from the various congresses of the Communist Party, but all new decisions coming before the People's Congress naturally undergo previous review by the Party organs.) A main item of business was the New Constitution, which in essence departed from the Constitutional Charter of 1975 and moved back to the more liberal provisions of the Constitution of 1954. Citizens were given the right "to speak out freely, air their views fully, hold great debates and write big-character posters." The individual's right to defense in a trial was restored. Minority ethnic groups were given guarantees that they could "preserve or reform their own customs and ways." Perhaps as important as any new provision, citizens were to be allowed to enter complaints against prejudicial conduct of government officials. These were valuable attempts to protect citizens' rights, but the prevailing attitude of respect for, even fear of, local Party officials often caused a gap between theory and practice, as was seen when in 1979 demands for personal rights became even more evident.

At the Congress of 1978, Hua Guofeng was continued as Premier. Some had expected Deng to be given the post, but he, with his supporters in key positions, found it politic to have the reality of power without its appearance. Another major item was the promulgation of a ten-year plan for development, with the ultimate aim, which Zhou Enlai had first proposed, of making China a fully modern country by the year 2000. The ten-year plan envisaged an agricultural growth of 4 to 5 percent per year and a corresponding industrial growth of 10 percent. Plans were made for large-scale mechanization on the farms and a rise in industrial wages if the aims for increased production were realized.

There was a more moderate and liberal spirit in the air, as well as a sense that certain injustices and excesses of the recent past should as far as possible be corrected. "Detainees" numbering 110,000 were reported in May 1978 as released and rehabilitated. Some of them had been imprisoned since 1957, but the majority were victims of the Cultural Revolution and of the radical campaigns of 1975–1976. It was admitted that prisoners had been tortured and died or had become insane. Earlier in the spring of 1978 considerable efforts had been made to reinstate purge victims, some of them former employees of the Academy of Sciences in Shanghai. By the late fall there was an outbreak of posters carrying messages unprecedented in the history of the PRC to date, some criticizing Mao Zedong and linking him to the errors of the Gang of Four, some calling for democracy and civil liberties, others praising America. A movement toward further restraint of expression began in spring 1979, and by the end of the year, posters were no longer allowed on the famous wall where

Hua Guofeng, Ye Jianying, and Deng Xiaoping.
"The reality of power without its appearance": Hua is Premier, Deng Deputy Premier.
Xinhua News Agency

they had been put up. Some who led protests against this action were tried and jailed. The grand continuity of the main policy, dignity, and infallibility of the Communist Party must be preserved. Signs of the more pragmatic methods now appearing were the admission of students direct from school to university, without the intervening two-year labor period; the operation of factories by managers rather than by the revolutionary committees set up after the Cultural Revolution; and the removal of the ban on Chinese making contacts with foreigners. (The isolation of foreigners from the mass of the people had been a predilection if not a policy of the Chinese authorities from the days of the empire.)

FOREIGN AFFAIRS

With the conclusion of the Cultural Revolution and the new leadership alignment, China was able to turn its attention again to foreign policy. The ruling factor was concern over Russia's perceived ambition for "hegemony." This in turn led to a desire for better relations with Japan and the United States; but in both these cases the need for trade openings also played a part.

In 1978 the PRC and Japan signed a Treaty of Peace and Friendship which had been in the making for six years, and did so in spite of warnings from Russia. Secretary of State Cyrus Vance had explored the possibility of closer relations with China in the summer of 1977, but the response had been cool; China was not yet ready for such a decisive step. Then in the fall of 1978 Deng Xiaoping announced three conditions that had to be met if China was to have normal relations with the United States: the abrogation of the U.S. treaty with Taiwan, severance of diplomatic relations with Taiwan, and the withdrawal of U.S. forces from the island. These demands were not new; the PRC had said it all before. But the United States administration had moved further in China's direction, and China appeared to be willing to be more flexible on details.

President Jimmy Carter made a historic announcement on December 15, 1978 that the United States would establish diplomatic relations with the People's Republic of China on January 1, 1979, severing relations with the Republic of China in Taiwan on the same date, and that the USA and the PRC would exchange ambassadors on March 1. The United States would also cease to recognize its 1954 defense treaty with Taiwan. In response, the PRC agreed to bypass the question of whether the U.S. would give military aid to the Republic of China in any future crisis. The U.S. administration promised to "maintain cultural, commercial, and unofficial relations with the people of Taiwan." Public statements by each side reflected the inward glance at probable opposition to be anticipated at home.

Reaction from the Republic of China was understandably bitter, but there was no appreciable effect on trade relations with the U.S. President Carter's actions were in the end endorsed by the U.S. Senate. Press opinion in Asia was in favor of the move, which also found support in West Germany and Britain.

President Carter had invited Deng Xiaoping to visit the United States at the end of January 1979, and when he did so, he proved to be a very popular figure. Small, compact, and extremely alert in spite of his 74 years, he evidently enjoyed the visit and adapted his words effectively to his various political and commercial audiences, who were surprised to find him witty and charming. His flexibility was tested when he was compelled to ride in a stagecoach in Texas and wear a ten-gallon hat. (Some hats for the entourage had to be hastily discarded when it was discovered, just in time, that they had been made in Taiwan). He toured America, visiting factories, including Boeing's, where commercial planes for China were being built, and throughout his visit exhibited that practical approach for which he had once been severely criticized in China: "I don't care whether the cat is black or white; what is important is that it catches mice." He made guarded references to the danger posed by Russia, but was not as outspoken as he had once been in the Philippines, when he warned that Russian power must not be allowed to take the place of American power in the Pacific region, saying, "We must avoid letting the tiger in through the back door while repelling the wolf through the front gate."

No sooner was Deng Xiaoping back in Beijing (Peking) than China advanced in a large-scale attack across the Vietnam border. There were a number of factors which the Chinese had found provoking: Vietnam's ingratitude

Deng Xiaoping with President Jimmy Carter in Washington, January 31, 1979.

A historic moment, for no Chinese of comparable power had visited the United States since the founding of the People's Republic in 1949. Mr. Deng was warmly welcomed, but in making the visit he was taking a risk, staking everything on the new policy of economic and technological advance which carried with it openness to the West.

Xinhua News Agency

for continued Chinese aid, not to mention loss of Chinese lives, in the wars against France and then against the U.S.; Vietnam's turning away from China to conclude a treaty with Russia; Vietnam's assertion of control over Laos, and then its recent Russian-supported invasion of Kampuchea and consequent overthrow of the Pol Pot regime; and the mistreatment of Chinese residents in Vietnam.

Chinese troops crossed the border on February 17, 1979, and were soon twenty-five miles into Vietnamese territory. They encountered considerable resistance, and only with difficulty captured several key towns, including Lao Cai and Lang Son. They did not attempt any attack on the capital, Hanoi, and withdrew their forces just one month after the onset of the hostilities. This nineteenth-century-style war to teach the Vietnamese a lesson and vindicate Chinese status in the region was not without risk; the USSR might have intervened, but did not. The lesson learned by China was that its army had to be streamlined and outfitted with more modern weapons. But the problems China had with Vietnam and Kampuchea were by no means settled; they were to reemerge later in a wider setting involving the United Nations.

16

THE NEW COMMUNISM

1980–1992

The members of the Gang of Four (see pp. 220–21), although purged in 1976, just after the death of Mao Zedong, were not formally put on trial until November 1980. Near the end of the trial in December, Jiang Qing, Mao's widow, defiant to the last, shouted out in court: "It is more glorious to have my head chopped off than to yield to accusers. I dare you people to sentence me to death in front of one million people in Tiananmen Square." On hearing the call for the death sentence, she cried out, "I am prepared to die," and was removed from the court. Among the charges against the Gang of Four and the others tried with them were sedition, conspiring to overthrow the government, persecution of party and state leaders, suppression of the masses, persecuting to death 34,380 persons during the Cultural Revolution (among them 16,322 in Inner Mongolia), plotting to murder Mao Zedong, and fomenting an armed rebellion in Shanghai.

Jiang Qing and former Vice-Premier Zhang Chunqiao were condemned to death, the remaining two members to terms of imprisonment. Jiang Qing posed a problem to the authorities, for she refused to confess, insisting that everything she had done during the Cultural Revolution had been at Mao's request. Jiang Qing was raised in a very poor family and became an actress in Shanghai in the 1930s. She met Mao Zedong and lived with him, later becoming his third wife when he was forty-five and she twenty-four. The marriage was opposed by his Communist Party colleagues, but finally accepted, provided she agreed to take no part in politics, a condition she fulfilled until the onset of the Cultural Revolution.

In October 1982 six persons involved in the Lin Biao plot against Mao were released from prison, as was Mao's secretary Chen Boda. And in January 1983 the sentences of Jiang Qing and Zhang Chunqiao were reduced from death to life imprisonment. The authorities publicly made it plain that she had not shown "sufficient repentance," but on the other hand they thought it wise not to make her a martyr. The end of this remarkable tale came when Jiang Qing committed suicide, reportedly by hanging herself, on May 14, 1991, at the age of seventy-seven. Her prominence and the impact of her forceful personality on the public prompted the government to withold news of her suicide until after June 4, the second anniversary of the 1989 crackdown on students in Tiananmen Square. Her purging and sentencing, followed by the powerful public statement of suicide, might have reflected adversely on Deng Xiaoping.

POLITICS IN THE EARLY 1980s

The episode of the Gang of Four was a pivotal event at the conclusion of the Cultural Revolution. It was put to political use, beyond its immediate significance, as a catch-all explanation for much that seemed to have gone awry in the society. In a theoretical system in which the pattern of events must be accounted for, the actions, actual or presumed, of the Gang of Four, and their ultimate fate, served as a purgative for the Party. The episode also marked a real change of policy direction. The first open signs of a change in thinking came at the time of the trial itself, when, on December 22, 1980, the *People's Daily* carried a front-page article saying that Mao Zedong had made mistakes in his late years, especially in initiating and leading the Cultural Revolution, mistakes which had brought grave misfortunes to the Party and the people. But the article was careful to distinguish between Mao's political mistakes and the counter-revolutionary crimes of his wife and the other defendants.

This reassessment of the great leader was spelled out in more detail in April 1981 by General Huang Kecheng in articles appearing in the *Liberation Army Daily* and the *People's Daily*. The general stated that Mao's merits outweighed his mistakes, and that his thought would continue to guide the Party and the people. His two main errors had been in pursuing the socialist revolution and socialist construction too far and too fast, and in pushing the class struggle in absolute terms. The articles mentioned the excesses of the Anti-Rightist Campaign and the Great Leap Forward of the late 1950s, saying that the entire Communist Party Central Committee shared the blame but that Mao was responsible as the leader. This new policy line, however, did not command universal assent in the inner circles of the Party. The Central Committee on December 25, 1981, declared that Mao's doctrine of "politics in command" was correct. Mention of "laxness in ideological and political work" was read as an attack on the policies of Zhao Ziyang, who had been appointed Prime Minister in place of Hua Guofeng in September 1980.

Nevertheless the pragmatic line of economic development and "socialist modernization" favored by Deng Xiaoping and Zhao Ziyang had been implicit all along in the reassessment of Mao Zedong's legacy. It was given a more stable foundation in the new constitution passed by the Twelfth Party Congress, which met in September 1982. The Congress denied the importance of the class struggle in contemporary China, restructured the party organization to eliminate the Maoist cult of personality, and abolished the post of Party Chairman, replacing it with that of General Secretary. "Secretary" sounded more modest, but the power of the position remained the same. The Congress decided to continue limited free enterprise in the economy, and decreed a switch of emphasis from heavy to light industry.

An important occurrence in 1983, which received little notice abroad, was a purge of the Communist Party. This was not a purge by violence, but rather a complete review of the membership, conducted in order to eliminate extreme right- and left-wing elements. It was aimed principally at those who had gained membership during the Cultural Revolution, and who therefore might be expected to oppose Deng's reforms. Reeducation through study of the works of Deng and Marx was required, and there was a nod to the hardliners in the form of a warning against "spiritual pollution" through the corrosive influence of China's contacts with the West. All members of the Communist Party were considered to have resigned en masse, and Party leaders in factories and offices decided on ideological grounds who could rejoin and who would be dropped and thus lose valuable privileges. No figures were published, but foreign estimates indicated that from one million to three million probably lost their membership.

AGING LEADERS

Since the eruption of the Democracy Movement and its suppression in 1989, the Western world has been aware of the stress placed by Chinese students and others on the "old men" ruling China. Deng Xiaoping had in fact long been aware of the need to bring younger men into the governing circle. He himself had resigned as Vice Premier in 1980 because of old age (he was then seventy-six), along with two other vice premiers, Li Xiannian and Chen Yun. (This is not to say that Deng gave up the reins of power, for he retained, among other official posts, the chairmanships of the PRC and of the Central Military Commission until 1989.) In the same year, 1980, it was arranged that five deputy chairmen of the Standing Committee of the National People's Congress, whose average age was eighty-four, should resign in favor of five men whose average age was sixty-five.

Retirement had to be a selective process, but that the program was serious became clear in April 1985, when 1,000 young officials were chosen to be prepared for future ministerial and provincial posts and thousands more for work at prefectural and county levels. They would form the third echelon. The first had been the revolutionary generation; the second, those who had held office after the 1949 establishment of the Communist state. General Secretary Hu Yaobang stated that 70 percent of all officials down to the municipal level would be replaced, and that 900,000 (if the figures can be held as accurate) had retired during the long campaign to replace aging and unqualified leaders.

Not even the Army was exempted. In 1984, forty top officers at the rank of general who were over sixty were retired.

Factors other than age were clearly involved in the move for retirement and replacement. One was an individual's attitude toward Deng's program of economic reform. Age was given here as the excuse for dismissal, but an aversion to the politics of modernization was frequently the real reason. Another factor was the person's level of education. In June 1985 the government mandated higher education and age below fifty-five as requirements for new appointments to ministries dealing with aeronautics, railways, electronics (including radio and television), coal, and state commissions doing research for the military. However, there were certain leaders who were too powerful to be dismissed—too valuable, too respected—whether they were hardline and opposed to reform or not. Marshal Ye Jianying, for example, had had a long and distinguished career in the People's Liberation Army from the time of the Long March of 1934. The eighty-one-year-old veteran was commended as a "shining example" of one prepared to resign, but was retained in the Standing Committee of the Communist Party Congress in 1980, and in the Party's Central Military Commission and the Politburo until 1985.

ENERGY

The above changes in leadership and policy positively affected the direction of the Chinese economy; but in China, as in every nation, the extent to which the economy could expand was strictly determined by the amount of energy available. China has always depended heavily on coal to fuel its industry but has made increasing use of oil since the late 1970s. Coal accounted for 96.7 percent of the energy total in 1952, and other sources for only 3.3 percent; but by 1987 coal supplied 72.6 percent and other sources 27.4 percent.

The PRC regarded oil as of special importance in the growth of the Chinese economy, since the financial return on rising oil exports would pay for modernization. To promote export, China's first 50,000-ton-capacity oil tanker was launched in the northern port of Dalian. In April 1976 China sank its deepest oil well to that date in the province of Sichuan. But because the mineral-rich northeast province of Heilongjiang contained the largest reserves of crude oil, the government gave priority in the introduction of advanced technology to factories and oil fields in the northeast, especially in the region of Daqing. In the early nineteenth century the whole province of Heilongjiang, where Daqing is situated, was still the hunting ground of Manchu tribesmen; it now became the major producer of crude oil and natural gas in China.

In 1983 the deepest offshore well came into operation in the East China Sea. China began accepting bids from foreign companies for offshore drilling, with Prime Minister Zhao Ziyang promising that no large fields would be nationalized. By 1984 eighteen foreign companies had signed up, including firms from Britain, Spain, Australia and France. The terms were very favorable to China, for it was to receive 51 percent of any oil found, while paying none of the production costs. Possible sources were reported off Tianjin in the Yellow Sea, off Hainan Island in the South China Sea, and in the Pearl River Basin. By 1988 oil, at annual total value of $3.4 billion, ranked second after clothing in China's list of exports.

Still, the high expectations on both sides were not all realized. Offshore oil field yields were disappointing, and offshore commercial oil was not obtained by the French group Total until 1986. Pennzoil withdrew in that year from dry wells in Guangdong on the mainland. China then opened a second round of bids, but was compelled to offer better terms, since the first round had yielded such meager results. Thus, although the figure quoted above for oil exports in 1988 was a sizeable one, the hoped for major financing of modernization from oil was not fulfilled.

Since output in mining and industry had been maintained during the Cultural Revolution in spite of the general chaos, there was a quantum leap of three times the total energy production by 1978. In these critical years of 1965 to 1978 the proportion of coal declined and that of oil rose by a factor of 2.75. China's oil consumption was reported in 1990 to be growing at the rate of 10 percent a year. Although China was able to export 500,000 barrels a day in 1990, by the year 2000 it is expected to be *importing* 1.3 million barrels a day, or the equivalent of almost all the oil exported by Kuwait per day. In the 1980s the use of natural gas and hydropower increased. Nuclear power plants were being built in the early 1990s but were not yet in production. Overall, coal remained the dominant source of energy in China, and a severe pollution problem was the inevitable consequence.

REFORMS IN THE ECONOMY

Zhou Enlai had long proposed that China should aim to become a fully modern country by the year 2000. Central planning would have to be supported by individual incentive if this goal was to be achieved. To this end the National People's Congress announced in 1975 that farmers could cultivate small private plots and engage in "sideline production," such as raising pigs and silkworms, and that factory workers could work for themselves, provided they did not employ others to work for them (see p. 218). These changes sowed the seeds for the later economic reforms of Deng Xiaoping, who was a protégé of Zhou.

A further step toward the fulfillment of Zhou's vision was reached with the adoption of a ten-year economic plan in 1978. The plan was to mechanize farming on a large scale; increase industrial production and raise wages accordingly; have factories controlled by managers and no longer by revolutionary committees; and abolish the ban on contact with foreigners.

But despite all efforts, the centrally controlled command economy was not functioning well. Valuable natural resources were badly allocated or simply wasted, government pricing by a rigid bureaucracy often lacked any rationale, and workers had little incentive for greater production. The standard of living for the common people in town and countryside thus lingered at unnecessarily low levels, and the export trade suffered.

A new experiment in Sichuan province sought to overcome some of these problems. Zhao Ziyang was Communist Party Secretary and Political Commissar there from 1975, and by 1979 he had substantially reduced centralized planning in that province. Certain factories were allowed to keep some of their profits instead of turning them all over to the state. If production exceeded the planned amount, managers could increase bonuses to their workers. They could begin to set their own quotas and product prices. At first 100 factories were involved in the scheme; by 1980 the number had doubled. Output in 1979 was up by nearly 15 percent and profits by 33 percent. Farmers were given more liberty in their choice of crops to plant and could sell private produce in markets at noncontrolled prices. Private ownership of land was planned to rise from 7 percent to 15 percent of the whole. Total grain production increased by 24 percent between 1976 and 1979, and industrial production by an astonishing 80 percent in the same period.

Sichuan had traditionally been a rich province, but had declined perilously during the lean years of the Cultural Revolution. The experiment there proved so successful that the province advanced from being one of the poorest to a position of comparative prosperity. The government decided to apply certain of the Sichuan principles of decentralization and reform to the nation as a whole. In August 1980 Finance Minister Wang Bingqian announced some major changes in economic practice:

1. Economic authority would be dispersed from the central government to provinces, counties, and businesses.

2. Banks would operate independently, and be responsible for loans and cash flow.

3. State-owned factories and enterprises would pay the state certain new taxes and fees.

4. Provinces would receive funds from the state in proportion to the money collected from their enterprises. (Two provinces, Guangdong and Fujian, had already been given responsibility for their own finances after turning over fixed sums to the state).

5. Farmers and workers would be encouraged to form partnerships, cooperatives, and individual enterprises, such as family stores.

6. Tax incentives would be offered "to promote the development of the collective economy."

None of this loosening of strict party control was easily gained; behind the walls of the Forbidden City the pendulum still swung secretly between the hard, orthodox, Communist line and a cautious opening toward a market economy. Mao's doctrine of self-reliance had played to an ancient tune of pride in China and deep distrust of foreigners. But it was by now quite clear to Deng Xiaoping and his supporters that China could not prosper without access to foreign technology, foreign expertise, and even foreign capital. In fact, in view of the ever-increasing population, the issue was not so much prosperity as sheer survival. Therefore a large part of reform had to be a new "open door" policy to Japan and to the West.

As a result of his success in Sichuan, Zhao Ziyang was promoted to the post of Prime Minister in the fall of 1980, and in his first speech he stressed increased decision-making powers for enterprises and a wider role for workers and staff in factory management. He reaffirmed the new economic guidelines of Deng Xiaoping to "make China a modernized, highly democratic, and civilized socialist state." The implementation of the unfamiliar ideas in these guidelines undoubtedly varied widely in different parts of the country.

One of China's first "open door" successes was a five-year series of low-interest loans from Japan, which ran from 1979 to 1983 and amounted in the end to $1.5 billion.* In 1980 China was admitted to the International Monetary Fund and the World Bank which qualified it for loans. There was encouragement for the Chinese leadership in the World Bank's 1981 development report, which stated that, although the poorest developing countries with annual per capita income of less than $370 were dropping behind, China was something of a success story because it had made the poorest of the population "far better off in real terms than their counterparts in most poor countries."

To obtain access to needed foreign technology, China was willing to offer foreign firms the chance to enter into joint ventures. For instance, in May 1983 American Motors Corporation entered into a joint venture with Beijing Automotive Works to build jeeps. Since jeeps were already being produced in the Beijing factory, the objective was not the acquisition of basic, but of the latest advanced, technology as well as access to an expanded market. The plan was eventually to use AMC engines in the cars, and after seven years to produce an improved model based on an American design. But such a plan was not easy to steer through the labyrinthine delays of a state-controlled economy.

An even more complex joint venture was the building of China's first nuclear power plant at Daya Bay in Guangdong. China owned 75 percent of the project and the Hong Kong Light and Power Company the remaining 25 percent. Negotiations took seven years, culminating in 1985, and provided for obtaining nuclear reactors from France and turbines and generators from Great Britain.

In all such arrangements for foreign investment in China the PRC was eager to secure imported equipment and the initial expertise to operate it, as well as to acquire modern management skills, so that at the earliest opportunity the Chinese themselves would become expert and hence independent in various industrial fields. The incentives for foreign firms considering investment were entry to an immense but strictly controlled market, cheap labor, and certain tax breaks offered by China. The PRC recognized that foreigners ran considerable risks and would require both accurate accounting and legal protection. China's application for IMF loans made it

*All figures are given in US dollars.

necessary for it to meet the accounting requirement, and legal protection was officially initiated in September 1983 by the promulgation of Regulations for the Implementation of the Law of the PRC on Joint Ventures using Chinese and Foreign Investment. It is not surprising, however, that civil disputes arose over foreign trade, joint ventures, maritime transport, insurance, patent rights, and copyright. But the desire to trade and to enjoy its benefits usually enabled merchants on both sides to overcome, quietly or openly, all obstacles. Such has been the case since the Tang dynasty and earlier, through the troubled years of the nineteenth century in Canton and Hong Kong, and up to the present day. Mutual understanding has always been easier in the mercantile city of Canton than in the political city of Beijing.

The easing of controls over domestic markets brought greater prosperity to China. But the rising demand for consumer goods led to inflation. To the concern of the government, inflation in 1980 was up by 7 percent, and consumer prices rose by 10 percent to 12 percent. Economic anarchy, so greatly feared, seemed to be looming on the horizon. The authorities therefore took steps to slow the economy by making cuts in oil and coal production, capital construction, and defense. But freedom in the private sector for farmers and businesses was not unduly curtailed.

Another attempt to attract foreign capital was the opening of special economic zones that offered preferential tax treatment. Four of these areas on the coast were established in 1979, and four more were added in 1985. Among the locations chosen were the Pearl River estuary close to Canton, Shantou in northern Guangdong, Xiamen (formerly Amoy) in Fujian, and the peninsulas of Shandong and Liaodong opposite one another in the north. One of the principal sites, Shenzhen, just over the border from Hongkong New Territories, became a boom-town, with many of the characteristics of its wealthy neighbor. Foreign investment began slowly in the 1980s, increased in 1985, but fell off again in the first half of 1986, prompting China to devalue its currency by almost 16 percent and to offer still further advantages to overseas firms locating in the special zones.

In spite of China's efforts to keep open the path to joint ventures, a new difficulty arose in the fall of 1993 with an austerity drive, put in place to curb an inflation rate which had reached 13.9 percent and to cool down an overheated economy. The joint business of General Motors and Jinbei Automotive Company in Shenyang suffered at once, since for the time being the government would no longer purchase any trucks.

SOCIAL POLICY

The fluctuating process of imposing and releasing controls took a new and important ideological turn during the period 1982 to 1984. In 1982 an employment merit system was introduced. The first experiment was conducted in Beijing, where 200,000 new workers were given an entrance examination. If accepted, they began a period of probation, after which they signed a contract in which they accepted certain conditions set by the employer. This new merit system was openly stated to be the "end of the iron rice bowl"—that is, a guaranteed job at a guaranteed wage—which Mao had sought to give every worker. Mao's egalitarian ideal had been to accord an opportunity to everyone down to the very poorest, and to eliminate, by deliberate policy, the distinctions between urban and rural workers and between rich and poor. The extremes of the Cultural Revolution had tarnished this ideal and set China back ten years economically in the unforgiving global competition. Now one-quarter of state-run enterprises were reporting annual losses, and this was attributed not only to mismanagement, but also to inefficiency and to workers' carelessness and laziness. The overstaffing of industries had tended to make workers feel nonessential and thus bored and complacent.

Although conditions of employment had been altered, this did not mean the end of any safety net for the distressed. While the PRC did not institute a system of social security with full coverage, workers in industry did receive pensions (usually about 40 percent of their regular pay) and sick pay through their trade unions. Nonunion members were not covered. There were relief funds for extreme hardship cases such as widows, war veterans, and the severely disabled. About 60 percent of these funds came from the national treasury and the remaining 40 percent from local government sources. In cases of widespread rural poverty caused by flood or famine the state might provide national finance for relief.

In most Western democracies the employment of workers is a matter for the private sector, while the concerns of unemployment and welfare are relegated to the government. Under the Chinese system the work unit, or *danwei,* handles these matters together at the local level. It has wide control over the workers in their private as well as their working lives. The work unit regulates the entitlement to rations, the allocation of housing, permission for marriage and divorce, and the crucial matter of assessing a person's political reliability. The distribution of relief at the local level is also a part of its responsibility. With the growth of free markets in the 1980s, the work unit was deprived of some of its functions, but it was retained in the system by the conservative leaders as a part of true socialism and a means of social control.

The new management/labor plan, now called the "responsibility system," was said to be working well. Managers in all state-run enterprises could hire and fire workers and set wages. They could award bonuses without regard to earlier limits and could retain part of the profit after taxes for worker benefits, new equipment, or other use within the firm. Workers' wages were to be proportionate to their level of performance on the job. On the other hand, workers had some protection, since a new trade union constitution of 1983 allowed unions to remove workers from factories that had unsafe working conditions. The constitution also called on workers to end remaining discrimination against women.

The introduction of the "responsibility system" led to fluctuations in employment. Unemployment, with estimated rates of 2 percent to 3 percent in previous years, had not been a major problem. But the years 1987 and 1988 saw internal migrations of millions of part-time workers and unemployed persons from both rural areas and cities in search of work (see p. 239). The increase in private industry and state-run enterprises could absorb these numbers only gradually.

The leadership used the slogan of the Four Modernizations to impress national goals on the consciousness of the ordinary man during the 1980s. These areas of modernization were: industry, agriculture, defense, and science and technology. The first two of these have been mentioned above; the latter two, now to be briefly considered, also saw significant changes.

DEFENSE

A reform of the military command structure in 1980 was followed two years later by a more thorough reorganization of the armed forces under General Yang Dezhi. Without mentioning the Soviet Union, he warned of the danger of a "well-trained and powerful enemy." To fight a modern war, he said, China must upgrade the organization and discipline of its forces, maintain high morale, and acquire expertise in handling modern weapons. Both the hierarchy of military ranks and the use of distinctive uniforms for officers, abolished during the Cultural Revolution, were restored in this period. But in 1985 financial constraints caused the reduction of the 4.2-million-man Army by one-quarter to just over three million, (still the largest in the world). The discharged soldiers added to the problem of unemployment.

The Army under Mao had had its own schools, farms, factories, and many other ancillary operations. In the changes of 1985 some of these support groups were reduced or eliminated, some Army factories were diverted to the production of consumer goods, and certain ports and airfields were opened to civilian use. The Army changed from a people's militia dominated by ideology under Mao to a much more professional force equipped with increasingly modern weapons. The national self-strengthening, so contentious and difficult in the nineteenth century, had now visibly matured and become effective with the introduction of modern armed forces. How far the military would go in submitting to civilian control was still not clear.

In the two decades prior to 1990 China acquired or built a range of sophisticated weapons. (Here the updating of defense overlaps with advances in China's science and technology). Clues to the nature of this armament, kept as secret as possible, can be gained from a study of some international arms sales. Here are a few examples. Between 1984 and 1986 the United States sold to China naval antisubmarine weapons, antiaircraft missiles, and antitank weapons, as well as half a billion dollars worth of radar, navigation and computer equipment, to upgrade the fifty F-8 interceptor aircraft in China's possession. Between 1986 and 1988 China, now a manufacturer of sophisticated weaponry, proved to be the largest supplier of arms, including the J-6 jet fighter aircraft, to Iraq. China also provided immense quantities of arms, including Silkworm antiship missiles, to Iran, the enemy of Iraq. China assisted Pakistan to produce a short-range missile and supplied Saudi Arabia with Chinese-made CSS2 ballistic missiles with the considerable range of 1,600 miles.

China was at the same time developing the ultimate military capability, a nuclear arsenal. Its scientists were successful in designing, building, and then testing an atomic bomb by October 1964. It was not until August 1981 that the PRC announced that it would sign the 1968 Nuclear Nonproliferation Treaty. France had just indicated in June its willingness to sign; thus China had stood out as the last of the major nuclear powers—and the last of 140 countries in all—to agree to the treaty banning the export of nuclear weapons technology. After a series of test firings monitored by other nations, it appeared certain in 1988 that China possessed a system of long-range strategic nuclear missiles of its own.

SCIENCE AND TECHNOLOGY

As was to be expected, China went shopping widely in the Western world for items of the latest high technology. Equipment purchased served not only for use, but even more for models to be copied. China aimed to become, as quickly as possible, independent and able to compete on equal terms with the rest of the world. The policy was similar to that of the modernizing young leaders of Japan in the midnineteenth-century Meiji Restoration. Japan had then brought in foreign advisors from several nations to jump-start a technical revolution; but at the same time it sent many more Japanese abroad to acquire the necessary scientific and practical know-how that would make the expensive foreign personnel unnecessary. China has been following the latter path. Of 433 students going to the United States in 1978–1979, the six highest choices for fields of study were, in order: physics, radio-electronics, computer sciences and engineering, chemistry, mathematics, and medical- and life-sciences. It is not hard to see national policy reflected in these choices.

But, for the government, students who had lived abroad posed a dilemma; a number returned not only with valuable knowledge but also with subversive ideas. This had happened before, as when Chinese students had been caught up in the fervor of democratic and revolutionary theories in Japan and elsewhere before and after the turn of the century. It had happened in the 1920s when Zhou Enlai and Ho Chi Minh were active in the Communist Party in Paris. So, in the decades from the 1950s to the 1990s, numerous students returned to China with dreams and plans about democracy.

Many students and intellectuals who went to Europe or the United States did not return to China but remained abroad to pursue a career. The brain drain was significant enough to cause grave concern in the PRC, so much so that in 1992 the government granted top research scientists and scholars a salary bonus and more freedom to choose their area of work in order to encourage them to stay in China.

However, access to scientific knowledge through students who did return and through the vast network of international science information enabled China to make the important technological advances indicated above. Much of this progress occurred in the military field, and in this respect China is not alone. But in other areas as well the PRC has begun to catch up with the advanced industrial nations. Some examples are the building of oil tankers in Dalian, the advanced steel-making capacity at Baoshan, airline traffic expansion both domestic and foreign, a submarine cable link to Japan, offshore drilling for oil, and significant progress in superconductivity research.

POLITICS AND ECONOMICS IN THE LATE 1980s

China's leaders had decided to move from total central planning in their economy to a measure of private enterprise. With this went the momentous decision to open the door to the outside world, to acquire foreign technology, and to seek foreign investment. In their contacts with other nations the leaders had managed among themselves to present a consistent, united front. But in the decade of the 1980s at home they were forced to perform a delicate and somewhat perilous balancing act.

The principal domestic economic issue was also a political one—free enterprise within a socialist state. The problem was how to allow the individual entrepreneur enough operating space to enable him to make money and thus benefit both the state and himself, yet at the same time to maintain the social-ist framework of the nation to which the leaders were committed. Thus an official statement at the Sixth National People's Congress in June 1983 denied that economic reforms, such as the introduction of taxes, interest rates, float-ing prices, and other components of capitalism, were eroding socialism. Rather, it stated, the reforms were designed to improve socialism by making it more efficient.

There were other economic problems facing the government, some of which were only gradually becoming evident. How should the public and the private sectors be balanced? The rigidity and inefficiency of state planning and administration had led to unemployment. Abolition of the "iron rice bowl" (a guaranteed job and wage) was intended to be an incentive for hard work and efficiency and did produce some good results. But there were many who were unable to work at any given time because of shifts in industry, lack of trans-portation, or other reasons, and provision of government welfare for them was a drain on state and local funds. Vast amounts of consumer goods still had to come from state factories, and where planning was poor or production below normal, there were shortages. Too much new, privately earned money chasing too few goods in turn led to inflation. But at least it can be said that that China's gradualist approach—private plots and sideline production, more power for managers to hire and fire and retain some profits, doing away with

job guarantees, and at the same time permitting freedom of travel and residence—was much more successful than Russia's rapid plunge into economic
reform had been.

By late 1985 Deng Xiaoping's position and policies were secured and
consolidated. (One sign of this had come in June, when communes were abolished and a greater number of smaller townships were put in their place). At a
special conference in September supporters of Deng were elected as members
of the Central Committee, the Politburo and the Secretariat. There was, however, one orthodox Marxist, Chen Yun, who was prepared to come out and
publicly criticize Deng's policy on agriculture, his stress on market forces, and
his neglect of ideology. Chen Yun said the new line was blindly allowing supply
and demand to determine production. He condemned speculation and corruption in pursuit of personal gain by those who had "turned their backs on
serving the people."

Chen Yun had struck a sensitive chord. In 1986, the CP Central Committee stated that "socialist morality rejects both the idea and the practice of pursuing personal interests at the expense of others, putting money above all else,
cheating and extortion, and abusing power for personal gain." At the same
time the Central Committee statement emphasized the point that "the economic modernization program to raise living standards through foreign contacts was a basic, unalterable policy." This policy would not negate the socialist
system in favor of capitalism but, while China was still in the early stages of
socialism, it "must allow individuals to become prosperous before prosperity
for all could be achieved." The last statement was the hint of a swelling ripple
of private production, which in a few more years became an overwhelming
wave.

The difficulty of the balancing act between a more liberal economic openness and a more conservative political hardline came out in the National People's Congress of 1987. Prime Minister Zhao backed economic reforms and
foreign investment, but acknowledged Party concerns that such moves could
lead to social instability. He attacked "bourgeois liberalization," (which just
previously had led to the dismissal of Hu Yaobang as General Secretary of the
Party). "Bourgeois liberalization" were the code words for the spread of Western political and cultural beliefs. Deng Xiaoping himself, for all his desire for
foreign investment, had spoken out the year before against bourgeois liberalization, saying, "We cannot adopt Western ways, because if we do, it will mean
chaos." "Chaos," interpreted in China as any widespread opposition to the
official orthodoxy, had always been the nightmare of the former autocratic
rulers of the Chinese Empire.

During 1987 Deng Xiaoping stepped down from membership in the Central Committee, removing himself from the Politburo and its powerful Standing Committee. The first Communist leader to resign voluntarily from the top
posts in the leadership of the Party, he nevertheless retained much of his
power, working from behind the scenes. The constitution was amended to
enable him to retain the chairmanship of the Central Military Commission.

Zhao Ziyang replaced Hu Yaobang as Party General Secretary, and Li Peng, more conservative than Zhao in the matter of economic reform, replaced Zhao in the post of Prime Minister.

During this transitional and experimental period, politics and economics were more than ever interdependent, a state of affairs that had a significant impact in the social sphere and on the lives of the people as the economic swings of the 1980s proved difficult to control. For example, the favorable economic situation of 1983 still obtained in 1985. But in that year retail prices rose nearly 9 percent, the highest increase since 1950, and inflation stood at about the same figure. Then, in 1987, an economic downturn affected people's livelihood even more directly when certain food staples were in short supply and pork had to be rationed in Beijing and Shanghai. In 1988 the government went ahead with its program to move from central planning to a free market and for that purpose removed price controls on certain foodstuffs. Prices at once soared by 30 to 60 percent in some cities on staples such as eggs, sugar, pork and vegetables. In July 1988 inflation rose to 19 percent over that of July 1987. In response the Central Committee abruptly postponed the disturbing removal of price controls and restored them for at least two years.

There was worse to come. Droughts and flooding throughout the country, particularly in Fujian and Zhejiang, brought twenty million people to the brink of starvation, and left another eighty million short of food.

By 1989 the mood had become somber and cautious. With inflation now a serious threat, the government tightened economic controls and reduced construction projects. Another problem involved the austerity regulations of September 1988 which had resulted in the cancellation of several large-scale rural development projects. Unemployed peasants seeking work and wealth had begun moving en masse into Canton in early February 1989, sometimes at the rate of 100,000 a day. Similar movements were taking place around Beijing and Shanghai. The central government gave orders for local officials to prevent people from leaving their province and to compel those who had gone to neighboring cities to return home to the countryside. But it was obviously easier to give the orders than to carry them out.

THE DEMOCRACY MOVEMENT

Such was the backdrop against which the drama of the student protests of 1989, the Democracy Movement of Tiananmen Square, and the subsequent violent crackdown by the government and the army were played out. It was a struggle in which neither side seemed able to understand the attitude of the other. The students and their supporters were *not* aiming to overthrow communism or the Communist government, but were asking for an extension of their freedom, attention to the material needs of the people, and an end to the growing corruption in high places (see pp. 269–270). The government, however, saw a basic challenge to the Party and to its authority to govern—a threat to law and order and the possible onset of total chaos.

Both students and members of the government were powerfully reminded of a precedent—the May Fourth Movement of 1919—when student protests succeeded in overthrowing the government of the day and forcing upon it a new nationalist policy, which involved a denial of certain provisions of the Treaty of Versailles. The students alone could not have accomplished this; but they had been joined by a significant number of businessmen and the general public (see p. 184). Similarly, at Tiananmen Square in 1989, the government was well aware that a large number of ordinary citizens, many of them intellectuals and even more of them members of the new moneyed middle class (which the government was sedulously encouraging) had now come out in vigorous support of the students. Meanwhile the rural population was in a very restless state. The tinder was there for a conflagration. But, in an irony worthy of a Greek play, what seemed (at first) to the government to be one more incident like many others, to be quickly suppressed, appeared to an attentive world public to be a titanic struggle for "democracy," deserving of every possible support.

In order to understand the violent events triggered by the student protests of 1989, it is necessary to go back to the period between 1986 and 1988, when China was going through a time of rapid economic development. As a result of more emphasis being placed on wealth and less on ideology, there was a growing uncertainty about the future direction of the country, even among the leaders themselves. Students began to perceive this and sought to press their demands for greater freedom of thought and action. High inflation and corruption in politics and business troubled the waters still further.

The hardline wing among the Party leaders sensed the dangers in this situation and took advantage of the meeting of the CP Central Committee in September 1986 to attack "bourgeois liberalization," defined as a trend "negating the socialist system in favor of capitalism," and to put through a resolution on the spiritual construction of socialism. This was a blow to those seeking democratization and progressive reforms. It formed the background against which students reacted in large numbers in December of that year, when enormous demonstrations broke out involving a 100,000 students from 150 colleges and universities in fifteen cities. The students demanded freedom of speech, assembly, and the press, plus democratic elections. The first protest took place in Hefei in Anhui province at the University of Science and Technology, sparked by the university's vice-president, Fang Lizhi, a famous astrophysicist. He called for action, and said that democracy could not be bestowed from above, but must be won from below. What was bestowed could be withdrawn, but what was won could not.

The hardliners criticized the comparatively lenient way Hu Yaobang handled the student unrest, and persuaded Deng Xiaoping to deal sternly with the students and to oppose Western-style liberalization. Hu Yaobang was fired from his post as General Secretary of the Party in January 1987, to be succeeded by Zhao Ziyang. Hu's dismissal immediately made him a hero to the students. On his death in April 1989 prodemocracy demonstrations broke out again on April 17, first in Shanghai and then in Beijing, where students laid wreaths in Tiananmen Square for him (just as other students had done for Zhou Enlai in 1976) and chanted, "Long live democracy, long live freedom!" Two days later, on April 19, they marched to the Zhongnanhai compound of the Forbidden City, where many of the CP leaders lived, staged a sit-in, and shouted for the Prime Minister, "Come out, come out, Li Peng!" The trouble had started, and the revolt was on.

TIANANMEN SQUARE

Events began to move fast. The first stage of the main student-led movement for political and social reform began with a rally of 100,000 in Tiananmen Square on April 21, 1989. This rally intentionally coincided with the official memorial service for Hu Yaobang. The student demands included freedom of speech, press and assembly, increased funding for education, the rehabilitation of Hu Yaobang, and publication of the incomes and assets of the top leaders of the government. The cheering crowds gave new significance to the rally and to the whole movement now under way, since they included large numbers of workers and students from other parts of China. Television introduced a new factor into the equation, with riots and attacks on the police erupting in Xian and Changsha after people saw a broadcast of the memorial service. Meanwhile, in Beijing, tens of thousands of university students began an indefinite boycott of their classes, and a number of professors supported them.

This was serious, and the government's reaction marked the beginning of the second stage. The Politburo met and decided that the Party "must be prepared to spill some blood if necessary." On April 25 Deng Xiaoping declared over loudspeakers and on TV that "a conspiracy of unlawful elements" required "grave political struggle. . . . A handful of people with ulterior motives," he said, had set out "to poison minds, create turmoil, and sabotage political stability." His statements provoked the largest rally to date. Close to a million workers and citizens turned out to support the students, marching for twelve hours through the streets of Beijing. The size of the demonstration overwhelmed the police, and troops were called in, but workers formed human blockades to prevent troops from halting the march. There were further demonstrations to celebrate the seventieth anniversary of the student-led May Fourth Movement of 1919, including rallies in Shanghai, Dalian, and Changchun.

The students in Beijing petitioned for a meeting with Li Peng, following a useless meeting with lower-level officials (for which the student representatives had been picked by the government). But then came a crucial move: students went on a hunger strike in the square on May 13, and by May 17 their numbers had risen to 3,000. Not long after that some had to be hospitalized. As public sympathy and support mounted, Li Peng and Zhao Ziyang made visits to the students in hospital. An irony and embarrassment for the government was that these events coincided with the arrival of Mikhail Gorbachev in Beijing for a summit conference. His visit was completely overshadowed by a climactic rally of over a million people on May 17. The circle of support had widened; in addition to the students, participants now included workers, intellectuals, professional people, journalists, teachers, schoolchildren, and even some soldiers and low-ranking Party officials. A thousand journalists signed a petition asking for greater freedom for the press. Gorbachev could not get to an opera performance taking place beside Tiananmen Square because of the crowds of demonstrators. (There was always the Great Wall, several miles outside Beijing, to which he was conducted.) Li Peng met with the student leaders, but without any positive result.

At this point there was a power struggle in the Communist Party. A day-long debate took place in the five-member Politburo Standing Committee, in which Zhao Ziyang spoke in favor of moderate measures. But the final decision was for martial law, announced by Li Peng on May 20. The decision for the definitive use of force may be considered the opening of the third and final stage of a gathering drama truly extraordinary in the setting of an authoritarian state.

In reaction to the imposition of martial law, the students called for Deng Xiaoping and Li Peng to step down. It was rumored that the commander of the 38th Army from Baoding had refused to move against the protesters. Troops of the 27th Army from farther away in Hebei province were called in to deal with the main group of 200,000 students and hunger strikers still encamped in Tiananmen Square. But the soldiers found buses, trucks, and taxis blocking the streets; hordes of ordinary citizens implored the soldiers to turn back saying, "The students are our children." Many soldiers gave their tacit support simply by inaction. But the hardliners among the leaders appeared to be gaining ground. News and television reports were suppressed. And on May 21 the hunger strike ended after a nine-day fast. There were rumors of an attack to come that night, but it did not materialize.

Rallies in twenty cities in China, including a crowd of half a million in Shanghai and 300,000 in Xian, and supporting demonstrations in Washington, London, Paris and Tokyo made abundantly clear the world-wide appeal of the students' ideals and aims. In one last effort they enshrined these ideals in a thirty-three-foot plaster and styrofoam statue of the Goddess of Democracy erected by groups of art students in the square. The tension increased. Zhao Ziyang, advocate of reason, had been deprived of all his powers and placed under house arrest. Deng Xiaoping was marshalling hardline support for extreme measures. He now had 200,000 troops surrounding Beijing, and on May 30 the first arrests were made.

By June 2 troops were stationed at ten key points in and around the city, and after midnight on June 3 a large force marched unarmed down Chang'an Avenue. Blocked by jeering students and workers, they retreated. Many soldiers were stripped of their backpacks and uniforms; some were reduced to tears. That was the last straw for the government. By 2 P.M. there were the first reports of violence. Police and Army troops used tear gas, truncheons, and electric cattle prods near the Zhongnanhai officials' compound.

On the night of June 4 an all-out military assault was launched, with tanks, personnel carriers, and troops armed with machine guns and assault rifles. Citizens moved to block the advance, but this time the troops did not back off. Bloody fighting broke out along Chang'an Avenue and in a ten-block radius round Tiananmen Square. The crowds fought back with sticks, rocks, pipes, and firebombs. One old woman lay down in the road in front of an Army vehicle. Soldiers who fired on unarmed civilians were twice set upon by the crowd and hanged. Hundreds of protesters and bystanders were killed, and by 3 A.M. on June 5 Tiananmen Square was sealed off. After some negotiation, the students remaining in the square were told they could leave. They voted to withdraw and most had departed by early morning. At 7:40 A.M. it was announced that the rebellion had been suppressed. There were sporadic confrontations and firing into crowds through June 5. In one incident a student stood in front of an advancing tank and halted the whole column until he was dragged away by his friends; a picture of this went around the world.

The story of Tiananmen Square speaks for itself, but a few points should be placed in context. First, modern means of communication played a greater part in this uprising than in any previous one in Chinese history. The use of loudspeakers gave a certain control advantage to the authorities; but television proved to be a double-edged sword, when a broadcast of events set off further riots in Xian. During the demonstrations materials faxed by dissident supporters in the United States and Britain were a valuable source of information and encouragement to the protest movement in China. Secondly, the students from Beijing University and other universities in the city behaved with considerable restraint in the early stages; it was students in other cities, such as Changsha, who gave some color to the government's accusation of promoting instability when they looted shops and attacked police. It was, as ever, chaos which the authorities dreaded most, for that spelled not only loss of power for themselves but also, they believed, the possible demise of communism and the breakup of China. Third, the popular grapevine in Beijing and around the country functioned with extraordinary speed and efficiency. Even with only limited telephone connections, enormous crowds took to the streets on short notice, day and night. Fourth, the government feared the participation of workers—the basis of a Communist state—in these protests far more than they feared students; that was why the number of workers supporting the students, especially in Beijing, was of grave concern. Protests on May 4, which included workers in Changchun and Dalian in the heavily industrialized northeast, only increased this concern. Lastly, the government apparently held off from arresting students until May 30, presumably recognizing to some degree the people's traditional respect for scholars.

What lay behind the drama played out in the streets of Beijing was the ancient Confucian model of the parent-child relationship. It had a powerful effect upon the ordinary citizen. The parent should provide for the child's needs and the child should respect and obey the parent. The students desired one thing above all, an open dialogue with the rulers. They did not advocate the overthrow of the whole Communist system; they just wanted reform. They raised the stakes by the unprecedented action of a hunger strike, and they waited in vain for a government response. When the citizens saw a total lack of concern and parental compassion on the part of the leaders, they turned spontaneously to help the students to resist the government. The authorities reckoned without the depth of the people's concern for students. It was not only because "the students are our children." Students are the leaders of the future, and scholars in the past had always been considered to have some right to advise the government. And when the hardline leaders called in the Army and used tanks and bullets against students fasting from patriotic motives, public outrage was unbounded. The authorities won, but they lost face; they were morally shamed in the eyes of the people.

After extraordinarily courageous resistance, the students ultimately retreated. Calm was restored by force. The Chinese at every historical crisis have been pragmatic about power, but a corner had been turned. Sadly in one sense, but necessarily, the people had lost confidence in the People's Liberation Army, which had ended up firing on its own citizens. Cynicism about the Communist Party leaders had clearly increased throughout the country. The leaning of the people towards more democratic freedom, combined with the government's own support for a limited free market economy, meant that fresh doubts began to spring up in many minds about the whole Communist ideology at all levels of society. The Communist system was still in place and might be expected to continue for an indefinite period; but things would never be quite the same after the events of 1989 in Tiananmen Square.

A Summary of Chinese Leaders

The GENERAL SECRETARY of the Communist Party, usually the single most influential figure in the leadership. The post (originally that of Chairman and changed to General Secretary in 1982) was held after 1976 by:

Hua Guofeng, successor to Mao Zedong,   1976–1981
Hu Yaobang   1981–1986
Zhao Ziyang   1987–1989
Jiang Zemin   1989–

The PRIME MINISTER (also Premier), top post in the national government, was held after 1976 by:

Hua Guofeng, successor to Zhou Enlai,   1976–1980
Zhao Ziyang   1980–1988
Li Peng   1988–

Note: Although Deng Xiao-ping's name does not appear in this list he was the *de facto* leader in the hierarchy during the 1980s and 1990s. For some of his positions, including the important one of Chairman of the Peoples' Republic of China Central Military Commission, see the text.

17
CHINA, THE PACIFIC RIM, AND THE WORLD COMMUNITY

After the foundation of the PRC in 1949, China was concerned to establish and maintain its own security and to win a full measure of respect in the international community. In working toward the second goal, the PRC preserved throughout a strong attitude of independence, unwilling to make any compromises which were not in its long-term interest or which would appear to diminish its national dignity. Foreign policy issues for China involved relations, first with the USSR and the USA, second with its own East Asian neighbors—chiefly Japan and Southeast Asia—and third with Europe, the Third World, and other countries.

In the second half of the twentieth century China moved from intense preoccupation with its internal affairs (including a civil war) to becoming a world power engaged in forming a web of international ties, many of them quite new. One of the key themes in the emerging design was strategic security, maneuvering between two superpowers while remaining faithful to ideology and China's own practical needs.

RELATIONS WITH THE SOVIET UNION

Soviet Russia had been Communist China's first and principal ally. But the formal Sino-Soviet alliance, signed by Mao Zedong in Moscow in 1949, had broken down by 1960 (see p. 209); by the next year there were armed clashes along the lengthy frontier between the two countries. This enmity across Asian frontiers had a long history, made no easier by the fact that nomadic tribes in inner Asia took their herds where there was grazing and had little concept of exact frontiers. China was especially nervous about a Russian presence anywhere near its nuclear testing grounds in Xinjiang province, and relations became even more strained when the USSR invaded Afghanistan in 1979.

The USSR made some quiet approaches toward improving the situation, and Prime Minister Zhao Ziyang responded in 1982. But relations could not be normalized, he said, unless three conditions were met, namely: withdrawal of Soviet troops from the Sino-Soviet and Sino-Mongolian borders; an end to the occupation of Afghanistan; and a halt to the Soviet-supported Vietnam invasions of Kampuchea (Cambodia). Talks aimed at normalization on political and strategic issues took place on several occasions but with little result until the mid-1980s. However, a need for trade was common to both countries, so an agreement was reached to increase the exchange of goods in 1983 by 150 percent. China would import lumber and steel from, and export textiles and food to, the USSR.

The Russians agreed to a further positive step in 1984, sending economic and technical experts to China to help modernize several dozen factories and projects originally built by the Soviets in the 1950s. In spite of the intervening years of rivalry and disagreement over the correct Marxist line, the PRC and the USSR had a common interest in modernization, cooperation, and social reform. Yet this common interest was constantly overshadowed by China's fears of Russian "hegemony," a code word frequently applied to Russia in Chinese negotiations with Japan and the USA. In 1986 Mikhail Gorbachev brought a conciliatory tone to the discussions with the PRC, and Deng Xiaoping made a positive, if guarded, response. During Gorbachev's visit to Beijing at the height of the Tiananmen Square crisis in May 1989, both countries declared that relations had been "nornmalized."

By the 1990s the USSR had dissolved into its constituent parts. The world, one might say, was left with a China too big to ignore, strongly ideological but also pragmatic enough to lay aside differences, look for areas of mutual advantage, and exploit them. Abundant evidence of this is to be seen in China's relationship with the United States.

RELATIONS WITH THE UNITED STATES

In the period after World War II relations between the United States and China suffered from a great gulf in ideology; the civil war in China and the war in Korea caused further alienation. But gradually the mutual benefits of trade, the advantages to China of imported new technology, and opportunities for Chinese to obtain advanced education abroad led to an improvement in relations. And American students, professors, and researchers were given more access to study in China.

In the commercial sphere, the goods most desired by China were high-technology products from the United States. In 1981 the U.S. government decided to ease the regulations governing the export of microprocessors, computers, and machine tools. The first use China made of these sophisticated products was in the field of defense (see p. 235). But the leadership, concerned at the size of the trade deficit with the United States in the high-technology field, decided to open the door to foreign investors coming to China. (See joint ventures and special economic zones, p. 233). Such investors would serve China's constant aim to become less dependent on imports from abroad. Thus China used the time of slowly increasing détente to build up its defense and its economic strength in order to insure its future security against all comers.

In 1983 there was pressure on the U.S. government from American manufacturers of high-technology equipment who wanted export restrictions eased still further, even though the sensitive devices they exported were capable of military as well as civilian use. The U.S. government proved willing, but the PRC held up the agreement by refusing to give assurance that such technology would not be transferred to a third country. Disputes regarding the import into China of military hardware, the export of weapons and of the sensitive manufacturing technology which China then mastered, continued to be an irritant in relations with the United States.

The Chinese, in their turn, had acquired a large trade surplus in the export of textiles to the United States. Sales of $69 million in 1979 had grown to $834 million by 1982, and U.S. manufacturers were seriously alarmed, blaming the U.S. government for being too soft on China. The two govern-

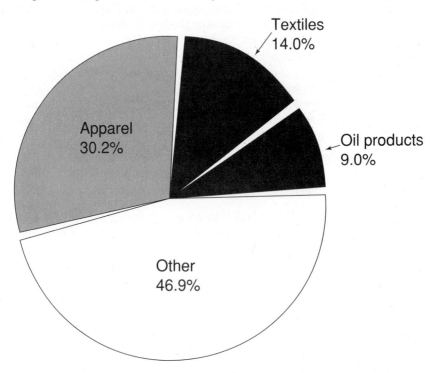

United States Imports from China, 1983.

SOURCE: Immanuel C. Y. Hsü *China Without Mao: The Search for a New Order,* second ed. (Oxford University Press, 1990), p. 199.

ments arrived at an agreement permitting Chinese textile exports to the United States to grow at an average rate of 3.5 percent a year for five years. South Korea, Taiwan, and Hong Kong had accepted similar limitations the year before. Forty-four percent of all Chinese exports to the United States in 1983 consisted of apparel and textiles.

HUMAN RIGHTS IN CHINA

World opinion after 1989 was particularly concerned over the violation of human rights in China. And the United States went further than most countries in its determination to tie trade relations with the PRC to a closer observance of human rights.

Immediately following the crackdown in Tiananmen Square, some student leaders managed to escape to Hong Kong and to the United States and Europe. From these bases they spread word of the struggle, which in turn enabled foreign governments to exert some pressure on the Chinese authorities. But those who escaped were only a fraction of the number who were arrested and imprisoned as dissidents. An Australian human rights mission secured information from Chinese officials that indicated there were still 4,000 convicted prisoners in detention in 1992. The Chinese denied that political prisoners were tortured, but there was convincing evidence that mistreatment, solitary confinement, and torture were widespread, and that prison guards were frequently out of control. A typical victim of this mistreatment was Wang Juntao, one of the founders of the Beijing Economic and Social Science Research Institute. Though seriously ill with hepatitis B, he was kept in punitive solitary confinement in a tiny airless cell under unspeakable sanitary conditions. His requests for medical care were denied. It was only as a result of continued international pressure that he was moved to a prison hospital.[*] He was released in 1994.

Camps for "reform through labor" *(laogai)* were notorious, with prisoners suffering from cold, starvation, and illness. In one of these camps, hungry inmates working in the fields were reduced to eating earthworms.[†] In another, in the northeast province of Liaoning, a political prisoner was tortured with a high voltage electric baton, known as a cattle prod, until he went into spasms and lost consciousness.[‡]

Prison songs, which had developed even before 1949, became a distinct genre in China. As prisoners were moved, the songs spread from prison to prison, and then were picked up by the general public when prisoners were released. One of the songs, more poignant in the original, reads in part:

---

[*]Human Rights Watch, *New York Times,* May 19, 1992.
[†]*New York Times,* September 10, 1991.
[‡]Bai Yong (pseudonym), verified by Asia Watch, *New York Times,* September 2, 1992.

> Bitter tears wash me as I pace to and fro.
> The sun shines outside, but my heart is icy.
> Darkness looms up before me.
> I am stuck here inside the prison.*

A letter smuggled out of prison in the spring of 1993 quotes a guard as saying, "If you refuse to bow your head, we'll grind you slowly to death." Yet a leader of the 1989 Democracy Movement, Shen Tong, rearrested in September 1993 after a period in the United States, recommended to Americans: "push China towards democracy, peacefully."†

Wei Jingsheng, the best-known dissident, released in September 1993 after almost fifteen years in prison, wrote an article published in the *New York Times*‡ in which he said:

> China not only doesn't understand reason but also does not intend to reason. . . . The present leaders [of China] were the most outspoken . . . shouting their support of human rights and democracy before they came to power. But their subsequent dictatorship made clear that they have no intention of making good on the promises they once made to the masses.

In the same article, he said of the United States:

> The new direction of U.S. policy toward China leads them [the Chinese people] to believe that the party was right all these years in saying that the American government is controlled by rich capitalists. All you have to do is offer them a chance to make money and anything goes. . . . I don't really believe in this kind of understanding—or rather I'm not willing to believe in it.

After the appearance of this article, Wei Jingsheng was forbidden to write anything for publication in China or abroad. In the spring of 1994 Wei was again placed in detention.

President Clinton said in 1993 that the U.S. would only renew the Most Favored Nation (MFN) status of China's trade if China made significant improvements in human rights enforcement. The main U.S. concerns were the sale in the United States of goods made by Chinese prison labor and the continuance of torture and inhumane prison conditions; the administration demanded free entry for prison inspections by the Red Cross.

There has always existed a wide gap between the Western and the Chinese view of human rights. Emphasis in the West has been upon the rights of the individual to life, freedom, property and self-defense. In China the rights of the individual have often had to give way to the rights of the community, as in Article 51 of the constitution: "The exercise by citizens . . . of their freedoms

---

* *New York Times,* July 6, 1992.
† *New York Times,* Op-Ed page, September 2, 1992.
‡ *New York Times,* Op-Ed page, November 18, 1993.

and rights may not infringe upon the interests of the state, or society and the collective . . ." It is the state that provides and witholds rights, the state that stipulates duties. China considered the use of foreign pressure from outside inadmissible when applied to its internal dealings with its own citizens; trade sanctions became in the 1980s an example of such pressure. The Chinese insisted that trade and human rights should have no linkage whatever. The United States, on the other hand, frequently included a universal moral imperative in its foreign policy. This contrasted not only with the policy of China but with the practice of many nations in the world, including European countries. Moral considerations and demands for reform in China had already been a part of the debate concerning the massive American aid given to Jiang Jieshi (Chiang Kaishek) and his government over several decades.

In 1990, however, the PRC sent a delegation abroad to study the human rights policies of other countries. It appeared that Deng Xiaoping could no longer allow China to continue to avoid the topic. Soon articles in the Chinese press criticized the human rights failures of the West in Northern Ireland and Los Angeles. The next year an official "white paper" published in Beijing made claims, some considerably exaggerated, about China's progress in human rights; but at least the matter was now on the PRC agenda. From time to time the Chinese government released political prisoners as an example of concern for civil liberties. The PRC's main stress, however, was on a people's rights to free development and on the violation of rights which arose from the unjust economic order prevailing in the world.*

HUMAN RIGHTS IN TIBET

Tibet was the scene of some of the worst Chinese violations of human rights, a tragedy in which geographical and historical factors played a part. Tibet is isolated in a high mountainous region, and highlanders have never been easy to control. The Picts in the Scottish highlands beyond the Antonine Wall gave even the Roman legions trouble. The Swiss on their Alps have always been proudly independent. And no one could fully control the Vietnamese mountain tribes. Similarly the highlanders of Tibet had frequently been a thorn in the side of Chinese administrations seeking to assert their authority in the far west of the country. During the Ming dynasty Tibet accepted a tributary relationship with China. As a rule this meant only a recognition of the Chinese emperor's culturally superior position as the Son of Heaven, a means of conducting diplomatic relations, and an official approval of mutual trade. It did not involve nor lead to invasive procedures to take over Tibet's internal affairs. The Ming emperor Yongle conferred titles and confirmed appointments within Tibet as part of his activist policy in the north-

---

*I am indebted on the question of human rights to *The Crux of the Struggle,* a seminar paper given at Columbia University by Professor James D. Seymour, Dec 9, 1993—Author.

west. During the Qing dynasty, however, the level of interference rose. The Tibetan politico-religious system concerned the Chinese authorities because of its disturbing extension into the affairs of Mongolia. The Qing sent several military expeditions into Tibet and at length established the Dalai Lama in political as well as religious leadership under a firm Chinese protectorate. Republican China was unable to maintain control in Tibet, but the PRC claimed to be the superior power on the basis of past history. Chinese Communist troops invaded Tibet in October 1950 in order to "liberate" the country from "imperialist oppression," although the Tibetans were not conscious of any need to be liberated. The Chinese claims went far beyond historical precedent and generally ignored Tibetan culture and Tibet's Buddhist form of theocracy in order to absorb the country into China and the Communist system.

In 1955 the PRC set about establishing the Tibetan Autonomous Region. They proposed the Dalai Lama as Chairman of the Preparatory Committee for that purpose, but this move had no chance of success. In March 1959 the Tibetan capital, Lhasa, arose in serious armed rebellion against the Chinese overlordship. The Chinese quelled the revolt in two weeks, and the Dalai Lama took refuge in India. The PRC then secured the Panchen Lama, second in ecclesiastical rank, to head the Preparatory Committee. The United States and other governments protested that China was violating Tibetan human rights, to no avail. But twenty years later, in May 1980, the PRC declared that it would ease central government control and promote the economy and culture of the autonomous region. It allocated more funds to Tibet, and gave more government posts to Tibetans. Chinese working in Tibet were ordered to learn the Tibetan language. Even the self-exiled Dalai Lama said China's attitude had become more moderate, realistic, and understanding.

But a protest by the Dalai Lama on China's harsh policies in 1987 was followed by several demonstrations in Lhasa, in the largest of which two thousand monks and others took part. In clashes with Chinese security forces then, and again in March 1989, Tibetans looted houses and shops belonging to Chinese. These disturbances were the worst since those of 1959. The PRC declared martial law, which lasted until January 1990.

In 1988 the international body Asia Watch had already denounced China for making arbitrary arrests of supporters of Tibetan independence, for using torture on prisoners, and for inducing abortions without the mothers' consent. The Chinese claimed there were inaccuracies in these reports and that the sources behind them were questionable. In any event, Chinese control was maintained and Chinese cultural influences continued to spread in Tibet.

THE PACIFIC RIM

A second key theme in foreign affairs was China's relations with its closest Pacific Rim neighbors. Although there were security considerations here, particularly in regard to Japan, the main emphases were cultural and commercial.

For much of their history, China and Japan had endeavored to ignore each other, but their geographical proximity and mutual needs frequently brought them together. In the distant past Japan had received its writing system and much of its high culture from China, and the Japanese had all along had a respect, sometimes a rather distant respect, for the Chinese. The Chinese had not, in the main, reciprocated this feeling. From the late nineteenth century onward, Japan's success in modernization and its aggressive stance created severe problems for China. Signposting China's ever-deepening hostility toward Japan were a number of developments: the disgrace of being defeated by Japan in 1895; indignation at Japan's gains in the Versailles Treaty, expressed in the May Fourth Movement of 1919; the humiliation attendant on Japan's creation of Manzhouguo (Manchukuo) in 1932; and the hatred engendered by Japan's role in World War II. More recent causes of disaffection were China's trade deficit with Japan ($2 billion in 1984, rising to $4 billion in September 1985), and Prime Minister Yakasone's visit to the Yasukuni Shrine in Tokyo honoring the Japanese war dead, the first such visit by a prime minister since World War II.

Japan came gradually to recognize these feelings and tried to reach out to the Chinese and the other peoples of East and Southeast Asia. Conciliatory visits were crowned by apologies offered by Japanese prime ministers and even by Emperor Akihito himself. After considerable pressure by the Chinese, the Japanese Ministry of Education altered the wording of school textbooks to correspond more closely to the facts of Japanese aggression and cruelty during World War II.

In the commercial field, Japan's efforts before and during World War II to promote the idea of a Greater East Asia Co-Prosperity Sphere under its leadership had met with little success. But as soon as Japan had made an industrial recovery after the war, Japanese firms, particularly pharmaceutical companies, quickly found markets in Southeast Asia. Trade with China began again, and in 1978 Japan offered China a five-year series of low-interest loans for development; these amounted to $1.5 billion by their end in 1983. Projects thus financed included the construction of a railway in Shandong province and the updating of a number of factories. The Japanese also supported Chinese steel, coal, and oil development. In 1983 arrangements were made for a second round of low-interest loans, a clear indication that Japan was satisfied with China's performance.

On their side, the Japanese also had anxieties about China. When the General Secretary of the CCP, Hu Yaobang, visited Japan in November 1983, one of his main objectives was to allay Japanese fears of instability on the continent. The Japanese felt uncertain about the succession to power after Deng Xiaoping and about whether the intentions of North Korea towards South Korea were to be peaceful or not.

But leaders on the Chinese as well as the Japanese side realized the clear necessity of a cooperative relationship, particularly for the sake of trade. In April 1992, as the inner circle of the PRC government was engaged in debate over the degree and the forms of free enterprise to allow, Jiang Zemin, the CCP General Secretary, paid a goodwill visit to Japan to allay its fears. He praised the high level of Japan's economic development and said that Japan "has had many experiences China can learn from." He may have had in mind the fact about Japan most admired in China: namely, the coexistence of free markets with a strong central government dominated for a long time (until the summer of 1993, in fact) by a single ruling party.

Main Destination/Origin of Exports/Imports in 1988

DESTINATIONS OF EXPORTS		ORIGINS OF IMPORTS	
COUNTRY, REGION	PERCENTAGE OF TOTAL	COUNTRY, REGION	PERCENTAGE OF TOTAL
Hong Kong and Macau	38.4	Japan	21.7
Japan	16.7	Hong Kong and Macau	20.0
United States	7.1	United States	12.0
Singapore	3.1	West Germany	6.2
Soviet Union	3.1	Canada	3.4
West Germany	3.1	Soviet Union	3.2

SOURCE: Mackerras, Colin and Yorke, Amanda, eds. *The Cambridge Handbook of Contemporary China*. (Cambridge, 1991), p. 168.

The export/import table above reveals some interesting points about China's part in Pacific Rim trade. (Of the countries listed, only West Germany is not geographically connected to the Pacific Ocean). China exported to Japan more than twice the amount of its exports to the United States and received from Japan almost twice what it received from the United States. Much of the export to Hong Kong went for reexport elsewhere (see graph on p. 259). Imports at this date were still in large part destined for development within China and consisted to a great extent of machinery and raw materials.

SOUTHEAST ASIA

China had long had trading connections with the lands of Southeast Asia. Song dynasty porcelain was exported in large quantities. Ming dynasty ambitions brought states in Southeast Asia into the tribute system, which implied a two-way trade. And by late Ming, a spreading junk trade took merchants from China into nearly every port in the region.

Militarily, China dominated its near neighbor, Vietnam, throughout much of China's history. The part of the country formerly called Annam was conquered by the Tang in the seventh century (in Chinese, Annam means "pacify the south"), and the Mongols sent four expeditions against Annam late in the thirteenth century. In modern times, Vietnam was involved in frequent warfare: a war of liberation against the French, ending with the battle of Dienbienphu in 1954; the protracted and devastating civil war in which South Vietnam was aided by the United States, and a brief invasion by China in 1979 after Vietnam had invaded Kampuchea (Cambodia) (see pp. 224–225). The Chinese had much to answer for in Kampuchea, since they had backed the Khmer Rouge which killed one million Kampucheans during their reign from 1975 to 1978.

In 1988 China proposed a settlement plan for Kampuchea involving a four-party provisional government which would include the Khmer Rouge. Building upon this, the five members of the UN Security Council called for greater UN involvement and proposed the withdrawal of foreign forces, a cease-fire, a UN presence during a transition period, and then free and fair elections. This was significant, because China had decided to support UN involvement. On October 23, 1991, the Paris Accord on Kampuchea along these lines was signed by the five members of the Security Council, the Kampuchean government, and nineteen other nations, many of them Asian. The three rebel factions agreed to merge their political branches with the Kampuchean authorities in the capital, Phnom Penh, under the leadership of Prince Sihanouk, the only political figure acceptable to all parties. China and Vietnam thereupon agreed to normalize relations.

Vietnam welcomed a bold, conciliatory action by President Clinton in February 1994, when he lifted the trade embargo which the United States had imposed on Vietnam after the war in order to force that country to give a full accounting of Americans missing in action. President Clinton's move gave Vietnam, united after the war under Communist leadership but now turning toward a market system, a new opportunity to revive its economy. The common people seemed glad and relieved that their long chapter of war was closed, but the leaders were treading with caution lest a sudden boom in the economy lead to high prices and inflation. Many in the country felt relief that the new American umbrella might help to protect them from China, their traditional enemy to the north.

What, then, is going to be the importance of Vietnam, with its seventy-one million people, to China and to other Pacific Rim nations in the future? It may prove to have a purely commercial impact, as a competitive source of markets and materials. Or it may become a successful manufacturing center itself, employing for this purpose its hardworking and relatively well-educated labor force. Or it may turn out to have a mainly strategic importance, as a buffer zone for China's own defense or as a point from which an outside power might threaten China.

Since 1945 and the end of World War II—a decisive hinge in all geopolitical events—the Pacific Rim nations have been frequently singled out as the likely shapers of the future. The two large land powers at either end of the huge semicircle, the United States and Australia, had been aware of the presence of Russia on the Pacific coastline, but they had also awakened to the incalculable power of Japan and China. A new factor in the uneasy equation characterizing the period from the 1970s to the 1990s was the rising significance of the Newly Industrialized Countries or NICs—namely South Korea, Taiwan, Hong Kong, Singapore, Thailand, and the Philippines. The list could be extended to include Indonesia and Malaysia. The first four of the countries listed above have been called The Four Little Dragons, and three of these—Taiwan, Hong Kong and Singapore—have inhabitants who are predominantly Chinese, while the fourth, Korea, shares many cultural features with China.

TAIWAN

Taiwan, seat of the Republic of China, is an oval-shaped island 250 miles long and 80 miles wide, with a mountain chain running down between the center of the island and the east side. The agricultural plain on the west, with plentiful rainfall and a semitropical climate, yields rice, vegetables, and fruit in abundance. Taiwan is about a hundred miles off the China coast, lying opposite the province of Fujian, and Chinese have been emigrating to the island since the seventh century. They now form the vast majority of the twenty-million population, speaking the dialects of Fujian and Hakka.

The Portuguese in the sixteenth century named it the "beautiful" island, Formosa, and Taiwan has also been a prize in the hands of other nations—the Dutch in the seventeenth century and the Japanese from 1895 to 1945. The presence of the U.S. 7th Fleet prevented the island from being attacked by the PRC in 1950, and the Mutual Security Treaty between Taiwan and the United States was not only a pragmatic way of defending American interests in the Pacific but also an expression of long-standing American sympathy and support for Jiang Jieshi (Chiang Kai-shek) and his government.

During the dying years of the Nationalist government on the mainland, the governor of the province of Taiwan (which was recovered from the Japanese in 1945) permitted callous exploitation of the native Taiwanese. On February 28, 1947, a street confrontation sparked a revolt which spread across the island. The arrival of Nationalist reinforcements in mid-March initiated a brutal repression in which at least eight thousand Taiwanese were slaughtered (some estimates go far higher). Memories of this "2-23 Incident" continue to smolder in the minds of Taiwanese and have found an outlet in the new party politics of the 1990s.

Economics in Taiwan

Nationalist policy in Taiwan altered radically when General Chen Cheng was appointed governor in January 1949. (Jiang Jieshi evacuated from the mainland to Taiwan in December of that year). Among the initiatives of General Chen which were vital to restoring confidence in the government was a reduction of the rent paid by farmers to 37.5 percent of their main crop from the previous figure of 50 to 70 percent.

This was the beginning of a land reform program which proved to be the foundation of Taiwan's rise to prosperity and civic stability, despite lingering resentment against the incoming mainlanders who controlled the government. The next stage of land reform was the redistribution of land which had formerly belonged to Japanese, amounting in all to 20 percent of the total available for agriculture. This land was sold to 140,000 farmers on very favorable terms, with repayment in twenty years at an annual interest of only 4 percent. The final step in land reform came in 1953, when the government bought up all the land held privately or worked by tenants, then resold it to those who actually worked it. Tenancy was radically reduced, so that by 1960 it was claimed that 90 percent of the agricultural land was in the hands of the farmers who cultivated it.* The results were spectacular. Even as early as the first half of the 1950s, agricultural yield rose by 25 percent, and farmers were able to plant two and even three crops a year. One of the great ironies of history is that, if the Nationalists had carried out the ideas of land reform implicit in Sun Yat-sen's Principle of the People's Livelihood (see p. 179) in the early years of their rule in China, the history of that country and of their governing authority might have taken a very different course.

Along with the improvements in agriculture went the development of light industry, as metal cans were manufactured to export specialized and luxury cash crops such as mushrooms and pineapples. Further expansion included the production of sewing machines, then refrigerators and air conditioners. Bicycles made in Taiwan captured a sizeable share of the world market. Government-planned heavy industry followed, including the construction of a large steel mill at Gaoxiong and the China Shipbuilding Corporation, which erected the second-largest dry dock in the world. A vast export industry in clothing grew up; television sets and computers were also large export items.[†] Export processing zones, where simplified customs and export regulations were an encouragement to foreign investors, played a part in this phenomenal industrial growth. Three of these zones were set up in the 1960s, and by 1974 there were almost three hundred in existence. During the years 1974–1984 Taiwan had the second-highest economic growth rate in the world, exceeded only by that of Singapore, and the per capita GNP figures showed remarkable gains: $2,100 in 1980, $3,046 in 1984, $6,053 in 1988. But even more important, there was a reasonably fair distribution of the new wealth. If one takes the highest 20 percent and the lowest 20 percent of wage earners, their incomes in 1952 stood in a ratio of 15 to 1; but in 1987 the gap had shrunk to a ratio of only 4.69 to 1—less than the gap between rich and poor in the United States.[‡]

---

*See Rafe de Crespigny, *China This Century* (Oxford, 1992), p. 313.
†op.cit. pp. 323–324.
‡I am indebted for many of the figures in this section on Taiwan to Immanuel C. Y. Hsü, *China Without Mao: The Search for a New Order*, 2nd ed. (Oxford, 1990), pp. 248 ff.

A progression from agriculture to computer manufacture was, of course, impossible without an educated workforce. And here Taiwan had an excellent record. Almost all children were enrolled in the first stage of nine years' free education. Of those between fifteen and seventeen years of age, 51 percent went on to senior high school, and of those aged eighteen to twenty-one, 25.2 percent attended college and university (figures for 1977–1978). The national literacy rate in 1987 was an astonishing 97 percent.

Politics in Taiwan

Jiang Jieshi died in 1975, and the real power of leadership devolved on his son, Jiang Jingguo (Chiang Ching-kuo). At first Chairman of the Guomindang, GMD (KMT), he was elected President of the Republic of China in 1978. His emphasis was on the economy, while his father's had been on military affairs. Jiang Jingguo was sociable and friendly, and he made it a point to introduce native Taiwanese into positions of leadership. He was nevertheless strong in his defense of the ruling party and the Three People's Principles of Sun Yat-sen; which made it all the harder for him to accept the United States' recognition of the PRC in January 1979 and the consequent downgrading to unofficial status of its relations with the Republic of China (see p. 223).

Jiang Jingguo's liberal politics were carried on after his death in 1988 by his Vice President and successor, Li Denghui (Lee Teng-hui). Li had very good credentials for his position in a new Taiwan; he was scholarly and trustworthy, with a doctorate from Cornell University and previous political experience as Mayor of Taipei and Governor of Taiwan. He was also a convinced Christian. During his presidency the Central Standing Committee of the GMD had a majority of Taiwanese-born members for the first time. In May 1991 a decree of Li Denghui formally accepted the existence of the Beijing government, ending the state of civil war. The question of the eventual unification of the PRC on the mainland with the Republic of China on Taiwan was always present in the background. Neither country wanted permanent division into two Chinas, but up to 1994 there was no evidence of any imminent attempt to unite. This question of reunification was a factor in the historic Taiwan elections in December 1992, the first full and free elections in the history of the island. The principal opposition, the Democratic Progressive Party, campaigned for a Taiwan entirely independent of mainland China, a position that contributed to its defeat, with the GMD winning with 70 percent of the vote.

HONG KONG

Hong Kong, a barren rocky island, began as a haven for refugees. They were rather well-off British merchant refugees, who, after a showdown in the nineteenth century with Commisioner Lin of the Qing dynasty, had to flee from Canton. From the island they carried on their trade with the cooperation of some American merchants, selling opium and buying tea (see p. 153). The island was ceded to Britain in perpetuity by the Treaty of Nanking, which ended the Opium War in 1842. In a second agreement, the Treaty of Peking which ended the Anglo-French War in 1860, Britain obtained the southern part of the Kowloon peninsula opposite Hong Kong. Finally, in 1898, the British colony of Hong Kong secured a ninety-nine-year lease on the New Territories extending north of the Kowloon peninsula, and of 235 islands in the vicinity. This last acquisition covered ten times the area of the first two. The entire territory was integrated under one system of colonial government, which would all return to China by June 30, 1997. The PRC had from the beginning made known its refusal to recognize the validity of the unequal treaties extracted from a weak Qing regime. And since mainland China had control of water and food supplies for Hong Kong and could overwhelm the island militarily at any moment, there was no question that the 1997 deadline for withdrawal would be met.

Hong Kong harbor is one of the most valuable deepwater ports in the world, and one of the most picturesque. It is crisscrossed by a great variety of junks, smaller sampans, modern ferries, international freighters, and, formerly, ocean liners from Europe and Japan. The island's Peak climbs steeply from the harbor and is ringed at night by necklaces of lights, while at its base rise gleaming office towers, growing in number and height year by year, and clinging somehow to the sides of the mountain. The upper part of the Peak is dotted with the luxury houses of *taipans* (heads of merchant houses), both Chinese and foreign, including the residence of the British governor of the Crown

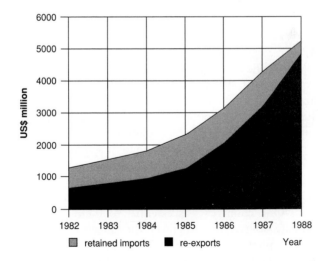

Hong Kong's Imports from China

SOURCE: Mackerras, Colin and Yorke, Amanda, eds. *The Cambridge Handbook of Contemporary China.* (Cambridge, 1991).

Colony of Hong Kong. Residential areas and Chinese fishing villages, such as Aberdeen, now crowded with floating restaurants painted in gaudy hues, are scattered around the indented coastline.

The population of Hong Kong grew rapidly with the influx of refugees from China in the 1940s and early 1950s. Great efforts were made to house the immigrants, but in 1953 the Hong Kong government had to halt the flow. The people thus added to the existing workforce helped to increase production in clothing, handicrafts, various forms of light industry, sugar processing, and the manufacture of electrical equipment, television sets, and computer components. On the managerial side, British commercial law allowed the formation of corporations and the accumulation of capital without the restrictions which applied in China. Firms from the United States, Europe, Japan, mainland China, Taiwan and elsewhere set up branches in this briskly expanding free market for goods and currency. Risks for investors were reduced because the Hong Kong currency was pegged to the U.S. dollar. As a result of this activity and these advantages, Hong Kong ranked at the top of the PRC list of trading partners, as indicated by the table on p. 254 and by the graph on p. 259.

Return of Hong Kong to Chinese Rule

The coming restoration of Chinese authority over Hong Kong in 1997 has affected every aspect of its life—political, commercial, and social. After Prime Minister Margaret Thatcher's visit to Beijing in 1982 and the subsequent series of talks on the subject between Britain and China, feelings ran high, for the life plans of thousands of families were adrift on a sea of uncertainty. A draft agreement restoring Chinese sovereignty over the former colony on July 1, 1997, was initialed in the Great Hall of the People in Beijing in September 1984. The Legislative Council in Hong Kong and the British Parliament both approved the draft, and the final accord, the Joint Declaration, was signed on December 19, 1984, in Beijing by Prime Minister Thatcher and Prime Minister Zhao Ziyang. The agreement stipulated that Hong Kong was to "enjoy a high degree of autonomy, except in foreign or defense affairs," as well as "executive, legislative and independent judicial power," with its current laws remaining basically unchanged. The capitalist system was to continue, and rights and freedoms such as those of speech, press, assembly, travel, and religious belief were to be ensured by law.

The PRC leadership characterized the new situation as "One Country, Two Systems." "One country" was essential to them, a matter of national pride and ultimate sovereignty whatever the intervening stages in practice might be. But the phrase "two systems," though it sounded good, was not reassuring to the people of Hong Kong. The matter of travel documents, which would give them freedom of movement after 1997, had not been settled; and worse, the PRC spoke of the stationing of troops in Hong Kong.

Hong Kong residents' most serious concern was the Basic Law for Hongkong as a Special Administrative Region of China, upon which a committee of legal and political experts (thirty-five members from the PRC and twenty-three from Hong Kong) had begun work in 1983. The first draft of the law was released in 1988, and the final version, passed by the National People's Congress of the PRC, was promulgated in 1990. But despite the joint consultation, inhabitants of Hong Kong were afraid that provisions of the Basic Law—and possible future amendments to it—might weaken or nullify promises made in the 1984 Joint Declaration concerning the handover of power. Particular concern centered on the weakness of the legislature and the judiciary in the new system of governance. Many of the young and vigorous Chinese leaders pointed out that official PRC visitors to Hong Kong met only with pro-China leaders and did not understand the Hong Kong justice system, especially the high value placed upon the rule of law.

The Hong Kong public also became concerned about the increase of corruption and violent crime. These had always been present, but became worse with the arrival of criminal gangs from the mainland, such as the notorious Triads. For instance, there was a regular market in stolen luxury cars, transported to China by means of boats that were often fast enough to outrun customs vessels. But that was only one example of the crime attendant on the moneymaking fever both in Hong Kong and on the mainland.

Nevertheless, during 1993 foreign observers in Hong Kong noted a surprising investment confidence, especially among the Japanese. The colony enjoyed such a close link with the apparently unstoppable economic surge in south China that it was expected that the Hong Kong economy would simply continue to grow. Also expected, however, was a future decline in business efficiency and honesty, as well as in the desirability of Hong Kong as a place to live for all classes in the community. After Tiananmen Square, distrust of the Chinese government increased because of its use of force against its own people. Distrust of the British government also grew because of its too ready compliance with China's wishes. The people of Hong Kong seemed more than ever prepared to take their destiny into their own hands wherever possible. But in the early 1990s manufacturing moved increasingly from Hong Kong into China, leaving the colony more dependent upon service industries. There was some speculation that Singapore, where the English language and modes of thinking were more familiar, might become a strong competitor in the service sector.*

These combined anxieties about the future led to the flight of many residents from Hong Kong. A large number of them preferred to move to Canada or Australia rather than to the United States or Britain. One of the oldest firms, Jardine Matheson, transferred its headquarters to Bermuda as a precaution, but continued to function otherwise as before in Hong Kong. In a simi-

---

*Personal correspondence Feb. 5, 1992 with Alison Hardie, businesswoman and China scholar, who is a resident of Hong Kong and travels constantly in China.

lar vein, some individuals moved out but made property arrangements with friends who were staying, to enable them to return to Hong Kong if the future were to look brighter.

The leaders of the PRC, in their turn, had some cause for anxiety when, in September 1991, sixteen of the eighteen seats up for election in the Legislative Council went to prodemocracy candidates. Twelve of the sixteen belonged to the United Democrats of Hong Kong party, led by a prominent liberal lawyer, Martin Lee. No pro-PRC candidate won a seat in spite of efforts by newspapers, labor unions, and businessmen who were backed by China. Government policy, in actual fact, was not going to be materially altered by this result. The remainder of the sixty members of the Legislative Council were still appointed by the Governor directly or appointed to represent various interests, such as business, the medical and legal professions, and tourism. The balance of power remained with the colony's business elite. In an article in an influential journal, Martin Lee said, "Virtually every economically advanced nation in East Asia—as in the West—has recognized that prosperity and democracy are not mutually antagonistic but are in truth inseparable."* Although ultimate power remained with Beijing, the extent of the liberal vote and statements such as Martin Lee's showed that the transition in 1997 would be far from easy.

The British government was embarrassed by the liberals' criticism that it had given in too easily to demands from Beijing in the last years under the governor, Sir David Wilson, a Sinologist and an old-line civil servant. In July 1992 a new Governor, Christopher Patten, arrived. His policy, more assertive and independent, further aggravated the tension with Beijing when he proposed to increase the proportion of freely elected seats in the Legislative Council due to be voted on in 1995. This would make Hong Kong still more difficult for China to govern along its lines of strict control. In November 1992 China threatened to repudiate altogether the agreement of 1984, which had promised fifty years of political and economic freedom after 1997. But few believed the threat would be carried out. China needs Hong Kong, not only as a window on the world, but still more as an economic partner. Sixty percent of the huge investment in the Chinese economy made by overseas Chinese in the 1990s came from Hong Kong.

RELATIONS WITH OTHER NATIONS

The third key theme in China's foreign relations was its shifting global strategy. Relations with Europe, for example, were governed in the 1980s by commercial needs and scientific/technological considerations, not by ideology. In establishing relations with various countries (of which only a few examples can be given here), China relied on visits and on some extensive tours by

---

*Far Eastern Economic Review, September 26, 1992, p. 31.

senior officials. In May and June of 1984 Prime Minister Zhao Ziyang visited France, Belgium, the Netherlands, Germany, Sweden, Denmark, Norway, Italy and Great Britain to encourage foreign investment in China and trade relations generally. The PRC's wider objectives in Europe were to seek a counterweight to the United States and the Soviet Union and to find a source for new technology other than Japan. But China's trade with Europe in 1983 comprised only about 17 percent of its total volume.

Zhao Ziyang also made an extended tour of Africa, not so much for trade as for purposes of public relations, exhibiting China as the champion of the Third World. In African countries also, a more practical strategy replaced the Cold War maneuvers, of which the Chinese construction of the TanZam Railroad for Tanzania was a part.

Back in the Pacific Rim, Australia negotiated an agreement to export iron and steel to China. And both Canada and Australia became major suppliers of wheat to the Chinese market. In this trade connection it is important to note that, from the early days of the PRC, the Canadian people and their government have shown much less opposition to the Communist regime than has the United States. As the end of the century approached, the United States seemed to be drawing closer to a similar pragmatic view.

18

CHINESE SOCIETY

Study of the politics, economics, and foreign relations of a country tells us a good deal about the leaders and their aims but not much about the ordinary people, their daily life, their struggles, and their sources of contentment. This is especially true of a country such as China, where information which might adversely affect the prestige of the nation is strictly controlled. Looking more closely at some positive factors, some major problems, and some particular facets—such as education, the family, and contemporary culture—may give us a clearer view of this elusive society.

PROSPERITY

During 1993, groups of small investors would crowd around the door of Mr. Yang's office in a Shanghai securities firm. At lunchtime he would leave his computer and the flow of price quotations to stand at the door, answer questions, and give market advice to individuals before the afternoon session of the stock exchange opened. His success story and his good humor were the reasons for his position as an oracle. A Red Guard in his youth, he had used his business acumen to rise to the position which earned him the name Yang Baiwan, "Millions Yang." The Shanghai Stock Exchange, which carried him upwards, had grown in two years to the point where, in May 1993, it had two million shareholders, with the number growing by 50,000 a week. The market index had shot up 167 percent in 1992.

Then there was the young Mr. Wang Junjin, a traveling salesman dealing in badges and insignia. By the age of twenty-three he and his brother had been able to found an airline, the Sky Dragon Charter Airline Company, with a 1992 revenue of $2 million. His motto could apply to a host of entrepreneurs,

Rice paddies, an age-old geometric pattern.

Planting, tending, and harvesting rice in the paddy fields in the hot sun has been going on for centuries and still continues in the PRC. Much of the labor of rice cultivation cannot be done by machines, even if they were available, and must be done by hand.

Photo: Richard Balzer

"If the Government lets us do it, we'll do it." Perhaps never before in history have so many risen so rapidly out of poverty.

But prosperity is not confined to a few outstanding individuals. In the early 1980s, Qiaotou, a town in southern Zhejiang province, began making buttons as a sideline to increase its peasants' earnings. China's general prosperity and opening to the West was having an interesting side effect: people were wearing fewer Mao jackets and more shirts with more buttons; and buttons were easily transported, even though Qiaotou had poor roads and no rail link. By 1993 the town was producing twelve billion buttons a year in more than a hundred factories, seven of which were joint ventures with Taiwan and Hong Kong companies.

Numbers in China can be numbing, but perhaps the most interesting point is that the local Communist Party secretary, Chen Jianlin, owned a factory. His words might be taken as a succinct summary of the new Party line. "My most important job is building up the economy. People here say, 'If you push the economy along, you're a good leader. Otherwise, you're not.'" Mr. Chen's salary was only $20 a month. Qiaotou's 20,000 workers, most of them migrants from elsewhere, earned three times as much. But the Party provided Mr. Chen with the following useful perquisites: most of his expenses, a house,

Wheatfields.

Wheat is also an important staple food source in central China. A modern combine harvester is used by the Qiliying People's Commune in Henan province. Many former communes still have to rely on more primitive agricultural tools.

Xinhua News Agency

an Audi car and chauffeur, a telephone with international direct dialling, a beeper, and a Mastercard.

Since 1980 the economy of China has grown by an average 9.5 percent annually (in 1993 by 13 percent), rivalling the figures for Japan and South Korea at their highest in the postwar period. Some experts hold that a growth figure of 6 to 9 percent may be sustainable on average for ten years into the future, in part because the levels of efficiency and productivity can still be raised considerably.

Everyone visiting China in the early 1990s was struck by the extraordinary speed of change. Paul Theroux described driving through a new city site in south China*:

> Everything was being built at once—the roads, the pedestrian bridges, the apartment houses, the factories, the stores. The buildings were thirty or forty

*Paul Theroux, "Going to See the Dragon," *Harper's,* October, 1993, p. 37.

stories high and still clad in spindly scaffolding. . . . I had never seen anything like it in China, or the world, a whole city under construction, and what made it strangest of all was that no heavy machinery was in evidence—no bulldozers, no cranes. . . . In a short time—months maybe—the town would be inhabited and brightly lit.

Apart from the move toward a market economy and the expanded legal space in which to make money, a random list of improvements in the quality of life in the new China might include the extension of roads and electric power lines to remote villages, health benefits such as free prenatal checkups for mothers and wheelchairs for the disabled, and preferred admission to university education for minorities, including Tibetans. Down at the basic level in the villages the objects most desired used to be "the Three Rounds": a watch, a bicycle, and a sewing machine (all of which revolve). Then, in 1984, a remarkable parade in Beijing marked the thirty-fifth anniversary of Communist rule, with the customary quota of tanks, guns, and missiles in the front, but followed by floats adorned with a twenty-foot high chicken, a stereo system, and a huge refrigerator stuffed with food and bottles of beer. In the villages of the 1990s one had to list as goals a brick home, preferably of two stories, fitted with electric light, a refrigerator, a television set, and, some would add, foreign romance novels. Black-and-white TV sets were to be found in only a few homes in, say, 1987. Six years later the great majority of homes, except for the poorest, had TV sets, about half of them being color televisions. The rise in the general standard of living has been phenomenal, even though there are still many pockets of poverty.

ENVIRONMENTAL PROBLEMS

Chinese society also faced many problems in the decade of the 1980s, some due to natural disasters, others man-made, the former all too familiar in Chinese history, the latter associated for the most part with contemporary prosperity. Hubei province in 1980 was hit by flooding of the Yangzi River, with a consequent loss of 550 lives. China, for the first time since 1949, applied for international relief funds to meet this disaster. In April 1981 a severe drought affected nine northern provinces, subjecting 130 million people to food shortages. There was no starvation and government relief was said to work well, but again Hubei province was one of the worst hit. In July of the same year the Yangzi rose again, flooding parts of Sichuan and Hubei, causing 753 deaths and rendering 1.5 million people homeless as the river reached its highest level since 1905. The Gezhou Dam under construction at Yichang survived. But the flooding was blamed on Mao's policy of making "grain the key link," causing indiscriminate deforestation. The melancholy tale continued, with floods in the southeast in July 1981, in Guangdong in May 1982, and in Sichuan in July 1989.

Yet reports of the opposite problem, water shortages, were not reassuring. In 1993 the Water Resources Minister of the PRC said, "in rural areas over eighty-two million people find it difficult to procure water." The cities were worse off; the minister cited three hundred cities short of water. Water sources were also increasingly affected by pesticide contamination and industrial pollution, the latter caused by the recent erection of hundreds of new factories. Problems like these are familiar in the experience of other countries. But in China the pressures of an expanding population (despite strenuous birth control efforts) make them more than usually serious.

China's historic concern about water—its benefits and its dangers—is reflected in the veneration paid to an early culture hero, Yü the Great, who devoted his life to organizing irrigation and flood control (see p. 14). Preliminary work has begun on a modern equivalent to his achievement which has been under consideration for over thirty years: the Xiaolangdi Dam on the Yellow River, designed to generate electricity, mitigate silting, control flooding, and make irrigation easier. A proposed Three Gorges Dam on the Yangzi River, just below the mountain gorges where the river runs onto the southern plain, is a much more controversial affair. It would produce an enormous supply of electric power and greatly reduce the chances of large-scale flooding. However, apart from the estimated financial outlay (on the order of $11 billion) on the dam itself, building it would involve the relocation of 1.1 million people over a 375-mile stretch of riverbank and would destroy some of China's most spectacular scenery. A third project—namely a 730-mile canal to send water from the Yangzi near its mouth to Beijing and the dry north China plain—has received preliminary approval. One argument in favor of this canal is that use could be made of most of the route of China's old, hand-dug Grand Canal, begun in the seventh century and extended in the thirteenth.

If China's first problem is water, its second is air pollution. In Chongqing, Sichuan, for example, the surrounding mountains trap air severely polluted by coal burned in factories. The city's death rate from lung cancer has been reported at 47 per 100,000, while in a town just twenty miles away the rate is twenty per 100,000.

The voice of the common people, as distinct from that of the students and intellectuals, has not been directly heard in recent years. But in the early 1990s radio stations began broadcasting call-in talk shows, which were for many ordinary people a welcome relief from the standard, bland overoptimism of the government stations. One of these independent stations even broadcast citizens' complaints about such problems as illegal smoke emissions and garbage dumping that attracted rats. The offenses were minor; the new freedom to air complaints about them, however, was major.

But popular resistance to the degradation of the environment has sometimes taken much more determined forms than radio complaints. For instance, on August 14, 1993, workers in a former nuclear plant in distant Gansu province actually fought a battle with the workers of the Lanzhou Chemical

Company which was poisoning their air and water. The company had not bothered to secure the necessary environmental permits when it had obtained its land; it had simply begun producing sulfuric acid and carbon disulfide. The workers in the nearby nuclear factory and their families began to complain of an intolerable stench, dizziness, fatigue, and respiratory trouble. Some parents even outfitted their children with gas masks. The local authorities finally agreed to shut down the factory, but the owners brazenly put it back into operation three weeks later. The government's environmental authority was apparently unable to assert itself when faced with a successful commercial enterprise. But the victims of the plant's pollution refused to put up with the situation any longer, attacked the chemical plant, and shut it down by force.

CRIME AND CORRUPTION

Another problem area for contemporary China is that of the growth in crime and corruption which has accompanied the increase in economic freedom. In August 1981, the Mayor of Beijing and other leaders called for a campaign against urban crime on the grounds that gangs were making the capital of the nation unsafe at night. In November 1981 smuggling was reported to be rampant in the provinces of Fujian, Zhejiang, and Guangdong. Eight hundred boats, both foreign and Chinese, were seized within eight months. Some 26,000 prisoners were reported jailed in the first nine months of 1982 for economic crimes such as embezzlement, smuggling, bribery, and tax evasion; this number increased in 1983. Foreign influences and "unhealthy tendencies" within the Party were officially assigned as causes. Children and adults were warned against Western pornography, which included rock music. A booklet was issued in 1982 entitled "How to Distinguish Decadent Songs." The key was to note "unclear, loose, drunken pronunciation and quivering rhythms." Jazz was "against the normal, psychological needs of man."

A crackdown on crime began in August 1983, and punishments were sometimes severe. Thirty persons were executed on one day for murder, arson, rape, and robbery, and 80,000 delinquent or unemployed youth were sent to work in the remote western province of Qinghai.

One notorious white-collar crime scheme involved a number of Party officials on the island of Hainan, which is a duty-free zone. They imported cars, motorcycles, television sets, and other expensive items, and then sold them illegally at inflated prices in inland cities all over China. Transportation to Sichuan was provided by Chinese Navy planes. The disclosure of such corruption increased the disillusionment of the population with the officials and with the Communist system. Public outrage demanded that offenders be given the harsh punishment of prison sentences. Conditions in Chinese prisons have long been lamentable, including undernourishment, beatings, solitary confinement for years on end, and, at times, confinement in cells about the size of a coffin. (Executions were reckoned in 1993 to amount to about 1,000 a year.) But apparently the Chinese public wanted even more severe measures against crime by officials. A major problem was that the government had never distinguished between regular criminals and political prisoners, although many ordinary folk in China were well aware of the difference.

White-collar crimes seem to be a part of free market economies everywhere. They may be more common in this period of transition in China. But many such crimes in the grey area of stock manipulation have only recently begun to be prosecuted in the United States. Economic crimes, even crimes by officials, are not subject to simple assessment in China. For instance, during a government anticorruption campaign, auditors in Guangdong uncovered nearly $14 million in bribes to officials by businessmen in two thousand enterprises. But what were the bribes for? Not directly for power or perquisites; they were bribes to obtain raw materials to keep production going in their factories. The ultimate aim was to make money; and to make money was the goal most encouraged by the society and its leaders. Bribes were expected, and this may be deplored. But when a midlevel bureaucrat is making a salary that is one-third of what a waitress receives, what is he to do to feed his family?

China is in a *partial* free market phase, still yoked to a rigid, inexperienced, inefficient centralism, not merely subject to government advice, but under government control. Part of the trouble in the 1990s, finally recognized and being faced by Deng Xiaoping and the other leaders, was that a place in the saga of the Long March and loyal Communist service did not automatically endow an official with economic knowledge or experience. And in the minds of the general public—our chief focus here—there is a bewildering confusion of values: first Confucian, then Communist, now just Market Economy? Many Chinese are thinking deeply about what the new values are to be, and how they are to be inculcated.

WOMEN AND THE FAMILY

In China kinship groups, clans, and the extended family have traditionally been important determinant factors, not only in marital, but also in political and economic affairs. Family connection was often a main reason for preferment in office and success in commercial life. In the affluent extended family, living in separate courts and rooms in one large, common compound, the men dominated the women, for the Confucian ethic stressed filial piety and the father-son relationship. Under this Confucian system the worship of the ancestors, which assured the welfare of the family, could only be performed by the senior male.

For centuries women, already dependent, had been rendered even more so by the cruel custom of foot binding, in which the toes were bent and crushed under the foot by constant tight bandaging from the age of five, a process that caused excruciating pain. This practice, deemed necessary for a girl to get a husband, turned women into comparatively helpless objects of luxury—an indication of the husband's wealth—and came also to have erotic associations in the minds of men. The custom came in with the urban gentry of the Song dynasty in the tenth century, spread through the upper and middle levels of the society, and was only abolished in the twentieth century.

The situation in poorer peasant families was different, because women worked in the fields, and therefore foot binding could not as a rule be practiced. As elsewhere in the world, women whose labor was required in order for the family to exist acquired thereby a higher status relative to the men than women in upper-class situations. (Nevertheless, in the poorer peasant families in China incessant labor and grinding poverty meant a wretched existence for most women.) A widow of the senior generation, however, where age took precedence over gender, was in the best position. In all families, rich or poor, the grandmother who survived her husband often assumed a position of considerable authority. Literature and history provide instances of a great officer returning home and showing extreme deference, not to say fear, before the matriarch who ruled her household with a rod of iron.

The least fortunate person in the household of the past was the new daughter-in-law. She was regarded more as the servant of her mother-in-law than as the wife of her husband, who might in any case be often absent from the home. Her life was frequently one of sustained misery, and suicide was not uncommon. Yet many homes reflected a peace, serenity, and degree of cooperation which showed that some arranged marriages could work as well as love matches. Couples unacquainted with each other would marry first and fall in love afterwards. The wife who bore a son would acquire great "face" and find herself more fully and readily accepted in the household. But for most women, their low status was the cause of deep frustration and sorrow. Women in poorer families may in some instances had a happier lot than those in wealthier ones, for they were spared the jealousy and strife which go with polygamy and concubinage, a way of life which only the rich could afford.

WOMEN AND CAREERS

In 1924 a young woman who was forced to marry before she was fifteen and who was beaten by her mother-in-law, ran away and found a job in a factory. She expressed her feelings thus:

> My life at work is truly happy—compared to all the humiliations and hardships I had at home, it's like I'm in some kind of a fairyland! . . . If a woman can obtain economic independence she can be a human being."*

During the Maoist years, from 1949 on, the status of women improved greatly. Prostitution, child marriages, and concubinage were all banned by law

*Li Yuning, ed., *Chinese Women Through Chinese Eyes* (Armonk, N.Y.: M.E. Sharpe 1992), p. 173.

and the sale of brides forbidden. In the moral climate of the period sexual discrimination was a serious breach of Communist principles, for the constitution of the PRC stipulates complete equality between men and women. But there are always exceptions in practice; the weight of centuries of tradition still hangs heavily on women.

In recent times the nuclear rather than the extended family has become predominant, sometimes with the addition of one or more grandparents under the same roof. Where this is accepted as a normal arrangement, as it usually is in China, child care within the family is a built-in advantage for the working mother. Moreover, a grandparent can give the children a sense of reassurance and stability through sharing old songs, folklore, and family traditions. Marriages are still arranged, but the personal preferences of the parties assume a much greater role than in the past.

Preschool child care is provided in factories and certain farming communities, so that women are free to enter the job market even if there is no one at home to look after children. Yet in actuality the women may be working harder than the men, for many families are able to return home at for the midday meal. This means that the wife may be preparing two main meals a day in addition to her farm or factory work. The consciousness of the men has not been raised to the point where large numbers of them help with child rearing or household tasks. Many fathers, however, can be seen in the streets and parks carrying around their small children with great pride. Children, "little emperors," are now valued more highly than ever because of the strict limitation on births.

By the 1990s the position of women at work had again changed vastly. The workforce by then was 50 percent female. Women held positions in the Party and government, although not in great numbers, and many women entrepreneurs had launched successful businesses. Among urban women, 82 percent held jobs outside the home, as opposed to 29 percent in 1949; this gave them a new measure of self-confidence and economic independence. Maternity benefits were good, and the maternity death rate was declining. But it was also true that when there was a local economic downturn, it was the women who were fired first.

Yet in spite of these undoubted gains, distinct signs of a reviving bias against women reappeared from about 1992 onwards. Women were discriminated against in jobs, in housing, and in the allocation of land. For example, at a point when 180 government positions were opened for applicants, 80 percent were available only to men. One woman reported being told by a private firm that she would only be hired if she agreed not to have children for three years. Physical attractiveness became a vital factor in the hiring of women for positions in business offices. And there was evidence that women were again being sold as brides. Taken together, these examples suggest that the renewal of bias against women is connected to the new emphasis on a money economy and the concomitant decline of central ideological control which had improved the position of women.

BIRTH CONTROL

Population control is taken with the utmost seriousness by the government of the PRC. The number of persons living in China reached 1.07 billion in 1988, and the plan was to hold it to 1.2 billion at the year 2000; otherwise the food supply would simply be inadequate. Policy varied on the number of births allowed, often to the confusion of the uneducated; but in general one child per family in the city and two per family in the countryside was the rule. Various means of birth control have been employed—pills, intrauterine devices, tubal ligation, vasectomies, abortion, and the promotion of late marriages—age twenty-eight for men and twenty-five for women, sometimes expressed as a combined age of over fifty. In 1982 the ages were reduced to twenty-two and twenty respectively. Probably one of the most efficient means of control has been what might be termed a neighborhood advisory service, but one armed with the authority of the local Communist Party. This neighborhood counseling is, of course, but one facet of the universal Party guidance of the lives of all citizens. According to a Chinese professor returning from a visit to his native village in the mid-1970s, certain older women visited the young wives house by house, or gathered them in small groups on a particular street. They then explained the policy of small families of two children and discussed, or rather laid down, a quota. "You have one child; you could have one more." "You already have two; you must stop." Then later, if a couple "entitled" to a child failed to have one, it might be permissible for another couple to have a third baby and still keep the street or village within the quota. If a child died or proved to be deformed, the birth of another was permitted.

This raises at once in the Western mind the question of invasion of privacy in its most acute form. It cannot be doubted that resentment must be aroused in the secret thoughts of a large number of Chinese couples also. But privacy as a right is not regarded in the same light in China as it is in the West. Nor is it even expected. In the Manchurian countryside in the 1930s strangers one met on country bus rides, both men and women, would feel free to finger one's woolen suit and ask the price, or would make detailed inquiries with perfect openness about one's age or salary. In China everyone's life was lived communally long before communism.

The program for population control, although successful, was fraught with dangers and subject to abuse. In 1983 female infanticide was reported to be widespread. According to the law, an infant who died within three days of its birth was considered stillborn, and this made it easier for a midwife to drown a female and report a stillbirth, which gave the couple a chance to try again for the much desired son. There was a harsh crackdown at that time on people having several children; women were sometimes dragged off for forced abortions. In the 1990s, under Peng Peiyun, the sixty-four-year-old woman Minister of the State Family Planning Commission, the emphasis shifted to sterilization. Once or twice a year local cadres came to a village and rounded up the women to take them to a clinic for the fitting of IUDs or compulsory sterilization if they had reached their legal limit of successful pregnancies. Disobedience to the regulations was punished by fines, sometimes so impossibly heavy that they had to be paid over a decade, or by the destruction of the family's house and meager furniture. This severity was due to the new "responsibility system" (introduced also in the economic sphere), which insisted that local officials meet birth control targets, with bonuses for success and fines and threats of dismissal for failures.

The fertility figures obtained by such draconian measures were impressive. The birthrate declined to an extent which surprised both Chinese and international experts—from 23.3 births per thousand in 1987 and 21.1 in 1990 to only 18.2 in 1992. Based on this last figure, each Chinese woman can expect to have, on average, 1.8 or 1.9 children in her lifetime, a fertility rate approximately the same as that in the United States or Britain. The average woman in India by the same reckoning would have four children.

The gravity of China's situation is apparent in the future projections. With 22 percent of the world's population (the 1989 figure was 1.11 billion) on only 7 percent of the world's arable land, the Chinese will continue to increase because of the present high proportion of youth. The numbers are expected to peak at 1.9 billion about the middle of next century, then become stable and begin to decline.

HOUSING

Family life was intimately affected by changes in the housing policy of the PRC in the late 1980s. The earlier situation can be represented by a rural commune outside Shanghai in 1981, where a newly married couple would pay for the materials for their house and then the whole commune would join in to help erect the building, as in a cooperative barn raising in the United States. Urban houses, until the late 1980s, were generally built and maintained by the factory or the government and allotted to workers and their families at a very low rent, usually 2 percent of their income. Some dwellings rented at under $2 a month, but were extremely cramped and in poor repair. Most had no indoor toilet. But as the market economy increased, the government decided that the housing sector should become a part of it and that workers should be encouraged to buy their own homes. Many desired this change and the greatly improved conditions offered; but even with subsidized and interest-free mortgages, purchases could only be slow. New houses for rent were still being constructed. For these also there were rent subsidies, and the government expected rents to reach the market level without subsidy in about ten to fifteen years.

EDUCATION

The more closely one looks at contemporary China, the more crucial appears the Cultural Revolution of 1966–1968. A watershed both in theory and in practice, its most active phase lasted two to three years, but its effects continued until 1976 and were still being felt in the 1990s. Nowhere is this more true than in the field of education.

The "two lines" of Liu Shaoqi and of Mao Zedong in the 1960s differed fundamentally on educational policy. Liu and his faction felt that China's limited resources had to be mobilized for modernization. Since not everything could be done at once, the important thing was to concentrate on the most able students and train them in special schools. If this were not done, Liu asserted, everyone would suffer. Once China was able to overcome its backwardness in relation to the rest of the world, education could be broadened and ultimately made universal. Mao and his supporters, on the other hand, maintained that the perpetuation of an educated elite must be avoided at all costs. That was precisely where China had gone wrong in its past history. A truly egalitarian society, based on nothing less than a new type of human being, was the only guarantee of the continuance of the new state, already founded on socialist principles. Education was vital to this goal, but it must be a new kind of education, less academic, more linked to work in the real world. This made some sense for China, since increased skills through some basic education for everyone would strengthen the development of the nation. "Red" was more important than "expert." Liu's immediate aim was national construction; Mao's was cultural transformation.

Mao won. On August 8, 1966 the CCP Central Committee decided to make

> education serve proletarian politics and [have] education integrated with productive labor, so that those who get an education may develop morally, intellectually and physically and become socialist-minded, cultured laborers. . . . The academic course must be shortened and the curriculum simplified. . . . Besides studying academic subjects, [the students] should also learn to do industrial, agricultural and military work.

Thus, during the Cultural Revolution, with young people involved in "criticizing the bourgeoisie," the educational system ground to a halt. Schools and universities were closed for years. When they reopened, the time to be spent in primary school was cut from six years to five and that spent in junior and senior secondary school from three to two years each. Thus pre-university schooling was reduced from twelve to nine years, and of that school time a good proportion was destined to be expended in work in field or factory. Even after the Cultural Revolution, university education was at first only two years, then increased to three. In addition, a number of short college programs were offered in such fields as agriculture, industry, teaching, and health care.

But by 1975 voices were being raised in criticism the dismal results of the educational system as it had been set up by proponents of the Cultural Revolution. Liu Bing, deputy head of Qinghua University in Beijing, wrote to Mao saying that unless the system was changed, "people will be leaving the universities without being able to read a book." Through all the tug and pull of rival policies, the need for thorough academic education was becoming more evident.

A new opportunity came when the radicals lost power after the death of Mao in September 1976. But the moderates could only move slowly; it was not until 1978 that Deng Xiaoping made a major pronouncement on education in which he said that the main task of students was to study and that examinations were essential. (Regular examinations had earlier been characterized as "ambushes" and "sneak attacks"). Students would be required to spend only a small amount of time on manual labor and would not be discriminated against because of family background. Fifty-five new universities were to be founded, the status of teachers raised, students divided into classes of fast, normal, and slow learners, and better teaching materials provided.

Because of China's lag in technological development (estimated at fifteen to twenty years behind that of the developed nations), the government would encourage research and set up special crash programs in laser technology, computer development, and genetic engineering. For a Communist country the social sciences normally represent the most sensitive area, but a freer pattern appeared even in this field. In February of 1978 it was announced that university graduate schools in the social sciences would reopen for the first time since the Cultural Revolution and that they would teach history, law, religion, philosophy, literature, and economics.

Smiling schoolchildren in a group activity.

Photo: Richard Balzer

The educational situation was further stabilized by laws promulgated in 1985–1986 setting the period of compulsory attendance at six years of primary school and three years of junior secondary—nine years in all. This period could be preceded by three years of preschool and succeeded by three years of senior secondary school, followed, for those qualified, by university.

Preschool education became widely available in the 1980s for children between the ages of three and six, to the benefit not only of the children but also of the many women in the labor force. At this early stage in life much emphasis was given to social and moral training.

By 1992 primary school education was almost universal in urban areas. In the countryside, however, the children often entered school only at age seven, and the requirement was then reduced from six years' schooling to five. Even so, the rural dropout rate was high. Mao Zedong's aim had been to reduce the age-old gap between the city dwellers and the farmers, particularly in the opportunity for education. But the more elitist China emerging under Deng Xiaoping's policies charged fees in the public schools, even at the primary level, as part of the cost for both tuition and board, which caused the gap between city and country to widen again in many instances. In a number of backward rural areas, bright children, especially girls longing for an education, had to drop out of primary school because peasant families with an average income of $60 a year could not afford $13 for their tuition and board. (Most rural children lived too far away from the school for daily attendance and had to board at the school during the week.)

The first stage of schooling past the compulsory level, namely the upper secondary, both general and technical, was the key to China's reaching the position of an advanced society. Most of the important field of technical education was covered in the secondary stage; but under the new laws the number of university students admitted to technical and vocational education was also increased. Demands on the upper secondary students were steep and challenging, and they extended to women as well as to men. One special girls' upper school in Shanghai, for example, sent two graduates to Harvard University in three years. Standards and motivation were high in such schools, and the workload heavy. Some seniors preparing for tests spent twelve hours a day at school, and a half day of school on Saturday was a regular feature. The study of English began in second grade, and in the Shanghai girls' school already mentioned there were three foreign teachers of English on the staff.

Literacy, Chinese leaders recognized, was clearly the key to development. In 1949 the new Communist government claimed that the illiteracy rate was 80 percent; others estimate it was about 75 percent. In the 1920s, under the Nationalists, James Yen of the YMCA had designed a simplified vocabulary of a thousand characters and run a successful literacy campaign. But political changes in the country had left little time to extend it widely. The PRC decided on a three-thousand-word vocabulary and simplified the writing of many common characters. By 1964 the rate of illiteracy (those over twelve years of age who were illiterate or semiliterate) had been reduced to 38.1 percent; by 1982 it had gone down to 23.5 percent. But in 1988 the figure rose again, to 26.7 percent. The presumed reasons for this downturn were the "responsibility system" in rural areas and the privatization of land (both of which carried a high incentive for the use of child labor), as well as the increasing requirement to pay school fees.

To summarize, it is evident that both the PRC central government and the local authorities who control much of the operation have made immense efforts to educate the youth of the country and have achieved considerable success. According to United Nations figures, 83 percent of Chinese children are enrolled in school. The historical increase is indicated by the following tables.

Total Enrollment of Students

	1952	1987	FACTOR OF INCREASE
Primary	51,100,000	128,360,000	x 2 1/2
Secondary	3,145,000	54,030,000	x 18
Tertiary (university)	190,000	1,950,000	x 10

SOURCE: Mackerras, Colin and Yorke, Amanda, eds., *The Cambridge Handbook of Contemporary China*, Cambridge, 1991, p. 221.

Number of University Students per 10,000 People

1949	1978	1980	1987
2.2	8.9	11.6	18.2

SOURCE: Mackerras, Colin and Yorke, Amanda, eds., *The Cambridge Handbook of Contemporary China*, Cambridge, 1991, p. 224.

Although university enrollment also increased significantly, the number of students in China was small compared to other similar low-per-capita-income countries. By 1992 a considerable number of students who did not pass the entrance examination were being admitted to university on condition that they pay tuition. Those who passed received their education free.

RELIGION

Freedom of religion was written into the constitution of the PRC, a fact that its representatives often refer to in international discussions. But this freedom is interpreted by the Chinese authorities as freedom to practice personal devotion and spiritual self-development, not to preach on behalf of social justice or to offer any religious critiques of government policies. That would be to trespass on the function and powers of the state. The sensitivity of the PRC leaders in this matter was evident in their treatment of Buddhist monks in

Tibet in 1989–1990. Martial law was declared after riots there, and the mere presence of monks in peaceful protests was construed by officials as a symbol of nationalism and an incitement to anti-Chinese violence.

A keystone in the religious policy of the PRC, and a necessary condition for the continued existence of religious bodies, was the "Three-Self Patriotic Movement," sometimes called the "Three-Self Movement," instituted formally in 1954. It required religious entities to be self-governing, self-supporting and self-propagating—in other words, not to allow foreign direction of policy, not to depend on foreign funds, and not to rely on foreign influence or ideas in efforts to expand. These requirements obviously applied mainly to Christian churches. For Roman Catholics a consequence was the ban on Vatican control; this has led to a recognized "patriotic" Catholic Church in China, and an "underground" church whose members profess allegiance to the Pope. A Monsignor Tang Yiming's experience illustrates the seriousness of this split. Released in 1980 after twenty-two years in prison, Monsignor Tang was acceptable to the government-recognized Catholic church. But when the Pope appointed him Archbishop of Canton—the first such papal appointment since 1955—the Chinese Church denounced the appointment as "the Pope rudely interfering in the sovereign affairs of the Chinese Church." One reason given by the government for its refusal to recognize Catholics obedient to the Pope is that the Vatican maintains official relations with the government of the Republic of China in Taiwan.

Many Protestant missionaries were at first opposed to the Three-Self Movement, but the mainstream Protestant churches later came to see it as the only possibility—and indeed, as a necessary, healthy, and ultimately beneficial policy for the Christian Church in China. Bishop K. H. Ting (Ding) adhered to it from the beginning, and has been the main liaison between the united body of Chinese Protestants and the PRC government ever since. But he has also maintained an independent stance where possible. Although interference with government policy is forbidden, Bishop Ting on May 23, 1989, issued a public statement in support of the hunger strikers in Tiananmen Square.

Churches were suppressed and Christians persecuted widely during the Cultural Revolution, but there was a marked revival of Christianity all over China thereafter. The many church buildings returned to their congregations were filled to capacity for services two and three times a Sunday. The historic Beitang Catholic church, for example, closed in 1958, was restored with funds from the Beijing city administration and reopened in 1985 in a service attended by thousands. Some consider that people have turned to religion as a fellowship, a source of strength and of moral values, at a time of disillusionment with the Party and with Communist ideology. It is perhaps significant that 1.2 million Chinese copies of the Bible were printed in 1990 alone.

Whatever the reasons, certain facts not widely known in the West made it clear that the churches were meeting a need in the 1980s and 1990s. Wenzhou, for example, is the largest port and industrial city in southern Zhejiang and a noted center of Christianity. There were Nestorian Christians in Wenzhou in the Yuan dynasty (1280–1368) and a long Catholic presence later. The first Protestant missionary arrived in 1867. A foreign observer, fluent in Chinese and having close ties with the Chinese Church, estimated that in 1949 there were 100,000 Christians in Wenzhou and probably 400,000 in 1990.*

The churches provided a strong social center around which many gathered for religious education, musical and other activities, and meals in common. In 1993 in the province of Zhejiang as a whole there were estimated to be 1,040,000 Christians, about 2.5 percent of the population. In other parts of China also Christianity has found a recent response. In Shenyang, a hub of the industrial north, the number of church adherents tripled during the 1980s. It is difficult to arrive at a national figure, but the official numbers given in the 1982 census were 5.5 million Protestants and 3.5 million Catholics. A combined total for 1994 varied "between 10 million according to the official statistics and 30 million according to the unofficial estimates."†

After the watershed of the massacre in Tiananmen Square and the overseas reaction to it, the PRC exerted tighter control over religion. This was evident in the case of Buddhism in Tibet and Islam in the northwest of China. Yet overall, Chinese Muslims were reported as being allowed the greatest freedom of worship. Christians had to be especially careful, again because of a suspected foreign connection. Police checked worshippers going into services, and there were cases of pastors being forbidden to preach. The Party leaders were apparently afraid that what they viewed as Western influence in the churches might subvert Communist authority, and this fear was increased when they noted the role played by the Catholic Church in the revolutions in Poland, Romania, and other parts of Eastern Europe.

A new law of 1994 further limited religious activities by foreigners and overseas Chinese from Taiwan, Hong Kong, and Macao. "No one may use places of worship to destroy national unity, ethnic unity and social stability, to damage public health or undermine the national educational system." Underground "house churches" were banned. The language used here is significant at several points. Schools and house churches were singled out as possible sources of subversion. What was taught in the national schools must in no way be undermined. And regularly designated religious buildings could be supervised, but small gatherings in private houses would be dangerous. Government concern for "social stability" recurred once again as an ever-present anxiety.

"In China everything is true somewhere, but nothing is true everywhere." Zhejiang and Wenzhou may—or may not—presage the future of Christianity in China. Buddhism, imported from India, has for centuries been accepted and indigenized in the country, and in recent decades shown a considerable increase in the number of its adherents. Islam has penetrated China from surrounding Asian countries and found a home chiefly in the border regions. But Christianity had up to 1950 remained mainly, though not entirely, a foreign-sponsored

---

*Philip L. Wickeri, "Christianity in Zhejiang," in *China Notes*, Vol. xxviii, no. 2 and 3, (Spring and Summer, 1990), p. 1.
†Xinzhong, Yao, "Success or Failure? Christianity in China," in *History Today*, Vol. 44(9), (September 1994), p. 7.

religion. Yet since that date, the affairs of the Christian denominations, their growth and their destiny, have been entirely in the hands of the Chinese. In the 1990s there were undoubted signs of the flourishing of an *indigenous* Christianity in China; it remains to be seen whether it will strike deep roots.

THE LAW

In every land there is a fine line between government control which is seen to be beneficial and government control which is resented as arbitrary. This line is drawn at very different places in differing societies. The Chinese people have in the past been comparatively tolerant of government control within certain traditional limits, and this is apparent in the Chinese view of law. For one thing, many disputes never reached a court at all. Customary law, functioning within the family and clan, or through merchant guilds, could often dispose of cases within their competence without the need for official judgment.

The government of Imperial China was viewed—or viewed itself—as a parent, wisely restraining unruly and ignorant children. The district official was known as the "father-mother official"; he had judicial as well as civil powers and was judge and administrator at the same time—and often military commander as well. In a paternalistic mode the way to govern was by moral example; if the power of the law had to be invoked, this was in a sense an abnormality and a sign of failure. The tendency was thus to regard the prisoner as probably guilty, because otherwise he would not have found himself in the position of being accused. Torture to obtain confessions was allowed, but only in the court itself, and theoretically only by certain limited methods. The prisoner did not have the benefit of legal counsel, although he could bring forward character witnesses. Nor had he any protection against self-incrimination in his statements to the judge.

The judge, on the other hand, was, at least in theory, prevented from acting in a completely arbitrary manner. For one thing, there were rules of evidence, a series of regulations, and a scale of punishments worked out in precise detail to cover a great variety of situations.* These were all embodied in a sophisticated code dating from the Tang dynasty in the eighth century. The code also provided for a check on the judicial system through the threat of a visit from the Censorate, an independent body which investigated the conduct of officials and was empowered to criticize even the emperor himself. In periods when the empire was strong and efficient (which was less and less the case as the nineteenth century progressed), extreme popular discontent could lead to relief and the punishment of evil or corrupt officials.

In the Communist period the legal system evolved to function through three divisions: the public security system to investigate crime and detain suspects; the people's procurators to approve arrests, establish an a priori case

---

*Some punishments were extremely severe, particularly those known as collective punishment. If a man were convicted of treason, not only he but all his male relatives over sixteen years of age could be executed, and the female relatives made over to "meritorious officials" as slaves.

against suspects, and prosecute; and the people's courts, to pass judgments. Hence the majority of those who reach a court trial are convicted, and the role of the defense lawyer is in most cases expected to be an attempt to obtain a reduction of sentence rather than to establish innocence. In this there is a parallel with the traditional Chinese legal system.

During the Cultural Revolution, formal law fell into total disarray, but in 1978 the legal framework was reconstituted. In the 1980s it was greatly expanded beyond criminal law to include such civil matters as commercial law, contract law, and family law, especially divorce. The independence of the judiciary was a disputed question. Article 126 of the 1982 constitution states: "The people's courts shall, in accordance with the law, exercise judicial power independently and are not subject to interference by administrative organs, public organizations, or individuals." The Anti-Rightist Campaign of 1957 and the Cultural Revolution of 1966–1976 had been fatal to the sense of this provision; but in the 1980s the trend was to recognize that the law should be independent of the Communist Party and the state. However, after the Tiananmen massacre of June 1989, the current was again reversed, and leaders began using the law to promote the interests of the Party or the state, not to mention their own.

LITERATURE AND THE ARTS

In the first triumphant flush of revolutionary fervor, the Communist Party had downgraded most of China's literary and artistic past as belonging to an age of feudal oppression. Confucian philosophy and its outcome in the mandarin bureaucracy were condemned. Everything connected with religions, whether Buddhist, Daoist, or Christian, was at that time totally rejected as superstition. But gradually certain writers and poets in China's past were recognized as being on the side of the common people. It is easy to see how the poet Bo Juyi of the Tang dynasty, for instance, would be highly valued for his deep concern for social justice and his sympathy with the peasants.

> The strong reapers toiling on the southern hill,
> Whose feet are burned by the hot earth they tread,
> Whose backs are scorched by the flames of the shining sky . . .
> A poor woman with a young child at her side
> Follows behind to glean the unwanted grain.

And the translator goes on to comment that Bo asked himself "in virtue of what right" had he escaped the toil of "tending field and tree"? Elsewhere Bo describes his horror at seeing his underlings beating up the peasants in order to wring out of them the last handful of requisitioned grain. Later on, when he was in a position to influence government policy, he did not forget the common people of Zhou Ji.* (See also Bo Juyi's poem on pp. 92–93.)

*Arthur Waley, *The Life and Times of Po Chu-I* (London: George Allen and Unwin, 1949), p. 46.

Figures from *The Rent Collection Courtyard*, Sculptures of Oppression and Revolt, 1968.

The authorities of the People's Republic of China have portrayed, with life-size clay figures, cases of oppression by a former greedy landlord and the results among the angry peasants. (a) Peasant straining to push his wheelbarrow. (b) Worker, Soldier, and Peasant (the three types of "the masses") go forward under the banner of Mao, the Great Helmsman.

Foreign Languages Press, Peking

Similarly, in the realm of pictorial art, the style of the past as seen in scrolls of landscapes, birds, and flowers was abandoned in favor of "socialist realism" and poster art, designed to appeal to the common man and encourage a sense of pride in the successes of the new era. Art in the service of politics and ideology was but one more means employed in the vast task of renewal. Unfortunately, the quality of this politicized art was as deplorable in China as elsewhere.

Once the Communist leaders had firmly established the new regime and were less afraid of the revival of old artistic values, the nationalist sentiment of pride in the past began strongly to reassert itself. This is clear in Chinese archaeological and art historical scholarship, which justifies works of art and craftsmanship as products of the common man's genius and toil. Continuous archaeological excavations went on almost from the beginning of the PRC era, but little news of it reached the outside world until the 1970s. Astonishment and delight were all the greater when a superb exhibition of recently excavated art objects was sent on a tour to several major European and American cities, beginning in Paris in 1973. The objects displayed included burial suits of jade hitherto unknown save in literary references, a bronze "flying horse" at full speed, amusing actor figures, exquisite vases, and miniature chariots and cavalry of the Han period. Most impressive of all were representative pieces from an army of approximately 6,000 life-size terra-cotta figures fitted out with actual metal weapons and valuable objects in jade and gold. The army was unearthed near the tomb of the emperor Qin Shi Huang Di (221–210 B.C.) and the objects were assumed to have been buried on his orders. Excavations in the years following the mid-1970s have yielded artifacts of a kingdom in the former Nanyue region of modern Guangzhou. In 203 A.D., at the end of the Han period, a king named Zhao Mo, was buried in a magnificent tomb with unusual stone chambers. When found, the tomb was relatively undisturbed and contained in their original placement over a thousand precious objects, many of gold. These included two hundred jade articles of high-quality workmanship—and this in an area previously regarded as only semi-Sinicized. Another find in the Ordos/Ningxia region of north China cast a new light on early trade with the West. A large ceramic ewer, dating from 567 A.D. in the Six Dynasties period, depicted in high relief bare-chested figures whose dress and appearance clearly indicated a Mediterranean provenance.

It goes without saying that in the Cultural Revolution years neither traditional Chinese art nor art showing international influence could be practiced. But by the 1990s gradually easing controls resulted in such surprising developments as the emergence of soap operas on television, kung fu films from Hongkong, a rock star concert in Beijing, the opening of discos, and the operation of amateur radio stations. A journalist said, "We can breathe again." All this was a signal that pictorial artists could once again let their imaginations run free.

To contemporary Chinese painters Bada Shanren (1626–1705) is an inspiration from China's past—not because he belongs the past, but because he was a rebel, both politically and artistically. Born a prince of a branch of the Ming imperial family, he was active in the long resistance against the conquering Manzhou (Manchu) dynasty. As an artist, he moved away from the traditional towards impressionism, even abstraction. He delighted in eccentricity. One of his paintings shows a bird on a rock, its eyes peeking upwards at a fish swimming unconcerned above it. Small wonder that a superb technique, a spirit of revolt, and a crazy streak have made this artist a major influence in Chinese art of the twentieth century.

In the post-Tiananmen world of literature the students renewed their determination with some lines from another dissident writer: "Lies written in ink can never disguise facts written in blood. Blood debts must be repaid in kind; the longer the delay, the greater the interest." The writer was Lu Xun, who has been called the greatest Chinese author of the twentieth century. The lines were written in 1926 about forty students, also killed in Beijing, and also by Chinese security forces—those of the Guomindang regime of Jiang Jieshi. A fierce critic of the Gnomindang, Lu Xun sympathized with the Communists, although he never joined the Party. Mao Zedong said of Lu Xun: "On the cultural front, he was the bravest and most correct, the firmest, the most loyal and the most ardent national hero . . . without parallel in our history." There were museums, research institutes and journals devoted to the life and works of Lu Xun. But because he was so ardently opposed to tyranny in all forms, his words could easily be turned against the Communist Party long after his death in 1936. When he wrote, "Before the revolution we were slaves. And now we are the slaves of former slaves," Lu Xun was referring to the revolution of 1911, but the cap fitted the Party in power in 1989 only too well.*

Another writer who began work before the Communist era and who, like Lu Xun, was biting in his commentary on social injustice, was Lao She. His novel, *Rickshaw,* which is the one best known in the West, depicts the exhaustion and sickness of the rickshaw-pullers, and the often bitter love and humor they share in the tough world of the Beijing streets.

Two contemporary writers who were able to criticize and remain free and published were Wang Shuo, because he used comedy and satire without direct confrontation, and Rong Zhang (Jung Chang), because the Cultural Revolution, the climax of her powerful family history, had already been condemned by the Party.

Wang Shuo never went to university; perhaps for that reason he was able to capture the accent of the factory workers in the city and have his books sold on the streets. He made fun of the Communist Party's by then well-known habits, such as the necessity of having a designated culprit for anything that went wrong. In his satirical novel *No Man's Land,* a character is imprisoned because he has been accused of individual responsibility for the failure of the Boxer Rebellion! The author prided himself on writing "hooligan literature" and said he was never arrested because "They think I'm not a thinker."

*See Nicholas D. Kristof, *New York Times Book Review,* August 19, 1990, pp. 15–16.

Thinker or not, Wang's comment "I can't stand people with a sense of mission" reveals a cynicism which runs counter to the hopes of common people as well as to the aims of the Party leaders.

Jung Chang's *Wild Swans: Three Daughters of China* concerns the lives of her grandmother, her mother, and herself. It stands in a new literary tradition, that of the personally documented need for the emancipation of women, along with such books as Li Yuning's *Chinese Women Through Chinese Eyes,* although in quite a different style. As recounted in *Wild Swans,* the experiences of the Cultural Revolution—a revolution in which Mao deliberately pitted one half of the population against the other—are full of horror. But worse still is the book's accusation that the weapon of fear used in the Cultural Revolution was for decades previously employed by the Party to exploit the loyalty of its most fervent young supporters. When the author's father and mother were sent as a young couple from north China a thousand miles to Sichuan, he rode in a jeep but compelled her to walk most of the way because party discipline required it. He, like everyone in the Party, feared more than anything else in the world the ostracism that would follow disobedience. And when in Sichuan her father was inspecting vast areas where peasants were dying of famine by the thousands and could not reveal this fact even to his family, he lost his reason under the strain.

The most prominent example of a writer who remained active from the 1950s to the 1990s and was both a Party member *and* a dissident, is Liu Binyan. As a roving reporter for the *People's Daily* in 1956, he wrote some pieces of what became his distinctive genre of "reportage fiction." In response to the call of Mao Zedong and Zhou Enlai for criticism of bureaucratic style of work in the Party, Liu wrote *On the Bridge Construction Site,* with a young work leader as hero and an old middle-level cadre as his opponent. The older man has one motto: "Make no mistakes." When a river flood carries away part of the bridge under construction, the older cadre does nothing until he has got through to his boss to ask for instructions. He cares nothing for the fact that valuable equipment is meanwhile lost. The young, idealist work leader spurs his men on, and by innovative and unorthodox methods manages to save a major section of the bridge. But despite this he is accused of "arrogance, self-satisfaction, and individual initiative" and demoted to a lower job elsewhere.

Liu Binyan's *An Inside Story* concerns a young woman reporter struggling against the bureaucratic apathy, callousness, and corruption of Party hacks who are running a local newspaper. The Party will not admit her to membership because her reports of the truth are too disturbing. In particular she writes about the wretched working conditions of miners and of their resentment at the required attendance at constant political meetings, which often leaves them only four hours of sleep a night. The paper will not carry her stories of vast unemployment, shocking waste of manpower and resources, and failure of communication between different levels of officialdom. Although the reporter finds allies, the entrenched Party cadres condemn her by refusing her Party membership with all its benefits because of her "lack of respect for leadership, organization, and discipline"—in reality, simply for taking the workers' side against the Party leaders.

Liu Binyan's own experience was similar but worse. In 1958 he was "sent down to the country" and then condemned as a "mouthpiece of the bourgeois rightists." He was briefly released and then again imprisoned, so that he spent all the years from 1958 to 1979 as a prisoner, except for two months' freedom with his family. He did not give up either his writing or his belief in the ultimate good intentions of the central leadership of the Party, whatever the local cadres might be like. In 1979 he wrote his most famous work, *Between Men and Monsters,* a powerful indictment of the Maoist Party system and the decade of the Cultural Revolution. The villain of the story is a woman paymaster of a coal company in the industrial northeast who builds an organized crime network worth millions, with first the connivance then the support, of the local Party chiefs. On its publication, Liu immediately received floods of grateful letters from all over China, saying that the picture he had painted was accurate.* There are other contemporary writers and other themes, but ideology, or the release from ideology, colors the literature of a new age.

FILM

Philosophy, literature, and painting all reached their high points in various periods of China's cultural past. Today, cinematic art may perhaps be taken as typical of the twentieth century worldwide maturing in Japan in the 1950s and 60s, and in China from the 1980s. New films coming out of China in the 1980s were distinguished by stunning visual effects and by story lines which take the viewer—even the foreign viewer—right into the reality of Chinese social life. We see expanses of green millet fields, double takes of figures behind sheets of flame, aerial views of the sea stretching from a diminutive wharf past cliffs and craggy little islands into an unfathomable distance, and quiet, intimate glimpses of old stone houses in Beijing alleys. So much delights the eye and draws one into the lives of the people—sunsets, wine, fire, opera costumes; there are blazes of color everywhere, and then dim night and lurking violence. In scenes of cruelty and extreme misfortune a sense of fatalistic inevitability is heightened by the sheer ordinariness of everyday Chinese speech, which tends to be lost in the English captions.

Several of the best directors have belonged to the Fifth Generation—that is, they are graduates of the fifth class coming out of the Beijing Film Academy. Since the fourth class graduated before the Cultural Revolution, the fifth group reached maturity in the new age after that fatal divide and became known for a high degree of originality, imagination, and creativity. A few of the best-known directors and their films are listed on the following page:

*For further material on Liu Binyan and his times, see Michael S. Duke, *Blooming and Contending, Chinese Literature in the Post-Mao Era* (Bloomington, Ind., 1985).

Zhang Yimou	Red Sorghum	1987
	Ju Dou	1990
	Raise the Red Lantern	1991
	Qiu Ju	1992
Chen Kaige	Yellow Earth	1984
	Farewell, My Concubine	1991
Wu Yigong	My Memories of Old Beijing	1982
Tian Zhuangzhuang	The Blue Kite	1993

The New Wave directors, as they are also styled, have broken away from the older dramatic sources and focused on personal experience, contrasting town and country, the role of women in the past and the present, and such issues as the stagnation of bureaucracy and the long-lasting effect on the people of Mao Zedong's policies. A number of the films have been set in the recent past, enabling the director, while dealing with universal human experience, to comment by indirection on political and social aspects of the contemporary world which were too hot to handle directly. (This had long been a practice of the literati in novels and essays of the past). For example, in the film *Ju Dou,* the heroine, in fear of village gossip, seeks a secret abortion by using a painful folk remedy. Is this a comment on contemporary birth control and barriers to woman's freedom? The compulsory requirement of another old custom that the young couple "block the path" (as a sign of grief) forty-nine times at the funeral of a tyrannical family elder may be glancing at the tyranny of communism's total control of people's lives.

In the same film the dye vat, the symbolic center of the action, is the scene of two deaths, both ironically at the hands of the much desired little son. They are reminiscent of the deaths of despairing characters who traditionally drown themselves in wells; only this time the victims are men, not women. Indeed, in three of Zhang Yimou's films, *Red Sorghum, Ju Dou,* and *Qiu Ju,* the principal woman, played by Gong Li, is a stronger and more resolute character than the men who surround her, without in the least losing her feminine attractiveness. In strength delicacy is not lost. When in *Ju Dou* Gong Li is observed through the peephole, her slow and hesitating gestures gently display the struggle between modesty and desire.

The crude and brutal facts of life are faced very directly; in *Red Sorghum* a bully urinates into the wine vats to demonstrate his power and contempt, and a man is shown in the early stages of being flayed alive. But one sees also gentler scenes of everyday life. In Wu Yigong's *My Memories of Old Beijing,* there are water sellers wheeling up their barrows with buckets to get water at the street well, visually effective as a regular punctuation in the life of the neighborhood. The lead character, a little girl, goes through all the experiences of growing up without ever leaving the quiet alleys where she lives. She is the only one to understand a young woman who has lost her reason; she sees a thief whom she has befriended arrested; and then she visits her father when he is dying of TB. The natural acceptance of life to be found in the child of a secure home is subtly evoked. The girl seems to emerge relatively unscathed and ready for her future.

Technically the films are a delight—with the camera dwelling in a leisurely way on faces, impassive but with flickers of feelings; with cuts to bright red and yellow dyestuffs hanging to dry at moments of emotion, of love and death half seen indoors a second before; with the sweep of landscape embracing those small human figures familiar in Chinese landscape painting; and with the look and sound of old wooden machinery in the distillery of *Red Sorghum* and the dye works of *Ju Dou.* The young director, Zhang Yimou, born in 1952, is already nostalgic about the wooden tools of old rural China.

Taiwan and Hong Kong have also produced noteworthy films. The Hong Kong director Kong Hu's masterpiece, *A Touch of Zen* (1975), was a tour de force, combining scenes of palaces, mountain landscapes, romantic gorges, and flashing martial arts fights which featured its female star, Xu Feng, as one of the combatants. This film was less well known abroad than the martial arts films of a cruder but more popular type. Some of these starred Bruce Lee, whose combat skills were called "a choreographic delight." Hong Kong films virtually pioneered the international kung fu genre. There has been cooperative effort in East Asian film production. The credits in the films produced in one of China's main studios in Xian contained many Japanese names, and Zhang Yimou's *Raise the Red Lantern,* filmed in the PRC, was a Taiwan-Hong Kong coproduction.

The film world in the People's Republic reveals an interesting pendulum oscillation between economic reform and ideological control, between artistic freedom and censorship. After Tiananmen Square, the hard-liners, losing ground as entrepreneurial freedom expanded, tried to keep a grip on the purity of Chinese Marxist culture. Even though Zhang Yimou's *Raise the Red Lantern,* a film about sexual politics involving a fourth wife in a rich home, was set in the pre-Communist era, and was nominated for an Oscar abroad, its domestic release was held up. Then, in June 1992, a top official of the Ministry of Radio, Film, and Television said films not released previously were being reevaluated, noting at the same time that the film industry was in a financial crisis. Attendance at cinemas had dropped by 20 percent in 1991, and was expected to decline by a further 30 percent in 1992—probably because the "approved" films with a higher ideological content were not box-office successes. *Raise the Red Lantern* was soon afterwards released for viewing in China.

The influence of the rest of the world was more clearly evident in the case of Chen Kaige's *Farewell, My Concubine.* One can understand why this film was considered contrary to the Party's principles on "art and socialist spiritual civilization," for parts of it deal with cruelty practiced during the Cultural Revolution, with homosexuality and a suicide. It was also said to "mix up justice with injustice;" but that is what real life tends to do. The film was shown in China in July 1993, and then promptly withdrawn. But it had shared the top award at the Cannes Film Festival in May, and, moreover, China wanted approval in the West in order to secure the Olympic Games for Beijing in the year 2,000 (China's bid was unsuccessful). So, after some changes and cuts in the film had been made, it was allowed to resume domestic showing in September 1993. But the censors warned that the ban would drop again on films that showed the Communist system in a bad light.

CONCLUSION

The more farseeing Chinese statesmen at the end of the nineteenth century, fully aware of Western threats to China and somewhat aware of the sources of Western power, set about "self-strengthening." There were two schools of thought on the lines of the reform that would be required (see pp. 159–160). The less radical group proposed to build a stronger China upon a revived Confucianism, but also to adopt certain Western methods. These would include the promotion of industry, the founding of an imperial university to teach the Confucian classics and Western technology, and even the building of a railway through central China. But they were opposed to democracy, a constitutional monarchy, a parliament, or any form of people's rights.

They used a phrase which became popular in the 1890s, "Chinese learning for the essential principles, Western learning for the practical applications." The idea had its roots in a Song dynasty notion of *ti*, "substance," (literally "body,") and *yong*, "function," (literally "use.") Western technology had its uses, but *ti*, the central, spiritual core of "Chineseness," the Chinese spirit, had to be kept intact. When the Japanese encountered the West, they had exactly the same idea, defining it as "Eastern ethics and Western science." Later, during the militaristic phase of the 1930s, the Japanese Army, equipped with the most up-to-date Western weapons, laid the stress on *Yamato damashii*, "the spirit of Old Japan" in an extreme interpretation of that term.

Every nation tends to practice exclusivity in sane or insane forms. But the PRC leadership of the 1990s was caught, quite seriously, in a dilemma not unlike that of *ti* and *yong*. The essential *ti* was defined not as Marxism nor just as "Chineseness," but as a combination certainly existing nowhere else, namely "socialism with Chinese characteristics." The leaders faced a daunting task: how to keep the economy growing, feed and clothe all their people, and bring China into modern international society on an equal footing with other nations. But at the same time, in order to maintain the essential *ti*, they had to hold back democracy and retain the Communist ideology and system of control. The essential *ti*, by this reckoning, legitimized the Party, for when there is one ideology, there can only be one party.

Some theorists in the West are persuaded that it is only a matter of time before economic success and the broadening of the middle class in China will lead inevitably to a more open and democratic form of government. They speak of the demise of the old men in power; but by the deliberate policy of Deng Xiaoping over several years many younger men are already in positions of authority. While the projected political change in the direction of democracy may take place, there is an obstacle: the apparent inability of a totalitarian regime to grasp, or an unwillingness to adopt, the notion of a "loyal opposition." The Chinese word for a political party or group, *dang,* has always carried the flavor of subversion, for in China's past there was only one national orthodoxy, and there still is. Any opposition to the agreed or imposed line of policy is considered equivalent to treason. And this attitude comes out very clearly in the almost paranoid objection by the PRC to the recently suggested extension of democracy in Hongkong.

Nevertheless, in every nation, China included, there is such a thing as public opinion, however inchoate and unorganized. To call this "the will of the people" in China's past would be to use a term that is much too exact. Yet Confucian philosophers, and Mencius in particular, spoke of a dynasty whose emperors were consistently evil and unjust as having forfeited "the Mandate of Heaven." And those who determine the mandate are, in the last resort, the people of China. Rebellions of desperate peasants, combined with the skill of generals and statesmen, have brought about changes of dynasty in China's past. The question in a very different contemporary China is how far demonstrations, protests, boycotts, strikes, or open rebellion would have to go to engage the gears of real political change. Change may after all be evolutionary and gradual; no one knows.

Meanwhile one form of change began taking place in the 1990s through the medium of economics, namely the immense increase of wealth in south China. There is evidence* that businessmen and officials in Guangdong province pay lip service to Beijing and its edicts, then simply go on in their own way making money. And since making money is by government definition good, Beijing looks the other way. How far do both sides realize they are winking at each other?

Few would want a full break between north and south; that would open the door to widespread regionalism and the *luan,* or chaos, which is most feared by all Chinese. Thus the regional breakups that have occurred in Russia and Yugoslavia are perhaps less likely to happen in China.

Yet mere economic success will not suffice China as a sole or permanent goal. Somehow there has been a loss of purpose, even a loss of morality. In 1975 there was more honesty among the general populace, in 1993, more corruption. Thoughtful Chinese want their country to have modern technology, a solid economic base, and the ability to offer all its citizens the chance of a decent livelihood. But, it would seem, they also long for the renewal, in a contemporary form, of the culture, the moral strength, and the distinctive civilizing influences which China, at its best, was able to offer its Asian neighbors in the past.

*Personal conversation, 1993, with a reporter for *Fortune* magazine who visits China frequently.

What is clearly evident in today's China, despite its national problems, is the remarkable vitality of the Chinese people. This energetic life force—artistic, intellectual, and entrepreneurial—has risen and fallen in an extended wave motion throughout a long history. If today it leads to a cultural renaissance, then China will again benefit its neighbors, and even the world.

Yangzi Gorges. Zhong Ming. Oil Painting, 1978.

Zhong Ming, One of China's younger artists, born in Beijing, has had exhibitions of his work in China, Japan, London, Taiwan, and Hong Kong. He remarks of this picture: "Chinese painting is not normally done from life, but I painted this, standing on the banks of the Yangzi, going against tradition. Thus it has a Western feeling."

Horse 馬   Brush painting 1992.   Wang Fangyu

The pictograph from which the cursive form of this character evolved is found on oracle bones dating as early as the thirteenth century B.C.

The artist has exhibited widely in the United States, Europe, and China.

"In Wang Fangyu's highly innovative calligraphy, the imagistic dimension of Chinese characters is once again visible even to the uninitiated onlooker as a source of visual delight."

C.T. Hsia, Columbia University.

CHRONOLOGY

The entries in this chronology make no claim to completeness. They are limited for the most part to dates mentioned in the text. All dates B.C. are so marked. After the occurrence of the first dates A.D., the letters A.D. are omitted. "First" in the chronology means only "first in China."

DATE	HISTORY	CULTURE
1523–1027 B.C.	**Shang** (or Yin) **Dynasty**	Bronze culture (from 17th century B.C.)
		Oracle bones (c. 1300 B.C.)
1027–221 B.C.	**Zhou Dynasty**	Beginning of accurately dated history (841 B.C.)
	Eastern Zhou period (771–221 B.C.)	
	Spring and Autumn period (722–481 B.C.)	Laozi, philosopher (?6th century B.C.)
		Confucius, philosopher (551–479 B.C.)
		Iron first mentioned (513 B.C.)
	Warring States period (403–221 B.C.)	Mozi, philosopher (470–?391 B.C.)
		Mencius, philosopher (372–?289 B.C.)
		Shang Yang, statesman, dies (330 B.C.)
		Cavalry introduced (c. 300 B.C.)
		Zhuangzi, philosopher, dies (c. 300 B.C.)
		Xunzi, philosopher (c. 300–237 B.C.)

DATE	HISTORY	CULTURE
		Han Fei Zi, philosopher, dies (233 B.C.)
221–206 B.C.	**Qin Dynasty**	
	Qin Shi Huang Di, founder	The Great Wall completed
206 B.C.–A.D. 221	**Han Dynasty**	
	Earlier Han period (206 B.C.–A.D. 8)	
	Gao Zu, emperor, reigns (206–195 B.C.)	Steel manufacture begins (2nd century B.C.)
	Wu Di, emperor, reigns (141–87 B.C.)	Dong Zhongshu, scholar (?179–105 B.C.)
		Sima Qian, historian (c. 145–c. 85 B.C.)
139–126 B.C.	Zhang Qian's first expedition to the West	
111 B.C.	Nan Yue in south China conquered	
A.D. 9–23	Wang Mang on the throne	Wang Mang era; water mills first mentioned
A.D. 23–221	Later Han period	Capital moved from Changan to Luoyang
A.D. 25–57	Guang Wu Di, emperor, reigns	
97	Ban Chao, general, reaches the Caspian Sea	Invention of paper (A.D. 105)
		First seismograph constructed (132)
184	Rebellion of the Yellow Turbans	
222–581	**Six Dynasties Period**	
222–280	Era of the Three Kingdoms: Wei, Shu-Han, and Wu	
386–534	**Northern Wei Dynasty**	Tao Yuanming, scholar (365–427)
		Pilgrimage of the Buddhist monk Faxian to India (399–414)
589–618	**Sui Dynasty** China reunited	Changan rebuilt as Sui capital and developed under Tang dynasty
618–907	**Tang Dynasty**	
618–625	Gao Zu, emperor, reigns	Pilgrimage of the Buddhist monk,
626–649	Tai Zong, emperior, reigns	Xuanzang, to India (629–45)
649–683	Gao Zong, emperor, reigns	Block printing begins (?680)
683–705	Wu, empress, reigns	Wang Wei, poet and artist (699–759)
712–756	Xuan Zong, emperor, reigns	Li Taibo (Li Bo), poet (701–62)
		Du Fu, poet (712–70)
755	Outbreak of the rebellion of An Lushan	Nestorian Church stele at Changan (781) records 631 as

DATE	HISTORY	CULTURE
		date of introduction of the church
		Han Yu, essayist and poet (768–824)
		Bo Zhuyi, poet (772–846)
881	Capital, Changan, sacked	Major persecution of Buddhism (841–45)
907–960	**Five Dynasties,** North China	Li Cheng, artist, active (940–67)
907–970	**Ten Kingdoms,** South China	
960–1126	**Song Dynasty**	Compass used in China, in large oceangoing junks with sternpost rudders (990)
1021–1086	Wang Anshi, statesman and reformer	Xu Daoning, artist (c. 990–1010)
		Fan Guan, artist (990–1030)
1067–1085	Shen Zong, emperor, reigns	First paper money issued by the state (1024)
		Use of movable type (1030)
1100–1125	Hui Zong, emperor, reigns	Sima Guang (Ssu-ma Kuang), historian, (1019–1086)
1126–1234	**Jin Dynasty** (Jürchen) North China	Gunpowder as propulsive force (1132)
1127–1279	**Southern Song Dynasty** South China	
1127–1162	Song Gao Zong, emperor, reigns	Zhu Xi, philosopher (1130–1200)
		Ma Yuan, artist (1190–1224)
		Xia Gui, artist (c. 1180–1230)
1167–1227	Genghis Khan, Mongol	Liang Kai, artist, active (c. 1200)
1215	Peking captured by the Mongols	Mu Qi, artist, active (c. 1220)
1215–1294	Kublai Khan	
1260	Kublai Khan becomes Great Khan	Kublai Khan sets up Imperial Library in Peking (also known as Yenjing or Cambaluc) (1238)
1271	Kublai Khan becomes Emperor of China	
1280–1368	**Yuan Dynasty,** Mongol, set up after all China conquered	Giovanni de Piano Carpini reaches Karakorum, Mongol capital (1246)
1274, 1281	Two unsuccessful attempts to invade Japan	Marco Polo in the service of Kublai Khan in China (1275–92)
1300–1368	Floods and rebellions, some under White Lotus Society, White Cloud Society, and Red Turbans, weaken Mongol control	Luo Guanzhong, novelist (1330–1400)
1368–1644	**Ming Dynasty**	
1368–1398	Zhu Yuanzhang, Hung Wu emperor, reigns	
1387	Reconquest of China by the Ming completed	

DATE	HISTORY	CULTURE
1403–1424	Yong Le, emperor, reigns	Construction of Forbidden (Imperial) City, Peking, begins (1421)
1406–1427	Vietnam occupied by the Chinese	
		Chen Xianzhang, philosopher (1428–1500)
1405–1433	Great maritime expeditions under Zheng He	Wang Yangming, philosopher (1472–1528)
		Francis Xavier, Jesuit, lands in Japan, then attempts to enter China (1549)
1522	Single-Whip Reform	
1550	Altan Khan lays siege to Peking without success	Wu Chengen, novelist (?1500–1582)
1550 on	Japanese pirate raids on the coast	Matteo Ricci (1552–1610), Jesuit, lands at Macao; later in Peking (1582)
1559–1626	Nurhaci, Jürchen Manzhou leader	
1621	Liaoyang and Shenyang fall to Nurhaci	
1628	Famine in the northwest; Rebellion under Li Zicheng	
1592–1643	Abahai, successor to Nurhaci	
1644	Li Zicheng captures Peking but is defeated by the Manzhou and Wu Sangui	
1644–1911	**Qing Dynasty**	
1681	Qing suppress the Revolt of the Three Feudatories in South China	
1683	Taiwan captured from Guo Xingye (Koxinga)	Kang Xi promulgates the Sacred Edict (1670)
1661–1722	Kang Xi, emperor, reigns	James Cuningham, pioneer botanist, in China (1698–1708)
1699	British East India Company establishes a trading "factory" in Canton	Papal bull, *Ex Illa Die,* angers Kang Xi (1715)
		Christianity named as heterodox (1724)
1723–1736	Yong Zheng, emperor, reigns	Encyclopedia published (1728)
		Cao Xueqin, novelist (?1724–64)
1736–1795	Qian Long, emperor, reigns	Four Treasuries (encyclopedia or MS. Library) completed (1789)
1755–1759	Chinese Turkestan brought under Qing control	
1760–1770	Marked increase in tea trade with Europe, mainly London	
1793	Lord Macartney's embassy to Qian Long, emperor, unsuccessful	

DATE	HISTORY	CULTURE
1816	Lord Amherst's embassy unsuccessful	
1839	Lin Zexu appointed commissioner in Canton; opium burned; British retreat to Hongkong	
1839–1842	Opium War	
1842	Treaty of Nanjing	
1850–1864	Taiping Rebellion, led by Hong Xiuchuan (1813–64)	
1856–1860	Anglo-French War (also called Arrow War and Second Opium War)	
1860	Ratification of Treaty of Tientsin, drawn up in 1858; Summer Palace looted and burned by French and British troops; Prince Gong, acting head of state	
1851–1862	Xian Feng, emperor, reigns	
1811–1872	Zeng Guofan) leading scholar	
1812–1885	Zuo Zongtang) officials and	
1823–1901	Li Hongzhang) modernizers, involved in suppression of the Taiping Rebellion	
1861	Zong-li Yamen set up	
1853–1868	Nien Rebellion	
1868–1873	Muslim Rebellion	
1865	Jiangnan Arsenal in Shanghai	Tong Zhi Restoration (1862–75)
1866	Navy Yard at Fuzhou	Wei Yuan, author (1794–1857)
1872	China Merchants Steam Navigation Company	
1870–1895	Li Hongzhang, as governor-general of Hebei Province, develops coal mines, railroad, telegraph lines	Robert Morrison, first Protestant missionary, arrives in Canton (1807)
1861	Chinese Maritime Customs Service set up, from 1863 under Robert Hart (1835–1911)	
		Timothy Richard (1832–1919), director of the Christian Literature Society
1870	Tientsin Massacre	
1875–1908	Guang Xu, emperor, reigns	
1896	Postal Service set up	
1838–1908	Cixi (Tz'u Hsi), empress dowager	
1894–1895	Sino-Japanese War	

DATE	HISTORY	CULTURE
1895	Treaty of Shimonoseki	
1898	June to September, Hundred Days Reform, under leadership of Kang Youwei (1858–1927) and Liang Qichao (1873–1929)	
1898–1900	Boxer Rebellion	
		Traditional civil service examination system ends (1905)
1904–1905	Russo-Japanese War fought in Manchuria	
1866–1925	Sun Yat-sen, "Father of the Republic"	
1894	Sun forms Revive China Society (Xing Zhong Hui)	Liang Qichao, Yen Fu (1853–1921), Lin Shu (1852–1924) write and translate in Japan
1905	Sun forms United League (Tong Meng Hui) in Tokyo	
1911	October 10: Army revolt in Wuchang marks the end of the Empire and the beginning of the Republic	
1912	January: Sun, first provisional President of the Republic; Guo Min Dang (KMT), National People's Party, formed	
1912	February: Xuan Tong, emperor (Pu Yi), age 6, resigns; Sun resigns, and Yuan Shikai becomes provisional President	
1915	Twenty-One Demands presented by Japan	
1916	Death of Yuan Shikai; struggle among warlords	
1919	May Fourth Movement	Writers active during and after the May Fourth Movement: Lu Xun, Wang Guowei, Ding Ling, Mao Don, Bajin, Hu Shi, Guo Moro
1921	Foundation of the Chinese Communist Party (CCP)	John Dewey in China (1919–21) Bertrand Russell also lecturing
1921–1922	Washington Conference and Nine-Power Treaty	
1923	Jiang Jieshi (Chiang Kai-shek) (1888–1975) sent by Sun to Russia to study, then becomes commandant of Huangpu (Whampoa) Military Academy	

DATE	HISTORY	CULTURE
1925	March 12: Sun Yat-sen dies; May 30th Incident (strikers fired on by British and Japanese troops)	Opening of the Museum in the Imperial City in Peking (1925)
1926	July: Northern Expedition of KMT with CCP moves off from Canton	
1926–1927	Mao Zedong organizes peasants in Hunan	
1927	Jiang Jieshi breaks with the Communists and labor unions and kills the leaders; first Chinese Soviets in the Jinggang mountains	
1928	October: KMT under Jiang Jieshi in control of most of China; capital at Nanjing	Discoveries at Anyang of oracle bones and Shang artifacts (from 1927)
1928	Japanese blow up Zhang Zuolin's train	
1929–1931	Disastrous famine in North China	Foundation of League of Left-Wing Writers (1930)
1931	September: Mukden Incident and Japanese Army takeover of Manchuria	
1932	February: Creation of Manzhouguo	Chinese Chemical Society founded (1933)
1930–1934	Five encirclement campaigns of Jiang Jieshi against the CCP	New Life Movement founded (1934)
		Chinese Mathematical Society founded (1935)
1934	The Long March of the CCP	
1936	Xian coup; Jiang captured, then released	Death of writer Lu Xun
1937	July: Marco Polo Bridge Incident sets off the "China Incident," an undeclared war	
1938	Japan occupies major urban centers of China; KMT retreats to Sichuan and Yunnan	
1940	Puppet government in Nanjing under Wang Jingwei	
1941	July: Japanese extend war to Indochina December 7: Japanese attack Pearl Harbor	
1945	August: Japanese surrender	
1946	January: Cease-fire in civil war between KMT and CCP arranged by Gen. George C. Marshall but proves abortive	
1948	October: CCP victorious in Manchuria and (December) in north-central China	

DATE	HISTORY	CULTURE
1949	December: Jiang Jieshi and KMT retreat to Taiwan; CCP takes over mainland China	
1893–1976	Mao Zedong	
1949	Sino-Soviet Alliance signed by Mao Zedong in Moscow	
1950	Agrarian Law (land reform): period of terror	Three-Self Movement in religion set up
1950	October: Chinese "volunteers" enter Korean War	
1951	Three-Anti, Five-Anti, and Thought Reform campaigns	
1953–1956	Cooperatives set up, the beginning of collectivization	
1956–1957	The "Hundred Flowers" period	
1958	The Great Leap Forward	
1960	USSR withdraws technicians from China	
1966	June: Beginning of the Great Proletarian Cultural Revolution	Suppression of liberal tendencies in art and literature and increased criticism of all things foreign
1969	March: Drive to reopen schools	Chinese scientists synthesized a structural component of insulin (after 1967)
1970	Universities reopened	
1971	October: PRC given the China seat at UN; Republic of China (Taiwan) excluded	
1971	September: Lin Biao killed in a plane crash while reportedly escaping to Russia	
1972	February: President Nixon's visit to China	
1973	Tenth Congress of the CCP; Anti-Lin Biao and Confucius campaign; Deng Xiaoping rehabilitated after ouster in Cultural Revolution	
1975	January: Grant of certain civil rights at National People's Congress	
	Death of Jiang Jieshi (Chiang Kai-shek)	
	Sideline private production permitted	
1976	January: Zhou Enlai dies, age 78	

DATE	HISTORY	CULTURE
	April: Riot in Tiananmen Square in Peking; Deng Xiaoping ousted; Hua Guofeng made Premier	
	July: Zhu De, veteran general, dies; Tongshan earthquake	
	September: Mao Zedong dies, age 82	
	October: Arrest of the Gang of Four	
1977	July: Deng Xiaoping rehabilitated for the second time	
1978	February: New Constitution passed by the National People's Congress; Treaty of Peace and Friendship with Japan signed	Greater freedom in art and literature and in certain religious observances
1978	Jiang Jingguo elected President of Republic of China, Taiwan	Reform of education after damage of Cultural Revolution
1979	January: United States and PRC establish diplomatic relations, and United States severs diplomatic relations with ROC in Taiwan	Release of dissident writer Liu Binyan, imprisoned since 1958
	January 28–February 4: Deng Xiaoping visits US	
	February 17: Chinese armed invasion of Vietnam	
1980	Liu Shaoqi posthumously rehabilitated	
1980	Trial of the Gang of Four	
	Economic reforms, and "open door" begun	
	China admitted to IMF and World Bank	
1981	April: Drought in nine northern provinces	
	July: Severe flooding of Yangzi River	
1982	Employment merit system	
	End of "iron rice bowl"	"Fifth Generation" or "New Wave" film directors begin production
1983	Purge of the Communist Party	
	Trade agreement with USSR	
1984	December: Joint Declaration signed between Great Britain and China concerning restoration of Hong Kong to China in 1997	

DATE	HISTORY	CULTURE
1985		Beitang Catholic Church, closed in 1858, restored and reopened
1987	Riots and repression in Tibet	
	"Bourgeois liberalization" attacked	
1988	Li Denghui (Lee Teng-hui) elected President of Republic of China on death of Jiang Jingguo	
1989	April–June Democracy Movement and massacre at Tiananmen Square	
1991	Suicide of Jiang Qing, Mao's widow	
	China and Vietnam normalize relations	
	Opening of Shanghai Stock Exchange	
1992	December: First free elections in Republic of China	

SELECTED BIBLIOGRAPHY

This is a suggested list of books for the reader who may wish to go further in the study of Chinese history and culture. The dates are usually those of the first edition; in many instances, later, revised editions are available.

Balazs, Étienne. *Chinese Civilization and Bureaucracy: Variations on a Theme*. Trans. H. M. Wright. New Haven, Conn.: Yale University Press, 1964.

Barnett, A. D. *Communist China: The Early Years*. New York: Praeger, 1964.

Beers, Burton F. *China in Old Photographs 1860–1910*. New York: Scribners, 1978.

Binyon, Laurence. *The Flight of the Dragon: An Essay on the Theory and Practice of Art in China and Japan, Based on Original Sources*. London: J. Murray, 1911.

Birch, Cyril, comp. and ed. *Anthology of Chinese Literature*. Vol. 1, *From Early Times to the Fourteenth Century*. New York: Grove Press, 1965.

Boorman, Howard L., ed., *Biographical Dictionary of Republican China*, New York, Columbia University Press, 1976 ff.

Cameron, Nigel. The Face of China: As Seen by Photographers and Travelers, 1860–1912. Millerton, N.Y.: Aperture, 1978.

Carter, Thomas Francis. *The Invention of Printing in China and Its Spread Westward*. New York: Columbia University Press, 1925.

Chan, Wing-tsit, comp. and trans. *A Source Book in Chinese Philosophy*. Princeton, N.J.: Princeton University Press, 1963.

————, et al., ed., comp. and trans. *The Great Asian Religions: An Anthology*. New York: Macmillan, 1969.

Clubb, O. Edmund. *Twentieth Century China*. New York: Columbia University Press, 1964.

Clyde, Paul H., and Burton F. Beers. *The Far East: A History of Western Impacts and Eastern Response*. Englewood Cliffs, N.J.: Prentice-Hall, 1948.

Cohn, William. *Chinese Painting*. London: Phaidon Press, 1948.

Creel, Herrlee Glessner. *The Birth of China: A Study of the Formative Period of Chinese Civilization*. New York: Reynal and Hitchcock, 1954.

———. *Chinese Thought from Confucius to Mao Tse-tung*. Chicago: University of Chicago Press, 1953.

Crespigny, Rafe de. *China This Century*. Hongkong: Oxford University Press, 1992.

Cressey, G. B. *Land of the 500 Million: A Geography of China*. New York: McGraw-Hill, 1955.

Dawson, Raymond, ed. *The Legacy of China*. London: Oxford University Press, 1964.

De Bary, William Theodore, Wing-tsit Chan, and Burton Watson, eds. *Sources of Chinese Tradition*. New York: Columbia University Press, 1960.

Duke, Michael S. *Blooming and Contending Literature in the Post-Mao Era*. Bloomington, Ind.: Indiana University Press, 1985.

Fairbank, John K. *Chinese Thought and Institutions*. Chicago: University of Chicago Press, 1957.

———. *The United States and China*. Cambridge, Mass.: Harvard University Press, 1948.

Fung Yu-lan, trans., Derk Bodde, ed. *A Short History of Chinese Philosophy*. New York: Macmillan, 1953.

Fitzgerald, Charles Patrick. *China: A Short Cultural History*. London: Cresset Press, 1935.

———. *Revolution in China*. New York: Praeger, 1952.

Gernet, Jacques. *Le Monde Chinois*. Paris: Armand Colin, 1972.

Giles, Herbert A. *Gems of Chinese Literature*. Vol. 1, *Prose*. Shanghai: Kelly & Walsh, 1923.

Goodrich, L. Carrington. *A Short History of the Chinese People*. New York: Harper & Brothers, 1943.

Goodrich, L. Carrington, and Fang Chao-ying, eds. *Dictionary of Ming Biography*, New York, Columbia University Press, 1976.

Hay, John. *Ancient China*. London: Bodley Head, 1973.

Herrmann, Albert. *An Historical Atlas of China*. Chicago: Aldine, 1966 (based on 1935 edition).

Hightower, James R. *Topics in Chinese Literature: Outlines and Bibliographies*, Rev. ed. Cambridge, Mass.: Harvard University Press, 1953.

Hsia, C. T. *The Classic Chinese Novel: A Critical Introduction*. New York: Columbia University Press, 1968.

———. *A History of Modern Chinese Fiction, 1917–1957*. New Haven, Conn.: Yale University Press, 1961.

Hsü, Immanuel C. Y., *China Without Mao: The Search for a New Order*, 2nd ed. New York: Oxford, 1990.

————, ed. *Readings in Modern Chinese History.* New York: Oxford University Press, 1971.

Hummel, Arthur W., ed., *Dictionary of Ch'ing Biography,* Washington D.C., Government Printing Office, 1943.

Latourette, Kenneth Scott. *The Chinese: Their History and Culture.* New York: Macmillan, 1934.

————. *A History of Christian Missions in China.* New York: Russell & Russell, 1967.

Lau, D.C., trans., *Tao Te Ching,* Hongkong: Chinese University Press, 1981 (including new material).

Lee, Sherman E. *A History of Far Eastern Art.* Englewood Cliffs, N.J.: Prentice-Hall, 1964.

Levenson, Joseph R. *Confucian China and Its Modern Fate.* 3 vols. Berkeley: University of California Press, 1958–1964.

Li Yuning, ed. *Chinese Women Through Chinese Eyes.* Armonk, N.Y.: M. E. Sharpe, 1992.

Lin Yu-tang. *The Gay Genius: The Life and Times of Su Tungpo.* London: Heinemann, 1948.

Link, Perry. *Evening Chats in Beijing: Probing China's Predicament.* New York: Norton, 1992.

Loewe, Michael. *Everyday Life in Early Imperial China During the Han Period, 202 B.C.–A.D. 220.* London: Batsford, 1968.

————. *Imperial China: The Historical Background to the Modern Age.* London: Allen & Unwin, 1966.

Mackerras, Colin and Yorke, Amanda, C. eds. *The Cambridge Handbook of Contemporary China.* Cambridge: Cambridge University Press, 1991.

McAleavy, H. *The Modern History of China.* New York; Praeger, 1967.

Moore, Charles A. *The Chinese Mind: Essentials of Chinese Philosophy and Culture.* Honolulu: East–West Center Press, 1967.

Morton, W. Scott. *Japan: Its History and Culture,* 3rd ed. New York: McGraw-Hill, Inc., 1994.

Needham, Joseph. *The Shorter Science and Civilization in China: An Abridgement of Joseph Needham's Original Text by Colin A. Ronan.* Cambridge: Cambridge University Press, 1978.

Noss, John B. *Man's Religions.* 3rd ed. New York: Macmillan, 1963.

Prawdin, Michael. *The Mongol Empire, Its Rise and Legacy.* Trans. Eden and Cedar Paul. London: G. Allen and Unwin, 1940.

Reischauer, Edwin O., John K. Fairbank, and Albert M. Craig. *East Asia: Tradition and Transformation.* Boston: Houghton Mifflin, 1973.

Rowley, George. *Principles of Chinese Painting.* Rev. ed. Princeton, N.J.: Princeton University Press, 1959.

Schram, Stuart. *Mao Tse-tung.* Baltimore: Penguin Books, 1966.

Sickman, Laurence, and Alexander Soper. *The Art and Architecture of China.* Baltimore: Penguin Books, 1956.

Snow, Edgar. *The Battle for Asia.* New York: Random House, 1941.

————. *The Other Side of the River: Red China Today.* New York: Random House, 1961.

————. *Red Star over China.* Rev. ed. New York: Garden City Publishing Co., 1939.

Terrill, Ross. *800,000,000: The Real China.* Boston: Little, Brown, 1972.

————. *The Future of China, After Mao.* New York: Delacorte, 1978.

Waley, Arthur, trans. *The Book of Songs.* New York: Grove Press, 1960.

————. *Three Ways of Thought in Ancient China.* London: G. Allen and Unwin, 1946.

————, ed. and trans. *The Analects of Confucius.* London: G. Allen and Unwin, 1938.

————, trans. *A Hundred and Seventy Chinese Poems.* London: G. Allen and Unwin, 1946.

————trans. *Monkey.* New York: John Day, 1943.

————trans. *The Way and Its Power.* London: G. Allen and Unwin, 1934.

Wango Weng. *Chinese Paintings in the Collection of John M. Crawford, Jr.* New York: Dover, 1978.

Watson, Burton. *Ssu-ma Ch'ien, Grand Historian of China.* New York: Columbia University Press, 1958.

Watson, William. *Ancient China: The Discoveries of Post-Liberation Archaeology.* London: BBC Publications, 1974.

————. *Early Chinese Civilization.* London: Thames and Hudson, 1966.

Wright, Arthur F. *Buddhism in Chinese History. Stanford, Calif.: Stanford University Press, 1959.*

Yule, Henry. *The Book of Sir Marco Polo.* 3rd ed. London: J. Murray, 1903.

Zagoria, Donald S. *The Sino-Soviet Conflict, 1956–1961.* Princeton, N.J.: Princeton University Press, 1962.

INDEX

Index Note: *The* pinyin *spelling currently in use is given in the Index. For a conversion table for the Wade-Giles spelling still found in many books, see the Note on Pronunciation and Spelling at the beginning of this book. A few Wade-Giles entries are given in the Index in parentheses for clarification of certain names.*